29 50

D0811811

CAMBRIDGE COMMONWEALTH SERIES

General Editor: Professor E. T. Stokes

# THE MAKING OF MODERN BELIZE

CAMBRIDGE COMMONWEALTH SERIES

*Toward 'Uhuru' in Tanzania:* G. Andrew Maguire

*Developing the Third World: the experience of the nineteen-sixties:*
Ronald Robinson (ed.)

*Mackinnon and East Africa 1878–1895: A Study in the 'New
Imperialism':* John S. Galbraith

*The Durham Report and British Policy: A Critical Essay:* Ged Martin

These monographs are published by the Syndics of the Cambridge
University Press in association with the Managers of the Cambridge
University Smuts Memorial Fund for the Advancement of
Commonwealth Studies.

# The making of modern Belize

*POLITICS, SOCIETY & BRITISH COLONIALISM
IN CENTRAL AMERICA*

C. H. GRANT

Associate Professor, Department of Political Science
University of Waterloo

CAMBRIDGE UNIVERSITY PRESS

CAMBRIDGE

LONDON · NEW YORK · MELBOURNE

Published by the Syndics of the Cambridge University Press
The Pitt Building, Trumpington Street, Cambridge CB2 IRP
Bentley House, 200 Euston Road, London WNI 2DB
32 East 57th Street, New York, NY 10022, USA
296 Beaconsfield Parade, Middle Park, Melbourne 3206, Australia

First published 1976

Printed in Great Britain by
Western Printing Services Ltd, Bristol

*Library of Congress cataloguing in publication data*

Grant, Cedric Hilburn.

The making of modern Belize.

(Cambridge commonwealth series)

'Derived primarily from... [the author's] doctorral
dissertation . . . University of Edinburgh . . . 1969.'

Bibliography: p.

Includes index.

1. Belize – Politics and government. I. Title.
F1448.G73   320.9′7282   75-36022
ISBN 0 521 20731 2

For Lorene
Adèle, Denise and Gayle

# CONTENTS

# ILLUSTRATIONS

# FOREWORD

There is still a great deal to be learnt about the period of European break-out into the Oceanic world, and about its abiding consequences. The labels 'imperialism' and 'colonialism' are convenient, and need not be mislead-ing so long as one remembers that the conquest of empires, the founding of colonies, were only part of the show; the most conspicuous, but not necessarily the most appropriate for a radical analysis of what happened.

There were two factors common to this and to all previous periods of 'folk-wandering': the search for loot, and the search for land. It is easy to trace these characteristic features: the former primarily where armed adventurers broke into the territory of ancient empires, the latter in 'new found lands' where scattered aboriginal populations were pushed aside by superior technique and weight of numbers. Analogous episodes can be traced in human history back to the dawn of literacy and beyond; but this episode was radically new in that the wanderers were also merchants, investors, and in the end industrialists. Even in the first phase the mer-chants were prepared to invest three or more moves ahead of the ultimate market; to build ships, to hire crews, with which to buy slaves, with whom to open up new lands for tropical agriculture, whose products would sell richly in European markets. And so round the cycle, a cycle lubricated by the growth of an extremely complex international money market.

The effects of these movements of population and investment were com-plex and dynamic, and the process that created them cannot be reversed. The heritage now exists independently of its history and the receding tide of empire has left castaways who can justly blame long-dead colonizers, but must now lead their own lives.

I am glad that Cedric Grant (himself from Guyana, 'B.G.', to use the old name) introduced me to the story of the country that was known as British Honduras ('B.H.') and recently renamed Belize, when he was a Ford Foundation Fellow at Edinburgh University. In a sense Belize has nothing: a strip of not very fertile Caribbean coast in the path of hurri-canes, some sluggish rivers, a large area of tropical forest (looted rather than harvested), enough archaeological remains to show that a thousand years ago its people were on the fringes of the great Mayan culture. It was a scrap of the Mosquito Coast, a resort of fugitives and broken men; its new name, Belize, is vaguely reputed to be that of an obscure Scottish adventurer called Wallace. There was once (in 1798) a little and decisive sea battle with the Spaniards (the Spanish Field-Marshal was called Arturo O'Neil) at the entrance to its port; but it was virtually outside the colonial wars of the eighteenth century, outside the general history of the Caribbean. It was with difficulty that the British were coaxed, perhaps tricked, into annexing it in 1862: ever since then they have been trying and failing to get rid of it.

Why then study this assembly of some 130,000 descendants of castaways? I have myself been fascinated by Cedric Grant's account because of the complexity of the situation contrived here by the events of history, almost without the intervention of collective human will or reason. There was no loot and no systematic murder of native Indians. There were no minerals to speak of, and therefore no use for slave labour in the mines; no plantations to speak of, and therefore no use for slave labour in cultivation. Slaves were used in the search for valuable timber trees, but this required initiative and work in small groups. Slaves in Belize did not remain so for very long, and the dominant racial group was of mixed mulatto blood, and Creoles, as they are called, moved into the lesser professions and into trade. One of the oddities of British colonial history is that the elite secondary school (the *Alma Mater* of the revolution, in so many colonies and which provided the nationalist leaders) was in this case a Catholic school (St John's College) run by Jesuits from the American Middle West (Irish or German, not highly regarded within the Order, an ex-Jesuit once told me).

This Creole elite can be distinguished quite clearly from the black Caribs, peasant farmers and fishermen, whose legend is that they are descendants of Carib women and of African slaves who escaped elsewhere in the Caribbean. Thus they can claim in a sense to be autochthones, more ancient in lineage than the elite, and they are a substantial influence, now moving in to take a place by the side of Creole teachers in primary education.

Finally, there are the *mestizos*, Spanish speakers of mixed blood, to whom Spanish and Indian languages are more familiar than English. The Premier, and firmly recognized leader, George Price, has an English (or rather Welsh) name, but claims mestizo ancestry, and is proud to press the claim of Indian blood for a share in government. But these are primarily Indians who moved in from Mexico along the northern coast. Their ancient history does not relate them very closely to the largely Indian state of Guatemala, which has for long contested the legality of Britain's claim to 'the Mosquito Coast', an issue which has become a classic case in international law.

Indeed, where are these descendants of castaways to find a home except in Guatemala? In the days when a federation of the British West Indies was on the agenda they rejected it, fearing an influx of West Indians, culturally alien to a sizeable section of the population. If one looks at the Isthmus on a small-scale map, it seems reasonable to tag Belize to Guatemala: a larger scale reveals that practical connection depends on building a road – a political question – and on finding traffic for a road when built. Commercially, to add nothing to nothing equals nothing; Belize has very little more economic connection with Guatemala than it has with Britain (there are no golden beaches around which to build the economy of a tax haven).

Why then study Belize? What has been written about the place I find of deep interest, yet I should not rank it high among attractive places. Why bother? I can think of three reasons. The first is that in spite of all the fierce and random accidents of history Belize exists. It is people in association with a place: a unique and true entity. It is itself, and nowhere else.

Secondly, it is a meeting place for strands of history. Personal pedigrees do not exist, but if they could be traced for 500 years the threads would lead back to a diversity of cultures, peoples and economies, widely displaced in space and time.

And, finally, there is a future. How far can a social future be chosen and shaped, how far is a social entity merely a leaf driven by the winds and currents of the ocean of history? Belize has set out to sail that ocean in a flimsy and leaky vessel. But so have we all: you too, *hypocrite lecteur*, are in essence a Belizean, *leur semblable, leur frère*.

*Glasgow,*                                                 *W. J. M. Mackenzie*
*July* 1975

# PREFACE

This book is derived primarily from a doctoral dissertation that I completed for the University of Edinburgh in late 1969. In that work I attempted to combine a general political history of Belize in the modern period with a structural analysis of its main institutions such as political parties, trade unions, and local authorities. The broad assessment was dictated by two considerations. First, Belize was and is still largely virgin territory for the social scientist and much of the spade work has yet to be done. Most of the published work on the country is concerned with the juridical aspects of the Anglo-Guatemala dispute, now more than a century old. It is essentially as an adjunct to this dispute that the internal political history of Belize has received attention. Those who take the view that the internal affairs of Belize merit a study in itself have either selected a narrow specialized topic or a part of the country as the unit of analysis. Together, these studies do not provide a composite picture of Belizean society, still less its politics. There have been exceptions, the most notable being D. A. G. Waddell, *British Honduras: A Historical and Contemporary Survey* (1961), Wayne Clegern, *British Honduras: Colonial Dead End 1859–1900* (1967) and more recently Narda Dobson, *A History of Belize* (1973). The first and third works provide little more than a historical overview. The second is more penetrating in its account, which is however confined to the latter half of the nineteenth century. In a way my dissertation picked up the history at this point and as the first attempt to analyse systematically contemporary political developments, particularly after the rise of a nationalist movement in 1950, it was essentially exploratory in character.

The second reason for giving breadth to the study is that spade work of this kind is virtually a prerequisite to fruitful comparisons with territories in the Caribbean that share with Belize its British colonial experience. As Lloyd Braithwaite points out, the institutional differences among the West Indian countries are sufficiently significant for us to guard against generalizations based on the data for one country.[1]

Extensive changes have been made to the original work to bring it to its present form. I have reorganized the material so as to avoid the criss-crossing of themes and chronology which was inherent in the combined analysis of a general political history with the analysis of the institutions. There is a greater degree of historical continuity, as is evident in the division of the book into three parts – the Crown colony period, the process of decolonization in the 1950s, and the move towards independence from 1961 onwards. As a result of the rearrangement the interrelationship between institutions is more fully established. I have also recast the study in terms of Belize being a cultural borderland, a meeting place for the British-oriented Creole and the Latin complexes in the Pan-American area, without sacrificing its broad orientation. Finally, I have included developments that have occurred since the dissertation was completed, up to the general election in October 1974.

The task of updating such a study is unrewarding and thankless. In a sense, fundamental changes seldom occur to justify the exercise. Yet I found the urge to undertake it irresistible. In the process I fell into an all-too-common trap. I was unwilling to call a halt although I realized that no published contemporary work is ever completely up to date. The constant revision and reworking was eventually overtaken by a constitutional event of symbolic importance. This was the change of the official name of the country from British Honduras to Belize, which was the name of its capital city, in June 1973. Rather than use the old and new names where appropriate I have at the risk of historical anachronism discarded the old except in direct quotations and endnotes. Belize is therefore used throughout the study to refer to the country, and to complete the change the former capital will be referred to as Belize City.

# ACKNOWLEDGEMENTS

Professor Lloyd Braithwaite, Pro-Vice Chancellor of the University of the West Indies, suggested this study of Belize to me in 1966. At that time he was the Acting Director of the Institute of Social Economic Research in the University where I was a Research Fellow. He also nominated me for a Ford Foundation Fellowship in 1967 which made it possible for me to complete the study as a doctoral dissertation at the University of Edinburgh. The updating of the study was facilitated by a Canada Council grant in 1970 and was undertaken at the University of Waterloo, where my colleagues in the Department of Political Science provided much intellectual stimulation.

Many people in Belize have aided me in my work. My friend and colleague, Vernon Leslie, Resident Tutor of the Department of Extra-Mural Studies, University of the West Indies, placed his office at my disposal. Being a Belizean, he was an asset to my work in many other ways. Gilbert Rodwell Hulse, a former Anglican Archdeacon, was a mine of information and an engaging story-teller. Sir Harrison Courtenay, a lawyer and former Speaker of the House of Representatives, was never too busy to share with me the entire fifty-odd years of his political experience. His private collection of newspapers and rare official reports saved me many inconveniences. Without the co-operation of other political veterans such as the late E. O. B. Barrow, a retired District Commissioner, James Meighan, also a retired District Commissioner and People's United Party Senator, and Edgar Gegg, proprietor of the Vogue Commercial Store, I would have been unable to evoke the political climate of the 1930s. Miss Alice Gibson, the Deputy Librarian, Belize National Library and Archives, was also of invaluable assistance in making material available. The PUP government proved to be an admirably open administration. I was granted frequent and informal interviews with members of the political executive, including Premier George Price.

I should also like to thank Professor Harry Hanham, formerly head of the Department of Politics, University of Edinburgh, and now at the

Massachusetts Institute of Technology, Professor D. A. G. Waddell, formerly a Senior Lecturer in History, University of Edinburgh, and now at the University of Stirling, and Professor W. J. M. Mackenzie, Department of Politics, University of Glasgow, for their interest in the work. With his encyclopedic knowledge the latter reminded me, in the process of raising several comparative questions, that Belize, though on the periphery of the colonial world, was just another colony. He also readily consented to write the foreword.

Several typists have been associated with the revision of this work and at the risk of being invidious I should like to thank Mrs Sandra Fauquier for undertaking the bulk of the typing.

Finally, I am deeply indebted to my wife, Lorene. She collaborated in data collection, typed and edited crude drafts and above all endured the deprivations which I inflicted during the period that the book was written.

*Lusaka* 1976                                                    C.H.G.

## PUBLISHER'S NOTE

The Publisher and author are grateful to the Central Information Office, Government of Belize, for permission to reproduce the photographs in their copyright.

# Introduction

*The geographical and historical background*

Belize occupies an area of 8,600 square miles and is a British possession in the Spanish-speaking sub-continent of Central America. It is bounded on the north and north-west by Mexico, on the west and south by Guatemala and on the east by the Bay of Honduras in the Caribbean Sea. The nearest British-oriented territory, Jamaica, lies about 600 miles to the east in the Caribbean Sea. Along the coastline are a number of cays or coral islets. The coastlands are mostly a few feet above sea-level with numerous lagoons. This ecological situation is compounded by the periodic occurrence of hurricanes in the area. Rivers also abound and two of them, the Hondo and the Sarstun, separate Belize from Mexico in the north and Guatemala on the south respectively. A third river, the Belize, flows from the Guatemala frontier to the Caribbean Sea and has at its mouth Belize City which was the administrative capital until 1970.

The swampy coastlands in the north give way to flat, low, fertile land. They are replaced in the south and west by pine ridges, scrub forests, savannahs and arable lands in a landscape of valleys and mountains which reach 2,700 feet above sea-level. The highlands are less exposed to the fury of the hurricanes than the low-lying coast, and after a hurricane, 'Hattie', devastated Belize City for the second time in thirty years, in 1961,[1] it was decided to relocate the capital some seventy miles inland in the western part of the country and to name it Belmopan.[2]

The country has a small population of 120,000[3] which is concentrated on the coastlands. About 39,000 or 33 per cent of the total population lived in Belize City in 1970. Another 16 per cent or 19,444 inhabited the smaller coastal towns of Corozal (4,724), Orange Walk (5,698), Stann Creek (6,939) and Punta Gorda (2,083). About eighty of the one hundred or so villages in Belize surround these coastal towns and Belize City; they also include the largest villages and together accommodated 45,465 or 38 per cent of the total population. A mere 5 per cent or 6,257 lived in the two inland towns of San Ignacio and Benque Viejo. Approximately 8 per

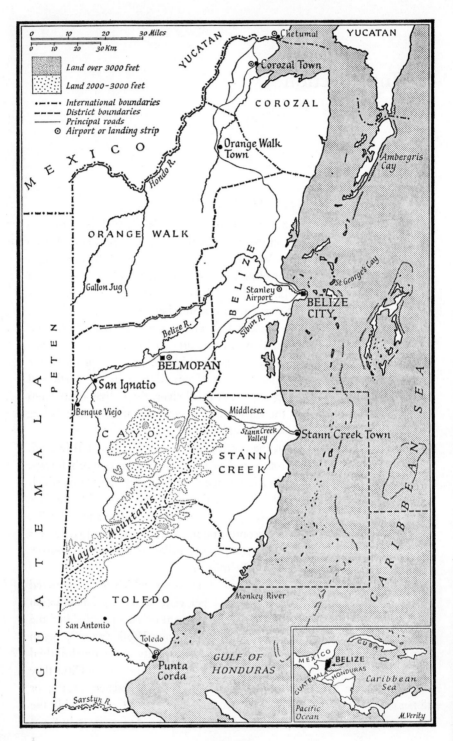

**BELIZE**

cent or 9,500 nearby rural residents complete the sum since the ridges and more mountainous areas are virtually uninhabited.

Belize is unusual in the Pan-American area. This is not because her problems and development are different in kind from those of the Central American and Caribbean territories. They are not. The country is typically underdeveloped. From the moment a British settlement was established around 1638 a whole way of life developed on the untrammelled exploitation of man and nature alike – of African slave labour and of the more valuable forest trees: logwood, mahogany, rosewood and sapodilla. The trees were scattered, and extensive forest holdings were an economic necessity. These holdings were owned by the individual settlers but most of them eventually fell into the hands of a single absentee corporate owner. This was the Belize Estate and Produce Company Ltd (BEC) whose headquarters is in London.[4] It was established in 1875 by the Hoare family;[5] in 1942 it became a subsidiary of the giant multi-national corporation, J. Glicksten Property and Investment Trust Ltd,[6] which has more recently become part of a new United Kingdom based conglomerate, the International Timber Corporation. At the time that it was acquired by J. Glicksten and Sons Ltd, the BEC owned more than 1,000,000 acres or one-fifth of the colony.[7] The properties included some of the more fertile lands that provided access to the forests but were never put to productive use.[8] Because of its vast forestry and agricultural holdings, the BEC has forced the peasant farmer and forestry worker into a dependent relationship with it. The farmer operates on a minute scale on relatively infertile land and the forestry worker functions at best as a contractor in the extraction of timber from the company's land. Indeed, as part of the dependency syndrome entire villages were established as tenants on company land. Their tenure was also at the mercy of the corporate landlord, and the eviction and the removal of large blocks of population from one estate to another were not unknown. The overall arrangement bore some resemblance to the plantation system in the West Indies. Indeed, Beckford, in a world-wide study of plantation economies, firmly cast Belize in the plantation mould from its inception, even though its main economic activity was non-agricultural.[9] Even if a different categorization of the forestry economy is preferred, the fact remains that Belize was, in Carey-Jones' words, a 'classic example of colonial exploitation, of taking away and not giving back...in the way of permanent improvement and capital development'.[10] From being prized in 1671 as the settlement which 'increased His Majesty's Customs and national commerce more than any of His Majesty's colonies',[11] Belize suffered so much at the hands of imperial economic interests that it is considered to have reached 'a colonial dead end'[12] by the turn of the twentieth century. As Carey-Jones indicates, the process of decay began with the exhaustion of the forests.[13] The dismal picture persisted well into the 1950s when there was a compensating rise in agriculture, with each of the two major industries, sugar and citrus, dominated by a single overseas company, the Belize Sugar Industries, a subsidiary of the British Tate and Lyle, and Salada Foods Company, a Canadian concern, respectively.[14] One sector has therefore replaced another as the mainstay of the economy and with it a distinctive feature of the colonial economy remains intact. The emergence of agriculture has also brought to an end perhaps the only important economic difference between Belize and the rest of the West Indies. The sugar industry, which is more important than citrus in terms of value of production, number of wage-earners employed and general influence, is organized on a plantation basis. It has unmistakably placed Belize in what Wagley calls the plantation culture sphere of the Americas[15] and has augmented the country's economic ties with the Commonwealth Caribbean.

Nor does Belize's uniqueness depend on its basic institutions. Its colonial experience has produced political, social and legal institutions that are common to the Commonwealth Caribbean and indeed to the British colonial world. Nor can its claim to a place of special interest in the region be based on its movement for self-determination. Nationalist politics in Belize forms part of the general response to British imperial policy in the West Indies and elsewhere, even though the colony was not the most precocious in the period between the two World Wars.[16] During the economic depression of the 1930s there was less nationalist argument and a lower political awareness than in the West Indian colonies, and Belize stood on the edge of the path of the disturbances that swept the other territories in the region during this decade.[17] Nonetheless, it was by no means a late starter in developing an organized nationalist movement after the Second World War. With little warning, the People's United Party (PUP) and its progenitor, the People's Committee (PC), burst upon the political scene in 1950 under a very young and zealous leadership.[18] This was the same year that a nationalist political party, the People's Progressive Party (PPP) was formed in Guyana[19] and some six years before the ruling People's Nationalist Movement (PNM) emerged in Trinidad.[20] In its development, the PUP has manifested many of the characteristics of its counterparts in these territories and other new states.[21] It gathered momentum with astonishing speed and easily became the dominant force in the country's political life. It has not merely won the six elections that have been held since its inception, but captured almost all of the seats in the first five, with the result that the parliamentary opposition has only since the last election in

December 1974 been more than a token force. At the same time, however, the PUP could not always count on the full support of strategically important segments of the population.[22]

Perhaps more than many of the other ruling parties in the Caribbean, the PUP has had its fair share of conflict with the colonial power before the latter came to terms with the changing political situation. This conflict reached its climax in December 1957 when the PUP leader, George Price, was expelled from the Executive Council,[23] and the situation was not resolved until 1960. The party also shares with many of its kind the experience of rivalry for its leadership that invariably results in a party split. This occurred in 1956 and led to the formation of the Honduran Independence Party (HIP) and the eventual consolidation of the opposition forces into the National Independence Party (NIP) in 1958. It is also possible to trace in Belize the familiar pattern of organizational disarray and fragmentation that overcome opposition parties that have known no experience other than endless electoral rebuffs in the pre-independence period.

Whether they are of the ruling or opposition parties, few political leaders in the West Indies rose from obscurity. Most of them were and are middle-class, either by birth, wealth, education or occupation and confirm the elitist character of political leadership in new states. George Price, the PUP leader, is no exception. His father 'came from an old Colonial family of distinction who were closely identified with the economic, social and religious life of the colony'.[24]

The elder Price was an auctioneer, a Justice of the Peace and 'had a unique record of outstanding public service'.[25] He sent his son to one of the 'select' secondary boys' schools, St John's College, which the Jesuits had established in 1887.[26] The young Price aspired to the Jesuit Order and tested his vocation for the priesthood in the United States of America and Guatemala in the late 1930s. On his return to Belize in 1942 he worked as secretary to a local multi-millionaire businessman, Robert Turton, who was an elected member of the Legislative Council from 1936 to 1948. Price was also engaged in the municipal politics of Belize City and was elected to the Belize Town Board in 1947 after an unsuccessful attempt in 1943.[27] Price was therefore well established and known when, together with John Smith, a cinema manager and member of the Legislative Council, Leigh Richardson, a journalist and a former primary school teacher, and Philip Goldson, also a journalist and a former civil servant, he formed the People's United Party in September 1950.[28] As one of the more influential leaders Price held the key posts of Secretary and Treasurer. He gradually established his pre-eminence as the party lost first Smith in 1951 and then Goldson and Richardson in 1956 over a protracted struggle for the leadership. From then on it is around his personal influence that the party has developed. He alone can claim a certain natural legitimacy or authority owing to his leading role in the movement for self-government. For it was after the split in 1956 and under his undisputed party leadership that the major constitutional advances occurred.

The concentration of power in Price's hands was to some extent the result of his conflict with the British government. Already weakened by the split, the truncated PUP could not survive further factionalism while it was under siege from 1957 to 1960 without totally destroying itself. Paradoxically, the resolution of the conflict in the party's favour in the 1960s enhanced Price's personal authority to an extent that the party is seen as little more than an extension of his personality. Price's personal hold on the PUP is not an uncommon phenomenon among political parties in the West Indies, especially those which have their origins in a nationalist movement and are still to survive their founders. For example, his counterpart in Trinidad, Eric Williams, has, according to Selwyn Ryan, been accused of 'instituting a personal monarchy and deliberately creating an image of an omnipotent superman'.[29]

At the minimum, the political culture as a whole in Belize, with its implications for the process of decision-making and the creating of political responses within the society, is a variation on the West Indian theme. This is because at least three broad aspects of the Belizean society are common to the other territories. First, as a legacy of the colonial era a strong element of authoritarianism characterizes the relationship between political leaders and their followers. Despite an outward appearance of egalitarian principles, there is little mass participation in the making of decisions which could affect the total society in fundamental ways. Second, there is the syndrome of 'sociological smallness' which Burton Benedict and others have identified as characteristics of certain small-scale societies such as those in the Caribbean.[30] P. J. Wood notes that in this situation 'private roles of kinship and obligation are entangled with public roles of office.... Personal antagonism can poison public affairs while disagreement over policy can estrange private lives.'[31] Such a situation is hardly conducive to public debate and collective responsibility. Third, the economies of these societies are unable to provide a reasonable level of employment to the majority of its citizens. This has tended to increase the importance of the government's role as an employer and dispenser of patronage. Governmental institutions inevitably become ubiquitous and this leads to further accretion of authority and influence to those who govern.

As in the case of its political culture, there is little that is singular in Belize's constitutional advance. The colony has had three transitory constitution's, in 1954, 1961 and 1964. All were fairly orthodox. The first introduced adult suffrage and a quasi-ministerial or membership system of government, the second a full ministerial system of government, and the third internal self-government.[32] At the time of the last constitutional change early independence was anticipated. The PUP government is however deterred from making the final move by the century-old Guatemala claim to Belize.[33] The claim, which was dormant for several years, was revived with varying degrees of intensity after the Second World War, and accompanied with threats of annexation by military action if Belize were to be given independence. In 1968 the dispute defied a diplomatic solution put forward by the United States of America at the request of the two high contracting parties, Guatemala and Britain.[34] External threat to a society usually serves to bring together contending forces within it into a common front, but in Belize the effect has been the exact opposite. The PUP's initial response to the claim was not clear and unequivocal, and although it is now unquestionably committed to the view that the country's independence is not negotiable, it has been unable to win the unqualified confidence of various opposition elements in its handling of the problem. The strain on national unity which the claim exerts adds to the PUP's reluctance to end its dependence on Britain's ultimate authority and military strength.

The protracted delay of independence, as distinct from the reason for it, is not peculiar to Belize. The smaller territories in the region have been in a state of constitutional limbo for an equally long period. After the failure of the West Indies Federation in 1961 these territories, doubtful about their economic viability, opted for a political formula that, in the mid-1960s, conceded internal self-government to them and kept intact British control over their defence, and external affairs.[35] Any one of these territories can withdraw from this arrangement at any time and become fully independent. Like these Associated States, as they are called, the initiative for arranging the final constitutional conference rests with Belize since the British government has repeatedly stated that the country can have its independence whenever it is ready.

Finally, Belize's distinctiveness is not derived from its geographical position on the coast of Central America in the heart of the Caribbean Basin.[36] The position is strategic for providing a link between the Caribbean and Central America but no more so than Jamaica or, to a lesser extent, Cuba.

Belize is unique in that it is a meeting place, a borderland of two quite different cultural worlds. These are the White–Creole–Carib and the

Spanish–Mestizo–Indian complexes. Together, these complexes give Belize a racial, linguistic and cultural heterogeneity that is unusual in either the West Indies or Central America. The relatively small population consists of such racially diverse groups as the Africans, Caribs, Chinese, East Indians, Europeans, Lebanese and Syrians, Kekchi, Mayan, Waika and Mopanero Indians.[37] Its diversity confirms the country's contiguity to Mexico and Guatemala, its colonial affinity to the West Indies and imperial attachment to Britain.

*Cultural Groups*

Further elaboration of the country's place of special interest in the Pan-American area is hampered by the problem of determining the numerical strength of the two broad cultural groups, classifying them by race and indeed of assessing the value of race as a basis of cultural differentiation. Belize is perhaps one of the few countries in the region in which there is very little up-to-date statistical data on the racial origins of the population. The last population census was taken in 1970, but the available information is preliminary and does not refer to ethnic origins except in the breakdown of the working population, which was 31,465 or 26 per cent of the total population.[38] Apart from pertaining to a relatively small section of the population, the data are of limited value in determining the numerical strength of each racial group. Negro or Black, East Indian, Chinese, Syrian/Lebanese, and White are the only racial groups specifically identified. Categories of 'Mixed' and 'Other races' cover the other groups including the Indians. The previous census in 1960 was completely silent on the racial composition of the society.[39] This silence is consistent with the PUP government's policy of de-emphasizing racial differences in the pursuit of a common identity: 'Do not say Creole, or Carib, or Mestizo,' Price told an interviewer, 'Use the expressions Afro-Belizean, Carib-Belizean or Maya-Belizean. Or better still, use only the word Belizean.'[40] The omission in the 1960 census is perhaps also a response to the difficulties of neatly allotting individuals to racial groups in a society where there are no rigid barriers of legal status or social discrimination and where miscegenation among the racial groups is not uncommon.

Some idea of the problems of establishing racial origins and allocation may be gained from the 1946 census.[41] This census divided the population into: Black 22,693 (38.39 per cent), Mixed or coloured 18,360 (31.01 per cent), Aboriginal Indian 10,030 (16.94 per cent), Carib 4,112 (6.94 per cent), White 2,329 (3.93 per cent), East Indian 1,366 (2.3 per cent), Syrian 128 (0.41 per cent), Chinese 50 (0.08 per cent), not stated 15 (0.05 per cent). Those described as black are the descendants of the African slaves who were imported mainly from Jamaica and also the more recent immigrants from the Commonwealth Caribbean territories. The white population included the descendants of the early British settlers, and more recent arrivals from Britain, the United States and Canada. It also included persons of Spanish origin whose ancestors migrated as refugees during the War of the Caste in the middle of the nineteenth century to the northern districts, Corozal and Orange Walk, from Mexico.[42] The 'mixed' or 'coloured' group included the two main sub-groups, persons of mixed European and African descent and persons of mixed European and Indian descent.

Although it reveals the complexity of racial origins, the 'mixed' category cannot cover in two sub-groups the bewildering variety of racial admixtures. There is a significant number of visible cases of individuals who straddle these two mixed categories of European and African, and Mestizo and Indian. It is, however, not possible to arrive at a more precise description of the various intermixtures of races by observing inherited biological characteristics, in particular skin colour, hair formation and facial structure. It is not uncommon for members of a family to display the differing phenotypical characteristics within the society, their various con-figurations approaching the 'European', the 'Mestizo', the 'Indian' and the 'African'. Such a family can trace its ancestry to Britain and perhaps another European country, Africa, the West Indies, and to one or several of the neighbouring Spanish-speaking republics.

The problem of racial classification is not confined to the middle-range groups. It also exists between two different ethnic groups, the African and the Carib, who are both unmistakably black. To the casual observer the Caribs are not easily distinguishable from the Belizean or West Indian Africans. But the Caribs, who were warlike and driven from St Vincent by their European adversaries, first to the north coast of Honduras and later to Belize, owe their origin to miscegenation between the Arawak Indians from the Orinoco and the African slaves.[43]

Skin colour and other physical characteristics are therefore not reliable guides to racial origins. Nonetheless they played an important part in determining social and occupational status in the colonial society. The controlling and prestigious positions in the civil service and in business, particularly the foreign-owned, were filled by Europeans and persons of light complexion. This does not mean, however, that every racial group that approximated to the European configuration qualified for leadership in the colonial society. For such a society to function effectively it was necessary for the British colonial oligarchy to assign responsibilities to and confer rewards upon those with whom they felt the closest social and cultural affinity and who in consequence could be relied upon to safeguard the existing social and political system. This placed persons of Spanish origin and of Spanish and Indian descent at a disadvantage and at the same time gave upward mobility to the British section of the 'coloured' group and the African population that readily emulated the colonial values.

Sociologically, these cultural considerations further complicated the problem of racial classification. Despite the common racial characteristics between the British colonial oligarchy and the Spaniards, or rather persons of Spanish descent, the latter were always distinguished from 'Europeans'. In fact cultural and social distinction was, and still is, perceived primarily by Belizeans not in racial and colour terms of white and black, but between those who were British-oriented or Creoles and those who were not.

It is in fact less problematic to classify the population numerically by cultural affinity rather than by racial origin. Two valuable indexes are language and geographic distribution of the two broad cultural categories. Both indexes were used in the 1960 census and there is a high correlation between them. As the tables 1 and 2 indicate Belize City is essentially a Creole town and also the home of the majority of this group. To the west of the Belize District the Indians gradually predominate over the Creoles until around Benque Viejo in the Cayo District and the south-western corner in the Toledo District, near the Guatemalan border, the inhabitants are almost entirely Indian. The Mopanero Indians who migrated from the Petan area of Guatemala are concentrated in the rural areas of the Cayo District and San Antonio, which is the largest Indian village in Belize. The Kekchi Indians, who are from the Vera Paz area of Guatemala, have tended to confine their residence to the Toledo District. To the north of the Belize District the settlement pattern is the same. The population of Orange Walk Town, the nearest town to Belize City, is composed of Indians, Mestizos and Creoles, with the former group constituting almost exclusively the rural population of the Orange Walk District. The population of the Corozal District in the extreme north consists mainly of Mestizos in the town and of Indians in the surrounding villages. The Indians in these two northern areas are the descendants of the Yucatan Mayas. The other major cultural group, the Caribs, is concentrated on the south coast of the country in the Stann Creek and Toledo Districts. Stann Creek is almost exclusively Carib and so to a lesser extent is Punta Gorda, the administrative capital of the Toledo District.

As table 1 indicates, over one-third (36.3 per cent) of the total population lived in Belize City in 1960. Jocelyne Kharusi has also pointed out that 'the rate of population increase of Belize City has always been greater than

the country as a whole, despite a net outflow of immigrants from the city
to the district'.[44] It should also be observed that Creoles are predominant
in the rural sections of the Belize District, particularly along the banks of
the Belize River, and are numerically significant in the towns of Orange

Table 1  *Distribution of main cultural groups, 1960*

| Districts and sub-divisions | Population | % | Main cultural groups |
|---|---|---|---|
| BELIZE | *90,505* | *100.0* | *Creoles and Mestizos* |
| *Belize District* | *40,084* | *44.2* | *Creoles* |
| Belize City | 32,867 | 36.3 | Creoles |
| Belize Rural | 7,217 | 7.9 | Creoles |
| *Corozal District* | *9,730* | *10.8* | *Mestizos and Indians* |
| Corozal Town | 3,171 | 3.5 | Mestizos and Indians |
| Corozal Rural | 6,559 | 7.3 | Indians |
| *Orange Walk District* | *10,306* | *11.4* | *Mestizos and Indians* |
| Orange Walk Town | 2,157 | 2.3 | Creoles and Mestizos |
| Orange Walk Rural | 8,149 | 9.1 | Indians |
| *Cayo District* | *11,764* | *13.0* | *Indians and Creoles* |
| Cayo Town | 1,890 | 2.1 | Creoles |
| Benque Viejo Town | 1,607 | 1.8 | Indians |
| Cayo East Rural | 3,199 | 3.5 | Creoles |
| Cayo West Rural | 5,068 | 5.6 | Indians |
| *Stann Creek* | *10,906* | *12.1* | *Creoles and Caribs* |
| Stann Creek Town | 5,287 | 5.8 | Creoles and Caribs |
| Stann Creek Rural | 5,619 | 6.3 | Creoles and Caribs |
| *Toledo* | *7,715* | *8.5* | *Creoles and Caribs* |
| Punta Gorda | 1,789 | 1.9 | Creoles and Caribs |
| Toledo North and Central | 6,950 | 5.5 | Creoles |
| Toledo South | 976 | 1.1 | Indians and Caribs |

Source: *Census of British Honduras, 1960*, Kingston, vol. 2, p. 1

Walk, Cayo, Stann Creek and Punta Gorda. These demographic patterns
suggest that the Creoles account for about 55 per cent of the population.
The second largest group is the Mestizos who make up about 20 per
cent of the population. The Indians and the Caribs make up some 15
per cent and 8 per cent respectively, and the other cultural groups account
for the remaining 2 per cent.

Table 2   *Residents classified according to ability to speak principal languages: minor divisions, 1960*

| Language | British Honduras | Belize District Belize Town | Belize District Rest of District | Corozal District Corozal Town | Corozal District Rest of District | Orange Walk District Orange Walk Town | Orange Walk District Rest of District | Cayo District Cayo Town | Cayo District Benque Viejo | Cayo District Rest of District | Stann Creek District Stann Creek Town | Stann Creek District Rest of District | Toledo District Punta Gorda | Toledo District Rest of District |
|---|---|---|---|---|---|---|---|---|---|---|---|---|---|---|
| Total | 90,505 | 32,907 | 7,217 | 3,171 | 6,559 | 2,157 | 8,149 | 1,890 | 1,607 | 8,267 | 5,287 | 5,619 | 1,789 | 5,926 |
| English only | 46,090 | 27,687 | 5,780 | 591 | 811 | 317 | 1,129 | 303 | 50 | 2,781 | 1,601 | 3,077 | 361 | 1,602 |
| Spanish only | 8,887 | 257 | 325 | 702 | 1,728 | 540 | 1,964 | 402 | 1,180 | 1,499 | 21 | 48 | 26 | 195 |
| Maya only | 2,810 | 3 | — | 3 | 358 | 1 | 131 | — | — | 93 | — | 5 | 1 | 2,225 |
| Carib only | 1,395 | 27 | 7 | 3 | 12 | — | 1 | — | 2 | 2 | 593 | 498 | 106 | 144 |
| English and Spanish | 17,824 | 4,576 | 1,007 | 1,750 | 1,705 | 1,162 | 1,575 | 1,165 | 371 | 2,671 | 214 | 749 | 334 | 545 |
| English and Maya | 839 | 10 | 1 | — | 6 | 1 | 10 | 2 | 2 | 51 | 4 | 8 | 2 | 742 |
| English and Carib | 5,025 | 148 | 53 | 2 | 24 | — | 66 | 2 | 1 | 65 | 2,619 | 1,086 | 1,276 | 183 |
| Spanish and Maya | 3,115 | 6 | 12 | 53 | 1,351 | 72 | 1,058 | 7 | 1 | 382 | 3 | 7 | 1 | 162 |
| Spanish and Carib | 41 | — | — | — | — | 1 | 6 | — | — | — | 7 | 16 | 18 | 1 |
| Maya and Carib | — | — | — | — | — | — | — | — | — | — | — | — | — | — |

SOURCE: *Census of British Honduras 1960*, table 2.5, p. 13

*The small cultural groups* While the numerical breakdown of population by culture rather than by race is less problematic, it nevertheless can be misleading. In our calculations the East Indians, Chinese and Lebanese are counted among the small cultural groups and they are of little importance to the political process. In fact their assimilation within the wider social system has proved easier than the preservation of their cultural identity. The most integrated group are the East Indians who are primarily peasant farmers in the sugar and rice industries in the Corozal and Toledo districts respectively. They were imported from Calcutta in the early 1880s to work the sugar estates throughout the country, especially those in the Toledo District which a number of southerners from the United States had established after the United States War of Secession in 1868.[45] East Indians also drifted in small numbers from the West Indies to the Toledo agricultural settlements.[46] But Belize was not an agricultural society, and the importation of East Indian labour ceased as the sugar industry declined in the late 1880s and the 1890s throughout the Caribbean. As a result of this short-lived immigration, and lacking systematic contact with other East Indian communities in the West Indies, this group lost most of its cultural characteristics. Its members speak no East Indian languages and have long abandoned their style of dress, religions and marriage customs in favour of the more common social values.

The Chinese, who were also brought in as indentured agricultural labourers in the 1860s,[47] and the Lebanese are more contented than integrated minorities since they are permitted to pursue their profitable commercial business in Belize City and the district towns. Perhaps the cultural group which occupies the most marginal position within the political and social system and which seems intent on maintaining its distinctiveness is the Mennonites. About four hundred families from two communities, the Reinland and the Kleingemeinde, emigrated in batches from Mexico and Canada from 1957 to 1959 and settled in the remote parts of the Orange Walk and Cayo districts after receiving firm assurances from the government of substantial autonomy in local matters. They are exempted from participation in insurance and social security schemes and for religious reasons do not participate in the political process.[48] The converting of virgin lands into highly productive agricultural areas is perhaps their main contribution to a society in which subsistence farming is the agricultural tradition. It is likely, however, that their children will establish a closer social relationship with the rest of the society as they are being educated within the normal school system.

*The Creole and Mestizo complexes: a static view* Neither complex is easy to define and of the two the Creole is the more difficult. The original use of the term Creole in the Americas and the Caribbean is obscure. The term is supposed to be derived from the Spanish *criollo*, meaning native of the locality and appears to have been used first by Spanish colonists in South America to distinguish their children from newly arrived Spanish immigrants and subsequently by and with reference to descendants of non-Amerindian and non-Asiatic peoples born and settled in the West Indies and in some areas of the Americas. Apparently, it is within the latter context that the term gained currency among the early British settlers, the Baymen, and their ex-African slaves in Belize. The original meaning of the term was probably also applicable in the sense that these inhabitants, who had found the territory largely unoccupied, witnessed the arrival of the Mayas and the Mestizos from North Yucatan, and the Caribs.

The term, however, developed into a concept with racial and cultural connotations. A precise racial definition of Creole is as elusive as its original usage is ambiguous, and it is significant that it was not used in the 1946 census. Africans constitute about two-thirds of this component but anyone with a generous admixture of African blood will answer the biological criterion.[49] It is however the cultural element that is emphasized since the complex is conceived and expressed more as a social and cultural than a biological phenomenon. The concept is therefore used primarily to identify a non-Indian and non-Mestizo way of life and a set of values derived, with local adaptation, from the Anglo-Saxon countries, mainly Britain, the West Indies, and from Africa. Thus the few British expatriates and the group of local whites, who are dwindling, form an integral part of this complex although racially they would be excluded from it.

The African element of the culture when not devalued has been subordinated to the British. This was largely the result of the socializing influence of the Protestant churches – Anglican, Scottish Presbyterian and Methodist – whose membership was predominantly Creole. As standard-bearers of British values and codes of behaviour these denominations channelled their efforts mainly through the educational system which they had shaped and controlled during the Crown colony period.

The local adaptation of an amalgam and mixture of African and British culture has, however, produced distinctive food preferences, social habits, and a dialect called 'Creole', which is the most obvious cultural characteristic within the group. It is the normal language of everyday discourse in the areas where the Creoles are concentrated. It is noteworthy that, unlike in the West Indies where the local dialect is regarded as the language of the working class, the Creole dialect in Belize does not suffer a social stigma.

It is embraced by the various social groups in the Creole complex and therefore helps to solidify the group.

The Creole culture also has a distinctive occupational pattern. The high and middle economic status groups opt for the elite positions in law, teaching and the civil service, with little interest in a career in business. The lower income group has traditionally pursued forestry operations as their main occupation. Since the decline of this industry they have found casual or intermittent employment as domestics, street vendors, unskilled labourers in the construction industry, longshoremen, fishermen and self-employed petty artisans. Only a small number are peasant farmers as most regard agriculture as an inferior and transitory occupation – a resting spell from the more vigorous forestry activity. The distaste for agriculture is so strong that few Creoles are attracted to the sugar industry despite its emergence as the main source of employment.

Apart from its distinctiveness the occupational pattern provides an insight into the system of social stratification among the Creoles. The findings of anthropologists[50] that occupation and colour are the main status determinants of stratification, and are closely correlated within the Creole social hierarchy in much of the former British West Indies, seem to be relevant here, even though it is usually pointed out that Belize lacked the plantation system and the comprehensive slavery system in which the social structure of the West Indies is rooted and does not therefore lend itself readily to a study within the plantation framework. A white skin usually means a high social and occupational position. People with this pigmentation are part of the commercial business element. They are the managers of banks, commercial houses and owners of the prestigious and expensive hotels. Those who have ceased to be affluent tend to maintain their position within the group by converting their large and spacious homes into exclusive guest houses for tourists. The white Creole element maintains its overall prestige by an institutionalized tendency to mutual supportiveness. In family structure it adheres to the model of the nuclear family.

The middle class whose members are brown and black in colour embraces the professions and has never displayed much entrepreneurial talent. In the heyday of colonialism it tended in a number of ways to be willingly dependent on the patronage of the upper class. It reacted to its precarious relationship with the upper class by frequent displays of antipathy and a discriminatory attitude towards members of the lower class. In family structure, the middle-class Creoles tended to resemble the upper class. Membership in the middle class is at least partly by achievement. Securing a coveted scholarship or losing a well-paying job can have immediate and dramatic consequences for an individual's position. The mobility that results between the middle and lower class explains the presence of a strong element of what M. G. Smith refers to as lower-class or 'folk culture' in the former stratum.[51]

The broad base of the Creole element is black in colour. Whether it is rural or urban the most important characteristic of this group is the range of occupation which it pursues in its effort to eke out an existence. Within this stratum, family structure tends to be characterized by non-legal marital unions, a preponderance of female-headed households and a high incidence of illegitimate births. These factors all predispose the lower-class family structure to instability. This socio-economic group is the least metropolitan-oriented in its cultural aspects and has retained a number of discernible 'Africanisms'.

The Caribs, who are a cross between runaway African slaves and Carib women, also share many African features of the Creole culture. Their inclusion in the Creole complex is, however, not straightforward. They possess their own language and their occupational pattern and social mores can be distinguished from the Creole and the Mestizo.[52] Fishing and subsistence farming, mainly of cassava, is their traditional occupation, but many also work in the citrus industry in Stann Creek. Although of mixed African and Indian descent, their culture is not simply a fusion of the two elements. By virtue of their unusual degree of cultural differentiation and the fact that the white ruling elite viewed them with distrust because of their rebellious and defiant past in St Vincent, they were ascribed from the outset a low social status. This has impelled them towards the maintenance of a strong group consciousness which their concentration in the Stann Creek and Toledo districts has reinforced. Like the Creoles, however, education ranks high in their value system. Many of them become primary school teachers and they are the only segment in the teaching profession which can be persuaded to work among the Indians in the rural areas. This at once confirms their low ascribed status and social aspiration. Since their desire is to break out of their social isolation and embrace the mobility aspirations of the Creoles they are included in the Creole complex.

If the Creole culture is a mixture of English and African, the Mestizo is a fusion of Spanish and Indian. Like its English counterpart in the Creole culture, the Spanish element in the Mestizo has been accorded a higher status value throughout South and Central America. Yet, more than the African in the Creole culture in the West Indies, the Indian element remains a conspicuous feature of the Mestizo way of life particularly in

Central America and more specifically in Belize. This capacity for long-term survival against the pressures of the European culture is due not so much to the Indian culture being indigenous as to the fact that Belize forms part of a concentrated area – which included most of Guatemala, the western parts of Honduras and El Salvador, and in Mexico all of the states of Campeche and Yucatan, the Territory of Quntana Roo and most of the States of Tabasco and Chiapas – which was initially occupied by the Toltecs, Aztecs and Mayas whose civilizations were remarkable for their scientific achievements and durability.[53]

Despite its durability the Maya civilization collapsed in the tenth century. There is uncertainty about the subsequent distribution and movement of the Mayas in Belize but archaeological evidence[54] discounts the view that they migrated in substantial numbers to Yucatan where the civilization flowered in a modified form in the thirteenth century. In Belize, however, the indigenous way of life remained unaffected by the Spanish conquest and colonization of Central America in the sixteenth century and also by the establishment of a British settlement around the mid-seventeenth century; for, although a Spanish possession, Belize was never administered or settled by Spaniards and the contact between the British colonial administration and the Maya population was minimal.[55]

The Indian population was reinforced by Maya refugees who had fled from eastern Yucatan in the wake of the Indian uprising, the Caste War of Yucatan, between 1847 and 1853.[56] The immigrants settled as villagers mainly in the northern districts, Corozal and in Orange Walk, which were parts of the ancient Maya province of Chetumal, the border town of Mexico. Some also found their way to the western district of Cayo, and a smaller number still to the southern district of Toledo. The stream of Indian refugees which continued as a migration movement well into the 1920s did not only consist of those who merely wished to avoid the aftermath of the uprising. It also included those who accompanied the Spanish colonists as sympathizers in the war.[57]

In terms of their cultural orientation the northern areas of Corozal and Orange Walk were more an extension of Mexico than part of the British settlement. In fact the waves of migration had by 1861 transformed the Creole population in Belize into a minority, and 37 per cent of the respondents of the census of that year were Spanish-speaking whites and Mestizos and 18 per cent were Indians.[58] Spanish local government institutions were legally established in the two areas in 1858,[59] and on the appeal of the refugees for pastoral care in their own faith, the missionary activities of the Roman Catholic Church began in earnest in Belize.[60] Clear regional differences between the two areas appeared almost from the outset. The

Orange Walk area had become a centre of labour recruitment in timber activities of both the Mestizos of the town and the Maya Indians of the surrounding villages. The Corozal area, already much more densely populated, had crystallized into a socially stratified agricultural community based on the production of subsistence food, notably corn and bean, and also sugar cane cultivation which was introduced by the refugees. At the top of the hierarchy were the Spaniards of pure European extraction, with their sugar estates or *ranchos* each with its own sugar mill. The middle stratum consisted of the bulk of the Mestizo who began as entrepreneurs in chicle extraction, and eventually accumulated sufficient capital to gain control by lease over large parcels of land in Corozal.[61] Because of the numerical decline of the full-blooded Spaniards mainly through miscegenation, it was easy for the Mestizos to penetrate the upper levels of the community or to move to Belize City where many of them now exert considerable social influence as prominent businessmen. The Maya Indians who lived either in the villages or the *ranchos* constituted the labour force, being dependent on cane cutting as their primary source of cash wages or entering the wider colonial economic system as chicleros, or bleeders of the gum of the sapodilla tree, or to a lesser extent as woodcutters.[62]

As social control was patterned after the pre-1847 sugar *hacendados* of Yucatan, and as was the case in the rest of Mexico, the Indians were exploited by the Spanish-speaking elite. According to Jones, debt peonage was commonly practised, and entire villages were tied by patronal relationships to powerful and influential Mestizos.[63] To some extent a series of economic changes – the establishment of a central sugar factory in Corozal in 1935, the decline of the small-scale family-owned plantations, the rehabilitation of the industry in the late 1950s and above all the expansion of the industry since 1963 under the corporate ownership of Tate and Lyle Ltd – have modified the social and cultural bases of control in the area. For one thing the Indians in the north are becoming more of an agroproletariat as they change from shifting subsistence farming of corn to the cultivation of cane either on their own land or as wage labourers on the lands of the large local growers. For another, the most important decisions affecting the cane-farmers emanate from the national and international centres of power and authority. It is in these external, bureaucratically controlled organizations rather than in traditional institutions that the formal structure of local associations such as co-operatives are rooted. Nonetheless, the number of Indians who have achieved upward social mobility within the Mestizo complex and the wider social system, or even emerged out of their rural habitat, is negligible. The opportunities for improving their economic and occupational status are limited by the considerable influence which the corporate plantation owner and the more established Mestizo cane growers exert on their own behalf in the utilization of the crucial resources such as land, cane licences, transport and credit.[64]

The Indians in the south are even more economically deprived. Their whole life is taken up with shifting subsistence agriculture and particularly with the clearing of the land or the 'milpa', as it is called. Perhaps more than their counterparts in the north, they have retained their dialects. This is not to say that their indigenous culture is less susceptible to a Spanish orientation. The ability to speak Spanish rather than an Indian language has been enhanced by the government's increasing use of it in the public media. The hispanizing tendencies are also facilitated not only by the relative geographic proximity of the areas to Mexico and Guatemala but even more by the virtual freedom of movement across the border of the former and easy physical connection with the latter. Indeed, the cultural affinity and familial ties of the entire Mestizo complex with Mexico and Guatemala, the increasing use of Spanish by the Indians and the actual contact have had a strong pull towards closer relationship with their Spanish-speaking neighbours.

Although it is marked, the differentiation within each cultural complex is overshadowed by that between them. It is possible to speak of two foci of social life with the Creole complex representing historically the dominant centre of gravity. Indeed, before the emergence of the PUP in 1950, political consciousness was a Creole and an urban phenomenon. The Creole elite acted and behaved as if Belize City was Belize with the result that the predominantly Latin peasantry was *in* the colonial society but not *of* it. Although the colonial political system was unitary the application of different methods of rural administration to the various communities strengthened and preserved the communal and cultural divisions. Rural organization in the Creole villages was informal and left to its own devices by the central government. In contradistinction the Spanish local institutions in the Indian villages functioned under a highly structured organization. The principal one is the Alcalde system. Although it was introduced in the north it is mainly found in the south and west. It was extended with limited success to some of the Carib villages in these areas. A kindred system, the Patron or Mayor, also existed in the north, but it was not as fully established as the Alcalde.[65] If coercive power, so often used elsewhere by colonial governments to regulate ethnic and cultural relationships, was noticeably absent in Belize it was precisely because the social and occupational distance separating these cultural groups was so wide that the need to invoke regulatory control seldom arose. Visiting observers, as Waddell points out, were impressed with the absence of racial and cultural frictions.[66] But this picture was deceptive in that it encouraged the ruling elite in Belize City to conclude that a highly integrated and cohesive society existed.

*The Creole and Mestizo complexes: a dynamic view*  This analysis, however, should not be pushed too far. Belize is not simply a collection of diverse cultural elements grouped into two main cultural complexes. The differences not only in race but also in culture, language, religion and occupation cut across each other to produce an extremely complex pattern of social and political life. The Creole language, for example, is more widely spoken than either English or Spanish. Essentially an adaptation and mixture of English and African dialects, it is enriched with terms from the Carib and Indian languages.[67] Likewise a number of Creole expressions have seeped into the Spanish spoken by Mestizos which is not that spoken in Spain or even in Central America.[68] This cross-fertilization has not escaped the Carib language. From the outset it had a small percentage of French terms, dating from the era of the French occupation of St Vincent, and to this a small number of English words have been added.[69] There is also movement across occupational frontiers, especially in business and some of the liberal professions. Above all, there are individuals who draw their identity from both complexes and cannot be exclusively allotted to one of them. The outstanding example is Premier Price. Not only does he belong to a prominent colonial family but reaches out on his maternal side to the indigenous Mayan for his heritage.[70] Few other political leaders in Central America or the West Indies would be equally at home in the social capitals of the Spanish-speaking Republics, Jamaica, England and the United States of America. Price has often stressed the country's Mayan identity as a basis for nationalism. This predilection was reinforced by his commitment at the outset of the nationalist movement to the development of the economy through links with the wider Latin American groupings rather than with the West Indian territories. Indeed his desire for a Central American orientation was equally matched by his opposition to political links with the West Indies Federation which the British government had begun to promote after the Second World War.[71] Price also conceived of the United States as a surrogate for Britain on the ground that this shift was much more consonant with Belize's regional orientation. Yet none of the other prominent leaders within the nationalist movement was a Mestizo or could have claimed affinity with this cultural complex. They were full-blooded Creoles. This fact at once dispels any notion that the ethno-cultural categories formed corporate political groups arraigned against each other.

If the stress on the Mayan identity appealed to the Indians and Mestizos, the opposition to political association with the West Indies found its principal support among the ordinary Creoles in Belize City who were apprehensive of labour migration from the overcrowded West Indian islands to Belize.[72] Despite its predominantly Creole leadership the PUP mass support was ethnically and culturally varied, and drawn from both the urban and rural sections of the society. The opposition to the party also came from the Creoles. To some extent it stemmed from the belief that Price's Central American orientation threatened the hegemony of the Creole culture. But the leaders of the opposition were not only members of the dominant cultural section of the society. They were also the urban elite that bolstered the colonial political system and were not dissimilar from their counterparts in other colonial territories in terms of their age, occupation, education and, perhaps to a lesser extent, wealth.[73] As we indicated in the discussion of the Creole middle class they were for the most part professional and salaried. Their leader was Herbert Fuller who formed the National Party (NP) in 1951. He came from a family that had a long tradition of public service and was one of the few Belizeans sent to England at an early age to receive a public school education.[74] On his return he became a commission agent and was elected in Belize City to the Legislative Council in 1948. In some respects, the experience of the Creole elite consequent upon the rise of the nationalist movement was uncommon to many West Indian territories. In most of these territories, the old elite was called upon to share its ruling status with the young intelligentsia. But in Belize this old elite was more or less displaced at least within the parliamentary system by a less prestigious group of politicians. Sir Hilary Blood, the visiting constitutional Commissioner, was in 1958 'astonished to find that there is among the unofficial members of the Legislative Assembly not a single lawyer, doctor nor person with a University degree'. 'This', he concluded, 'must be almost a unique condition of affairs.'[75] The new leaders could not only be differentiated occupationally from the upper ranks of the social elite but they were less affluent and more modest in their style of life.

It was not until the 1960s, when the colonial administration came to terms with the ascendancy of the PUP and brought the country to the penultimate stage of decolonization, that the PUP gradually attracted to its leadership members of various liberal professions and wealthy businessmen. This change in the social composition of the party leadership has strengthened the Creole representation within the ruling elite. For this group has retained its earlier educational advantage and therefore its domination of the professional, technical and bureaucratic skill upon which the government is so dependent. It cannot be overemphasized that identification of members of the Creole elite with the PUP came after the colonial government ended its negative attitude towards the party. This was the signal for them to do the same and to respond more positively to the nationalist political change if they were to retrieve and retain an important source of political power and influence.

The position of the Creole elite has been further reinforced by developments in the country's multiple orientation to external political entities. One of these developments is the response to the evolution of two regional economic groupings in the 1960s – the Central American Common Market (CACM)[76] and the Caribbean Common Market and Community (CARICOM) whose members are the Commonwealth Caribbean countries.[77] In 1961 the Economic Commision of Latin America (ECLA) decided to undertake a study of the possibilities of economic co-operation between Belize and Central America with a view to Belize joining what was at that time the Central American Economic Co-operation Committee.[78] Seven years later ECLA reported that the historical patterns of Belize's economic development and in particular its participation in the system of Commonwealth preferences did not favour its membership in the CACM.[79] This left Belize virtually no choice other than to move more in the direction of the Commonwealth Caribbean and join what was at that time the Caribbean Free Trade Association (CARIFTA), which it did in May 1971. The ECLA study was related to the unsuccessful attempt to find a diplomatic solution to the Guatemalan claim. The persistence of the claim does not only discourage Belize from taking its independence but also denies the government unrestricted participation in the inter-American system. Until the dispute is settled Belize cannot be admitted as a full member to the Organization of American States (OAS). In any case Price's desire to bring the country's colonial status to an end and to be more closely tied up with the hemisphere is tempered by the fact that, like the smaller territories of the Eastern Caribbean, Belize continues to be dependent upon Britain for most of its financial aid.

These developments keep Belize more in the Anglo-Saxon than the Latin sphere. The closer mainland attachments which would normally be expected to develop from the country's contiguity to, and the cultural and familial ties of the Indians and Mestizos with Mexico and Guatemala are being held in check by the legacy of British colonial rule in general and the closer identification with the Commonwealth Caribbean in particular.

The British and Anglo-Saxon orientation of the main institutions is intact. The legal system remains British and the law officers are mainly Creole and West Indian. The religious institutions which control the education system are also tied to the Anglo-Saxon countries. Furthermore, the orientation of these institutions provides the basis for 'models'. Despite their susceptibility to Latin American ideas and life-style, the young Mestizos, like their Creole counterparts, pursue their professional studies in Britain, Canada and the USA and to an increasing extent, the University of the West Indies[80] where they internalize the particular values of these educational and social institutions. The process of creolization is however taking place not only among the professional and other elite Mestizo groups. It extends to other socio-economic segments within the complex through the development and extension of the educational process. The school teachers remain predominantly Creole and Carib. The sole radio station, Radio Belize, provides 75 per cent of its programmes in English and most of the programmes are from Britain.[81] The radio is also the medium through which West Indian music has taken the country by storm since the development of closer economic association with the West Indies. Indeed, precisely because of its British and West Indian connections the influence of Radio Belize extends to Mexico, Honduras and Guatemala.

## Scope and purpose of this study

Although it has been indicated that Belize is in many ways simply another British colonial possession in the Caribbean and that its role as a cultural borderland gives it a place of special interest in the region, this study does not proceed within a comparative framework. No attempt, beyond the foregoing, is made to bring together those characteristics which the colonial and underdeveloped territories in the area seem to possess. The setting is Belize. And the purpose of the study is to describe the political institutions and process that have characterized political change in the country since the rise of a nationalist movement in 1950. The analysis is done in such a way that attention is focussed on the four aspects of the problem of political integration that emerged from the foregoing discussion. One involves the relationship between the two major cultural complexes, the Creole and the Mestizo, long separated by their settlement patterns, different occupational preferences and social values. Another involves the bridging of the elite–mass gap and the extent to which this relationship cuts across ethno-cultural lines. The third aspect of the problem of political integration is concerned with the conditions under which various parts of the country are brought within the national political system. A final aspect relates not merely to the country's relationship across its land boundaries but its multiple orientation to outside political entities – Britain, Guatemala, Mexico, the United States and the Commonwealth Caribbean. This last-mentioned dimension of the problem is closely related to the others because the country's regional attachment to Central America and the West Indies and its colonial connection with Britain in particular highlights the internal aspects of political integration.

Although the study is concerned with the broad analysis of political change it is not far removed from a theoretical issue. The issue is whether societies that are multi-ethnic and multi-cultural are 'plural' in character and dichotomized essentially into two culturally differentiated components or whether under the impact of colonialism and economic development all elements in these societies have increasingly come to share a commonality of values and aspirations so that differences in behaviour and conflicts are more meaningfully explained in the context of socio-economic classes. These two competing theoretical perspectives have characterized most studies of political and social change in the West Indies[82] and have given rise to a vast literature.[83] Of the two, the 'plural' notion has had a greater impact.[84] It is applied even to those territories where the population is not very racially mixed and is predominantly black. Its proponents argue that very little has conspired to modify the rigidity of the social hierarchy created by the plantation system and expressed in terms of the usual white–coloured–black ranking. This perspective has led M. G. Smith to divide the population of those territories that fall into this category, such as Jamaica and Grenada, into an urban, metropolitan-oriented elite and a rural 'folk' element, with each segment adhering to a unique value system and institutional forms.[85] In those territories that are multi-racial, such as Guyana and Trinidad, which both have two major racial groups, the Africans and East Indians, the proponents of this school of thought claim that the racial entities are so sharply divided by polarized values and institutions that their interaction is minimal and occurs more at the national than the local level of society.[86]

In the case of Belize, M. G. Smith, in a brief analysis of the process of decolonization, wrote in 1965:

The position and society of British Honduras are structurally unique. This territory straddles the boundary of two quite different worlds, the Negro–White–Creole and the Spanish–Indian–Mestizo culture areas. This cleavage divides Honduras culturally, linguistically, and by race. In consequence Hondurans hold conflicting loyalties and orientations. Many wish to quit the British Commonwealth and the Creole culture province for Guatemala and the Central American mestizo field. Others wish to remain Creole and British.

As Honduran autonomy increases, this cleavage will tend to deepen and some choice between association with the West Indies or with Guatemala will have to be faced. The final decision may then be determined by the balance of forces within Honduras.[87]

Our discussion so far suggests that this categorization of Belizean society and politics is too static. It distorts the reality of a more complex and dynamic situation in which, as we mentioned for example, the conflict relating to closer association with the West Indies in the 1950s arose over not only cultural but also socio-economic interests and over competition for political power among the old elite and the nationalist group which were both Creole. The firm alignment which Belize has eventually established with the Commonwealth Caribbean is also influenced by economic rather than cultural considerations although it reinforces the creolization process in the country.

The proponents of the plural school of thought are more prepared today to incorporate economic issues into their framework of analysis. Leo Despres recognizes that there are systematic political, social and economic forces which combine to upset the exclusive cultural relationships.[88] They prompt movement across environmental and occupational frontiers which in turn bring together members of different ethnic groups into various social and economic strata. This modification would appear to bring the 'pluralist' closer to the view that in the contemporary West Indian societies values and aspirations are based on an ever-growing awareness of the milieux of the western developed world, and involve the growing rejection at all levels of a life-style built around the deprivation of estate labour or the vicissitudes of grubbing for an existence on an acre of eroded hillside soil. But the conclusion which Despres draws from this more dynamic process of social action and change is not less but more racial and cultural cleavages. In his view, competition across micro-environment, especially where it takes the form of movement of population, must engender conflict. But the movement across environmental frontiers does not necessarily entail instability and even if it does its character is not primarily racial or cultural. Such movement, as R. T. Smith points out, gives rise to multiple group affiliation of individuals that reduces the salience and inevitability of racial and cultural differences and places segmented participation more on an economic, social and status basis.[89] Consequently deep cleavages along one axis are avoided. A kind of balancing mechanism of the Lewis A. Coser variety is achieved that at least arrests cultural fragmentation and political disintegration and therefore keeps the way open to a more integrative political system.[90]

PART ONE

# The colonial order, 1638–1949

# I

# Colonialism in historical perspective, 1638-1931

With Guyana and Surinam, Belize is one of the non-Iberian communities that breach the Latin continuum on the whole American continent from Rio Grande to Cape Horn. The breach is the least in Belize, where a sizeable element of the population is Latin in its linguistic and cultural orientation. It can also be more pertinently asked of Belize than of Guyana and Surinam, how is it that in the midst of the Spanish-speaking nations it did not become Spanish but, like Guyana, British? As Newton points out only history can tell us, and we must go far back into the seventeenth century to find the answer.[1]

Enclaves such as these are like chips split off in the carving of the great masses of rival empires. They changed hands with the military fortunes of European powers and were seldom claimed with the same tenacity as the larger colonial possessions. Belize fell into the second category. Throughout the eighteenth century England and Spain were almost constantly at war and the question of Spanish sovereignty in Belize was debated in most of the treaty negotiations between the two powers.[2] While neither England nor Spain would give way, Belize was not important enough for either to be willing to compromise by relinquishing valuable rights elsewhere, as was done between England and France in the case of Canada and Guadeloupe.[3] At the same time Britain recoiled from endowing Belize with a full paraphernalia of government until 1862 when it declared the settlement a colony.[4] Until then Belize offered an interesting study in primitive and spontaneous government set up without the sanction of the Crown, one that is unique and altogether anomalous in the story of the acquisition and development of Britain's colonial empire.[5] It is because of the manner in which British sovereignty was established that there exists to the present day the allegation of ambiguity in the British title to the colony so far as international law is concerned.[6] Britain was, however, less unorthodox and equivocal in its attitude towards the settlement's economic development in the seventeenth and eighteenth century. It recognized the territory for what it was: a primary producer whose logwood was to be fully exploited to meet the European demand for the dye which was extracted from the wood. It was the lucrative trade in this species of timber and later mahogany that had determined the foundation of the settlement and its retention in the late eighteenth century when its defeat by Spanish invaders seemed inevitable.[7] By the end of the nineteenth century the decline of this extractive industry was in full sight.[8] It was, however, not until the depression years in the 1930s that the full impact of the decline was felt. The straw which broke the back of the industry was a disastrous hurricane in September 1931. This event is a convenient point at which to end the analysis of the country's development from a settlement to a colony since it was a watershed.

*Disputed international status*

The beginning of the British settlement on Spanish soil in the Bay of Honduras is obscure. The records tell very little about it beyond setting 1638 as the date of the establishment of the settlement.[9] It is known, however, that the forestry pursuits were incidental to the original intention of the British who landed on the sea-shores.[10] Belize was valued for its location outside the principal shipping route and hazardous coral reef running off the shore line. It therefore provided a convenient hiding place from which the British buccaneers could launch their piratical attack from their base in Jamaica on the treasure-laden ships flying the Spanish standards along the two major Spanish galleon routes in the isthmus of Central America. Attacks on Spanish treasure, however, were not a full-time activity and it seems probable that several of the pirates found it lucrative to plunder also the trade in wood which the Spanish extracted from the Gulf of Campeachy.[11] The more enterprising adventurers discovered that it was easier and more certain to cut wood themselves. The British demand for the dye from logwood was growing with the expansion of its textile industry, and in 1655 the price paid for logwood in Britain was £100 per ton.[12] Forestry activities soon became the principal occupation and Belize City became an important centre for the export of logwood. The British woodcutters were so successful that they gained control of the logwood trade in many areas in the Bay of Honduras such as Cape Catocha, the Bay Islands and the Mosquito Shores of Nicaragua where they also settled. Belize, however, remained the 'central post' to which the woodcutters retired on their eventual evacuation from the outlying settlements.[13]

It was Elizabeth I who boasted in 1587 in her characteristic manner that neither the Pope's gift nor the Spanish King's claim to the Americas could prevent her subjects from settling on lands not occupied by Spain.[14] Some eighty years later Spain deferred to the British view. By the terms of the Anglo-Spanish or the Godolphin Treaty in July 1670 Spain recognized British sovereignty over Jamaica and also ceded to Britain all lands in the New World then occupied by British subjects.[15] A few months prior to the Treaty, Sir Thomas Modyford, Governor of Jamaica, had urged that Spanish recognition of the British settlement of Belize should be specifically included in any agreement with Spain.[16] The British government appeared to have ignored the advice or at best was indifferent to it. The claims of the settlers in Belize were neither respected by Spain nor consistently upheld by Britain. In 1713 Britain, for example, seemed to be in agreement with Spain that Belize was excluded from the places recognized by the Godolphin Treaty in 1670 as belonging to England.[17] By 1717, however, it was vigorously refuting Spain's contention that British subjects had no rights to the wood-cutting industry.[18] A diplomatic struggle ensued with Britain gaining the upper hand in 1763 when, in the Treaty of Paris, Spain recognized the economic activities of the settlers.[19] Spain, however, frequently abandoned diplomacy in favour of raids and incursions into various parts of the settlement, whereupon the settlers would withdraw from the area under siege.[20] In 1779, Spain, as an ally of France, declared war upon Britain and took opportunity of the hostility to drive the British inhabitants from Belize.[21] It was not until the Treaty of Versailles in 1783 that the settlers returned in substantial numbers from the Mosquito Coast where they had taken refuge.[22] It took another three years for Spain to explicitly sanction in the Convention of London the resettling of the British in Belize. But the 1786 Convention confined the settlers to the area between the Rio Hondo and the Sibun River,[23] a restriction which the settlers continuously violated by extending their occupation to the Sarstun River.[24] When the Spanish-American nations became independent in the early 1820s, Mexico acknowledged in 1826, in return for her recognition, British title as far as the Sibun river in conformity with the Convention of London.[25] Implicit in this acknowledgement was Mexico's view that it had inherited at least the section between the Hondo and the Belize rivers that was considered to be within the territory of Yucatan. But the Central American Federation and its successor state, Guatemala, withheld such recognition on the ground that it inherited all of the Spanish imperial possessions in the area which, if it was the case, also challenged any claim that Mexico was likely to lay to the northern part of the settlement.[26] Guatemala registered its claim in no uncertain manner. It menaced the British settlement on the Sibun River with a gunboat in 1827.[27] Eight years later it reasserted its contention by allotting about half of the land occupied by the Belize settlers, ironically, to a British commercial concern in

London.[28] Nothing, however, came of the arrangement which the British government had promptly denounced as 'a deliberate and insidious encroachment on British sovereignty'.[29]

The validity of British occupation was thrown into further uncertainty by the Clayton–Bulwer Treaty in 1850.[30] The Treaty, which provided for joint British–United States control of any inter-oceanic canal developed by them on the Isthmus, prohibited either nation from establishing or maintaining dominions in 'Central America'. At the same time the settlement of Belize was explicitly excluded from the scope of the treaty.[31] The two contracting parties, however, had disagreed about the southern boundary of the settlement. The United States contended that the settlement ended at the Sibun River as stipulated by the Convention of London in 1786 and that the territory between this river and the Sarstun belonged to Guatemala. But Britain had refused to accept this view. It upheld its objection six years later in 1856 in an unratified Treaty with the United States, the Dallas–Clarendon, which specifically identified the Sarstun as the southern boundary.[32] Britain seemed to be in firm possession of the entire area which it claimed when it negotiated a boundary agreement with Guatemala in 1859.[33] The first six articles provided that the boundary should extend from the mouth of the Sarstun, up that river to Gracias a Dios Falls, thence north to the Garbutt's Falls on the Belize River, and from that point due north to the Mexican border. A seventh article provided for the construction of a road from Guatemala City to the Caribbean coast by Britain. As far as the British were concerned the boundary treaty simply gave *de jure* recognition to a *de facto* situation. But Guatemala saw its acceptance of the convention as cession of territory that had to be disguised as Britain was precluded from acquiring territory in the area by the Clayton–Bulwer Treaty of 1850 and for which the construction of the road by Britain was compensatory.[34]

Instead of proceeding with the construction of the road, Britain made this commitment the subject of a further treaty in 1863.[35] Guatemala failed to ratify this second treaty in the stipulated time. When she eventually did, Britain claimed that the opportunity was lost and that for her part she had discharged her obligation. As Waddell points out the British attitude, however, 'legally defensible', was 'far from credible'.[36] Britain attempted to correct the diplomatic error when the matter was reopened in the 1930s by offering to consider means of implementing article seven or of making some financial adjustment.[37] By this time, however, Guatemala was even more intent on obtaining the territory for reasons which will be discussed in the next chapter. At this point it is only necessary to observe that the dispute was conceived in juridical terms by both Guatemala and Britain.

The former argued that the annulment of the convention restored her sovereignty over Belize which the British had never recognized.[38] Britain countered that the *status quo ante* 1859 was not Guatemalan sovereignty but British right to the territory by prescription, after Spain had tacitly abandoned her sovereignty over the area.[39] Guatemala had studiously refused to accept the British offer of submitting the dispute to the International Court of Justice,[40] and as mentioned in the introductory chapter diplomatic attempts to mediate the dispute have been unsuccessful.

The dispute is further complicated by Mexico's attitude. In 1893, after putting forward its own claim to Belize, Mexico signed a treaty with Britain defining the boundary between itself and 'the colony of British Honduras'.[41] This treaty was silent on the question of sovereignty; in defining the boundary it followed the line generally laid down in the Anglo-Spanish treaty of 1783 and the line thus defined is now in force. Recent Mexican governments have taken the formal view that in 1893 Mexico was gratuitous for the sake of friendship with Britain, and that they are prepared to leave their claim latent so long as the present situation is not altered in favour of Guatemala.[42] As we shall see in the final section of the book Mexico at times seems willing to sacrifice this attitude in the interest of its diplomatic relations with Guatemala.

## The forestry economy

If the profitable trade in logwood and mahogany firmly cast the settlement's pattern of economic development in the mould of forestry exploitation, Spanish injunctions and British reluctance to openly challenge them contributed to the imprint being indelible. In the Treaty of Paris in 1763 Spain limited its recognition of the settlers' economic activities to logwood cutting.[43] The mahogany operations which had begun to emerge as a more important trade than logwood remained outside the law. Even the legalizing of the logwood activities was not without its ambiguities. The area in which these could be undertaken was vaguely defined as between 'the Bay of Honduras and other places of the territory of Spain in that part of the world'.[44] Despite Spanish objection the woodcutters argued for the widest interpretation of this clause which was the right to cut the logwood wherever it was found. The Peace of Versailles in 1783 settled the boundary dispute to the advantage of the woodcutters, but not entirely so.[45] Many areas which the settlers had penetrated, including those over the Hondo river, in the Peten district, and above all over the Belize river to the Sibun, fell outside the boundaries.[46] The Treaty had also reiterated the prohibition of any forestry exploitation other than logwood on a commercial scale.[47] Three years later in the London Convention of 1786 the privilege was extended to mahogany.[48] But this merely confirmed an activity in which the settlers had been engaged for decades and which had definitely supplanted logwood – whose price had ruinously fallen to about £12 a ton in 1771 – as the principal and most profitable undertaking.[49]

The keynote of the Treaty however was the prohibition against commercial agriculture.[50] There were to be no plantations such as sugar, coffee or cocoa, and only fishing was permitted. This legal impediment, however, should not be overemphasized. For all practical purposes it was removed with the Spanish imperial presence in Central America in the 1820s. In 1839, the Secretary of State was confident that Spain 'will not raise any objections to the cultivation of the soil, having no longer any real interest in the maintenance of the former treaty'.[51] Furthermore by 1867, the Superintendent of the settlement recognized that the future of the mahogany industry was bleak and that agriculture 'was the only hope of the colony'.[52] Few paid heed to this warning. Extracting, with minimum effort, the natural resources for almost two centuries, the community had become accustomed to regard the forestry products as inexhaustible. Those who accepted the prediction merely aggravated the situation. The extractive nature of the forestry industry and the fact that a mahogany tree took about thirty years to mature produced a get-rich outlook among them that permitted little more than lip service to agricultural development.[53]

It is not surprising, therefore, that commercial agriculture owed its origin to two sets of immigrants. One was the Yucatan refugees who numbered about 12,000 in 1861.[54] They began the sugar industry as tenant farmers on cane plots in the 1840s. Large sugar plantations were out of the question because they were being ruined everywhere by the bounty system which protected beet sugar in Europe. By 1866 the industry had sufficiently developed into an export commodity for the Lieutenant-Governor to fling it in the face of the British settlers. In a speech he asked a series of rhetorical questions: 'Cannot you point with pride to the splendid cane fields at San Andres, Santa Cruz, Trial Farm and Indian Church? Has not costly machinery been erected...? Do you not already grow more sugar than suffices for home consumption, and are you not commencing to export?'[55]

The other group of immigrants was a number of Southern families from the United States who as we observed in the introductory chapter were resolved to leave their homes rather than submit to the victorious North. They were induced in 1867 by the offer of 100 acres of land to every male adult at a 'gratuitous' price in the virgin forest of Punta Gorda in the south.[56] The donor was one of the two large landed interests, Messrs Young, Toledo and Co. who eventually opened a private immigration agency in New Orleans. Most of the settlers, deterred by the hardships of a pioneer life in this area, soon abandoned their new homes, and either drifted back to the United States or moved further south to settle in Brazil. Those who persevered took advantage of the rich soil and rainfall and replaced the forest with maize, cattle and sugar-cane. The latter grew luxuriantly for twenty to thirty years and enabled the area to prosper. With it a social order developed that was not unduly remote from that obtaining on the old Southern plantations. Each plantation attracted the Caribs in the area as resident labour and later on recruited the East Indians who had drifted in small numbers from the West Indies and Guyana. The First World War, depression in the industry and the antiquated methods employed in the harvesting and preparation of the crop, brought decay upon the agricultural settlement and drove the younger agriculturalists to mahogany-cutting in the West of the District.[57]

The only commercial agricultural undertaking which the British settlers pursued was banana cultivation in the south. To encourage the industry, the price of Crown land was lowered, but this provoked the opposition of the mercantile interest which accused the government of being in alliance with the great landowners.[58] The development of the industry was contingent on the improvement of transportation between Belize and New Orleans to which the Central American banana trade was directed. Belize however did not have sufficient commercial activity and passenger traffic to make regularly schedule steamer runs economically possible without a government subsidy. To justify such assistance, the agricultural interest proposed in 1866 that the mail route to Jamaica be changed to New Orleans.[59] But although the shift would have further induced immigrants from the United States to settle in Belize, several objections were raised both in Belize and Jamaica between 1867 and 1879.[60] First, the change would have ended the direct transmission of despatches between Belize and Jamaica which also was an intermediary in the exchange of correspondence between Belize and London. Second, and more important than the effects upon the administration of government, the discontinuation of direct communication with Jamaica and the rest of the British West Indies would have disrupted the military arrangements with Belize. Above all, it was feared that the arrangement would make Belize substantially a dependency of Louisiana rather than of any British possession and that this would Americanize it. These objections were not upheld for long. As part of some sweeping reforms in agriculture, a strong-willed and resolute Lieutenant-Governor, Frederick P. Burlee, permanently changed the mail route soon after his arrival in 1877, and by 1883 hardly a day went by without a banana boat sailing from Belize to New Orleans.[61] The industry was buffeted by periodic fall in demand but it was sufficiently promising to induce the United Fruit Company to purchase the Middlesex estate of 12,500 acres in the Stann Creek Valley in 1911 and to begin operations on a large scale.[62] Prospects looked so favourable that a railway was built to join Middlesex to the port near Stann Creek Town twenty miles away. The industry, however, suffered a severe setback when Panama disease attacked the bananas in 1913 and caused the United Fruit Company to abandon its estates.[63] Up to the end of the period under review it had not recovered.

The chequered development of agriculture in the south reinforced the dominant view that logwood and mahogany would maintain the country for some time to come, if not indefinitely, even though towards the end of the nineteenth century the forestry industry itself was being subjected to periods of crisis and depression.[64] To note this reliance on the forestry industry is to indicate the emergence of a 'forestocracy', the imbalance in the ratio of ownership to the size of holdings and the system of land tenure. Originally, the British settlers disposed of land in Public Meetings by various resolutions which had the force of law.[65] The white population never exceeded two hundred and sixty except in 1742 when it was four hundred.[66] It could therefore afford to be a liberal distributor of the land. But perhaps a more important reason was that land *per se* was of little value to the woodcutters. What was of value were the forests. The first settlers were little more than squatters on Spanish territory and they initially determined their land rights in 1765 by occupancy. This merely involved the building of a hut.[67] Logwood extraction was conducted on a relatively small area of land since the wood grew luxuriantly in swamps where it formed immense thickets. When an area was exhausted it was simply a matter of moving to another one. But as mahogany replaced logwood in commercial importance there was a need for larger land areas because its distribution pattern was only one tree to every two or three acres of land.[68] Furthermore the location of the mahogany in the heart of the forests required additional areas of land in order to guarantee the woodcutter the unimpeded removal of his timber from the centre of operation to the river which was as important as the forests themselves. Thus a 'location' or a 'mahogany work', as each area of land was called, was defined in 1787 not only as the area of the forest operated but also a frontage of three miles on a river bank and a portion at the back which extended half way to the next navigable river or eight miles.[69]

One begins to see how a great part of the colony was alienated. In fact, the government only possessed lands which held little attraction for the woodcutter or which had been returned by him in lieu of the payment of land tax after they had been denuded of their wealth. The only redeeming feature was that the 'location' was not alienation in perpetuity. The grantee was a tenant at will and entitled to two locations on a river.[70] He forfeited his location if he acquired a third or left the country. These restrictions on ownership and the size of location were removed in 1812 when it was recognized that their effect was to encourage the registering of locations under fictitious names.[71] Crown grants replaced leaseholds, bestowing upon the occupier unconditional freehold title. The way was completely cleared for the more prosperous and favoured grantees to consolidate their holdings. Some distrained on the lands of their debtors. Others used the new land tenure system to force out their small competitors and to end disputes over land rights in their favour.[72] Lands were amassed on a scale that approximated to the latifundia. By 1927, as shown in table 3, 96.8 per cent of the freehold land was held by 96 owners, 2.81 per cent by 550 owners, and the remaining 0.32 per cent by 1,006 owners whose holdings averaged 8.72 acres.[73]

Table 3   *Statistics of freeholders, 1927*

| Acres | Total acreage | No. of freeholders | Average area held by each individual | Percentage of total |
|---|---|---|---|---|
| 5 and under | 1,842 | 465 | 3.9 | 0.07 |
| 5 to 20 | 6,947 | 541 | 12.8 | 0.26 |
| 20 to 50 | 8,756 | 273 | 32.0 | 0.33 |
| 50 to 100 | 9,240 | 121 | 76.3 | 0.34 |
| 100 to 500 | 27,645 | 120 | 230.3 | 1.03 |
| 500 to 1,000 | 29,785 | 36 | 827.3 | 1.11 |
| 1,000 and over | 2,599,156 | 96 | 27,074.5 | 96.86 |
| | 2,683,371 | 1,652 | 1,624.3 | 100 |

Source: Pim Report, p. 217

    The statistics are not as revealing as they might suggest. In 1871 most of the alienated land had fallen into the hands of two companies, the British Honduras Company and Young, Toledo and Company. In 1875 the first company became the BEC which acquired most of the land of the other company when the latter went into bankruptcy.[74] It was in this way that the BEC came to own more than one-half of the private lands or one-fifth of the colony, a fact obscured in the table. Furthermore, the company commandeered the northern area of the colony, Orange Walk, whose mahogany resources were equalled in quality throughout Central America only by those of northern Guatemala and Yucatan.[75] The company was indisputably the most influential concern which guided the colonial government. In fact its relationship with the government was overt and interlocking. The Conservator of Forests, Cornelius Hummel, OBE, who was appointed at the inception of the Government Forest Trust in 1923, was also a part-time employee of the company. He eventually resigned his government appointment to become the company's manager and representative in the Legislative Council in 1925. The secondment of assistant conservators of forests to the company was not unusual; and one of these officers spent his tour of duty in the service of the company.[76]

The control which this company exercised reinforced the virtual stranglehold of the forestry industry on the economy. Although a decline in the forestry industry was expected, the BEC was willing neither to enter into commercial agriculture nor to sell its arable lands. It contended that their retention was necessary to secure accessibility to its forest areas.[77] There was also no obligation to develop the land and the company leased the less valuable areas for both settlement and peasant cultivation to the extent that in 1933 more villages were estimated to be established on its property than on Crown lands.[78]

The withholding of permanent occupancy rights from the agricultural tenants was related to the labour needs of the forestry industries. As Sir Allan Pim noted in 1932, there was the tendency for 'the influential classes not to encourage agricultural production for fear of its diminishing the supply of labour available for the forest industries'.[79]

The BEC had a double vested interested in an unbalanced economy. It had diversified its activities to become one of the more important commercial and importing firms which viewed agricultural development as being inimical to their interests. For a concomitant of the neglect of agriculture was the country's inordinate dependence upon imported food. Although the interruption of food supplies during the First World War called attention to the dangers of dependence, little was done to diversify the economy beyond the commissioning of four government reports between 1917 and 1928.[80]

The reports were in part a response to the difficulties in the forestry industry. The industry was extremely sensitive to changes in world demand and therefore subjected to alternating periods of boom and slump. It was adversely affected by the lack of shipping facilities in the First World War and suffered even more from a trade depression in the immediate post-war years. There was a recovery in the mid-1920s but as table 4 indicates the slump returned by the end of the decade. The effect of the depression was so severe that the export of the principal commodity, mahogany, to its chief market, the United States, virtually ceased in 1931.

Concern for the mahogany industry was not only aroused by the depressed conditions in the United States. There had been a progressive depletion of accessible supplies due to the overcutting of trees during the four years, 1926–9, when the mahogany industry appeared to be reviving. In the process immature trees were recklessly felled. Furthermore the cost

Table 4   *Total quantities of the principal forestry exports, 1910–32*

| Year | Chicle (lbs) | Logwood (tons) | Mahogany (sq. ft.) | Cedar* (sq. ft.) |
|------|------|------|------|------|
| 1910 | 2,790,890 | 3,669 | 10,175,571 | — |
| 1913 | 3,163,129 | 2,812 | 15,027,520 | — |
| 1915 | 3,467,696 | 11,935 | 6,907,123 | — |
| 1917 | 2,266,621 | 5,260 | 9,933,269 | — |
| 1919 | 3,543,764 | 2,736 | 9,648,700 | — |
| 1920 | 3,690,641 | 1,570 | 9,773,150 | 674,485 |
| 1921 | 2,577,481 | 760 | 9,649,582 | 221,519 |
| 1922 | 2,132,252 | 1,350 | 9,755,263 | 561,791 |
| 1923 | 2,206,009 | 1,142 | 9,967,186 | 663,437 |
| 1924 | 2,462,667 | 1,311 | 12,857,845 | 641,517 |
| 1925 | 3,022,196 | 609 | 12,580,836 | 465,979 |
| 1926 | 3,260,172 | 667 | 18,745,537 | 292,741 |
| 1927 | 3,029,210 | 332 | 24,726,313 | 733,088 |
| 1928 | 3,103,798 | 1,064 | 16,362,280 | 578,368 |
| 1929 | 3,714,018 | 220 | 16,478,180 | 703,520 |
| 1930 | 4,094,415 | 225 | 10,829,331 | 382,198 |
| 1931 | 2,186,564 | 268 | 3,240,240 | 226,865 |
| 1932 | 1,029,473 | 103 | 643,593 | 1,476 |

ᵃ Figures for cedar from 1910 to 1919 defaced in copy of the report consulted.
Source: Pim Report, p. 128

of production was increasing because the trees were becoming very scarce within the limit of cheap haulage to a waterway. The industry was also suffering from the competition of mahogany from Peru and Brazil, and mahogany substitutes from West Africa. Finally, mahogany was being displaced by steel in the manufacture of furniture and the construction of railway carriages and ships.[81]

With the industry under siege, the colony which had hitherto only suffered from labour shortages became familiar with unemployment for the first time in its history. The number of mahogany labourers employed fell from 1,717 in the 1913–14 season to 714 in the following season.

There was a corresponding drop in average monthly wages from $12.64 to $8.21.[82] Improvements in the employment situation and wages were generally offset by alarming increases in the imported staples which had begun during the war.[83] It was to this depressing situation that some five hundred disbanded soldiers who had seen active service in Mesopotamia returned. In July 1919 they registered with a riot their protest of having to recognize unemployment as the order of the day and endure the rising cost of living.

The government was financially incapable of continuously relieving the social gloom. It depended for more than half of its revenue on customs duties which fluctuated with the exports of forestry products in the 1920s as the figures in table 5 indicate.

Table 5    *Customs duties as a percentage of ordinary revenue, 1920–32*

| Year | Customs (Belize dollars[a]) | Percentage of ordinary revenue |
|------|-----------------------------|--------------------------------|
| 1920–1 | 659,925 | 61.4 |
| 1921–2 | 490,163 | 51.5 |
| 1922–3 | 509,978 | 58.1 |
| 1926–7 | 681,879 | 61.2 |
| 1927–8 | 645,131 | 60.7 |
| 1928–9 | 626,895 | 60.5 |
| 1929–0 | 641,844 | 62.1 |
| 1930–1 | 711,745 | 61.9 |
| 1931–2 | 546,785 | 64.1 |

[a] Note that unless otherwise stated all dollars are Belizean.
Source: Pim Report, pp. 195–6

The true effect of the decline in the forestry trade on the colony's finance was concealed by an adventitious source of revenue. This was the proceeds from the liquor trade during prohibition in the United States. Belize was conveniently located for the enrouting of liquor from Canada to Mexico from where it was smuggled into the United States.[84] The government appeared to be conniving with the merchants in the evasion of the 1919 Volstead Act which prohibited the sale of liquor.[85] Although this was politically embarrassing it would have been an act of heroism for the government to co-operate with the United States. The budget by 1930 could not balance without the duties from the export of liquor although this item of revenue was 'deliberately obscured in the printed estimates'.[86]

As Governor Burdon reported to the Colonial Office in March 1931, 'Export duties have been increased to $180,000 in anticipation of the continuance of the export trade in liquor at the present rate. The total is made up of the following items: wood $15,000, chicle $45,000 and liquor $120,00.'[87] In the 1931–2 financial year the duty on liquor formed $89,878 or 11.75 per cent of the estimated ordinary revenue of $765,152, or 75 per cent of the export duties.[88]

The deterioration of the forestry industry, however, could not be concealed forever. For one thing the United States repealed the prohibition law in 1933. But even before this, the occurrence of the disastrous hurricane on 10 September 1931 and the onset of the world depression in the 1930s laid bare the short-sighted policy of dependence upon a monoculture that was exhaustive in nature and vulnerable to the vagaries of the world market.

## Social system based on slavery[89]

Just as the discussion of the economy must focus on the forestry industry, consideration of the social system must develop around slavery. The forestry economy had been built on African slave labour imported not directly from Africa but from Jamaica, with which the settlers had strong ties. So much has been written on the subject of slavery in the New World that there would be little justification to say much more here but for the fact that a myth pervades the social history of Belize during the slavery period in the West Indies.[90] There is the general notion that there was no slave system or if it existed it was administered with such compassion by the settlers that it was nominal. Almost every superintendent of the settlement reported to London that the woodcutters extended nothing but 'kindness, liberality and indulgent care. . . towards their Negroes, so that slavery can hardly be said to exist in the settlement'.[91] Colonel Arthur had 'in no part of the world seen the labouring class of people possessing anything like the comforts of the Slave Population of Honduras'.[92] Others who were less expansive in their comparison were nonetheless certain that slavery in Belize was milder than in the British West Indian islands.

This claim has been attributed to several factors that would appear peculiar to Belize. As in the West Indies colonization in Belize (or, to be more correct, occupancy) was conceived as a process of European settlement. The idea of settlement in the West Indies was replaced to a large extent by that of the absentee landlord who managed his plantation from a distance. In Belize a settler psyche developed in spite of or possibly because of the threatened existence which the woodcutters pursued at the hands of the Spaniards. Slaves were therefore not left to the mercy of the attorney and managers to the same extent as in the West Indies. Further, the very nature of the forestry industry as opposed to the sugar plantation in the West Indies imposed upon the master a judicious attitude towards his slaves.[93] The industry was carried out in remote and isolated areas where the slaves posed a constant danger since they were armed with machetes to clear the thickets to the forest, axes to cut the trees and guns to hunt the game. It is also claimed that the geographical and social isolation, which lasted for about six months each year, dictated 'mutual aid' between master and slave and produced a congenial atmosphere in the mahogany camps.[94] Also, with the proximity of Belize to Mexico and Guatemala the threat of slave desertion always hung over the woodcutters' heads.[95] This necessitated a continuous campaign for good industrial relations, especially as slavery was reputed to be more humane in the Spanish than in the British colonies in the eighteenth century[96] and as the Mexicans and Guatemalans held out the promise of freedom to the escaped slaves.[97] Related to this consideration was the comparatively high price of slave labour and the degree of skill involved.[98] The woodcutter had to be more discriminating than the sugar plantation owner in the West Indies in his recruitment of slaves. Work in a mahogany gang called for strong, healthy and ideally tall people. Not all slaves were fitted for the rigour of forestry work and those who did brought a good price. Transportation from Jamaica to Belize also added to the cost of a slave, and the training of the worker for the tasks in the forests entailed some investment. In the 1820s the average value of an inexperienced Belizean slave was about three times that of a Jamaican and of one 'accustomed to the labour' about seven times.[99] Furthermore slave property was almost the only security on which it was possible to raise a loan and which the merchants demanded from the mahogany woodcutter for advance in provisions and other perishable articles.[100] A runaway slave in Belize was therefore a serious economic loss.

The final consideration in support of the view of a liberal attitude towards slaves was the ease with which the slaves obtained their freedom. Dobson argues that the incidence of manumission in Belize was less than in the Spanish colonies but much greater than in the British West Indies.[101] The comparative figures for the years 1821–5 show that in Barbados 408 slaves were manumitted, in Demerara 142, in the Bahamas 176, and in Belize 141, which was impressive because the total population was much smaller than in the other territories.[102] The two customary methods of manumitting slaves obtained in Belize. One was by will and the other by purchase. It was usually the slaves who purchased their own freedom, but cases of another slaveowner paying for the freedom of a slave, especially of his children born to a slave woman, were not unknown in Belize.[103] But there was a third way in which the slave obtained his freedom. This was for him to enlist in the West India Regiment. He encountered obstacles to the extent that his labour was needed in the forestry industry, but whenever the community was threatened by Spanish attack the need to defend it operated in his favour.

The view that these peculiar conditions gave rise to a mild form of slavery in practice has, however, been accepted somewhat uncritically.[104] Slave rebellions were not unknown, and the first detailed information about one concerned the killing of two white men up the Belize River in May 1773. Rebellions became more frequent in the nineteenth century as a result of 'unnecessary harshness'.[105] The rebellions, however, caused less concern than the 'numerous desertions of slaves'.[106] As the reports of harsh treatment indicate, Spanish inducement did not entirely account for the desertions. Irrespective of their cause the desertions threatened to wreck the forestry economy and they had to be deterred. Every conceivable punishment, ranging from death and mutilation to perpetual imprisonment, was therefore employed.[107] In 1795 a Summary Court sentenced two slaves to flogging and transportation merely on suspicion of intending to escape to Spanish territory. The deterrent was applied to the 'field' and 'domestic' slaves alike, but the latter were often subject to much more ill-treatment. The sentence for minor offences, such as acting with 'insolence and bad conducts' to the mistress of the home could be one hundred lashes on the bare back and a 'tour' around the town at the cart's tail.[108] Physical cruelties were matched by the cultural. As elsewhere, slavery entailed the almost complete destruction of African institutions and customs. Of necessity, the slaves adopted the English language. Their religious beliefs and practices were suppressed. Obeah, which is of West African derivation and meant quite simply the practice of magic and sorcery, was legally condemned as 'a wicked art of Negroes'.[109] The obeah men were seen as an economic threat since they were accused of using their influence to 'advise, aid and abet' slaves to 'depart their Master's Service' and to promote rebellion.[110] Like every activity with adverse economic implications, the practice of obeah was punishable by death upon conviction. African music was also a casualty. Drumming or the playing of 'Gumbays' and other noisy amusements were prohibited after 9.00 p.m. and, together with dancing, could not be performed on Sundays. Much more than harmony and amicability, fear, suspicion and insecurity characterized the woodcutters' relationship with their slaves. Accordingly they requested, in 1825, three or four companies of white troops from Jamaica, 'in view of the fact that the Desertion of Slaves continues and the Slaves in the several Works of the Colony are openly threatening rebellion'.[111] They had little confidence that the 'Black portion of local Militia and also the Black Soldiers of the West India Regiment' would remain loyal to them 'in the event of a sudden rising of the slaves'.[112]

It was Superintendent Arthur who eventually exposed the myth about slave conditions. In 1822, six years after he had reported favourably on these conditions he admitted the slaves were deprived of all protection.[113] The courts were a mockery of justice and were the last place to seek redress. This could not have been otherwise since the magistrates were among the principal perpetrators of cruelty against the slaves. They had no qualms in delaying action in a case concerning a family illegally kept in slavery for fifty years after being manumitted.[114] This was in stark contrast to the expeditious manner in which they dealt with the case of a coloured woman who lived with one of the magistrates and was charged with 'punishing her slave girl in an illegal, cruel, severe manner by chaining her and repeatedly whipping her and for confining her for a considerable time in the said chains in the loft of her house'.[115] In less than five minutes the accused was acquitted on the ground that every slaveowner was entitled to give his slave up to thirty-nine lashes with a whip. It was not the business of the court to pronounce on the severity of the punishment but only on whether it was exceeded. This prompted Colonel Arthur to issue a proclamation declaring the Consolidated Slave Laws of Jamaica to be in force. He was 'astonished' at the number of slaves who came forward as a result of the proclamation and 'at the fraud and injustice so long secretly practised toward them'.[116] This he duly reported to the Colonial Office with his regret for having 'underrated the extent of the grievances of the Slaves'.[117] Unfortunately, but not unexpectedly, Arthur's administration ended in 1823 in a long and acrimonious dispute with the settlers. His reassessment of slave conditions is therefore vulnerable to a charge of personal bias.

The favourable view about slave conditions was allowed to gain currency and to become a popular stereotype because the settlement was relegated from the outset to a minor chapter in British imperial history. Few observers visited the country; fewer still visited the distant mahogany camps which an understanding, and much less the illuminating, of the situation required. The observers were like the latter-day social scientists who talk to the political elites in the cities of the new states and then write about the social and economic conditions of the rural poor.

Too often the picture painted of the regime of slavery is that of the slave-owner forming alliances with his slaves or violating them. Slavery was much more than a direct interaction between master and slave with deleterious effects on the latter. It was an institution which coloured the whole social structure of the society. Unable, like members of the 'true' upper classes, to import European wives, the slaveowners were forced into some sort of cohabitation with coloured women and the female slaves. The particular role which the free-coloureds came to play in the community was not unconnected with their relationship with the whites. Totally dependent upon the whites for their status they disparaged their ancestral past and were merciless towards the slaves who were the daily reminder of their negroid origin. It was therefore at the hands of the coloured population, as we saw in the case of the coloured mistress, that the domestic slaves experienced some of the worst excesses of slavery. Their inhumanity was only matched by that of the 'lesser' whites,[118] and the alliance between the coloured element and this sub-group of whites added to the richness and complexity of the social relations existing during the slave period.

On the whole the coloured population was a privileged group. 'The people of colour', Dr Lushington wrote in 1828, 'have privileges far beyond what are granted in any other part of the West Indies.'[119] To some extent this reflected their numerical and economic strength. In 1826 their population was 1,037, which was three times that of the white and more or less equal to the free blacks.[120] They owned nearly two-thirds of the private land and slaves, and used their wealth to educate their children in England.[121] But the top of the social pyramid was never fully within their grasp even though they were legally granted the civil privileges of the whites on the eve of emancipation in 1831.[122] They were subject to certain disabilities that rudely reminded them of their colour and intermediate position in the society. In times of military threat commissions in the militia were opened to them, but these were summarily withdrawn once the danger receded.[123] To add to the social injury, in the militia many wealthy coloured employers found themselves under the authority of one of their junior clerks.[124] And since God was supposed to have put the rich man in a castle and ordered the lot of his less fortunate 'bretheren', pride of place was legally reserved for the whites in the seating arrangements of the government-financed Anglican church.[125] The coloured group was also debarred from prestigious public offices such as the magistracy and jury service and, as we shall see in the next section, their qualifications for membership in the legislative body were more demanding than those for the whites.[126] Like the harsh conditions which the slaves endured, the indignities which the coloured population experienced tended to be ignored or to be dismissed as being less severe than those in the West Indies.[127] The essential point however is that they were poised between the white and the black population no less easily than their counterparts in the West Indies.

Although they were solidified by their attitude towards the coloured population and the slaves, the whites were by no means a homogeneous group. Status differentiation based upon nationality, residence, and occupational roles existed. Every effort was made to restrict the white population to British subjects even though there was a recognized need for a large white population to counteract the economic and numerical preponderance of coloured people. The uncertainty of the settlement's status and the fact that the sentiments of aliens towards it were unknown called for a highly selective immigration policy. In 1810 French immigrants from Jamaica were forbidden to land.[128] Americans from the United States were considered less of a political risk but they were discouraged from settling. Those who settled were denied citizenship, for fear that the mahogany industry would eventually fall into American hands.[129] Jews were disliked and it was not until 1814 that a law prohibiting them from becoming residents was annulled.[130] Nonetheless they were not accepted as 'whites' and suffered many of the indignities of the coloured population. The settlement's uncertain status and proximity to Guatemala and Mexico, however, imposed certain limits upon the restrictive immigration policy. The settlers conceded that Spanish subjects had a right to carry on any lawful business in Belize. They were also uncertain about the British government's authority to determine the rights of Spaniards who had become citizens of Central America or Mexico after these countries declared their independence in the 1820s.[131] Clusters of people of Spanish descent therefore began to develop along the borders with little interference from the settlers.

There was also a distinction between whites who were the original inhabitants, natives or Creoles, and those who were recent immigrants, including the British who had evacuated the Mosquito Shore in 1787. The newcomer was not entitled to the privileges of an 'Inhabitant' until he resided for two successive years since enrollment, possessed a house, land and slaves to the value of £2,000 (Jamaica), and was in business.[132] The period of residential qualification was eventually reduced to six months for British subjects.[133] This further marked off those of British origin from other whites. A part of the rationale for the financial and economic requirements was the attraction of the community as a British enclave to felons and the bankrupt from the neighbouring British, French and Spanish plantation islands. Such characters were socially unacceptable. They were likely to be a public burden to a community that was unwilling to spend money on any endeavour unrelated to the forestry industry.

The ownership of slaves, the most valued and valuable factor of forestry production was also an important status determinant. This conferred the advantage on those whites engaged in the mahogany industry, which employed most of the slaves, as opposed to those in commerce. The status distinction was not only between those who owned many slaves and those who did not, but also between whites whose slaves were Africans and those whose were Indians. The latter had been brought by the British evacuees from the Mosquito Shore in 1821. They did not figure prominently in the slave records until their status was queried in 1821 on the ground that the enslaving of Indians, particularly those from the Mosquito Shore, was illegal.[134] It was more prestigious to own African slaves since they were more suited to the rigour of mahogany work. The Indian slaves worked primarily as domestic servants and in the logwood industry which was not only less exacting than mahogany but also of less economic importance. The illegality of Indian slavery also enhanced the position of those whites who owned African slaves and whose proprietorial rights were therefore beyond dispute. It was the forest and the relations of production in and around it that determined in the final analysis the community's value system and its hierarchical social arrangement.

No analysis of the slave society would be complete without reference to the activities of the Christian missionaries. Throughout the West Indies missionary activities among the slaves were designed to ameliorate the slave conditions and to make the slaves tractable to the ideas and customs of European society. The majority of planters either openly opposed or viewed with suspicion the missionary activities on the assumption that the acquisition of Christian ideas would tend to induce dissatisfaction with a slave status.[135] Most of the missionary work was undertaken by the Dissenting Protestant Churches rather than the Anglican Church. Those missionaries who chose to disregard the slaveowners' sentiments were vilified and harassed. There is the celebrated case of John Smith, a Congregational minister in Guyana, who in 1813 was accused of treason on the ground that he was alleged to have known of a slave uprising and suppressed his knowledge. He was sentenced to death and died in imprisonment from consumption before news of his reprieve by the home government reached the colony.[136]

In Belize the spiritual welfare of the slaves was viewed as a nonproblem for the greater part of the slavery period. This was not so much because the missionaries accepted the popular view that slavery was virtually non-existent but because the Anglican church monopolized the activities until the Baptists[137] and the Methodists[138] entered the field, in 1822 and 1826 respectively. Almost from its beginning, Belize was provided with a government-paid Anglican chaplain from Britain. The settlement built a church, St John's, in 1812 from public funds and earned the distinction of possessing the first Protestant Episcopal church in Spanish

America.[139] Indeed, breaching the Latin uniformity in many ways, Belize was regarded by one of its chaplains, Matthew Newport, as a bastion of the Protestant faith, being 'the only Protestant settlement between the boundaries of the United States and Cape Horn'.[140]

It was the close relationship between the government and the Anglican Church that determined the extent of the missionary activities in the slave society. Indeed, being a member of the ecclesiastical and secular establishment in Britain, the government chaplain was essentially an office-holder and imbued with little missionary zeal. He was expected to confine his pastoral activities to the 'upper classes' which systematically opposed the religious instruction of the slaves, as well as of the adult population of the lower class generally.[141] Being 'bound hand and foot by the State'[142] he was obliged to the point where his own personal conduct was governed by the values of the slave society. His 'religious duties seem to have been over on a Sunday after he had read the Liturgy to a few hearers; then he could go and superintend his slaves working by the water side'.[143] Slaves were also denied the formal ceremonial sanctions of Christianity as a result of marriage and baptism fees which proved prohibitive to the extent that no marriages of slaves took place in 1826.[144]

The Baptist and Methodist missionaries entered expressly to fill the void among the slaves. In answering the call from an influential group of English Methodists in Belize to end 'the spiritual destitution and moral disorder' of the slaves, the Methodist Missionary Society in London specifically instructed its first appointee 'not to fix himself in the town, but itinerate along the river, seeking out the woodcutters' camps and evangelizing the Negroes remote from the means of grace'.[145] The missions prospered despite the Anglican Church's hostility which had its roots in the strained relationship between the Established Church and the Dissenters in England. Nonetheless not all of the Dissenting missionaries remained immune from the slave ethic of the society. In 1826, the Baptist missionary who claimed to have established a home for the care of patients stricken with cholera, was found on an unexpected visit by the Superintendent to be operating a workhouse.

The slaves, therefore, could hardly have viewed the missionaries with supreme trust and confidence. The group which seemed most favourably disposed to them was the government officials who arrived from Britain in the 1830s to assist in implementing the various imperial laws relating to the abolition of slavery. The business-like manner with which these officials undertook their work did not command the unqualified admiration of the slaveowners. The chairman of the Legislative Meeting, in a violent speech, saw in every new appointee from Britain an addition to a 'nest of hired and official anti-slavery spies',[146] even though the British parliamentary campaign against slavery and the Anti-Slavery Society which Wilberforce had formed in 1823 were less concerned with Belize than with the plantation islands in the West Indies.

The outburst was not isolated and it suggests that the slaveowners in Belize did not relish the prospect of the emancipation of the slaves any more than did their West Indian counterparts. Indeed since a slave in Belize was worth more than an equivalent slave in Jamaica and was difficult to replace, the slaveowners were also no less concerned than the West Indian planters with the British government's plans for compensating them for the loss of their slaves.[147] Belize, however, stood to benefit since the amount of compensation for each colony was to be assessed, not on the basis of number, but on the industrial value of the slaves. After the British Parliament passed the Abolition Act in 1833 and introduced a system of apprenticeship, the settlers took exception to the Order in Council that was to protect the ex-slaves during the apprenticeship period. In the first place the Order was drafted for Guyana and the settlers considered it too complicated and even 'unworkable' in a society where conditions were different.[148] Scattered as the labourers were in the forest, for example, it was not as easy to regulate their hours of work as on the sugar plantations. Second, and more important, the settlers refused to accept the notion, implicit in the application of the Order, that their former relationship with the ex-slaves warranted imperial protection for the apprenticed labourers. In their view the ex-slaves had long enjoyed conditions far better than what the law was intended to provide.[149] In any case no legislative precaution could influence their attitude towards the apprentice labourers more than the unalterable proximity of the republics. These views were made known to the Colonial Office some eight months before the apprenticeship system came into effect in August 1834, but with little impact. As in other colonies stipendiary magistrates were sent from England to ensure that the provisions of the ordinance were carried out.

## Emancipation and the Latin influx

The transition from a slave system to a free society was not as far-reaching in its impact on the structure of Belizean society as in the West Indies. In the latter territories the ex-slaves deserted the plantations, established their own villages and attempted to pursue a peasant life independent of plantation work.[150] This aggravated the labour shortage and necessitated the immigration of indentured labourers, mainly from India. In some respects the emancipated slaves in Belize responded in a similar manner with results that were only different in degree. Between 1832 and 1835 the total population of 'coloureds' and 'blacks' declined sharply from 969 and 2,602 to 670 and 1,651 respectively.[151] This suggests emigration on a relatively large scale, presumably to the neighbouring republics during the apprenticeship period. The emigration did not, however, approach an exodus. Nonetheless since the black proletariat was small in absolute terms, every loss was keenly felt. Furthermore since the ex-slaves were safely beyond their jurisdiction the settlers, unlike their counterparts in the West Indies, had little opportunity to force them to return to the mahogany camps. It was therefore with relief that the settlement learnt that Cuba was willing to dispose of captured male Africans who had been liberated by a Commission in 1836.[152] Five hundred of them were immediately requested to 'be introduced at once for employment', principally in the mahogany work.[153] Cuba again became a source of labour supply when the shortage was acute during a sharp increase in mahogany trade in 1845 and 1846. Over 1,000 emancipated slaves were recruited from Havana.[154] The settlement also had no compunction in admitting 250 Africans liberated, also in Cuba, from captured slaveowners.[155] Steps were also taken to procure labour from the United States and more distant places. However, since the British government was still unwilling to accept complete responsibility for the settlement it turned down most of the requests for labour on the ground that the settlers would be unable to cope with the 'dangers' to which they would be exposed both internally and from the neighbouring republics.[156]

It was more to solve its own problems than the woodcutters' that in 1858, after the Indian Mutiny, the British government transported to Belize from India 1,000 Sepoy mutineers and their families.[157] As late as 1883 it was still being vainly hoped that India would provide a regular and satisfactory supply of forestry labour on terms similar to those in the West Indies.[158] Even if the British government's policy had been more permissive it is doubtful whether indentured Indian immigrants would have solved the labour problem in forestry. For as has been indicated, most of the East Indians were attracted to the sugar estates and small plantations which the United States exiles established in the south in the 1860s. The British Honduras Company prevailed upon the British government to allow the importation of Chinese in 1864.[159] The experiment however failed. Many of them fatally succumbed to one disease or another or over-work. Those who survived were disappointed with the conditions and moved on to Spanish Honduras. Of 474 who landed in 1865 only 265 were left in 1868.[160] In this same year a number of Italian escapees from Guatemala arrived in Belize.[161] But like the East Indians they preferred farming to woodcutting and settled in Manatee in the south. Although the labour shortage in the forestry industry was never overcome it generated less anxiety than in the West Indies. For the emancipated slaves who remained in Belize stuck to the mahogany camps. This was not principally because the apprenticeship system appeared to have proceeded more smoothly in Belize than in the colonies in the West Indies.[162] Nor was it because the emancipated slaves had less of a desire to be independent of their erstwhile slaveowners. The principal reason for their continued attachment to the forestry work was the absence of alternative forms of lucrative wage labour. The mahogany workers' interest in agriculture had not developed over the years beyond the cultivation of a few subsistence crops such as rice, corn, beans and ground provisions. Moreover, neither the mercantile nor the landed interests were to be expected to give them the opportunity to take up farming as a way of life. One had a vested interest in the local demand for imported food and the other in retaining the labour of emancipated slaves for forestry work.

To maintain this hold the woodcutters developed a work arrangement whose main feature was the payment of wages on the system of 'advances'.[163] The 'advance' idea arose from the peculiar circumstances incidental to the remoteness of the forests. During slavery, the slaves had to be provided with a large part of their ration before they embarked upon the long isolation in the forests. With the development of a cash economy after slavery, the labourers were advanced a part of their wages to provide for their families during their long absence and to supplement their weekly ration of seven quarts of flour and four pounds of pork. Hiring was done at the beginning of December in Belize City for the two main seasons which began in January and August. This was the only holiday that workers did not spend in the forests and a spirit of dissipation overtook the labourers in their determination to 'keep Christmas' and have a final fling before taking leave of their families and friends in early January. The advance was therefore spent on the festivities and 'parting' sprees. Associated with the advance system, and indeed an integral part of it, was the so-called truck system, which required, or at least encouraged, the labourers to take a portion of their wages in goods from their employers' store or commissary as it was commonly called.[164] Being in the remote woods of the interior, with no other store within some thirty or forty miles, the employer charged exorbitant prices. The labourer was, therefore, doubly indebted to his employer for the wage advance and the credits. Somewhat akin to the indentured system of labour, the entire arrangement was 'pernicious'.[165] It placed the labourer permanently and more completely in the power of the employer. The Master and Servants Bill was passed in 1846 to enforce the arrangement.[166] The law included various penal clauses. It was revised on several occasions and in 1883, a breach of contract was made not a civil but a criminal offence, punishable by twenty-eight days' imprisonment with hard labour.[167] The provision, however, seemed unnecessary as the solidarity among the employers virtually rendered the erring worker unemployable in the forestry industries.

Unlike the rural peasantry in the West Indies, the emancipated slaves in Belize therefore never had the opportunity to entertain the illusion of an economic existence independent of the principal industry. The exploitative system persisted into the twentieth century. As the annual report for 1931 indicated the system brought out the worst in the labourer. In the chicle industry a spendthrift and improvident morale had been built up among the tappers which led to theft of other men's chicle and the sale of their own produce to some other contractor to obtain ready cash, until the dishonesty of the chicleros (as the chicle collectors were called) had become almost proverbial.[168] This reputation further stigmatized the forestry worker. The several years of depression in the forestry industry in the 1920s, however, largely rid the industry of the advance system which it was hoped would never be fully reinstated, to the ultimate benefit of the individual forestry labourer and his family.[169]

A development equally as important as emancipation and one which alleviated the labour problem in the forestry industry was the arrival of the Yucatan refugees after the War of the Caste in the 1840s. The refugees brought with them their own social milieu based on the plantation system. The major occupational interest of this complex was therefore different from that of the British settlers and their African labourers. The language and customs of the newly arrived group were different. The Spanish villages stood in 'violent contrast' to the Creole villages on the mahogany banks of the rivers, in the layout of the streets, the architecture and interior decoration of the house, and the style of dress. As Roman Catholics the Spanish community held to a different religious creed from the Protestant settlement of whites, coloured and black Creoles.

Neither of the two social milieux, although separated by distance and the difficulties of communication and transportation, was hermetically sealed. Both impinged directly on the other with consequences for the social relations within both the Creole and the Mestizo groups and society overall. To begin with, the sudden increase of the population and its remoteness from the principal administrative and social centre of Belize City necessitated a larger bureaucracy. The British settlers were too few in number and too business-oriented to staff the new posts that were created in the civil service. Many of the vacancies were therefore filled by the coloured element and the educated Africans in the Creole complex. This enabled the two sub-groups to come more into their own and to command a greater position of influence in society. The way was also cleared for the Spanish element to be considered for leadership roles. In 1886 a law was enacted to provide for the appointment of aliens to certain public offices in the settlement.[170] School-teaching also contributed to the interaction between the Spanish and Creole elements and came to offer at the same time an important avenue of upward social mobility for the African Creole. The occupation lay more in the sphere of the Church which had assumed responsibility for education. The Methodist Church was the pioneer of Protestantism in the predominantly Roman Catholic district in the north.[171] It also ran the only government-aided school in the area and drew the teachers from its predominantly Creole and Carib membership in the rural areas throughout the country. The Methodist Church also worked out a compromise with the Roman Catholic Church on the denominational allegiance of the children of religiously mixed marriages in the north. It was agreed that the male offspring of such a union 'may be a Methodist' while the female 'was to be handed over to the Roman Catholic faith'.[172]

The mandatory nature of the arrangement in the case of the females and the tendency for them to have a significant voice in the religious upbringing of children[173] contributed to the spread of Roman Catholocism throughout the country. The Church's first representative in Belize was a Franciscan priest in 1832 but its activities really began with the arrival of two English Jesuits in 1851 to undertake the pastoral care of the Yucatan refugees in the northern district. By 1856 the Roman Catholic membership outnumbered that of the Protestant churches everywhere except in Belize City where the Anglicans had the largest following.[174] The Church developed into a compact diocese until it became the largest single denomination in every administrative district except Belize. By 1921 it served 60 per cent of the total population, a proportion that it has consistently maintained.[175]

Despite the growth in the central government, the Indians, except in their occupational pursuits, were allowed to live under the guidance of their village elders, who were officially recognized as Alcaldes, and a parish priest. Economically they were subject to the control not only of the Spanish and Mestizo sugar planters, but also of the forestry owners. For the Indians were engaged in forestry industry, and more specifically the tapping of chicle and 'the monotonous drudgery of logwood cutting which principally passed into their hands'[176] by 1857. They worked under the same exploitative conditions as the black proletariat in the forestry industry but this did not necessarily engender solidarity between the two groups. On the contrary, the Indians were denied parity of status with the Creoles because they had succeeded them in the section of the industry that was the least economically important, and most poorly paid and boring. The blacks became acutely aware that in concentrating on the mahogany cutting they were a greater asset to the economy and that they were recognized as such by the socio-economic elite. In 1888 they were described as 'the main instrument in keeping the commerce of the colony and supplying the markets of England and the continent of Europe with the splendid mahogany and dye-wood of Central America'.[177] When combined with their lack of the cultural characteristics valued in the dominant Creole society and their basic identification with the relatively insignificant and undeveloped agricultural industry, the entry of the Indians into the lowest rung of the occupational hierarchy in the forestry industry encouraged the lower-class Creoles to feel that they were not the most inferior group in the society. Indeed, the official practice of distinguishing them from the whites and coloureds gradually fell into disuse as the whites, in dividing the increasingly heterogeneous population, racial and cultural, into four classes, identified themselves with the blacks on the basis of language. As early as 1859 'whites and blacks', or 'Africans and all who speak the English language'[178] were grouped as Creoles as opposed to the other three, Indians, Spanish and Caribs. These economic and cultural considerations prompted the black Creoles to assume a more positive outlook towards their social status and to put as much distance as possible between themselves and their African past in their attempt to achieve upward social mobility. This entailed the uncritical acceptance of upper-class behaviour as 'proper and right' and even the copying of it. The influence of certain upper-class patterns in the lower class became marked. Nonetheless there was a discrepancy between ideal and practice because of the impossibility of the black and the coloured Creole becoming white. However much the lower- and middle-class Creoles may have negatively associated their own distinctive and differentiating cultural characteristics with their social aspirations they had to accept their inevitability.

In sum, the social class structure remained predominantly Creole although the society had become much more culturally and racially mixed with the arrival of the Spanish–Mestizo–Indian element. The class structure was very much associated with colour and the relatively small group of white Creoles stood at the apex of the social pyramid with a feeling of inheritance. For their forebears had fashioned the society and given it its dominant British character in the Spanish sub-continent.

*Political development*

In a society that had been established largely for economic reasons and continued to conceive and justify its existence almost wholly in terms of trade, the distribution of economic and political power was highly correlated. For three centuries the governing of the country was virtually the preserve of the landed and mercantile interests. In the process of governing they instituted self-governing institutions. Their legislature possessed inherent constituent powers and had an unofficial majority except for a relatively short period of twenty-one years from 1871 to 1892. In brief they had determined the distribution of political power not only within the society but between the legislature and the imperial government. This final section explores the distribution of power in both the imperial and local context.

At the beginning of the chapter it was pointed out that the ambiguity in the British title to Belize can be explained to some extent by the equivocal manner in which British sovereignty was being established as late as the first half of the nineteenth century. A similar ambivalence characterized the British approach to the internal affairs of the settlement which resulted in a series of constitutional anomalies and struggles for supremacy between the Crown-appointed superintendents and the local political elite. For some purposes, such as imperial legislation dealing with the abolition of the slave trade and slavery, the British government dealt with the settlement as if the latter was in fact a British colony. For others it recognized that Belize was 'not within the territories nor dominions of His majesty'.[179] These included the trial for murders, violations and robberies and other crimes. It was not until 1817 and 1819 that the British government enacted legislation to regularize its jurisdiction over these specific matters in Belize.[180] At no time however did the British government remotely indicate any intention of providing the settlement with a regular constitution. The rules and regulations were formulated by the settlers. This was done in Public Meeting of the free inhabitants, at which about seven magistrates were elected to administer justice and finance.[181] One of these magistrates was chosen to be the Superintendent. These were the only administrative officers and were wholly unpaid. The informal Public Meeting had gradually taken shape as a Legislative Assembly by the middle of the eighteenth century and was restricted to British subjects with a year's income of £400.[182] All qualified persons in the community were not necessarily members because there was a 'club-like requirement'[183] that a prospective member had to be proposed by a member and receive at least twenty-six votes.

The British government refused to sanction this machinery of government, not so much because its beginnings were unprecedented, but because it did not wish to run the risk of violating the London Convention of 1786 which prohibited the formation of any but a rudimentary system of civil or military government.[184] The only recognition and protection which it offered was to make the settlement a dependency of Jamaica and to appoint a Superintendent to the settlement in 1784.[185] Distance however militated against the effective exercise of the Governor's powers. The visits of officials from Jamaica were rare and perfunctory although it should be noted that the Governor, Admiral Sir William Burnaby, on his visit in 1765, made to establish that Spain had fulfilled the conditions of the Treaty of Paris, codified the 'rules and regulations of the settlement'.[186] Although the British government declared the settlement a colony in 1862, it was still unwilling to place it on equal footing with the West Indian colonies. The Superintendent became a Lieutenant-Governor only to remain subordinate to the Governor of Jamaica. This political dependency lasted until 1884 when Belize was made a separate colony with its own Governor,[187] but it was not until 1911 that the final tie was severed by the abolition of appeals to the Jamaica Supreme Court; thereafter appeals went directly to the Privy Council in London.

What the settlers demanded above all, however, was military protection against the sporadic Spanish incursions. This was not forthcoming until January 1798 when a small British garrison was established.[188] In consequence what proved to be the final repulsion of the Spanish attack at the Battle of St George's Cay in September of that year was achieved by the settlers with the aid of their slaves, who numbered about 2,000, and British naval units.[189]

In 1851 the settlers made an attempt to regularize their constitutional relationship with the British government. They petitioned for a Legislative Assembly comprising eighteen elected officials and three ex-officio members partly because the Crown had no authority over their legislature and partly to communicate to the Crown-appointed Superintendent their conception of his role.[190] They had welcomed the British government's decision to appoint the Superintendent especially as the first incumbent, Colonal Edward Marcus Despard, had a military background. They saw in this particular appointee a response to their request for British support not to meddle in the internal affairs of the settlement but to withstand the external threat. Once, however, this threat had diminished after the Battle of St George's Cay the office of Superintendent reassumed its civil character, much to the concern of the settlers. Successive superintendents insisted, at times successfully, on appointing magistrates and other public officials, legislating by proclamation, controlling public expenditure, convening the Public Meeting and determining the matters which were to be debated. As far as the superintendents were concerned these functions were compatible with their position as representatives of the Crown. On the other hand whatever their conception was of this office when it was elective and filled by one of their peers, the settlers resented the attempt by the Crown-appointed superintendents from London to assume the initiative in government. In petitioning for a Legislative Assembly the settlers were in effect expressing their view that the Superintendent's function was what the title literally suggested: this was to superintend and not to govern.

Here again the British government failed to end the anomalous situation. It recommended the royal assent to the local act which established the Legislative Assembly. This represented a significant departure by the British government from its traditional negative approach and seemed to confirm the authority of the Superintendent. At the same time, however, the initiative for constitutional change and control of finance was left undisturbed with the local legislature. Indeed, being studiously reluctant to become too deeply involved with the colony's affairs the British government seldom supported the superintendents in their struggles with the settlers.[191] The extent, therefore, to which the thrust in administration came from the superintendents and their officials depended on their personal relationship with the unofficial members of the Legislative Assembly.

Despite the elevation of both the settlement to a colony, and the office of Superintendent to Lieutenant-Governor in 1862, it was not until 1871 that the way was opened for the Governor to exercise effective authority. And even then it was at the behest of his adversaries who were divided between the landed and commercial interests over the sharing of the taxation burden. Unable to reconcile their differences these interests voluntarily abolished the strife-ridden Legislative Assembly in favour of a wholly nominated Legislative Council and an Executive Council.[192] Provision was made for five official members, including the Governor as President, and not less than four unofficial members. As a matter of fact there were five unofficial members but since the Governor was given a casting vote there was in practice an official majority. The exercise of the casting vote on a financial bill in 1890 led to the wholesale resignation of the unofficial members and the formation of perhaps the first political organization, The People's Committee, whose aim was to redeem the country's political inheritance from the temporary custodian.[193] The Committee obviously received the solid support of the white community, as other 'suitable citizens'[194] refused to fill the void unless an unofficial majority was established in the Legislative Council. The Governor in a rearguard battle appointed civil servants to the Legislative Council but in 1892 a local commercial firm, Steven Brothers and Company, successfully challenged an amended customs tariff in the Supreme Court on the ground that the Legislative Council was illegally constituted.[195] Thereupon the British government advised the Governor to concede the unofficial majority.

A variant of the Crown colony system of government and its attendant anomalies had been established.[196] The colonial administration was hamstrung by the defects inherent in the separation of executive and financial responsibility. The Governor was still in the anomalous position of being answerable to the Crown for the administration of the colony but unable to compel local acceptance of imperial policy.

Although the problem of the country's international status had complicated the country's constitutional development the British government had only itself to blame for its predicament. By the time it took its responsibility for Belize seriously the territory's development from a woodcutters' camp to a political entity had been complete and the tradition of self-governing institutions was firmly rooted. Although the halcyon days of forestry were, like sugar in the West Indies, over by the mid nineteenth century, the social system in Belize was probably the least undermined by the abolition of slavery in 1833 and imperial protection in 1846. It certainly was never challenged by the black revolt of the kind which occurred in Jamaica in 1865. In consequence while the majority of West Indian oligarchies acknowledged the threat to their position by replacing their representative with Crown colony government between 1854 and 1875, Belize did not find it necessary to surrender its inherent constituent powers.[197] Indeed, as the constitutional impasse in 1890 demonstrated, the unofficial members had not enhanced the Governor's powers in 1871 to enable him to govern more effectively but to mediate the differences between the landed and commercial interests. So as not to be indebted to the Governor for their places, the unofficial members had also attempted to reintroduce the elective principle in 1890. When the request was turned down, they successfully insisted in 1912 that the practice of nomination for life to the Legislature, which had been abandoned with the abolition of the Public Meeting in 1854, be reintroduced.[198]

Although the constitutional status of the Legislative Council remained intact, social and economic changes impinged upon the relationship between the imperial government and the ruling group of whites. It was largely to prevent the domination of the non-European masses of some 29,500 by this narrow oligarchy that the British government did not reintroduce the elective principle.[199] As early as 1820 the ruling group had taken steps to stifle the emergence of the coloured population into public life. The Public Meeting had doubled the property qualifications for this racial group and restricted the magistracy to white British subjects.[200] Indeed, its club-like admission had reduced its membership from 63 in 1830 to 27 in 1853.[201] The unofficial members of the Legislative Council probably restored the practice of nomination for life not only to assert their independence of the Governor but also to exclude the growing class of *nouveaux riches* consisting mainly of African and Mestizo businessmen. Although the reinstituted practice was modified in 1912 to allow the Governor to determine appointments every five years except in the case of the then existing members, the old elite retained its hegemony.[202]

The need for a more open political system was dramatically emphasized in 1919 when the demobilized soldiers and the unemployed rioted. The political unrest was part of a pattern which the First World War nurtured in the West Indies. The British government and the unofficial members of the Legislative Council in Belize reacted independently; one sent a constitutional commissioner, Hon. E. F L. Wood (later Lord Halifax), who was then Parliamentary Under-Secretary of State for the Colonies, to the West Indies in November 1921[203] and the other, in the same month, requested the reintroduction of the elective principle.[204] Wood recommended that the retention of the existing official majority and a proportion of nominated members should be indispensable conditions of the introduction of the elective principle in the West Indies. In 1923 the British government was however prepared to waive the first condition in the case of Belize provided the Governor was given reserve powers.[205] It also established a local commission to work out the details of the constitutional change. In August 1923 the commission recommended a constitution similar to the one that had been adopted for the Windward Islands. It however insisted that the proposed reserve powers to the Governor should exclude financial measures.[206] As this stipulation rendered the reserve powers almost, if not wholly nugatory, the relevant constitutional bills which were introduced in 1924 were withdrawn in 1925.

In refusing to sacrifice their financial control for the elective principle the unofficial members appeared to be primarily concerned with preserving the country's political heritage. In effect, they were protecting their political monopoly which they feared was being threatened by the growing political awareness. As the Colonial Office noted, 'It appears clear from the contemporary papers that the clause [relating to the Governor's reserve power] was merely taken as a convenient excuse for the rejection of the [electoral] Bill, and the real reason was the fear of the Unofficial Members that the electoral and other qualifications would be reduced to a low level and an uncontrolled flood of democracy let into British Honduras political life.'[207] The Franchise Commission which the narrow oligarchy dominated had in fact recommended electoral qualifications that were in general more restrictive than those elsewhere in the West Indies. Indeed, the Colonial Office was certain that the 'very limited electorate' was bound to lead to 'the rise of an oligarchy [of white businessmen] of the kind existing in Barbados'.[208] As we have seen, the problem was not how to prevent the rise of an oligarchy but how to contain it. Although he controlled appointments to the Legislative Council, the Governor had to be wary in giving representation to the new wealthy businessmen and even the professional class. Lacking an official majority and faced with a group that automatically closed its ranks when in combat with the Governor, his position was likely to become untenable, as in 1892.

The abortive proposals in 1923 had in fact suggested that an attempt by the British government to initiate constitutional changes was likely to provoke a crisis. On the other hand, it was equally clear, as evidenced in the constitutional changes in Ceylon in 1924 and in Guyana in 1928, both of which countries were unyielding on this issue of financial control, that the British government would grasp the earliest opportunity, whether this was a political or economic crisis, to impose executive control on the Legislative Council. The opportunity arose in 1931 when the hurricane rendered the social and economic conditions acute and imperial aid necessary.

# 2

# Latent crisis of the colonial order: economic aspects, 1931-1949

Lucian Pye has observed that 'It has been customary to picture societies under colonial rule as having been politically dormant for a long time and then suddenly awakening when the silent effects of gradual social change dramatically came together to strike a spark over some handy political issue.'[1] This viewpoint is generally considered relevant to Belize. Except for the struggle for the assertion of local rights against the imperial power which was common to the West Indian colonies, the country led a quiet and unobtrusive political existence throughout the nineteenth century. The political calm remained generally unruffled throughout the first fifty years of the twentieth century and in particular during the 1930s when the West Indian colonies were engulfed in disturbances and riots that compelled the British government to appoint a Royal Commission to investigate their social and economic causes.[2] It was not until the Governor, Sir Ronald Garvey, announced on 31 December 1949 the British government's decision to devalue the Belizean dollar that Belize was rudely awakened from its apparent slumber. The devaluation was indeed politically significant. The necessary legislation[3] was enacted, in the teeth of unanimous opposition from the unofficial members of the Legislative Council, by the Governor's reserve power. More intensely opposed by the mass of the urban population, devaluation became the immediate occasion for the formation of the People's Committee in January 1950 which developed into the People's United Party. No other issue could have been more appropriate in stimulating the anti-colonialist movement. Devaluation of the dollar bound the country more closely to Britain, rather than to its traditional market and source of supply – the United States. In the short term at least, devaluation raised the price of imports, and thus the cost of living, at a time of acute economic depression. It also brought into the open the conflict of interest between the business community which was its immediate beneficiary and the working class. Finally, it had a similar effect on the opposing viewpoints of the

61

old political elite and the emerging group of young, nationalist politicians regarding the attitude to be adopted towards Britain.

While the issue should be recognized as a landmark in the country's political development its importance should not be overemphasized. No single event, however important, can adequately account for the political upsurge and the anti-British sentiments which were expressed at the time, and the devaluation is no exception. The roots of the resentment were deeper. They lay partly in the appalling social and economic conditions which had resulted from the world depression in the 1920s and were aggravated first by the disastrous hurricane of 1931, and then by conditions in the years immediately following the Second World War. The other important factor was the absence of an open, competitive political system, that was not unrelated to the system of social and cultural stratification. In discussing both factors, the aim of this chapter and the next is to put the devaluation issue in its correct perspective and to provide social depth and reality to political change after the Second World War.

### Social and economic decline, 1931–39

As we saw in the previous chapter the economic decline of Belize was already evident when the country was visited by the disastrous hurricane on 10 September 1931. Described in the official reports as 'the most awful calamity in the country's history',[4] the hurricane was perhaps even more responsible than the world depression for the country's deterioration of social and economic conditions in the 1930s. Having experienced no hurricane within living memory, Belizeans were unprepared and ill-equipped to meet the raging storm. Belize City, in which about one-third of the total population resided, was practically destroyed; over 1,000 of its inhabitants lost their lives and several thousands more were rendered homeless. The absence of even the most elementary drainage and sewerage facilities, coupled with the submerged corpses, constituted a public health hazard in the inundated city. The destruction was not confined to lives and buildings. Large areas of mahogany and pine trees in the accessible forests of the northern district which lay in the hurricane's course were devastated. As if fate had not been sufficiently unkind, a disastrous fire occurred in the city in April 1933. This greatly increased the hardship of many persons who were making efforts to recover from the hurricane. Within five months of the fire one of the highest floods in the country's history swept the Belize river causing distress and loss to farmers along its banks.

The hurricane disaster was of such extraordinary magnitude relative to the resources of the colony that it was impossible for the cost of relief and reparations to be met without assistance. The damage was estimated to be equal to one year's revenue, and the colony was already suffering severely from the effects of the world economic depression.[5]

Imperial aid which had been tentatively explored before the hurricane now became a compelling necessity. For constitutional and political reasons which will be discussed in the next chapter, the required loan of $1,100,000 was not made available until May 1932.[6] Here it is only necessary to note that a condition of the loan which the Legislative Council reluctantly accepted was the grant of the reserve power to the Governor and the assumption by the imperial Treasury of control of the colony's finance in 1932.[7] In terms of the prevailing economic conditions these constitutional and financial changes had their merits and disadvantages. They transferred the initiative in public expenditure from the Legislative Council to the Governor. This enabled the Governor to put an end to the discriminatory use of public funds by the business interests. As legislators, they were reluctant to tax their interests and seldom sanctioned schemes which brought them no obvious benefits. Their traditional

outlook...was that expenditure on public purposes must be limited by the amount which could be raised by a low level of indirect taxation and although they succeeded for a long period in maintaining a satisfactory financial position it was only at the cost of refraining from developing the country by means of roads, port facilities, technical departments of government to promote increased and diverse production and the provision of social services such as education and public health upon which a more progressive economy could be based.[8]

Indeed, as Governor Hunter observed in 1946, 'not a measure that was proposed had any chance of going through, no proposal had any chance of being accepted, unless they served the interests of the gentlemen in the counting houses of Belize'.[9]

If Treasury control rendered the equitable spending of public funds possible, it impaired the efficiency of the colonial administration which became a source of political discontent among the masses. Every item of expenditure required the prior approval of the British Treasury. Considerable time was lost in the approval of estimates. Machinery for public work which could have been easily obtained in the neighbouring United States had to be ordered through the Crown Agents in London. Moreover, this could be done only after the Treasury approved the estimates. The time taken between the approval of the estimate by the Legislative Council and the placing of an order for equipment varied between five and seven months. The delay reduced the effectiveness of the government's action at a time when, as we shall see, the provision of public works was the main palliative to the unemployment situation. The cumbersome administrative machinery was so irksome and frustrating that Governor Burns' comments are worth quoting in full:

The control of the Treasury over expenditure led to vexatious delays and a parsimony in administration at a time when the condition of the colony made it more than ever necessary that speedy and generous expenditure should be authorised. I can imagine nothing more deadening to a colony than 'Treasury control'. The object is, of course, to protect the British taxpayer from unreasonable or unnecessary burdens, by limiting the expenditure in a colony which cannot pay its own way; but I question whether this object is achieved by the method adopted. If a Governor cannot be trusted to use his discretion in the appointment of an additional junior clerk without reference to a Treasury official in Whitehall, then, in my view, that Governor should not have been appointed to the post he holds. And if the Governor and his senior officials and the members of the Legislative Council have examined the annual estimates of expenditure in detail, as they have to do, then it seems quite unnecessary that approval of these estimates should be delayed for months while comparatively junior Treasury officials check the details over again in London. So far as I can remember, in no instance did the Treasury disallow any item inserted in the draft estimates while I was Governor and nothing resulted from this scrutiny except delay. Year after year work was held up at the beginning of the financial year because the estimates sent home months before had not yet been approved; the result was that the dry season would end and the rains would arrive making it impossible to begin on outdoor work, such as the construction of roads, until the financial year was nearly ended.[10]

Perhaps a more important source of discontent among the ordinary people was the financial measures taken by the government to meet the depression years. The government aided the forestry interests by reducing the tax on chicle from 1½ cents to 1 cent per pound[11] and abolishing that on sawn timber produced by the BEC.[12] But this did not necessarily improve the employment situation as the bulk of the chicle exported from Belize was not of domestic origin, but from Peten in Guatemala and Yucatan in Mexico where Belizean contractors, though locally based, held concessions. The working class was even more aggrieved by the outcome of the increased land tax from 1½ cents per acre in 1920 to 2½ cents in 1931. Opposition to the increase was spearheaded by the BEC which contended that the increase was inimical to the recovery of the mahogany trade. The company further argued that since the proceeds of the additional 1 cent were in theory earmarked for road and agricultural development they would be expended outside of its estates.[13] As part of their protests the large landowners suspended payment of the tax in 1932 when the increase became effective.[14] The arrears tax for that year alone was $148,000 while the government estimate of collection of the arrears for 1933–4 and 1934–5 was only $18,000 and $26,000 respectively.[15] If from these modest estimates of collection the government appeared to have abandoned from the outset all hopes of recovering the outstanding taxes it was partly because the Land and Property Tax Ordinance[16] was not intended to facilitate the collection of arrears taxes. The law was designed to force the large landowners who were making little use of their lands to surrender them to the government. And of course the BEC which had made no payments since 1931 and whose arrears in May 1934 amounted to $114,933[17] was most obliging. It took the opportunity of surrendering several hundreds of acres of land of 'indifferent value'.[18]

The law, however, when indiscriminatingly applied, proved confiscatory to the small unemployed landowners and petty tenants of Crown lands. Under the law these unfortunate landowners were first served with a notice of distraint on their goods and chattels.[19] It was only after these were sold that the land could be attached. It was therefore possible for a person to be deprived of all his personal property in payment of arrears of tax before the land was sold. The peasant communities of Indians and Caribs in the western and southern districts were the main victims of the law. The yearly tax of $10 which the Indians paid for cultivating Crown lands in Toledo in 1934 was out of all proportion to land rent elsewhere which was 30 cents per acre.[20] Moreover, unemployment in the chicle industry robbed the Indian villagers of their main source of cash wages. The few chicleros who were able to obtain employment were still unable to meet their commitments to the government. The rate of pay for chicle collection was reduced from about $20 to $7.50 per quintal. From this amount the value of the labourer's ration was deducted and 'the remainder can only be described as starvation wage'.[21] Those Crown tenants who worked off arrears of rent by labour were allowed in 1934 credit at the rate of 50 cents or 75 cents per day depending on the district, as compared to $1.00 or $1.50 in 1929.[22]

The social and economic problems were perhaps more acute for the Caribs since they were more settled agriculturalists than the Indians. Many of the Carib tenants of Crown lands had cultivated permanent crops, such as coconuts, citrus, and other fruit trees. These crops were their only potential source of income. Yet the leases were cancelled, or worse, the leaseholders were evicted without being given the opportunity to reap the rewards of their labour.[23] The possible adoption of less drastic action by the government, though humane, posed its own problems. It was of little use to offer these peasants the sale of the lands at a reduced rate. They were unable to put down a lump sum and would have continued to fall into arrears with their instalments as they had done with their rent. A government declaration of amnesty to all debtors, which was probably the easiest and best course of action, would have been manifestly unfair to those who had paid their rents.[24] Still worse, it would have discouraged payment in the future.

Yet, in a sense, the government discriminated against the small land-owners who had felt the full weight of the law. It did not only accept from the large landowners overexploited and 'almost worthless'[25] land in lieu of their indebtedness but eventually yielded to their opposition to the tax increase. In 1935 it reduced the tax to its former rate of 1½ cents per acre with retroactive effect from 1931, thus annulling the increase imposed.[26] As Pim remarked in 1934, 'the criticism that they [the large landowners] had been treated with greater consideration than the petty tenants of Crown land is therefore not without substance'.[27] The rate of tax remained unchanged up to the end of the period under review in the chapter. In effect therefore, the landowners paid in 1949 the same rate which they had paid in 1920.

The rural communities were not the only group among the labouring class affected by government's fiscal measures. Individuals in Belize City who had mortgaged their properties to the Hurricane Loan Administration Board in order to repair their houses were in a similar position. Those who had become unemployed with the decline of the forestry industries were unable to meet their liabilities.

The Hurricane Board was also in a difficult situation. It was neither economic nor expedient for the Board to recover the outstanding loans by foreclosing the properties.[28] In the first place the debtors would have been thrown on an unabsorbed market. Secondly, selling the properties would have been equally problematic because of the depressed conditions. The renting of the renovated properties did not provide a solution either since rents had fallen and their payment was uncertain. Fourthly, the Board would have been responsible for the maintenance of both the unsold and unrented houses.

It was obvious that the solution to the social and economic problems did not lie in law enforcement. Yet the government harassed the Hurricane Loan Board for being lenient to its debtors. For the same reason in January 1938 it dissolved the Belize Town Board whose councillors were sympathetic to the ratepayers because they were also in heavy arrears with their repayments.[29] The taxpayers keenly resented the dissolution of the Board and the assumption of direct control of municipal affairs by an interim administration consisting of the Governor, members of the Executive Council and the Director of Public Works. The Town Board was the ratepayers' political pride. Though only partially so, it had been until 1936 the only elected political institution in the country. The interim Town Board predictably took action against the defaulters by instituting legal proceedings to recover the tax arrears. It discovered, however, that tax arrears for more than three years could not be recovered and for the first time was called upon to pay for court summonses which had been inadvertently overlooked in the past.[30] This further rendered the legal method ineffective because there was no guarantee that the Board would recover the legal cost even in cases for which judgements were obtained.

The colonial government had once more subscribed to its image of being punitive and somewhat oppressive. As was characteristic of the colonial political system the application and enforcement of the law developed as the main link between the ruler and the ruled. This assertion of authority far from humanizing their relationship polarized it.

Elsewhere in the British Caribbean similar social and economic conditions had stimulated industrial unrest – riots and strikes – and trade unionism among the wage labourers and the unemployed. The violent action which gripped the entire region burnt feverishly, if intermittently, for a period of about six years from 1934 to 1939. The leaders of several black middle-class groups took advantage of the situation to exert pressure upon the colonial system not only in their own interests but also on behalf of the disadvantaged and oppressed.[31] This marked a new phase of political evolution in the region in that it created a dichotomy by which economic power remained in the hands of a 'white' managerial class and politics was opened to a variety of black elements. It soon became clear, however, that the latter situation would not become a permanent feature. The middle class, mainly the professional element, emerged as the dominant political group, hardening in the process the divisions between the privileged few on the one hand and the disadvantaged mass on the other.

It is significant that mass responses to the overall situation in the 1930s were not as riotous as those in the other Caribbean territories. A disturbance in 1935 by the hastily formed Unemployed Workers' Association whose leader was Antonio Soberanis G, a barber, was the high point of several demonstrations which were not prolonged and never spread beyond Belize City. Furthermore Soberanis appeared to be a reluctant leader since he claimed that 'he knew that he was unsuited for this position of leadership'.[32] But this mantle had fallen on him, because unlike in most Caribbean territories, the middle-class politicians did not come forward as mass leaders for any length of time. As he and his co-author, L. D. Kemp, a colourful polemicist, observed in a book written in 1949, 'After the devastating hurricane of 1931 which ruined Belize, a few native intellectuals rallied the masses to protest against certain official impositions. The intellectuals withdrew at the height of "loyalty and devotion" to them, because they said they could not accomplish what the masses desired.'[33]

Apart from the lack of leadership the rudimentary industrial structure precluded more riotous forms of mass expression. In the first place the country lacked an industrial proletariat. Belize City was not an industrial but a commercial town which lived on the merchant business connected with the forest industries, by arranging and financing exports and providing for imports of food supplies.[34] The industrial centre was the forests. The method of production in the forest industries, however, effectively prevented the forestry workers from developing a strong group consciousness and still more from forging an alliance with other occupational groups in the city. Both the mahogany cutter and chiclero worked on a task basis. It was a question of the worker completing as many tasks as possible not only before the end of the day but also before the rainy season began. Though favourable to the strong and industrious, the method of production bred individualism. This situation was largely responsible for the absence of unionism among the forestry workers until the early 1940s. As the annual Labour Department report commented as late as 1942, there was a 'lack of the spirit of combination which will handicap any efforts at the formation of trade unions'.[35] Secondly, the worker had to contend with the many disadvantages of the advance system. Heavily indebted to his employer even before he commenced work, the worker tended to abscond in order to seek a job for ready cash.[36] This resulted in a high turnover of labour that was not conducive to workers' solidarity and concerted mass action.

Perhaps the forestry worker reacted moderately because the industrial evils appeared to him to lie at the feet of the rising group of local businessmen rather than in the colonial economic system. The system was perpetuated not only by the BEC but also by American concerns. The chicle industry, for example, was in the grip of an American cartel which took advantage of the fact that it had accumulated considerable stocks during the boom period to endeavour to depress the local price of chicle.[37] But the control which the latter companies exercised was remote and certainly not as visible as that of the BEC. Unlike their British competitor, they established no elaborate administrative machinery in Belize but functioned through the more wealthy local forestry owners whose operations they also financed.[38] These wealthy contractors also sub-contracted thereby pushing the American interests further into the background. It was, however, not without some justification, that the poor working conditions were readily associated with these middlemen. For the local contractors, conscious of their own vulnerability as debtors if operations were disrupted, were more resolutely opposed to industrial reforms, in particular trade unionism, than the established BEC. In 1941, for example, they defeated a bill which was designed to supersede the archaic labour law of 1883 and make the breach of contract remediable only by civil action.[39]

This widespread tendency to see the poor industrial conditions as a conflict situation between the local businessmen and wage-labouring element rather than primarily between Belize, as a colony, and the foreign-owned companies, was reinforced by the intervention by the colonial government to secure labour reforms[40] in conformity with the recommendations of the West Indian Royal Commission.[41] Trade unions were legalized in 1941 only when this was made a condition of the Colonial and Development and Welfare Fund.[42] The colonial government exerted considerable pressure before the local forestry interest agreed to the repeal in 1943 of the Masters and Servants Ordinance of 1883 and the Fraudulent Labourers Ordinance of 1922.[43] In insisting on the repeal, Governor Hunter stated,

So long as we have on our Statute Book those penal clauses (which, I must say, shocked me when I first came to this Colony) we cannot hold up our heads and say we are an enlightened community. There may not yet have been sufficient development of the trade union movement in this country to enable the workers to put their case forward in a dispute that might arise in a constitutional and orderly manner, but I see no reason to suppose that, because trade unions have not yet developed, they will not develop very quickly hereafter. The trade union ordinance has not been long on our Statute Book [1941], and, if you remove these penal clauses which go so far to nullify the provisions of that ordinance, the trade unions will surely come into being. I want it so, because I find it a very great difficulty in this Colony, that there is no real representative of labour from the ranks of the working classes, with whom I can discuss the conditions of the workers in this Colony.[44]

*Ameliorative measures*

Perhaps the government's image would appear less impersonal and soulless if we examine its own financial position and attempts to alleviate the social and economic distress. It can be reasonably argued that the government was compelled by its own financial problems to adopt the drastic legal measures to recover the arrears taxes. It undoubtedly was the largest debtor. The hurricane loan apart, the government borrowed funds on an unprecedented scale. Charges on account of the public debt more than doubled between 1931 and 1937.[45] On the other hand the decline in public revenue in the same period[46] reduced the government's ability to fulfil its obligation both to its creditors and the population. Moreover, the repayment of the instalments of the public debt was not susceptible to easy alteration.

Most of the loans, together with grants from the Colonial Development Fund, were expended on construction of roads. The government's emphasis on road building can be seen as an attempt to redress the imbalance in the country's infrastructural development. This form of transportation had been sadly neglected by the forestry-controlled government for the obvious reason that roads were not necessary to the transportation of timber. In the 1930s internal transportation was still by means of dories, pit-pans and paddle-propelled boats on the many rivers of the country. Despite the poor transportation system the forestry interest 'persisted in their opposition to road construction' on the ground that it was an 'unjustified expense'.[47]

The forestry interest would have been nearer the truth if it had criticized the expense as being unproductive and even wasteful. Road construction was conceived primarily as a form of unemployment relief. In order to spread the work among the unemployed the government adopted the rotation system of unemployment whereby the individual labourer was intermittently employed for about two weeks.[48] The social objective of road construction was so paramount that the use of machinery was avoided to a degree that precluded the introduction of modern methods in case it reduced employment. But the 'quincena' system, as the method of employment was locally termed, was to little avail. Had it not been disguised as a normal economic enterprise but recognized for what it was and given directly to the indigent, the relief benefit would have been more effective since the social distress fell more heavily on households in which a male was either absent or tended to avoid his responsibilities.

A more permanent solution to the problem of unemployment appeared to be the government's attempt to stimulate once more the agricultural industry and banana cultivation in particular.[49] For the twin problem of increasing local food supplies and of fostering a local peasantry could no longer be avoided if the social distress was to be arrested. Increased production required much more than the distribution of widely separated plots of leased land throughout the country. In consequence rural land settlement schemes were established. Several factors, however, militated against their success.[50] One was the government's ambivalence to agricultural development, another was the continued opposition of the mercantile and forestry interests to commercial agriculture, and the third was the discouraging features of the agricultural settlements. Although $203,075 of the hurricane loan had been earmarked for agricultural settlement, funds were not 'available at present [ 1935, i.e. within three years of the grant of the loan] from this source for Agricultural Settlements' because 'expenditure actual and authorised of [Hurricane] Loan Funds already exceeds the total amount approved, viz. $1,100,000'.[51] The government was therefore also unable to meet the farmers' requests for the creation of an Agricultural Loan Board.[52] On the other hand the BEC which had been originally allocated $100,000 from the Fund to build a local sawmill received $200,000 'to enable it to plan a comprehensive programme'.[53] Moreover, although the company immediately repaid $43,027 in order 'to reduce its interest charges. . .the government was bound by the agreement to keep this sum in reserve in case it is required by the company at any time and is thus precluded from using the money for development purpose'.[54] Denied government finance, the bulk of banana production was in the hands of peasant planters who for the most part cultivated the old diseased land. Other agricultural crops persisted on a limited scale, except for citrus which a Jamaican family, the Sharps, began to develop in Stann Creek in the mid-1930s.[55]

When the merchants in Belize City were not opposing agricultural development outright, they were influencing the location of the land settlement scheme to protect their trade monopoly. The first agricultural settlement scheme was established on Crown lands in the fertile Stann Creek Valley in 1932.[56] Sixty-one settlers, mainly from Belize City, were attracted to the area to cultivate bananas for export under relatively favourable conditions. The scheme, however, did not meet with much favour in Belize City whose principal merchants felt that it was too far away to attract people from Belize City. The real reason for their objection was their fear 'that trade will not all come to that town'.[57] Stann Creek, being a sea-port, was capable of attracting some of the import and export trade, which it eventually did with the establishment of the citrus industry in the Valley. Indeed, 'there was considerable jealousy between the Belize City and Stann Creek interests'.[58] The former interests being more influential, successfully urged the establishment of two other schemes at Salt Creek and Rockstone in the North, nearer to Belize City 'even though little was known of the land'.[59]

The merchants, however, did not accept the implications of their pressure upon the government. The government was compelled to rent private estates because most of the arable lands were to be found on them and not on Crown lands or even on such private lands as had and were likely to be offered to the government in lieu of taxes. But the mercantile interests objected to what amounted to the government subsidizing the development of private estates by land clearance and the construction of public access to them which in the final analysis served few interests other than those of the land owners.[60]

For its part the government, in submitting to mercantile pressures, revealed its ambivalence towards agricultural development. It recognized the importance of wresting the initiative from the powerful forestry and mercantile interests. At the same time, in determining the location of the land settlement schemes, it allowed itself to be influenced by considerations other than the agricultural suitability of the area. The urban Creole who had been attracted by the comparative ease of banana cultivation and its potential as an export crop to settle in Stann Creek was at best an improvised farmer. But the lands at Salt Creek and Rockstone yielded mainly the local staples – corn, rice, red kidney beans, and vegetables – and therefore did not give him the living standard which he enjoyed as a forestry worker. He experienced considerable difficulties in disposing of his small surpluses because the marketing organization, including transportation, was inadequate.[61] Periodical gluts of the more perishable products reduced prices to a point where the farmer could not sell except at a loss. There was also the prejudice in the towns, principally Belize City, against locally produced food – a prejudice the merchants had encouraged.[62] This offered little incentive to the farmer to produce beyond his own need. Furthermore, as the Governor observed, it was doubtful whether tenancy on private land 'offered that security of tenure without which no settler can be expected to put his best into his holding'.[63] Finally it was 'ridiculous' for the government to expect the urban unemployed to take up agriculture when it was at the same time ejecting from the land those who had been wedded to it for years and had made some sort of living from their farms.[64]

In general, the government seemed to be unaware of the full implications of establishing land settlement schemes. It seemed to be of the opinion that it had made its maximum contribution to the success of the schemes by launching them. Little attempt was made to increase the technical staff of the Agriculture Department with the constant supervision of these schemes required. Little consideration was also given to the social aspects of land settlement with the result that the government's immediate objective of relieving Belize City of some of its unemployed was not realized. The government catered for the farmer but not his family. There was no provision for educational and medical services. In consequence the farmer was compelled to leave his family in Belize City. This reduced the land settlement site to a camp. Under the slightest pretext the farmer forsook his agricultural holding for the relative comfort of Belize City.[65] Moreover, his separation from his family duplicated not only his personal expenses but his debt to the government, which included the rental of his agricultural holding and the city rates and property taxes. As the Governor observed, even those who made determined efforts to meet their liabilities 'found themselves handicapped by a millstone of debt from which it was difficult to escape'.[66]

Far from being resolved, the problem of the unemployed urban worker became more involved. His dilemma was that although agriculture failed as a palliative, it offered him the only long-term solution to his problem. For although there were hopes of a revival of the forestry industries there was no chance of their providing the previous high level of employment. Moreover, the neighbouring Central American republics which had once absorbed a large proportion of the country's labour force had been compelled by the world economic depression to close their frontiers.

The outbreak of the Second World War partially relieved the social and economic problem. Despite its many adverse effects, a fair measure of prosperity replaced the financial stringency, unemployment and depressed conditions of trade during the first three years of the war. The mahogany industry which was still the mainstay of the economy received a new lease of life. It was accorded the highest priority as an essential wartime commodity.[67] Chicle was also exported in greater quantities and at a relatively high price, mainly because of the partial failure of the Far Eastern sources of supply.[68] The war also offered employment overseas to thousands of labourers. Some were recruited to the armed forces. The migration of the unemployed in search of work in the canal zone in Panama came close to being an 'exodus'.[69] By June 1943, almost 2,000 Belizeans had made their way to the Isthmus. Exit permits had to be introduced in order to ensure that sufficient labour was retained in the colony.[70] As part of the imperial war effort a Forestry Unit of five hundred labourers was sent to Scotland.[71] Apart from relieving the unemployment problem in Belize the migrants positively helped the financial situation by remitting between $15,000 and $16,000 monthly to dependents in Belize.[72] These remittances were an indirect boon to the government since they reduced the necessity for a large measure of relief.

*Economic relapse*

The economic improvement which followed in the wake of the war was, however, shortlived. The colony relapsed into its depression with the entry of the United States into the war. Through its close trade relations with this country, Belize had been saved many of the inconveniences and hardships.[73] The wartime restriction and control which the United States government now imposed severely affected the Belizean economy. The United States restricted the importation of mahogany to that which was suitable for military and naval use. On the other hand the price of imported food soared. Essential commodities were subsidized[74] but renewed official efforts to promote agricultural development met with no more success than previously. The receipt of Colonial Development and Welfare grants and the extension of social welfare services which was recommended by the West India Royal Commission in 1940 made little substantial difference to the appalling social and economic conditions. The publication in 1948 of the Evans Commission Report, which had investigated the possibilities of the settlement in Belize and Guyana of the surplus populations of the British or other West Indian islands and of displaced Europeans of the Second World War, held out a ray of hope. The Commission fully covered the colony's potential for economic development and recommended several economic projects that were designed to realize the tremendous agricultural possibilities.[75] The announcement of the Secretary of State that funds would be made available to finance these projects in addition to those already allocated under the Colonial Development and Welfare Act was enthusiastically received. So too was the decision by the Colonial Development Corporation (CDC) to embark on a development programme within the framework of the Evans plan.[76] But by the end of 1949 there was no visual evidence so far as the public was concerned of the Corporation's activities or of any which the government might have taken. The failure of the CDC to commence work was a bitter disappointment to the hopeful. To the defeated the failure merely confirmed their belief that programmes meant nothing. As the Governor informed the Colonial Office, 'The public have heard about plans ever since the Royal Commission visited the colony in 1938, and they feel that so little has been achieved by the end of 1949 that plans are rather a form of procrastination than an indication of forthcoming activity.'[77]

The worst years, however, followed in the aftermath of the war. First of all the Belize Battalion which had brought an additional $30,000 monthly to the colony was disbanded in 1947.[78] The return of the ex-servicemen and other workers from abroad increased the ranks of unemployed. To many of the poor households the cessation of the dependents' allowances occasioned much distress.[79] Moreover, some of these people were still heavily indebted to the Hurricane Loan Board, a burden which they had carried for sixteen years and seemed destined to bear for a longer period.[80]

The year 1949 was particularly disastrous. Activities in the mahogany and chicle industries virtually ceased during the year because of a slump in the export trade.[81] There was also a failure of crops due to an unprecedented drought in the early months in the northern and western parts of the country.[82] The slump and the drought combined to create a more severe crisis than the colony had hitherto faced, with the exception of the 1931 hurricane. The Governor took immediate action and re-instituted relief work without the prior approval of his superiors in London. In a despatch primarily designed to justify his action to them, he vividly evoked the atmosphere of desolation bordering on despair:

That same day [when relief work was authorized] there was a procession of unemployed through the main streets of Belize [City], culminating in a mass meeting on the Battlefield. But while the tension in Belize [City] was not unexpected in the circumstances I was advised that a much more dangerous atmosphere was building up in the Western District. The Indians of that area usually maintain an attitude of aloofness towards the authorities, but circumstances had now compelled them to turn to Government for aid. Their two normal sources of livelihood, the chicle industry and the cultivation of their milpas, had completely failed them, and there is little doubt that if the Government had declined to come to their aid in this desperate situation, starvation would have stared them in the face. I cannot conjecture with certainty what their reaction would have been in such an eventuality, but those who know the Indians well have assured me that looting and violence would have been inevitable.[83]

During the year stricter measures of exchange control were also introduced to the chagrin of many thousands of Belizeans, who had fewer connections with the sterling area than with the neighbouring Republics and the United States.[84] Despite the exchange controls, it was cheaper to import certain essential goods from the dollar areas than the United Kingdom, but this was prevented by import restrictions. In fact in July 1949, the government suspended the issue of import licences from the dollar area because of the deterioration of the dollar position in the sterling areas. The restriction became punitive when trade with the United Kingdom was adversely affected by the devaluation of the British pound and other currencies in the sterling areas, except the Belize dollar, in September 1949.[85] The exemption of the Belize dollar also discouraged British investment upon which the economy was still dependent. More specifically, it was responsible for the inaction of the Colonial Development Corporation. The unfavourable rate of exchange also reduced the value of Colonial Development and Welfare funds which were in sterling by 30 per cent in terms of the Belize dollar unless they had already been received and converted into the local currency.[86] The exemption also threatened the future expansion of the citrus industry. Since the end of the war the British

Ministry of Food had become one of the principal citrus customers but it was not prepared to consider any upward revision of prices in respect of the Belize product since Jamaica and Trinidad could have made good any deficiencies in quantity at the existing prices.[87] Altogether, the imperial financial crisis further retarded the slow pace of economic development, and exacerbated the unemployment problem in the closing months of 1949.

In exempting the Belize dollar from devaluation the British government recognized the country's dependence on the United States for over 70 per cent of its imports.[88] But this consideration could not prevail over the more compelling British arguments for devaluation. Although at parity with the United States dollar, the local currency was backed by sterling securities and government investments were in sterling. The estimated amount required to make good the depreciation of all these investments and the Currency Board Special Account was $1,500,000.[89] Perhaps it was the subsequent recognition of the fact that this amount would have had to be met by the imperial Treasury which prompted the British government to vary its decision and devalue the Belize dollar on 31 December 1949. As we indicated at the beginning of the chapter the eventual devaluation of the dollar ensured the continued export of Belize products to the United Kingdom and other sterling areas and improved their competitive position in the United States. The local beneficiaries, however, in the short run were the merchants and investors since the immediate consequence was the rise of imported food prices and a decline in the real wages of the workers.[90] To the poverty stricken there seemed no way to end their problems except to turn to those political leaders who promised to solve them.

The foregoing account indicates that with the exception of the three years immediately following the outbreak of the Second World War the social and economic conditions from 1931 to 1949 were ones of unrelieved gloom. The situation described supports W. M. MacMillan's celebrated statement of the period that 'A social and economic study of the West Indies is...necessarily a study of poverty.'[91] The depressed conditions were partly caused by natural calamities – hurricanes, forest fires, droughts, and plant diseases. An overriding factor, however, was the narrow outlook of the forestry and merchant interests. They frustrated almost every attempt to diversify the forestry-oriented economy. In identifying the causes of the economic and social crisis, one must acknowledge that imperial neglect was paramount. Belize has been one of the most neglected territories in the history of British colonialism. It has received serious attention only after the liquidation of imperial rule elsewhere left the

Colonial Office to focus sympathy on the residue of the empire. The cumulative effect of centuries of neglect became manifest in the middle months of 1949. The demonstration in August on the day that relief work was reintroduced suggests that the breaking point had been reached. This was confirmed by the political outburst that accompanied devaluation.

# 3
# Latent crisis of the colonial order: political aspects, 1931–1949

The crisis of the colonial order was as much political as it was economic. It was inherent in colonialism that the basic problem would be the exclusion of the mass element from the exercise of political power and influence. But the problem was much wider in Belize. It also involved the local elite's loss of financial control to the British government in 1932. This at once placed the imperial authority within the country beyond doubt and undermined it in the eyes of those who had come to regard the country's self-governing institutions as part of a natural order. Even those elements who were not indignant over the shift of power from the unofficial members of the Legislative Council to the Governor took exception to the circumstance in which it was demanded.[1] The occasion seemed less than propitious. It raised the moral issue of whether a disaster beyond the country's control should have been seized upon to divest the legislature of its financial powers. Complete and unreserved support for the colonial order was therefore not forthcoming from the local elite at a time when the Governor needed it most. Indeed the relationship between the unofficial members of the Legislative Council and the Governor was subjected to considerable strain in the 1940s as the former seemed resolved to retrieve their political heritage.[2]

It must not be forgotten, however, that the local elite was never a homogeneous group, and this constituted another dimension of the problem of the colonial political process. The differentiation in terms of occupation, culture and social status soon encouraged those who were not within the inner circle to attend to the needs of those segments of the population which felt more denied. The result of this, in the absence of a fluid political process, was the gradual building up of the demand for political change which reached crisis proportions in 1950. These three issues – the relationship between the British government and the local elite, the basis of the distribution of political influence among the various components of the political elite, and the pressures for overall political change that were

78

imperceptibly exerted upon the colonial system – are discussed in this chapter.

## Power distribution between the imperial and colonial governments

*Constitutional change in 1932.* The British government had considerable difficulty convincing the Legislature that in seeking the reserve power for the Governor as a condition of the hurricane loan it was not 'exacting a price' but merely following the practice in other colonies of assuming ultimate control of finances as a measure of security.[3] It compounded its difficulties by proposing to the Belize government that $100,000 of the $1 million loan be made available to the BEC.[4] Three of the six unofficial members of the Legislature were adamant in their opposition to the proposal. For one thing they were local businessmen in the forestry industry and they regarded the BEC as their most formidable competitor. They therefore saw no reason to set the English company on its feet; more so as it was not the only firm that sustained losses in the hurricane.[5] For another thing the loan to the BEC would have entailed a reduction of expenditure on reconstruction items.[6] This would have exposed them to popular odium since no decision had been taken on the assistance to be given to the thousands of hurricane victims.[7] Holding to the view that the plight of the BEC was none of their business these unofficial members suggested that the British government make a loan direct to the BEC which the Belize government should not be called upon to guarantee.[8] But the British government considered this to be 'out of the question'; a direct loan would have been a precedent with untold political implications. The deadlock was broken when it was discovered that the exchange margin of the loan in sterling (£325,500) made it possible for the BEC to receive the extra $100,000 without reducing the $1 million to the Belize government.[9] Having taken care of the company's financial needs the British government intensified its demand for the reserve power. With the support of the other three unofficial members (who were Englishmen), the necessary legislation to amend the constitution was passed in March 1932.[10]

*Constitutional change in 1935.* This constitutional change revived local demands for elective representation. The British government was as ambivalent in this aspect of constitutional reform as it had been unyielding in its demand for reserve power for the Governor. By the attitude it had adopted to the previous demand some ten years earlier, the British government was committed to consider sympathetically the request. Nor did the example which it had set in other West Indian territories on Wood's recommendation 'offer the British government any other choice in Belize'.[11] On the other hand the Colonial Office believed that the unforeseen economic and financial deterioration of the colony had significantly altered the political situation. This was not a period for 'constitutional experiment' in elective representation but for firm, 'good and efficient government in the general interest of its very mixed population'.[12] Indeed, the Colonial Office doubted the value of the elective principle. It was certain that 'nobody better than the old gang' would be returned to the Council, and 'if there was to be any change in personnel' it 'would be for the worse'.[13] Moreover, the Colonial Office recognized that as elected representatives, the business element would be fortified in its claim to be articulating the interests of the people.

Against its better judgement, the British government introduced a new constitution in 1935 to permit elective representation.[14] The constitution provided for seven unofficial members, five of whom were to be elected and the other two nominated by the Governor. There was a clear majority of nominated unofficial members and ex-officio members in the Legislative Council. As we shall see later in the chapter the franchise qualifications were no less restrictive than in the other West Indian colonies. Nonetheless, the British government warned the local elite that it would not hesitate to have recourse to its reserve power in cases that it deemed necessary. Indeed the reserve power was no longer linked to Treasury control; it was to continue after this came to an end.[15] The constitution came into force in early 1936 when an election was held.

It should not be assumed that the sole or even primary objective of the British government's attempt to release the country from the grip of the unofficial members was to facilitate a more equitable distribution of political power in the colony, or to safeguard the interests of the poorer class. The uncertain future of the British financed interests was largely responsible for its attitude. As its financial problem and the response of the local vested interests to it indicated, the BEC was in serious trouble. Since the First World War it had been in danger of losing control of the forestry industries to the American companies. The chicle, and to a lesser extent, the mahogany industry was in the grip of American concerns.[16] Being a small-scale manufacturer of sawn timber, the BEC was unable to enter into direct world competition with American-sawn mahogany. Indeed, with its position rendered infinitely worse by the 1931 hurricane, the BEC claimed that the sale of its interests to a rival American concern, Messrs Mengel and Company, would have been unavoidable unless it had not received financial assistance.[17]

But British prestige and general confidence in an already weak economy

was too bound up with the activities of the BEC for the British government not to have rescued the company. The BEC was given the loan
primarily to erect a sawmill in order to 'reduce the existing dependence of
the mahogany industry on the American buyers'.[18] The British government also gave the BEC 'one of the few remaining areas of virgin
mahogany forests in the possession of the Crown in exchange for land that
had been over-exploited for some twenty years'.[19] Moreover, the Hoare
family claimed that the disposal of the company's assets to American concerns was the prospect which the Belize government wished to entertain
the least.[20] The American companies were more unscrupulous than the
early British pioneers in their exploitation of the country's natural
resources. And if the American companies enjoyed little confidence among
the colonial administrators they were also less susceptible than their British
counterparts to governmental pressures. In fact, the general political
climate remained conducive to the continuation of the commercial relationship characteristic of the European imperial system – with the difference that the United States was now becoming the major beneficiary. The
interest of the American concerns was confined to the extraction of the
country's timber and chicle for shipment to America where these raw
materials were converted into sawn lumber and chewing-gum respectively
and re-exported to, among other countries, Belize.

The American companies had little regard for the long-term future of
either these extractive industries or the inhabitants. Nevertheless, these
companies enjoyed considerable influence in the local business circle and,
therefore, in the Legislative Council which as we saw was divided in its
support for the rival British and American concerns. The American companies had created for the group of local entrepreneurs business opportunities which the dominance of the BEC and its influence both in London
and Belize City had so long denied them. They financed the entrepreneur's
operations and were his most profitable customers. One begins to understand better the businessmen's attitude towards the BEC. In having little
cause for regretting the likely collapse of the BEC they were protecting
more than their own interests.[21] As the Governor informed the Colonial
Office, opposition to the grant of the loan to the BEC was particularly
strong 'on the part of influential persons to whom American companies
are reputed to have offered inducement of gain if the company should be
closed down'.[22]

There was abundant evidence that the British government and the
Governor were as frustrated as the BEC by the factious opposition in the
Legislative Council. Reference to the unofficial members as 'corrupt', 'old
gang', 'gang of superior bootleggers' (an obvious reference to those

businessmen who had amassed their wealth from the illicit liquor trade during prohibition in the United States and the periodic depression in the forestry industries) punctuate the minutes in the Colonial Office files and the despatches of governors in the early 1930s.[23] Membership of the Executive Council did not prevent the local business interests from 'consistently opposing the government in every matter which has gone to the division, and [in taking] a leading part in the opposition to government measures'.[24] Any doubts that the BEC was out-matched were removed when the British government felt compelled to nominate the company's manager, C. H. Brown, to the Legislative Council immediately after his defeat in the 1936 elections by R. S. Turton, the multi-millionaire and one of the company's principal local business rivals. Turton's victory confirmed the political ascendancy of the local *nouveaux riches*, and, more important, provided the American concerns with another indefatigable parliamentary supporter. His election was also a personal triumph over the colonial officials since he had been refused a nominated seat in 1932.[25] Given the shift in political influence the safeguarding of British interest by a more positive assertion of imperial authority became a compelling necessity.

*Imperial hegemony*

Convinced that the British government had acted unjustifiably harshly, the unofficial members found it difficult to reconcile themselves to the loss of financial control and the use of the Governor's new 'reserve' power. A *modus operandi* could probably have been established had not successive governors taken a narrow view of their new responsibility. Armed with the 'reserve' power and answerable for the colony's finances, in the final analysis, to the British Treasury alone, they felt no compelling necessity to seek the advice and co-operation of the unofficial members.

Perhaps the most striking example of the Governor's attitude was the grant to the BEC in 1935 of an extension of three years for the repayment of its loan. The colony learnt of the extension from the West India Committee Circular in London which published the parliamentary replies to questions about the loan in the House of Commons.[26] It was stated that the agreed terms for the extension of the period of repayment were satisfactory to both the imperial and the Belize governments although, as was subsequently revealed, the Legislative Council was unaware of these terms. Perhaps it was because the loan to the company was unpopular that the extension of the loan repayment period was veiled in local secrecy. The disclosure, however, produced a strong reaction in a section of the local press which noted that

It is strange how information on local affairs is so difficult to obtain when it should be readily released by the Government for the benefit of the people. We had to wait until a member of Parliament took up the matter in the House of Commons. The local government must have had to furnish the necessary information to the Imperial Government and in like manner it should have presented it to the people here.[27]

Having been denied political responsibility and knowledge of most of the colony's financial affairs, the unofficial members repeatedly clamoured for their former constitutional rights. Their assertion, however, had little opportunity of prevailing against the authority of the Governor and in consequence the unofficial members resorted to the politics of protest. Writing about the colonial legislatures of the period, MacMillan states that every 'popular Assembly felt its work done and its privileges vindicated by vigorous resistance to all and any Government demands for rates and taxes'.[28] The statement implies that the unofficial members were content with their negative role and fails to recognize the frustrations which they actually experienced. The long period of Treasury control was irritating and politically frustrating, and in fact the Legislature was caught in a vicious circle. In 1945 the imperial government made the balancing of the budget a prerequisite of the resumption of local financial control.[29] Yet it denied the Legislature the opportunity to work towards this goal. In fact, the unofficial members claimed that the government was spending funds on services and developments which prolonged inevitably the period of financial tutelage.[30]

In assessing the merits of these criticisms however, it should be observed that they were made mainly by businessmen whose values, goals, and criteria of a successfully administered enterprise differed from those which guided the government bureaucracy. It was therefore not surprising that they were unimpressed with the methods of public administration and urged the government to 'discard its methods which are well established in government departments, but which might be considered wasteful and inefficient by businessmen who know from experience that such methods are not conducive to success in private enterprises'.[31]

The prolonged period of Treasury control, the high-handed actions of successive governors, the divergent values of the unofficial members and the Executive about government provided all the conditions for a crisis. The first sign of one was conveyed in the tone and content of the unofficial members' reply in November 1945 to Governor Hunter's address to the new session of the Legislative Council. They pointedly accused the Governor of not showing 'sufficient regard in the past to unofficial members and their opinions' and demanded 'a greater and more active part' in the government.[32] Not unexpectedly, the vexed issue of Treasury control was mentioned.[33] The unofficial members called for relief 'from the onerous debt-charges in connection with the [hurricane] loan which the colony was forced to contract'.[34] In support of this request the signatories referred to the recommendation of the West India Royal Commission that the imperial government should assume responsibility for these debts. Finally, the unofficial members warned that they 'ought not readily to consent to the imposition of further taxation without a return to the people of the effective control of the purse-strings which was their former right'.[35]

The crisis was brought to a head the following year on the very issue of taxation. It was the practice of the government to propose new taxation measures at any time during the financial year. In June 1946, the Colonial Secretary in his capacity as Financial Secretary introduced the Income Tax Amendment Bill.[36] His attitude when introducing the bill was indicative of the strained relations. He merely moved the second reading of the bill which immediately provoked Harrison Courtenay (later Sir), a lawyer, businessman and the spokesman of the unofficial members, to express 'disappointment and surprise' that the mover 'should be satisfied in making the motion...without any further explanation'.[37] It was clear from the other speeches that the unofficial members who had been placed in a majority by a constitutional change in 1945[38] had previously decided to vote against the bill. The Governor resolved the conflict by invoking his 'reserve' power for the first time to pass the bill while the unofficial members walked out of the Legislative Chamber in protest.

In the years between this crisis and the devaluation crisis in December 1949 the Executive Council made attempts to improve its working relationship with the Legislative Council. These attempts included the establishment of a Standing Finance Committee of the Legislative Council, the appointment of a Fiscal Review Committee in 1946, and the nomination of two members of the Legislative Council to the Executive Council. The most important outcome of the crisis, however, was the highly successful visit to the Colonial Office in 1947 of a delegation of three unofficial members to discuss the country's financial and constitutional position.[39] The delegation's outstanding achievement was undoubtedly the remission of the Hurricane Reconstruction Loan,[40] especially as the 1938 Royal Commission had apparently failed to persuade the British government to assume responsibility for the country's public debts.[41] Although its request for a loan for economic development was rejected, the delegation was promised every opportunity to balance the budget for three consecutive years after which the issues of Treasury

Control and the Governor's 'reserve' power were to be re-examined with a view to their withdrawal.[42]

The Colonial Office also agreed, in principle, to the delegates' proposals for constitutional reform and instructed the Governor to set up a local constitutional commission[43] whose investigation, as we shall see, was overtaken by the political upheaval in 1950. The proposals called for the introduction of universal adult suffrage, a reconstituted Legislative Council with its own President, consisting of twelve elected members and four members nominated by the Governor, and an Executive Council constituted with a view to establishing a quasi-ministerial system of government.

It must not be thought that the unofficial members in their opposition to the administration were either revolutionaries or radicals. They were a moderate group which simply demanded a greater share in, and a more businesslike approach to government. In terms of their self-serving approach, it is not insignificant that their relationship with the Executive foundered almost entirely because of financial issues. As moderates, their politics of protest never went beyond the resolutionary stage except over the income tax issue in 1947. Although many of them were opposed to the dominance of the BEC their attachment to the British colonial rule remained unshaken, and its strength was carried over into the 1950s to the extent that these leaders were among the chief apologists of the colonial political system.

### Components of the local elite

*The business element* There is little risk of repetition in discussing further the business element as it dominated almost every facet of social and political life. Despite the political ascendancy of the local business class of coloured and Spanish persons, the white Creoles, consisting of the established families of English and Scottish descent, retained much of their influence. In the first place they were nominated to the Executive Council which, as we have seen, was now the real locus of power. Of the three unofficial members of the Executive Council in 1937, Henry Melhado was a white Creole whose family held extensive lands in the Cayo District and commercial interests in Belize City, Frank Ellis was a local-born European, a lawyer and landowner who had been a member of the wholly nominated Legislative Council from 1932 until its dissolution in 1936 when the new constitution was introduced, and Charles Beattie was a white expatriate who was the manager of the only bank, the Royal Bank of Canada, and also a member of the Legislative Council in the 1920s.[44]

This old group also exerted considerable pressure through a variety of

economic organizations and informal contacts. Perhaps the most important of these organizations were the Chamber of Commerce and the
Belize Taxpayers' Association which jointly sponsored one of the two
successful candidates, Edward Usher, a wealthy planter, in the 1939
election. The pervasive influence of the group also touched the communication media. There were two newspapers in the colony, the *Belize
Independent* and *The Daily Clarion*. The latter was the only daily and the
leading newspaper. It was founded by the Woods family in 1897[45] and
up to the end of the period under review was still owned and edited by
them. A father, Philip, the editor, and his son Stanley, a lawyer, were
Legislative Councillors, one as a nominated member from 1924 until his
death in 1927, and the other as the Acting Attorney General in 1926.
Although or perhaps because it was the only daily newspaper, with a
circulation of 1,000,[46] *The Daily Clarion* kept the public in political
ignorance. Political issues were certainly not reported as extensively as
the Supreme Court proceedings in which the legal firm of Dragten and
Woods was involved. The pages were also filled with the social happen-
ings in the provincial towns of Britain with which many of the newspaper
subscribers had familial links and to which their children went for their
education. This elite group also provided many of the senior civil service
personnel. Since the family connections were ramifying, it was also not
altogether uncommon for two brothers or other close relations to be
members of the same committee, one serving in an ex-officio capacity and
the other as a representative of the business interests.

Profiles of the Legislative Councillors in the 1930s and the 1940s
would bring into sharp relief the change in the type of businessmen.
Space, however, does not permit their presentation although the number
of unofficial members varied from seven before the introduction of the
1936 constitution to ten at the end of it in 1954. A table which simply
indicates the extent to which the business group remained the major
element in the Legislative Council must therefore suffice (see table 6).

The change within the business group should not be over-emphasized
as the aims of the new legislative councillors, as we shall demonstrate in a
later section, were identical with those of the old. What is perhaps more
noteworthy was the failure of the elective principle to produce any new
occupational group in the Legislative Council. The special income and
property qualifications for candidates (an annual income of $1,000, or
ownership of real property valued at $500 and a deposit of $100)[47] could
only be satisfied by an unduly small class. Moreover, to facilitate their
election in the out-districts, the influential business group had as early
as 1922, when the Franchise Commission considered the elective prin-

ciple, decided against residence in the constituency being a qualification for candidature.[48] For although they possessed extensive property throughout the country the business group resided mainly in Belize City.

Table 6    *Occupation of elected and nominated unofficial members of the Legislative Council, 1933–1948*

| Occupation | 1933 | | 1936 | | 1939 | | 1942 | | 1945 | | 1948 | |
|---|---|---|---|---|---|---|---|---|---|---|---|---|
| | E | N | E | N | E | N | E | N | E | N | E | N |
| Big-business owners and representatives (mainly mahogany and chicle contractors, merchants and real-estate owners) | – | 5 | 4 | 2 | 5 | 2 | 5 | 1 | 4 | 2 | 1 | 3 |
| Small-business owners and representatives (bakers, tailors and employees) | – | – | – | – | – | – | 1 | 1 | 1 | 1 | 3 | 1 |
| Professions | | | | | | | | | | | | |
| Lawyers | – | 1 | 1 | – | 1 | – | – | – | 1 | – | 1 | – |
| Ministers of religion | – | 1 | – | – | – | – | – | – | – | 1 | – | – |
| Medical practitioners | – | – | – | – | – | – | – | – | – | – | 1 | – |
| | – | 7 | 5 | 2 | 6ª | 2 | 6 | 2 | 6 | 4 | 6 | 4 |

Note: E = elected; N = nominated
ª Membership increased with the division of the Southern constituency into the Stann Creek and Toledo constituencies (Ordinance no. 21 of 1938).

*The liberal professional element.* The professional group comprised another section of the ruling elite. This group consisted not only of members of the liberal professions – lawyers, doctors, clergymen, senior civil servants and primary school headmasters – but also the literary minded whose occupation was less prestigious. Perhaps the outstanding examples of the last sub-group were the Staine brothers, Calvert and Morrel, who were both tailors and musicians. Both were city councillors, and Calvert, who received the OBE in 1947, was also a nominated member of the Legislative Council from 1942 to 1947.

The humble origin of the Staine brothers was typical of the members of the educated class. Except for the few who were from the wealthy business families, persons within the professional category were usually the first among their kin to hold a high social status.[49] Their families were usually the lower- or quasi-middle class Creoles who were sufficiently appreciative of the role of education as the key to social advancement to make the necessary financial sacrifice.

One of the important features of the high status professional sub-groups was their overwhelming non-Belizean membership. In the 1930s only four of some twelve lawyers were Belizeans – Simeon Hassock, Harrison Courtenay, Arthur Balderamos and Ezekiel Grant.[50] Except for Grant who was a District Commissioner, these lawyers became elected members of the Legislative Council and two of them, Hassock and Courtenay, ended their political career in 1974 as a member of the Senate and Speaker of the House of Representatives respectively. The other lawyers were mainly West Indians who invariably served in the judiciary before entering private practice and politics.

The priesthood, the teaching and medical professions, and the upper echelon of the civil service were even more than law expatriate preserves. The expatriate monopoly of power and authority within the churches was virtually total; the only influential Belizean clergyman during the 1930s and 1940s being Gilbert Hulse, a Cambridge graduate, Archdeacon of the Anglican Church, and a nominated member of the Legislative Council from 1946 to 1948. The Roman Catholic structure, in particular, assigned a more or less passive role to the lay members as the American Jesuits dominated the ecclesiastical and the financial machinery of the Church.[51] It was very easy for the expatriate clergymen to extend their influence into the field of education. All of the schools, primary and secondary, were denominational.[52] The narrow outlook of the forestocracy was originally responsible for the firm hold of the churches on education. Since education could not improve the woodcutter's skill, it was one of those social services on which public funds were grudgingly spent.[53] The churches were by no means reluctant to assume the financial responsibility since they held the view that education was closely allied to evangelism and, in the case of the Jesuits, these two activities were conceived as being insolubly linked.[54] All of the denominations carried this view to its logical conclusion by appointing the clergymen as principals of the secondary schools.[55] The possibility of a professionally qualified local lay teacher becoming the head was even remote in some of the Catholic primary schools since these were traditionally managed by the American nuns.[56] Whether Catholic or Protestant, the dominant group of clergymen, nuns, inspectors of school, and a few lay West Indians who were primary school head teachers, had developed a vested interest in the schools which led a visiting educational expert, J. C. Dixon,

Georgia State Supervisor of Negro Education, to observe in 1936 that the pervasive expatriate control was

a tragic policy. It admits in effect that there are no available teachers in British Honduras; or that there is no available material out of which teachers can be made; or that government is not interested in a colonial self sufficiency or, as seems more likely to be the case, that the importation of teachers has resulted less from a desire to educate the children of British Honduras than from a desire to promote interests other than those of the children.[57]

The upper limit beyond which Belizeans could not advance was even more clearly defined in the civil service. As in other colonies, Colonial Office regulations gave priority to members of the Unified Colonial Service in the filling of senior administrative positions throughout the colonial world.[58] This meant that, for all practical purposes, non-Europeans would be excluded from such posts even in their respective colonies. The racial character of appointment to these posts which was usually cloaked in the regulations was at times laid bare in Belize even at the expense of the priority principle. Cases in the 1930s and 1940s are not unknown where jobs were immediately found for financially ruined Britons who had arrived from one of the Central American Republics with little claim to a civil service appointment other than their origin.[59] The office of District Commissioner was their principal haven, but since in these cases the criteria of recruitment could not ensure the selection of the most able candidates it was not surprising that the Colonial Office subsequently entertained doubts about the governors' choice of District Commissioners.[60]

The extent to which the professional and senior administrative positions were monopolized by the expatriates depended in the final analysis on the ability of the colony to attract and retain these officers. For the onus of territorial assignment seemed to rest largely with the officer since the Secretary of State for the Colonies seldom insisted on a transfer if this could be proved to be disadvantageous to the officer.[61] By no means one of the wealthier colonies, and with a small establishment and inferior status, Belize even in its halcyon days experienced considerable difficulty in attracting members of the Colonial Service.[62] The government therefore drew heavily on local personnel in the filling of senior vacancies, especially after salaries were reduced in 1933 below those of 1922 as a result of the economic depression and the disastrous 1931 hurricane.[63] This all but placed the country outside the competitive colonial world. Localization of the administrative service almost reached the summit when R. E. Gabourel was appointed Assistant Colonial Secretary in

1942 and Arthur Wolffsohn (later Sir) to the combined post of Colonial Secretary and Financial Secretary in 1943.[64]

Because it was the major outlet for their skills, the government service offered Belizeans most of their opportunity to fulfil their social expectations. But the high proportion of civil servants meant that the influence of the educated group could not permeate the political process as much as that of the business section of the ruling elite. This was because the civil servants were debarred from open political activity. A more important reason, however, for the limited influence of the educated group was the virtual monopoly given to the businessmen in the wholly nominated Legislative Council. It was exceedingly rare for more than one unofficial member to belong to the professional group.[65] Even more discriminatory was the tendency for the Governor to appoint to this high office Europeans, mainly clergymen and lawyers rather than retired local senior civil servants.

Until the restoration of the elective principle in 1935 the partially elected Belize Town Board was the only political institution through which the educated middle-class Creoles could advance their overall position. Indeed the Town Board members dealt freely with national issues[66] and as a taxing authority reminded the big-business owners that their political power was not total. From time to time, however, as the dissolution of the Town Board in 1938 demonstrated, the colonial officials felt obliged to curb the pretensions of the educated group.

The rebuffs, however, merely strengthened the resolve of the educated group to challenge the hegemony of the business group. Three of the six candidates in the two-member Belize District constituency in the 1936 elections were lawyers: F. R. Dragten and W. L. Thompson, who were West Indians, and Arthur Balderamos, a Belizean. From the time of his election in 1945 up to the dissolution of the Legislative Council in 1954, Harrison Courtenay dominated the parliamentary scene although the businessmen, notably J. S. Espat, a Lebanese chicle contractor, remained prominent.

It should not be assumed that the salaried and professional members of the ruling elite were as cohesive as the business group or were in conflict with them. In the first place, many of the lawyers were real-estate proprietors and their clients were mainly businessmen. F. R. Dragten, a Guyanese, 'owned considerable property in Belize [City] and...a grapefruit orchard in Stann Creek'.[67] He was one of the owners of the legal firm of Dragten and Woods and Woods, Philip, the editor, was one of his sponsors for the 1936 election. His other sponsor was Frederick Biddle who was also a wealthy proprietor and member of the Executive

Council from 1932 to 1936. On the other hand, Lucillio Ayuso, a Mestizo and owner of a commercial firm, was sponsored by Frank Ellis, the lawyer. Secondly, the more powerful sections of the ruling elite, in particular the colonial officials, could and did play upon the aspirations of individual members of the educated middle class. Thirdly, the latter group was continuously being infused with members whose occupation and intellectual achievement varied from the dominant sub-group of salaried and professional workers.

Electoral politics in the municipality brought to the fore the differences in attitudes and political views among the educated middle class. To this the formation of several political groups bore testimony, the best known of these groups being the People's Group and the Progressive Party.[68] Both organizations lacked the attributes of a modern party. They were committed to neither the broad objectives of political education nor to the search for a genuine popular feeling.[69] The groups certainly did not depend on the direct membership of individuals. Instead they had a distinct preference for working through a constellation of fraternities, religious organizations and voluntary associations such as the Ancient Order of Foresters, Eastern Star Lodge, Loyal and Patriotic Order of the Baymen, Good Samaritans, Methodist Sunshine League, Self Help Society, the Universal Negro International Association and the Black Cross Nurses.[70] These societies invariably touched the lives of a substantial segment of the population, providing financial assistance in times of crisis, performing community activities and even settling disputes. None of the party leaders could claim pre-eminence in politics, and the parties had little difficulty in surviving the removal of a leader. Indeed, there was a pattern of interlocking leadership between the parties and the major voluntary associations. But precisely because of the parties' ties to these associations, their existence could not be easily ascertained except during the municipal and (after 1936) national elections. Indeed, in 1936 *The Daily Clarion* bemoaned the absence of 'one functioning political party in the whole colony'.[71] These two political groups, however, survived the others and were only reduced to an anachronism on the rise of the People's United Party in the early 1950s.

This division of the ruling elite into two functionally specific groups – businessmen and salaried professional men – was merely one aspect of a more complex picture at this level of society. Communal and cultural interests vied continuously with economic and occupational interests for the social and political allegiance of the members of these groups. The relative importance of these cultural and economic bases of group consciousness cannot be understood outside the various institutions and organizations, ranging from the Church to the recreational clubs, in which this rivalry took place. We will, therefore consider the institutional manifestations of the differing cultural orientations of members of these groups and their implications for social status and political influence among the elite.

*Culture and social stratification: institutional manifestations*

*The Church.*    Writing about his experience in Belize in the early 1930s, Governor Burns observed:

> in no colony that I have served in has religious feeling run so high as in British Honduras, and this I attribute very largely to the fact that denominational adherence followed very closely on the lines of racial cleavages. Generally speaking, the Mayas, Caribs, Mexicans and Guatemalans were Roman Catholics, and most of them spoke Spanish while the priests were American Jesuits; the British and the Negro Creoles were Protestant, and spoke English.[72]

He should have added that this was due to the fact that the various denominations did not enjoy the same degree of intimacy with the colonial government, and that their individual relationships were determined by their external connections.

As we saw in chapter 1, the Roman Catholic Church had emerged as the largest denomination by 1931, serving 30,782 or 59.9 per cent of the total population of 51,347. Next in size were the Anglican, Methodist, Baptist and Scottish Presbyterian, claiming memberships of 10,813 or 21.1 per cent, 7,257 or 14.1 per cent, 1,224 or 2.4 per cent and 621 or 1.2 per cent of the total population respectively, or a total of 38.8 per cent.[73] The numerical minority of the Protestant denominations was no indication of their influence and status in the society. The official recognition which had been accorded the Anglican Church was extended to the Presbyterian as early as 1851 because the white community was predominantly Scottish.[74] Although both churches were disestablished in 1872,[75] they remained closely associated with the colonial government and retained their elitist character.[76] The Anglican Church possessed more foresight and gradually opened its door to the non-white Creoles according to gradation of their colour and position in the social and occupational hierarchy. The new adherents became the mainstay of the Church and by the 1930s counted its members from all social categories among its predominantly Creole adherents. At the same time its elite origins were still clearly discernible. In 1949, towards the end of the period under review in this chapter, S. L. Caiger, an Anglican priest, reported with satisfaction that the Church drew its membership largely from among the predominantly 'coloured people [who] have filled with conspicuous success important positions in commerce, the civil service and the professions'.[77]

An extension of links of the Anglican Church with the colonial government was its neglect not only of the ordinary Creoles but of the Mestizos and Indians. Its achievements in the Spanish-speaking areas were certainly not commensurate with its resources and personnel stability.[78] As Caiger admitted, 'the Church of England had little to do with the [Latin] section of the population in British Honduras'.[79] His explanation for this neglect was that Mestizos and Indians 'were well served by numerous [Roman Catholic] priests' and that it has never been the policy of the English mission to 'proselytise' in such cases.[80] His explanation ignores the fact that the Church could have afforded to confine its activities to Belize City and to respect the preserves of other denominations precisely because its influence did not depend primarily on the measure of zeal with which it fulfilled its divine mandate.

As we saw in chapter 1 it was the Methodist and Baptist churches which carried the Protestant religion to the lower social Creole stratum and the Caribs up and down the country. The Methodist missionaries were also conspicuous for their pioneering efforts among the Indians and Mestizos in Corozal. But this merely confirmed the less favoured position of these churches which was derived initially from their dissenting character. Within the colonial context, the Methodist Church may also have lost some more of its little influence when it gradually began to pass into the hands of West Indian clergymen in the late 1940s.

The differing status and social composition of the membership between the Anglican and Methodist churches should not be pushed too far. Both performed a socializing, and in the case of the Methodist Church, an integrative role. By disseminating English values, and making them acceptable to the lower social Creole strata, it helped to maintain a stable social hierarchy within the society. Caiger also draws attention to the inter-relationship between the external affiliation of the Protestant churches and the cultural and political orientation of their membership. In 1949 he wrote:

The great bulk of the population is either native Honduran or Negro, in both cases English-speaking and English-thinking by century old tradition. By the same token they are usually members of the Anglican church or to a lesser degree of the English Protestant denominations such as the Methodist or Baptists. They are extremely conscious and proud of their position as British subjects [which] they showed in no uncertain way during the two world wars, and even the imposing might and opulence of nearby America have not undermined their faith in the Union Jack, which has so noble a tradition in the West Indies as the standard of justice, liberty, and protection of the coloured folk.[81]

The difference between the Anglican and Methodist churches becomes less pronounced when they are compared with the Roman Catholic Church. The latter church stood at the other end of the spectrum because its external connection and orientations were non-British. It would be recalled that the first Roman Catholic missionaries were English Jesuits. In 1851 the shortage of personnel forced them to relinquish control of the Diocese to the Missouri Mission.[82] From then onwards the Church drew its priests, policies and funds from the United States.[83] In a very real sense the Catholic Church was the American Jesuits and from an imperial viewpoint was regarded as an alien institution in foreign hands. Apart from being unable to claim the same degree of legitimacy as their Protestant counterparts, the Jesuits' own dislike for British colonialism rendered their accommodation in the society difficult. Most of them were Irish- or German-born Americans.[84] They were, therefore, extremely conscious of their anti-British heritage as Irish or Germans, and of their marginal position, as Americans, in the colonial political system in Belize. From the observation of Governor Burns they were sufficiently passionate to communicate their political feelings deliberately to their religious charges. He wrote:

The [Catholic] Bishop [Murphy] was an Irish-born American, a true Fenian at heart, with a bitter dislike for everything British which he made no attempt to conceal; he told me on one occasion that he did not mind the children in his school singing the National Anthem as they did not understand it, but he himself would never soil his lips with it. I made real efforts to be friendly with the Bishop, not only because of his prominent position in a population more than half Catholic, but also because I am myself a Catholic; I cannot honestly say that I was successful. His priests were most loyal to him, but I feel that they themselves realised his tactlessness. It may seem absurd, but apart from my objections to his anti-British attitude I resented very strongly his assumption that because I was British I was therefore a 'heretic' at heart; he caused me to understand why so many practising Christians should be anti-clerical.[85]

It was not only the Jesuits who were on the periphery of the political system. Their adherents, Mestizos and Creoles, also occupied this position and thereby reinforced the view that among Belizeans there was a religious element in not only cultural but also class distinctions.

This association of the Catholic Church with the less influential sections of the society points to the activism of the Jesuits and in particular the several schemes they devised to fill the leadership void among these groups. In its drive to capture the imagination of the Indian villagers in the north and west, the Church ingenuously identified itself with the indigenous system of Patron or Mayor local government by assigning to the village leader (Mayor) the role of church leader (Mayordomo).[86] The combination of roles not only contributed to the spreading of the Roman Catholic faith but provided the Jesuits with a way into local affairs. It is no accident, therefore, that Belize has a thriving Credit Union Movement which has its origins in the modest efforts of a Jesuit priest, Father Marion Ganey, in 1945 in Punta Gorda, 'the most backward district capital in the colony'.[87] In fact the Jesuits claimed that they possessed the qualities of 'social leadership of the grass roots variety [which] the process of self-help for these poor people' demanded.[88] The economic depression throughout the 1930s could not have been more conducive to their activities. Their social and economic ventures were, however, not devoid of converting motives. These were vigorously promoted in the hope that 'with the gradual amelioration of their [the people's] economic lot, a new bond of closer attachment to the church will be forged and a deep and stronger Catholic culture will be built'.[89]

The activism of the Jesuits coupled with the relative neglect of the Protestant churches does not, however, provide an adequate explanation for the growth of Catholicism. The religion itself, with its ceremonials, images and mysteries, arguably has a greater inherent appeal than Protestantism. In acknowledging the decided magnetic effect of the ritual, the Jesuits stated in 1951, 'the turning point between the few struggling Catholics of the early days of the Mission and the strong, if financially poor, Catholic church in present-day Belize seems to have been a procession led by Bishop Di Pietro who carried the statue of our Blessed Mother through the muddy streets of the capital'.[90]

The Jesuits of course did not exclusively devote their attention to the poorer social classes. Among their active members were some of the wealthy Mestizo and Spanish businessmen who donated large sums of money and bequeathed valuable properties to the Church. The Roman Catholic Church also catered for the education of the sons and daughters of the wealthy class, at St John's College and at St Catharine's Academy respectively.[91] Both schools were residential and St John's College was known throughout Central America as it attracted a number of students from the republics.[92] As we shall see in the next section most of the Jesuits' political impact was made at St John's College which was the major focus of the social activities of the well-to-do and promising Catholic boys.

Whether in the parishes or the schools, as we shall confirm, the missionary success of the Roman Catholic Church was unequalled by the Protestant denominations. Its well-tested vitality was continuously engaged in the search for new outlets and means of attracting people to the faith.

Yet its influence within the colonial power structure remained incommensurate to its numerical strength. The Jesuits were under-represented on public bodies, although it should be noted that as American citizens they were excluded from certain appointments such as that of Legislative Councillor. From sentiments expressed by Edgar Gegg, the grandson of a Methodist minister and a Catholic convert, in 1947, the Catholic laity also believed that they were being denied positions of authority and influence. The situation, he suggested, would remain unchanged 'unless we [St John's College Alumni] come together in full numerical strength at fixed intervals to decide what our plans of action are to be'.[93]

*Education.* Education was the most important channel through which the denominations exerted their formative influence. Because the Americans and Britons, who headed and mainly staffed Roman Catholic and Protestant churches respectively, had very little in common save their vocation, each group tended to adopt a sectarian outlook towards the country.[94] Their general disinclination to look across denominational boundaries had unfortunate consequences for the educational system which they controlled.

Although their churches did not enjoy the same social and political status, the Roman Catholic and Protestant schools' management had developed a symbiotic relationship which rested upon the assumption that each had an ascriptive right to the loyalty of its adherents. This assumption led to a proliferation of schools throughout the country to the extent that the number of schools which a denomination owned and the enrolment in them were in direct proportion to the denomination's numerical strength. This struck Dixon, the visiting educational expert, as wasting and under-utilizing the country's already limited resources. 'Without decrying the value of the missionary efforts', he could not 'help asking whether education of the children or promotion of church interest and even proselytising are the objectives of the church when, in a small village where there are hardly enough children for one school, one finds two or more small schools of different churches competing for enrolment and attendance'.[95] It was not only in this manner that loyalty was fragmentary and divisive in character. The assumption also contributed to racial and cultural divisions. In the first place it kept the Protestant Creoles and the Catholic Indians and Mestizos apart during their formative years as students. In the second place, it enabled each denomination to impose whatever social and political outlook it wanted upon its students. Indeed, given the scant regard of the Protestant elite for the activities of the Roman Catholic priests, it was easy for the latter to bring their students at St John's College under the influence of a political education that was anti-colonial and anti-British in content.

The potential political conflict that inhered in the strong denominational ties, and their attendant divisiveness and permissiveness were recognized by the colonial administration. In 1945 Governor Hunter foresaw that in the absence of a more assertive government role in education the Protestant secondary schools, St Michael's College, Wesley College and St Hilda's College, which produced the Creole elite would be unable to keep pace with the two prestigious Roman Catholic schools, St John's College and St Catherine's Academy. As he observed,

the Creoles were not as fortunate as 'The Catholic community [which] is able to undertake such a liability [the running of schools] because it is much larger than any single Protestant community in the colony, it is helped with money from abroad and its schools are staffed by members of a religious order who live celibate and conventual existences, and are able to give their services more cheaply than the laymen or clergy of the Protestant denominations can afford to do.'[96]

In fact, the consequences of the Protestant Creoles' inability to keep pace with the Catholics were already evident since the 1930s. Much more than the Mestizo, the Creoles placed a high premium on education, presumably because they opted for the professions rather than business. There was therefore the tendency for even those who were active leaders in the Protestant churches and schools to place academic considerations above the denominational in the choice of schools, especially in the final years of their children's secondary education. They, therefore, had few reservations in enrolling their children at St John's College whose upper-form facilities were superior to those of the Protestant schools. This was even done in the face of strong opposition from their religious superior.

In general, however, the Protestant churches were paradoxically too denominationally bound to appreciate the Governor's argument that Protestant influence in education was bound to decline without government assistance. Thus he received little 'support from the public and from the ministers of the various Protestant denominations for an undenominational secondary school under government control'.[97] The Protestants had failed to recognize that for all practical purposes such a school would have been their own and would have guaranteed the dissemination of the British values which they so highly valued. However superior the facilities of the undenominational school may have proved to those of the Catholic, the Jesuits were unlikely to liberalize the attitude of their followers and endorse their attending a non-Catholic school.[98] Lamenting the short-sight of the Protestants, the Governor made 'it quite clear that the pastors who grew so concerned about this imminent danger [the undenominational school] to their flocks have little grounds as yet for their anxiety'.[99] We shall see in a later chapter whether this statement was prophetic and ominous.

*The Civil Service.* The close connection between the colonial government and the Protestant Creoles was even more evident in the civil service. Governors were highly selective in their choice of local administrative personnel. Priority went to those civil servants who were from the high-status Creole families with a long tradition of public service. And since within the Creole community there was a correlation between colour and class, a high proportion of the local senior civil servants were of unmistakable European descent or of light complexion. As members of the Creole elite they had traditionally lent support to the *status quo* and if they were not always rewarded with full admission to the inner circles of expatriates they at least won their social approval. Together the two groups gave leadership to the society. They set its social tone and values, worshipped in the leading Protestant churches, participated in inter-club activities, and held common membership to other prestigious organizations such as the Volunteer Defence Force.

The social background and career of the local Colonial Secretary, Arthur Wolffsohn, exemplify the close affinity between the expatriate officials and the local civil service elite. Born to a German–Jewish immigrant father and local mother of Scottish descent, both with extensive business connections, he was sent to Scotland at the age of seven to be educated. He attended the private school of Mrs John Jackson, the widow of Rev. Jackson, a former Presbyterian minister and Inspector of Schools in Belize. Wolffsohn completed his Scottish education at the Dollar Academy and entered the Belize civil service as a copyist in 1906. In the following year he was transferred to the Survey Department where he qualified as a surveyor in 1910. Wolffsohn then went into private employment and was on holiday in England when the First World War began. He saw active service as a second lieutenant before being appointed assistant engineer, Sea Defence Department, in Guyana in 1919. In 1922 he returned to the Surveyor General's Department in Belize and after becoming Head of the Department in 1934[100] he received the unusual promotion from a professional and technical post to the head of the civil service in 1943. Service in a colonial society, however, was not considered by a local official to have been adequately recognized, despite an impressive career, unless it was rewarded with imperial honours. The local Colonial Secretary was indeed twice the recipient of these honours, the OBE in 1943 and the CMG in 1947, before receiving the knighthood in 1961.

Not all of the local senior civil servants were white Creoles. Nor did all of them become members of the Colonial Service or have the benefit of Sir Arthur Wolffsohn's education and overseas experience. They however shared with him a similar family and social background and functioned as a privileged group. The bureaucracy in fact tended to develop a social stratification of its own, which, together with the limited number of senior administrative posts, rendered admission to the higher echelons of the civil service difficult.

The claim that social and cultural discrimination was practised should, however, not be pushed too far. In the first place the large number of Creoles in the civil service reflected their numerical strength and earlier educational experience. The Mestizos lacked the requisite educational qualification for entry into the civil service because the curriculum at St John's College, until the mid-1930s, was unsuited to the Overseas Cambridge Examinations syllabus.[101] The curriculum reflected the preferences of the American Jesuits, who encouraged and arranged for the more promising students to continue their studies in Catholic institutions in the United States.[102] This was another contributing factor to the relatively small number of Mestizos and Catholics in the civil service since few of them could be induced by the less lucrative opportunities to return to Belize. A third factor was the relative ease with which the Mestizos could have entered the family-owned business as well as the commercial banks. In this connection the Mestizos had not subscribed as much as the Creoles to the dominant English values of the colonial society. They were therefore less susceptible to the view that to be associated or identified with an institution where real power was supposed to reside was the most important way of either maintaining or enhancing one's status.[103]

It was not until the financial and economic crisis in the 1930s when many business enterprises failed that the Mestizos were inclined to embrace the civil service, as a career, in large numbers. Although the economic depression had necessitated a reduction of salaries in the civil service, the institution offered the security of tenure which the crisis denied the business sector. At the same time, however, it also limited recruitment. The resulting pressure on the few clerical vacancies, together with the continued tendency for the selection process to emphasize ascription rather than achievement and to be operated by a local personnel with strong and opposing denominational loyalties reduced the new group's chances of admission.

*The recreational clubs*

None of the other institutions that have been discussed reveals so clearly the complexity of the relationship between cultural orientation, social status and the absence of an open political system, even among the elites, as the prestigious social clubs in Belize City. The Belize Club which was established around 1940 was the preserve of the colonial officials and white businessmen, expatriate and local.[104] Despite their competition for control of the country's political institutions, these two groups were unanimous in their desire to preserve the *status quo*. The Belize Club may not have consciously assumed a political role; it nevertheless provided the businessmen with an informal but important link with the colonial bureaucracy. Official decisions affecting their economic interests were often a confirmation of hints given in the club or on the tennis court and cricket field.

Socially, therefore, the white businessmen were better placed than their Creole and Mestizo counterparts to influence the political process. The impact of the Creole and Mestizo businessmen on the political system was further reduced by their differing social and cultural ties. The Mestizo businessman shared almost exclusively with other members of his cultural group the membership of the Pickwick Club which was formed in 1938.[105] Whenever the Mestizo businessman acted within his cultural and social framework his political influence was negligible. This situation was inherent where the political influence of social organizations was in direct proportion to their position in the social system.

The influence of the Mestizo businessman was certainly less than that of the Creole businessman and salaried and professional middle class. This cultural group occupied the intermediate position in the social scale but its members were divided by their occupational differences into two distinct social sub-groups. The businessmen patronized the Newton Club which was formed in 1924.[106] Their devotion to sport and generous contribution to the club were perhaps unequalled by any of the other social groups. If the Newton Club members were noted for their wealth and interest in sport, those of the Colonial Band Association (CBA), which came into existence in 1911,[107] were noted for their intellect. Every important civil servant was a member of the CBA. The Association offered to the professional and the literary minded the social refinement of drama and music which were European in content. Pianoforte playing, in particular, was the flower of an education and the hallmark of a 'cultured' person. This interest in the classical model of European culture reflected much more than the roots of the educational system. It was also an attempt by the middle-class Creoles to consolidate their social position.

The last three clubs remain the most prestigious in the society. The dwindling of the white population, expatriate and local, first forced the Belize Club to lower its social barrier of admission and eventually forced it into inactivity. The other clubs are also less exclusive and multiple club membership exists. Nonetheless these clubs are still identified with a particular occupational or cultural group.

In conclusion, group consciousness or corporateness among the ruling elite could be measured by either occupation, race, or culture. Irrespective of their cultural origin the businessmen, a group which, it should be emphasized, included many lawyers, were inclined to seek alignments with other kindred groups in articulating their economic interests. But these lawyers also gave leadership to the professional group and, as Creoles, made common cause with the Creole businessmen on communally sensitive issues. Cultural loyalties cut across economic interests to the extent that they appeared to be a more important determinant of social ranking within this upper stratum of the colonial society. Thus although the well-off Mestizos being partly of Spanish descent were white, they were doubly marginal. They were a cultural minority and the social institutions with which they associated were accorded an equally low status in the social system. In this respect, it is significant that they did not receive education (which has been a most powerful agent of Creole acculturation) from Britons and West Indians. As Catholics they were the charge of the American Jesuits who, we observed, instilled little feeling of pride in British institutions and values. The different educational experience of the Mestizos and Creoles should not, however, be pushed too far. After all the Catholic secondary schools attracted many Creole Protestants who were converted in the process of their education to Catholicism and whose attachments to their British values were no doubt continually being tested. Perhaps the difference between the culture of the Mestizos and the Creoles was more a result of the difference in the average educational level among them rather than the differing educational orientations to which they were exposed. The Creoles were more educationally qualified irrespective of whether they attended a Protestant or Catholic secondary school. This advantage with all of its implications for their social status was not likely to be called into question until the Mestizos regarded education to be, as much as business, an important avenue of upward social mobility.

## Creole elite and electoral politics

The preoccupation with the elite in Belize City to the point where we established that its membership was almost entirely Creole is not mis-directed. As we mentioned at the outset of the study, political awareness was both an urban and a Creole phenomenon and also confined to a small social group. As Governor Kittermaster baldly put it in 1932 in connection with the proposed constitutional change, as far as 'opinion in Belize [City] is concerned' the other communities 'do not count'.[108] He suggested however that the feeling of superiority in Belize City was not entirely unfounded. In testing public opinion throughout the colony in 1932 on the proposal to introduce elective representation in Belize, he discovered that 'so far as the outdistricts were concerned the people were in many cases altogether at sea in understanding what the Magistrate [the District Commissioner] was talking about'.[109] In consequence neither 'the Caribs nor the Spanish Indians nor the Maya Indians made any definite representation'.[110] The Maya Indians in particular were not even superficially familiar with the rudiments of the colonial political system. Many of them were comparative newcomers from the neighbouring republics and 'unorganised and unvocal'.[111] The Governor, who had served in Africa, was inclined to regard these Indians as constituting a 'native problem' and seriously considered recommending to his superiors 'that representation shall be granted on a communal basis'.[112]

It is therefore only by equating national consensus with the decisions made in Belize City that the Governor, in responding to the Colonial Office enquiry about 'whether there is genuine and widespread feeling in favour of the proposed change'[113] could state that 'the vote of the Colony as a whole is unanimous in favour of a change to elected representation'.[114] Even the Governor's subsequent claim that this view 'may be said to represent the opinion, at any rate, of the Creole portion of the population'[115] was difficult to sustain *in toto*. There was little evidence, other than a Public Meeting in Belize City, to suggest that the ordinary Creole had participated in the decision. The Governor's view was based primarily on five memoranda from various organizations, four of which were received from Belize City and the fifth from Stann Creek. While the Stann Creek memorandum 'can be said to include Carib ideas'[116] the recommendations in the four memoranda from Belize City seemed, however, to be the product of the same Creole minds. This view is held not because the recommendations 'were similar in essence'[117] but because the Progressive Party provided the leadership to the other organizations. Apart from its own memorandum, the party submitted one in association with fourteen Friendly Societies which, in the absence of pension schemes, national social assistance and trade unions, fulfilled a useful role in the society. The Progressive Party also organized the public meeting on whose behalf it submitted the third memorandum. Finally, having distinguished itself in municipal elections, the party was represented on the Belize Town Board which submitted the fourth memorandum.

In general the rural population was left to fend for itself and responded accordingly. An idea of their insular political outlook in the early 1930s can be gained from the observation of the constitutional commission which visited the villages some fifteen years later in 1948 and 1949. The commission claimed that

In the districts [other than Belize] some enthusiasm was aroused in the capital towns and villages which we visited, but we cannot be sure that the interest created in the otherwise dull and monotonous routine life in a small community by the unprecedented arrival of a body of Commissioners from Belize [City] was not more important than the object of our visit. Most of the persons who attended our meetings were merely onlookers, and the few persons who gave evidence did so with much reluctance and only after considerable encouragement from the Commissioners. In most instances the meetings were in the nature of a seminar. Such interest as was evinced was more in local affairs than in the work of the Central Government. This was particularly so in most of the villages, where little or no knowledge of the working of government existed, and little or no interest even in the matter of district representation to the Legislative Council was shown.[118]

This lack of interest was perhaps much more mutual and pronounced in the 1930s. But the local government arrangement was not the only factor that encouraged the urban Creole elite to disregard the rural areas. Perhaps a more important factor was the rudimentary character of the rural economy. The subsistence way of life among the Indians was isolative. Apart from forestry, the outdistrict economy was too undeveloped to either command the interest of those in Belize City or to catapult the elite in the outdistrict towns into the national political arena. This elite consisted of the small-scale mahogany and chicle contractors who were invariably also the owners of the retail stores, sawmills and sugar distilleries, and also the money-lenders. Being at the top of the peasant-based outdistrict economy and, in the case of the Mestizo in the north, having determined the existing social order in the area with little interference from the central government, they had no compelling desire to extend their influence beyond their domain. As local notables they were appointed to the wholly nominated Town Boards which the government had established in the seven areas designated as towns – Corozal, Orange

Walk, San Ignacio, Benque Viejo, Stann Creek, Punta Gorda and Monkey River. This enabled them to help the District Commissioner to maximize the belief that all was well in the towns and thereby to minimize any likelihood of substantial change which might undermine their hold on the essentially peasant and inarticulate communities. Given this hold, they may even have welcomed the lack of interest of the urban Creole elite in the affairs of the outdistricts.

The notable exception was Stann Creek Town. The citrus industry was not only producing a Creole and Carib agro-proletariat but also attracted from Belize City a number of established businessmen, retired senior civil servants and other influential families as residents. Because of its social and cultural composition and economic advance the central government had conferred a higher status on the Town Board by making it partly elected. Indeed, it was the town's comparative economic and social development that finally prevented the Governor from recommending that 'representation be granted on a communal basis'.[119] He had observed that although the Caribs were in many respects culturally different from the Creoles they were sufficiently numerous and sufficiently organized to look after themselves in the event of elected representation being granted. Stann Creek, or more precisely its Creole elite, lived up to the Governor's expectations. Unlike the other outdistricts, it continuously produced its own elected representative to the Legislative Council under the 1935 constitution. The first representative was William Bowman, OBE, who was a local white Creole, a resident citrus planter, and a nominated member of the Stann Creek Town Board. He was succeeded in both offices by his son, Henry, who retired from active politics in 1948. Both were indefatigable fighters for the Stann Creek agricultural interests which, we have observed, the forestry mercantile interests in Belize City regarded as a potential threat.

Even though the Governor had decided against communal representation, the 1935 constitution did not altogether ignore communal and cultural differences. The Governor claimed that he had kept the qualification for the candidates moderate so as 'to make it possible for "a son of the soil" to be elected if he can persuade his constituents to vote for him'.[120] He, however, 'did not wish to see in the [Legislative] Council a man whose general education and qualification did not give him a higher value in the market than $1,000 a year. On the other hand if he has a genuine stake in the country as the owner of real property I must take the risk of the constituents electing a fool.'[121] The constitution discriminated against the Mestizos and Indians by requiring of the elected representative fluency in the English language to the satisfaction of the Governor. As the

Governor admitted, he had stipulated the language qualification 'to prevent the election of a Spanish-speaking member from the north and south to the detriment of facility of working the Council'.[122] This was the colonial period of what Pye calls 'administrative politics'.[123] What the Governor required primarily, therefore, was not genuine representation but an unencumbered Legislative Council.

In effect the objective ensured the continued political dominance of the Creoles, and it is therefore not surprising that those Creoles on the Executive Council did not object to the qualification. The Creole advantage was reinforced by the absence of a residential qualification for the candidates. Altogether these electoral conditions placed the outdistricts wide open to the Creole politicians in Belize City who feared electoral defeat in the Belize District, which was a two-member constituency.[124] Of the thirty-one unofficial members of the Legislative Council during the eighteen years that the 1935 constitution was in operation only one was a Mestizo. This was L. P. Ayuso, the founder of the Pickwick Club and resident in the Belize constituency, and one of its elected representatives from 1936 to 1939.

Little attempt was made in the selection of the nominated unofficial members to correct the geographical imbalance in representation and residence. It might be argued that the Governor's reliance on Belize City and the Creoles for nominated legislators was not unconnected with the lack of convenient and rapid means of communication and transportation. The Legislative Council met on an average less than once monthly and much of its work was done in committees.[125] The work of the committees would have been impeded if the members were scattered throughout the colony. Nor would the circulation of parliamentary papers have been expeditious. Nevertheless, in the final analysis cultural considerations were the principal criterion of the recruitment of nominated members since many Mestizo businessmen with an excellent command of English resided in Belize City.

There was also a literacy qualification for the electorate as a whole which conferred a further advantage on the Creoles.[126] The voter was required to sign the claim form in the presence of the registration officer or Justice of the Peace and also write the date and his signature on the form. Few of the Indian villagers could have satisfied the requirement, since illiteracy, which was determined by the non-ability to read or write in English, was highest among this racial group (42.48 per cent in 1946), followed by the Asiatic (26.30 per cent) and Carib (22.19 per cent).[127] In fact the illiterate proportion in the various districts followed the distribution of the races, being highest in those districts, Toledo and Cayo, where the Indians were most numerous and lowest in Belize where they were fewest.[128] As a basis of division the literacy qualification among the electorate was as much socio-economic as it was cultural. In fact the other electoral qualifications and the attitude of the Creole elite towards them emphasized the importance of the socio-economic division. The financial qualifications for candidature to the Legislative Council were outside the reach of the overwhelming bulk of the population, irrespective of the cultural orientation of the individual. It was the 'unofficial vote' that defeated a proposed amendment of the constitutional bill in 1935 to reduce the qualification of members from a clear annual income of $1,000, or ownership of real property valued at $500, to $750 and $300 respectively, and property ownership for voters from $500 to $300 and the rental qualification from $96 to $30 per annum.[129] Few persons, especially the small property owners who had suffered from the 1931 hurricane and the general economic depression, could however have satisfied the proposed requirements. Indeed, the general poverty of the entire population on the one hand and the comparatively high franchise qualification on the other, reduced the elective system to a farce. The out-districts returned four of the six elected legislators but only accounted for 30 per cent of the electorate. In the Corozal electoral sub-district of the Northern constituency there were in 1936, 12 registered voters in a popu-lation of 6,885.[130] The situation in the two-member Belize constituency was not substantially different. Of a population of 21,661 in 1936 there were only 772 voters.[131] The overall percentage of registered voters throughout the period of the 1935 constitution varied between 1.8 and 2.8 per cent.[132] The narrow electorate was compounded by the high incidence of unopposed candidates in the outdistricts. In these areas, once the contest had lost its novelty or a candidate had established his pre-eminence in his constituency the elections attracted few candidates. The virtual stagnation of the electorate and the extent of electorate activity are indicated in tables 7 and 8.

It should be emphasized that electoral politics was at once a Creole and an elite affair and hence the narrowness of the political process was two-dimensional. The upper and middle Creole stratum monopolized the access to political office. This stratum did not have to penetrate the lower social stratum to maintain its electoral support. Indeed their social and political aspirations left them with a vague feeling of solidarity with the urban Creole working class from which many of them originated. This feeling was not lost upon the Creole electorate. Although the number of votes polled in the Belize District constituency was high by any standards, ranging from 70 to 86.2 per cent, 'only a negligible proportion of the potential electors take the trouble to register as voters'.[133] The result was that the number of registered voters in the most politically aware constituency never reached five per cent. In the outdistricts where there was even less identity between the Creole elite and the Mestizos and Indians, the feeling among the electorate was one of complete impotence. For unlike their Creole counterparts these groups were told in no uncertain terms that they lacked the attributes of political office.

Table 7    *The population and the electorate, 1936–1948*

| Election | Population | No. of registered voters | Registered votes as percentage of population |
|---|---|---|---|
| 1936 | 56,071 | 1,035 | 1.8 |
| 1939 | 58,759 | 1,155 | 2.0 |
| 1942 | 61,723 | 1,383 | 2.1 |
| 1945 | 64,327 | 822 | 1.3 |
| 1948 | 63,139 | 1,772 | 2.8 |

Source: Courtenay Constitution Report, 1951, p. 26

*Incipient growth of political awareness*

It is clear from the foregoing analysis that politics in Belize was caught in a vicious circle. There was no organized public opinion to challenge the indifference that pervaded the atmosphere. On the other hand, because the electorate was small there was no compelling need to formally organize political interest. Against this general background of political quiescence the growth of political interest was discernible in Belize City in the latter half of the 1940s. The Second World War and its repercussion in the colonies played a part in stimulating this interest. The urban population was receptive to the idea of 'self-government' which the war had brought into prominence. It followed with interest the struggle for independence in Asia and noted approvingly that, nearer home, Jamaica had received an instalment of constitutional advance in 1944.

The emergent nationalist feeling abroad percolated into the urban community in Belize. An incipient nationalism found expression in the slogan 'Native First'. The slogan had been used spasmodically in the late 1930s by a few local-born aspirants to the Legislative Council and the Belize Town Board in their electoral campaigns against the European and the West Indian candidates.[134] The term gained more currency during the war, the principal advocate being Luke Dinsdale Kemp, commonly

Table 8   *Analysis of voting for Legislative Council elections, 1936–1948*

| | | Population | No. of registered voters | Voters as percentage of population | No. of votes polled | Voters as percentage of registered voters |
|---|---|---|---|---|---|---|
| Belize District | 1936 | 21,683 | 772 | 3.56 | 630 | 81.61 |
| | 1939 | 22,894 | 644 | 2.81 | 494 | 76.70 |
| | 1942 | 24,270 | 970 | 4.00 | 679 | 70.00 |
| | 1945 | 25,607 | 587 | 2.29 | 506 | 86.20 |
| | 1948 | 28,591 | 1,406 | 4.92 | 1,050 | 74.68 |
| Northern District | 1936 | 14,566 | 126 | 0.86 | 125 | 99.21 |
| | 1939 | 15,173 | 154 | 1.01 | * | – |
| | 1942 | 16,029 | 49 | 0.30 | * | – |
| | 1945 | 16,552 | 25 | 0.15 | * | – |
| | 1948 | 13,206 | 36 | 0.27 | * | – |
| Stann Creek District | 1936 | 6,250 | 155 | 2.48 | * | – |
| | 1939 | 6,561 | 289 | 4.40 | 268 | 92.73 |
| | 1942 | 6,802 | 204 | 3.00 | * | – |
| | 1945 | 7,053 | 44 | 0.62 | * | – |
| | 1948 | 6,765 | 134 | 1.98 | 128 | 95.52 |
| Western District | 1936 | 7,264 | 27 | 0.37 | * | – |
| | 1939 | 7,668 | 27 | 0.35 | 27 | 100.00 |
| | 1942 | 8,099 | 120 | 1.48 | * | – |
| | 1945 | 8,535 | 132 | 1.55 | 66 | 50.00 |
| | 1948 | 7,933 | 101 | 1.27 | 91 | 90.10 |
| Toledo District | 1936 | 6,308 | 7 | 0.11 | * | – |
| | 1939 | 6,463 | 41 | 0.63 | * | – |
| | 1942 | 6,523 | 40 | 0.61 | * | – |
| | 1945 | 6,580 | 34 | 0.52 | * | – |
| | 1948 | 6,653 | 95 | 1.42 | 75 | 78.95 |

* Candidate unopposed.
Source: Courtenay Constitutional Report, 1951, p. 26

known as Prince Dee. The slogan, however, was tinged with communal and racial overtones. For if its purpose was to reduce the prominence of non-Belizeans in the country's political life, it did not embrace all of the racial and cultural groups within the society. The local white Creole group certainly did not fall within the meaning of the term 'native'. The term was reserved for the Indian and black Creoles, the rationale being, as Kemp and Soberanis laboriously put it in 1949, that

when in 1821, Spain was expelled from Central America by efforts which included the flowing of the life-blood of African and Indian forebears of the present inhabitants, the equity of domicile which has devolved upon the descendants of Africans and Indians with no other place to call home and no prior allegiance to any other country, [provided] them with the equitable basis of a claim to a right of sovereignty or to a right of self-determination.[135]

For all practical purposes, however, the term was used with reference to the black Creoles even though it could be argued that the Indians, being indigenous to the region, had a more legitimate claim to the term. To be fair to the proponents of the slogan, their immediate purpose was not so much to ignore the Indians as to challenge the basis of British sovereignty, to foster an anti-colonial feeling among the Creoles who were the most articulate segment of the population, and to instil in them a pride in their history. Their starting-point of the pursuit of these threefold objectives was the victory of the Battle of St George's Cay which the British captain acknowledged was due almost entirely to the African slaves.[136] As far as Kemp and Soberanis were concerned this entitled the Africans to the land; it was theirs and not the British by virtue of the decisive role they played in the conquest. As they put it, 'How a victory in this "Battle of St George's Cay" could pass over the right of sovereignty to the British Crown and swallow up in victory all rights of self-determination of the descendants of the Negroes in Beymanduras is a real problem to justify.'[137] In their view the justification that the British had advanced over the centuries amounted to deception and a conspiracy between 'a few wicked half-breeds and white officials [who] seeing an opening because the mass of Negroes had no education or written records, decided to give such interpretations to what documents existed as would deprive oppressed natives of their right of self-determination'.[138]

Kemp and Soberanis were in effect contending that the time had come to reinterpret the history of the society from the standpoint of Belizeans. But the attempt to make the heroic accomplishments of the African slaves the basis of national identity promised a reinterpretation that was no less one-sided as far as the indigenous Indians were concerned. If the general thrust of their argument was disconcerting to this cultural group its negative aspects and tenor were also distasteful and even repulsive to the middle-class Creole elite who Kemp and Soberanis observed were too pre-occupied with their colonial attachments to 'unite in a native claim to self-determination'.[139]

Although the attempt to establish the Creole's political legitimacy was illustrative of what the 'Native First' slogan was all about, it was made within the context of two related issues that were to bring into much sharper relief than the 'Native First' policy the cultural as well as the socio-economic divisions of the society and its multiple connections with outside political groupings. One political issue was the British government's attempt to take Belize into the proposed West Indies Federation. The federal idea was not new; it was, however, the cornerstone of British post-Second World War policy in the region.[140] The underlying assumption of the proposal seemed to be that federation was the shortest path to political independence for the British peoples of the region. Even though the first Conference on the Closer Association of the British West Indian Colonies, held at Montego Bay, Jamaica, in September 1947, expressed the view that political development of the units must also be pursued as an aim in itself, some of the colonies, including Belize, were considered too small to aspire to independence on a unit basis.[141] The other issue was Guatemala's territorial claim which had been dormant for decades. In 1938 the Guatemala government published the 'White Book' in which it restated its case.[142] Whereas in the years following the treaty of 1859 Guatemala seemed prepared to accept a financial settlement of its claim, it now seemed to be only interested in outright acquisition. In 1945 Guatemala embodied in its constitution that 'Belice' is part of its national territory.[143] As Waddell observes, the position obviously admitted of no retreat with dignity, and indeed elevated the controversy to a level of fundamental principle.[144]

The federal proposal commanded little support except among the professional group of the urban middle-class Creoles which provided the two Belizean representatives, Harrison Courtenay and F. R. Dragten, to the British Caribbean Standing Closer Association Committee which drafted the proposals of the Federation.[145] The anti-federationists were vociferous from the outset in their denunciation of the proposal and summoned several impressive arguments to their aid.[146] Perhaps the most important argument was the country's geographical isolation and its unusual degree of cultural heterogeneity. With Belize lying outside the normal West Indian route, the movement of trade, people, and ideas to and from the West Indian territories was too limited to imbue Belizeans with a feeling of regional unity. Moreover, the country's contiguity to the Central American republics, and its Mestizo population, demanded of it at least a dual orientation to outside regional entities. The competitive nature of the economy of the West Indian territories, including Belize, also offered the latter little guarantee of an improvement in its economic conditions. The local insularity which federation was likely to, and did, encourage reduced the likelihood of a rationalization of the limited range of economic activity in the region. At best, federating with the other West Indian territories would have been of doubtful value. Thus there was considerable apprehension, even when allowance was made for regional economic co-operation, that the benefits accruing from federation were likely to offset the disadvantages that would have followed the dislocation of Belize's traditional trade with the United States. The anti-federationists also vigorously opposed for reasons of prestige the idea of changing the value of its currency. Being at parity with the US dollar the Belizean dollar was in a unique position in the West Indies and therefore a source of pride.

Still greater fears were expressed that there would be undue interference in the colony's affairs or even domination and exploitation by the larger West Indian territories. In this respect the urge to remain separate did not mean that the anti-federationists were content with their colonial status. On the contrary, they followed with interest the work of the constitutional commission of inquiry which was established in 1948.[147] But the hope that politics would become more competitive was overshadowed by the fear that the British had agreed to the idea of constitutional changes in order to bring the colony more in line with the larger territories in the West Indies and thereby facilitate federation.

Federation was also seen as an imperial conspiracy to facilitate the massive migration from the overcrowded West Indian islands which the Evans Commission had recommended.[148] This was perhaps the issue that aroused the most disquiet. Opposition to the idea of immigration partly reflected the country's political insularity and in part its negative views about West Indians. Neither the political activism of West Indian professional men nor the success of their ordinary compatriots who had been recruited to the police force from Barbados after the Second World War and as agricultural settlers from Jamaica in the 1930s won West Indians much admiration.

Opinion was no less divided on Guatemala's territorial claim. The pro-West Indian Federation group argued that federation was the solution to Guatemala's assertions.[149] Since this group comprised the essentially middle-class Creoles who constituted the political elite it was not surprising that in March 1948 the Legislative Council unanimously passed a resolution of loyalty to the British Crown and placed on record their unalterable desire to remain in the Commonwealth.[150] This strengthened the earlier action of the British government in sending warships to Belize in response to reported threats of invasion and also its offer to submit the dispute to legal adjudication.[151]

The group led by Kemp and Soberanis responded differently to the Guatemala claim. At best their response was non-committal, at worst it was ambivalent and ambiguous. They argued that 'The Guatemalan stand opens the gateway for natives to have legal rights to self-determination.'[152] But in asserting the principle of self-determination they did not make it clear whether their purpose was political independence or merely the right to determine their own destiny. Sections of their writings suggest that political independence was their goal. They claimed that in signing a treaty of boundary or cession in 1859, both Great Britain and Guatemala acted beyond the scope of their rights or equity by doing so without the knowledge or approval of the settlers of Belize. Such a convention was therefore 'without legal or moral foundation and is void or voidable'.[153] At the same time they were not unmindful of the importance of Belize as a transit route to the Caribbean Sea to the development of the hinterland of Guatemala. Nevertheless they urged that the 'orographic and political barriers existing should be removed without in any way affecting the right of sovereignty of each distinct unit or country'.[154] In contradistinction to this position, Kemp and Soberanis, stated that 'The Open Forum [which they organized] refuses to associate itself with the conspiracy to frustrate Guatemala in her claims.'[155] A third position could also have been identified from their argument. This was one which called for a politically independent Belize in 'Closer Association' with Pan-America. This position had been reached from a consideration of Belize's material interests. The republics had been lucrative avenues for Belizean labour. But, as Kemp and Soberanis observed, it was repeatedly brought to 'the notice of the entire country that natives travelling with a British passport find it difficult to get an even break in Pan America as against a Latin America passport'.[156] It was therefore in the country's economic interest to dispense with this liability, especially as 'No British opportunity in the past or apparent British effort is expected to compensate the masses of Belizeans for Pan American opportunities.'[157] Obviously taking to task the Legislative Councillors for having passed the resolution of loyalty to the British Crown, they concluded that their stand was 'based on "loyalty and devotion" to ourselves'.[158]

If this group was not in unequivocal support of the Guatemala claim, it was at least susceptible to Guatemala's overtures that were designed to exploit the unrest in Belize City by suggesting that in her hands the country could do better and to challenge the British government's claim that its stand was consistent with the wishes of the ordinary inhabitants. Thus a few Belizeans were arrested in 1949 for distributing to the general public in Belize City a leaflet, *A Downright Shame,* which commented on the colonial exploitation in Belize and was reproduced as a flysheet in Guatemala City for distribution in Belize after it had been published in the Guatemala press in August 1948.[159]

Public opinion on these and other issues was formulated by several organizations ranging from the Open Forum on the 'Battlefield' to the exclusive Christian Social Action Group run by the Jesuits. The role of each of these organizations was as different as the type of political mind which they attracted. The Open Forum provided a platform for the seasoned campaigners. Not the least of its patrons were the newcomers to the national scene who had acquired their political awareness under the stimulus of the Second World War. The Chairman of the meetings, for example, was Ethelbert 'Kid' Broaster who had been deported from the United States after imprisonment for advocating the non-participation of black Americans in the war.

Perhaps a much more influential organization was the General Workers' Union (GWU). The union catered for several occupational groups and claimed a membership of 350 when it was registered in 1943. Within the next five years its membership spiralled to over 3,000.[160] More important, it was the only urban-based organization whose influence spread to the outdistricts where it was engaged in protracted struggles with the BEC and the colonial government for the right of access to the company's lands to unionize the workers.[161] Their activities imbued the rural workers with a consciousness of their wretched conditions. As we shall see in the next section of the study, it was through this organization that in the rural areas the political movement in the 1950s first grouped the latent individual protest against the colonial institutions into an overt social struggle.

The 'Open Forum' and the nascent labour movement found the weekly *Belize Billboard* to be an asset. Founded by a Cuban national, Narciso Valdes, in 1946, the newspaper quickly developed an interest in the working class that marked it off from the two older newspapers, *The Daily Clarion,* and the weekly *Belize Independent.* It championed the cause of the GWU and in the process made the union a household name in various parts of the country. In so far as the ordinary people could grasp the essential features of colonial rule, the newspaper served another useful function by placing the social and political malaise in Belize in its wider colonial context.[162]

The other type of organizations were the study groups and debating societies which as we saw were the progenitors of political groupings. These commanded less public attention but were as influential as the Open Forum, the GWU and the *Belize Billboard*. The more established societies possessed their own publication outlets; the St John's Literary and Debating Society issued a quarterly journal, *Outlook*, which provided an excellent training opportunity for the determined coterie whose names reappeared continually as editors, poets and authors of the main articles on politics.[163]

Not all of the political views emanating from these societies were secular and non-sectarian. This was because the organizations were sustained largely by the social leadership of the clergy. For a feature common to most cultural and literary groups in Belize during this period was their association, however slight, with the churches.[164] When an organization did not owe its origin to the organizing skill of clergymen it at least received their patronage. There was indeed a ramifying connection between the churches, the societies, and the secondary schools which, we observed, were denominational. The societies attracted the secondary school leaders who had become junior civil servants and teachers, journalists and commercial clerks, and wished to maintain their literary and social interests. Their extra-mural pursuits were in a real sense the continuation of their scholastic relationship with their religious and educational superiors.

Perhaps the most outstanding society which bears out the foregoing analysis was the Belize Literary and Debating Club. Its origin was described as follows: 'A purely religious debating society instituted in 1912, had by 1928 turned into a society officered principally by civil servants',[165] who were staunch Protestants. That the society was engaged in a particular kind of political education is evident in its objectives which were 'to foster loyalty and devotion to His Majesty the King and the British Empire'.[166] But the Protestant clergy were outdone by the Jesuits in moulding the mind of the young. Catholic ideas on social justice, culled from the Papal Encyclical *Rerum Novarum* were the diet on which members of the Christian Social Action group were nourished. Indeed this group, which had grown out of another Jesuit enterprise, the Credit Union Movement, became the catalyst of nationalist growth and the rallying point of the Catholic young men in Belize City. John Smith, Leigh Richardson, Herman Jex, George Price, Philip Goldson, and Nicholas Pollard were members of this group. The Social Action group worked closely with the St John's Alumni Association which consciously advocated a concerted Catholic action in politics in its journal, *The Mangrove*, and took steps in this direction in 1942 when it sponsored candidates for the Belize Town Board election.[167]

The extent to which a liberal, religious and political education went hand-in-hand within the Catholic institutions cannot be over-emphasized. The comprehensive nature of the Jesuit influence produced a solidarity among their *protégés* that pushed into the background ethnic and other cultural divisions. Many of the members, such as Goldson and Richardson, were full-blooded African Creoles from Protestant families who became Catholic converts as a result of their association with the Jesuits. Others such as Price could claim racial affinity with White or African Creoles and Indians or Mestizos, and straddled both cultural groups. Although they were members of other societies, they appeared to be more active in the Catholic organizations. To some extent their prominence in the Catholic organization particularly as spokesmen reflected their earlier educational experience as Creoles. Nevertheless, their Catholicism seemed to be paramount. So much so that Edgar Gegg, who in addition to being a prominent Catholic is also a successful businessman and was a nominated member of the Legislative Council (1947–54), still felt denied as a Catholic. In 1947, as President of the St John's Alumni Association, he called upon Catholics to assume the political leadership of the country. His views were so representative of the Association's thinking on a number of related issues that they should be quoted at length:

Who are leaders? Or rather, who *should* be our leaders? Obviously, the ones best suited to lead, the educated class; men who in their youth received a complete and harmonious training of their every faculty; those who in their boyhood days were instilled with the right principles as regards their duty to their fellow men, to their country, and to their God. In a word, the Alumni of St John's College.

But do we take the lead in the affairs of our country, the lead that we should take? Is our leadership as outstanding, as pervading as it could be? Embarrassing questions these. It is true that we do really lead to some extent but ours is a timid, half interested, divided leadership, lacking in concerted and determined action toward a definite objective. A gross exaggeration, some will say. Yet the Alumni as a body think so little of the association that in the past it has been impossible to get more than a mere handful to attend meetings at which matters of importance not only to the association but to the state could be discussed, definite policies adopted and plans formulated to carry them out. In brief, how can we ever expect to work hand in hand toward a common goal with fervour and determination peculiar to that terrible Austrian referred to above [Hitler] unless we come together in full numerical strength at fixed intervals to decide what our plans of action are to be?

. . . what part do the Alumni play in the politics of British Honduras? The truth hurts terribly, since we have but one Alumnus on a legislature consisting of 7 elected and appointed members, and a single representative on our Town Board. It is obvious from this that we do not exercise the influence in the government of our country and in formulating public opinion that we should, and that as a body have seldom if ever had the temerity to raise our voices above a faint and ineffectual bleating against any measures which the government has decided upon. The result of this is that in the past, some laws have been enacted that have not evidenced the consideration for the common good which more Alumni surely would have brought to the consideration of our law makers. A glaring example of inconsideration for the best interest of natives, Alumni and otherwise, has been the laxity of our immigration laws.[168]

Such sentiments suggest that the conflict, actual and potential, was not so much between Creoles and Mestizos as between two opposing denominational groups of Creoles – Protestants and Catholics. One drew its strength from its colonial attachments, the other from the knowledge that its denominational group was numerically stronger, more widely distributed throughout the country, much more ethnically and culturally varied although predominantly Mestizo, and equally more representative of the lower class. Furthermore the second Creole group also had the advantage of some of its leading members not being exclusively committed to the Creole culture but being partially oriented toward the Mestizo. In calling attention to the limited influence of the Catholics in politics this Creole group was in effect aggregating and articulating the interests of several disparate groups. In fact its potential ability to make an impact upon the political process was slowly but surely being realized. Price was elected to the Belize Town Board in 1947 after having been defeated at the polls in 1943.[169] Smith, at his first attempt in 1948, became the senior elected legislative representative for the two-member Belize District constituency by topping the polls.[170] Richardson and Goldson forsook the security of their teaching and civil service positions respectively to pursue their political interests as journalists for the *Belize Billboard*.[171]

But these developments were either unnoticed by the colonial authorities or if observed, as was more likely, regarded as inconsequential. After all these were young men most of whom were of little social substance and whose mentors, the Jesuits, were not within the inner political sanctuary. The established Belize Creole elite however took the emerging political trend more seriously. The unofficial members of the Legislative Council not only discussed the political situation in the late 1940s with representatives of the various literary societies[172] but their unanimous decision to vote against the devaluation of the Belize dollar in December 1949 was partly influenced by the unpopularity of the measure with these young men.

## The politics of devaluation

The events between the devaluation of the British pound in September 1949 and that of the Belize dollar in December 1949 revealed the lack of popular confidence in the colonial political system. Few people believed that exemption was the ultimate fate of the dollar. The vast majority believed the *Belize Billboard's* argument[173] that devaluation was imminent as this was in the interest of the influential British-financed enterprises.

The first official attempt to confound these rumours had the opposite effect of maintaining public concern and scepticism. Within days of the devaluation of the British pound, Harrison Courtenay, who claimed to have been accused along with his business associates of 'exerting efforts to induce the government to devalue the dollar',[174] pointedly asked in the Legislative Council whether the Belize government had any proposal under consideration 'from any source whatever, to devalue the currency of the Colony?'[175] The Colonial Secretary replied in the negative and stated that the decision to change the rate of exchange was the responsibility of the Bank of England.[176] Implicit in the reply was the attempt to disabuse the people's mind that a decision on the future of the currency could be influenced, favourably or otherwise, by local pressure. There was also the obvious and related attempt to exonerate the colonial government from the responsibility for any decision on the issue. But those opposed to devaluation did not accept the official distinction between the Bank of England and the imperial government or between the latter and the colonial government. All were thought to be associated and in league, and all were destined to be blamed for the devaluation. Indeed, J. S. Espat foresaw this wholesale condemnation. He observed that 'if by choice His Majesty's government decides to devalue our dollar, there would be very little that we can do about it. And if that is done, the public will blame this council.'[177]

The business activities of the unofficial members of the Legislative Council were certainly not calculated to confound their critics. They exploited the situation by indulging in speculation.[178] Evidently, many of them fared well. The mercantile and commercial element purchased goods to cover import requirements for many months ahead to take advantage of the exchange rate. Overdrafts were raised with the local banks against sterling deposits in other colonies and Britain to cover the purchase of Belize timber for export. Some of the businessmen made payments locally in Belize dollars in advance to cover the purchase of US dollars and sterling which was necessary for financing approved imports into the colony. Some also contributed to the flight of the Belize dollar, estimated at $2 million,[179] by transferring their funds to Britain.

The fear and misapprehension of an impending devaluation of the dollar was partially allayed by the visit of Lord Listowel, Minister of State for the Colonies, in October 1949. Throughout his tour of the colony he was at pains to deny the rumoured devaluation.[180] If further assurance was needed from the British government it was immediately forthcoming in November 1949 from Mr Rees Williams, Under-Secretary of State for the Colonies, in a resolute parliamentary defence of the British government's decision to exempt the dollar from devaluation.[181]

The fear of devalution was, however, realized within five weeks of this latest assurance. Significantly, the unofficial members of the Legislative Council did not criticize the devaluation itself, but the Governor for not taking them into his confidence. It is difficult to see how the Governor could have acted otherwise if only because some of the unofficials were among the chief speculators. In fact, the Governor, in noting the lack of confidence in the Belize dollar, accused the speculators of precipitating the devaluation crisis.[182]

The British government's decision to devalue the dollar was not as sudden as it may appear. From the time the British pound had been devalued, the future of the dollar was 'under constant review',[183] as the Governor admitted. He had been 'in close consultation with the Secretary of State throughout the past three months' and the problem 'had been considered by all those officials both in the Colonial Office and in the Treasury at home who could be helpful in reaching a solution'.[184] These were astounding disclosures in view of the earlier assurances by the British government that the dollar would not be devalued.

The emerging group of young politicians were, therefore, justified in their lack of confidence in the imperial and colonial governments. These political leaders had been rudely reminded that the institutions which made the vital decisions were completely outside the people's control. Perhaps more important they were convinced that the unofficial members were unsuited to the task of correcting the situation. In fact, they were not impressed with the members' unanimous disapproval of the high-handed way in which the Governor had acted. They considered this a gesture to the outraged masses since many of the members stood to benefit from the devaluation. In forming the People's Committee on the night of the devaluation the emerging group of political leaders were setting themselves the task of gaining control of the country's political institutions.

## The summation

The devaluation was sufficiently important to be regarded as the watershed of Belize politics. It has been our contention, however, that this issue cannot adequately explain the political outburst in the early 1950s. The long-term explanation should take account of the British attitude towards the colony, the depressed social and economic conditions which the people had endured since 1931 and the absence of an open political system. These three factors cannot be separated. Once the British government began to take its responsibility for the colonial society seriously it took the necessary steps to further safeguard British economic interests against the more aggressive American concerns and their local business supporters. It is essentially within this context that the conflict between the imperial government on the one hand and the forestry and mercantile interests and the professional middle class in Belize on the other should be seen. The entire burden of the exploitative pursuits of both the foreign and local economic interests fell on the shoulders of the bulk of the population that appeared to be stoic. But the decades of comparative calm often masked a seething unrest and frustration within the ranks of the disenfranchised and disadvantaged. Indeed, the colonial authorities and the local elite had been more or less lulled by the apparent submissiveness of the masses into an unawareness of, or unconcern with, the latent hostility among the dispossessed.

The dynamics in such a situation seems to be the existence of leaders who would exert pressures upon the colonial system not merely on their own behalf but also on behalf of the labouring elements.[185] There is usually a correlation between the extremity of their demands and difficulties of their gaining access to the political process. Furthermore, for such a leadership to be truly national in a society like Belize and also seen as a genuine alternative, its aims have to transcend racial or cultural group interests. This type of leadership had begun to emerge within the study groups and debating societies in the late 1940s. The new generation of politicians such as Smith, Goldson, Price and Richardson recognized the necessity of demonstrating their interest in the various groups that were disparate and even divided in terms of race, religion, language and culture but which were relatively homogeneous in regard to their depressed economic conditions. They found in colonialism a ready explanation for all the misfortunes of not one cultural group but for all those people who felt economically and politically denied. Although largely academic and lacking the drama, force, and passion of later years their activities in the 1940s were as instrumental as the devaluation in bringing about the political crisis.

# PART TWO

# The decolonization process, 1950-1960

# An overview

This part traces the rise and development of the nationalist movement, the opposition which it encountered from the British government and the old political elite, the divisive impact of this rivalry upon its own leadership and the way in which the conflicts were resolved. It is interesting that although economic issues were the catalyst of nationalist growth they never sustained the conflicts that developed. There were no ideological differences among those who had plans for economic growth. All of them were agreed that Belize must rely upon expatriate interests in order to fulfil these plans, the difference being that the nationalist movement, the People's United Party which emerged, believed that the USA was more likely than Britain to respect its political aspirations and was more committed to the alleviation of the poverty in the underdeveloped countries. Far from implying local control of the country's economic destiny, the process of decolonization in Belize seemed to be essentially a question of imperial succession. While this may have had adverse implications for the British economic interests in Belize it did not necessarily stand in the way of a tacit agreement between the British government and the PUP about the progressive transfer of political power to the new Belizean elite during decolonization.

What prevented the agreement was the PUP's or, to be more precise, some of its leaders' attraction to a Central American destiny for Belize. This orientation was in conflict with the British colonial policy which was to guide the colonial territories to responsible government within the Commonwealth. Nor was the desire of the old Creole elite for a greater measure of political responsibility sufficiently strong to overcome their fears that the PUP's Central American outlook would result in the submergence of their cultural identity and an alteration of the social order. Indeed, the old political elite became a natural ally of the British government in the latter's bid to represent federation with the West Indian territories not as an end in itself but as the alternative to closer political relations with Central America and the answer to the Guatemalan claim. In this situation there was little basis for a partnership between either the British government and the PUP or the political groupings. Those PUP leaders who thought that a basis existed, co-operated with the colonial government in working out a new constitution which was introduced in 1954. But this put them at odds with their colleagues and this culminated in a major PUP split in 1956 and the loss of a considerable amount of their popular support. From then onwards the entire question of the country's relationship with external political entities, regional and metropolitan, did not only relate to the social and cultural differences in the society. It also assumed to a considerable extent a symbolic importance in a more purely local struggle for power which brought the opposition elements together into a single political party, the National Independence Party, in 1958. Even with the aid of the British government the opposition was still unable to find a popular answer to the PUP's commitment to political change through links with wider Latin American groupings.

An indefinite delay of the decolonization process could not, however, be part of such an answer without completely destroying the credibility of the element in the opposition that was previously associated with the nationalist demand for self-government. Recalling that their collaboration with the British government had paid few political dividends and recognizing that their legitimacy must ultimately come from within the society, the opposition joined in the call for internal self-government when Sir Hilary Blood undertook a review of the 1954 constitution in 1959. This homogeneity of interests among the political groupings was also facilitated by the willingness of the PUP to come to terms with constitutional change within the context of British colonial policy. The consensus was nevertheless in contrast to the tendency for colonial societies to fragment into distinct categories when basic constitutional change is in the offing. Indeed, the British government could not ignore the reconciliation of political differences in Belize. It therefore agreed in 1960 to a greater measure of constitutional change than the one which Blood had proposed a year earlier. Despite the resolution of the conflict, the question of the future of Belize was not completely settled because of the Guatemalan claim. On the contrary the issue persisted into the penultimate phase of decolonization in the 1960s with which the final part of the study will be concerned.

# 4
# The nationalist upsurge: the People's Committee in 1950

Once the political crisis had arisen it was only natural for the aspiring politicians to cohere into the distinct group to push still further their incipient movement for reform. On the same night that the dollar was devalued a protest meeting was held on the 'Battlefield' under the auspices of the Open Forum. The guest speakers were Smith and Price. The meeting was so well received that at its conclusion another was announced for the following night. It appears that within the first two days of January 1950 the organizers of the protest meetings formed a committee, for on the 3rd 'handbills told of the People's Committee [PC] with John Smith as Chairman and George Price as Secretary'.[1] In a sense the devaluation issue was the midwife of the PC for during its brief existence of nine months, it spearheaded the attack on the imperial decision.

The importance of the PC however does not lie so much in its genesis as in its being the progenitor of the PUP. It bequeathed to the party its leaders and supporters, its anti-colonial and anti-British sentiments, and some of its structural characteristics. To study the PC's posture therefore is to begin to understand the intentions and predisposition of the PUP at least in its formative years.

## Organization and appeal

From the inception the PC was a loose and informal amalgam of individuals. There was an appearance of a collective leadership of several people but in effect the internal organization centred around Smith, the Chairman, and Price, the Secretary–Treasurer. The former derived most of his influence from being a reliable spokesman of the PC in the Legislative Council. But the moving spirit of the Committee was Price. As Secretary, he devoted considerable time to the organization of the movement and it was at his home that most of the executive committee meetings were held. Apart from their joint desire for social reform, these two leaders shared at least one other feature with most of the other founding members. This was their Catholic belief which helped to stabilize the leadership.

125

The movement itself was sustained and unified by a popular desire to force the end of colonial rule. This was largely inherent in the situation. There was almost complete agreement among several disparate elements in Belize City – the unemployed, especially the youth and itinerant water-front labourers, small shopkeepers, manual government workers, clerical workers and young civil servants – that their disabilities and low standard of living were to be attributed to the colonial system. Among the more indefatigable supporters were the housewives. Perhaps more than any other group they struggled to make ends meet as the prices of staple food-stuff went up as much as 30 or 40 per cent because almost everything that was eaten was imported. Under these conditions the PC had little difficulty in rallying popular support in Belize City.

It was less easy for the PC to enlist popular support in the district towns and villages. The Committee lacked the organizational machinery to extend its appeal to these areas. The difficulties of transportation did not permit the deployment of the leaders with ease and speed, and, moreover, none of them was a full-time devotee to the Committee. Influential sympathizers from the outdistrict towns were instead invited to speak on the Committee's platform in Belize City. The *Belize Billboard* in turn gave prominent and extensive publicity to the 'impassioned addresses [which] showed an intimate grasp of the catastrophic con-sequences devaluation would impose on the people of Belize'.[2]

A more effective solution was, however, the PC's attempt to identify itself with the GWU which, as we observed, boasted of fairly strong district branches and which therefore was a potential asset. As a matter of fact from the outset the GWU supported the PC; its founder and only President during the seven years of its existence, Cecil Betson, having spoken at the first protest meeting. Furthermore the association seemed mutually beneficial. In addition to having a strong organizational machinery, the GWU had in its President and in its General Secretary, H. A. Middleton, national figures. Middleton had also in the first few weeks of the nationalist upsurge attended the World Confederation of Free Trade Unions (WCFTU) in England where he was promised support by the British Trade Union Congress. The union therefore was in a position to lend legitimacy to the activities of the PC. At the same time the union leaders were past their prime as both Betson and Middleton were about seventy years old. They therefore welcomed the energy of youth and were occasionally joint sponsors with the PC of meetings at the 'Battlefield'. They also entertained a suggestion from Nicholas Pollard, one of the founding members of the PC and President of the weak Mercantile Clerk Union (MCU) that his union be structurally associated with the GWU. But while Pollard conceived of a single union of which the MCU would be a branch, the GWU leaders spoke in terms of a confederation of trade unions. However the PC leaders were not content with either the GWU's voluntary support or its idea of a loose association. They sought complete control of the union's organizational machinery and if this could not be achieved by what Betson was to recognize as 'a subtle infiltration among the masses in the Union'[3] then a naked takeover of the executive council was seen as the alternative. Within four months of the Committee's formation the opportunity arose at the union's seventh annual conference. The outgoing President, in a rearguard battle to be re-elected, wondered 'if the working masses realise fully the aspect of this sudden appearance joining their fold'.[4] A lengthy reference to his achievements in office did not prevent the end of his seven-year-old presidential life.

The veteran leader lost to Nicholas Pollard. This was not the only important victory for the Committee. John Smith was named the Vice-President, while Price and Goldson were elected to the Executive Council.[5] The takeover had been accomplished. The new executive, confident and condescending, was benign enough to agree to a resolution of the General Secretary, Middleton, the long-standing colleague of the defeated presidential candidate that 'in recognition of his seven years as a "pioneer of the union" Betson be elected "Past President" with the right to sit on the GWU Executive Council'.[6] As if to remind Betson that his era of trade unionism was over, the Executive Council conferred upon him the doubtful honorific title of 'Patriarch of the Union' and voted a suitable purse for his 'distinguished service to the cause of labour'.[7]

The political leaders had assumed control of the GWU not only for its organizational value in the districts but perhaps more important because they believed that industrial objectives could be more effectively pursued by political means. As the union gained in strength it was increasingly dominated by politicians. These leaders extended their personal patronage to the GWU to such an extent that the fortunes of the union depended upon those of the individual politicians. Indeed this dependency, which the politicians seldom admitted, was the dominant feature of the trade union movement during the 1950s.

### Objectives and strategy

The Committee did not express its concern for social and economic reform in a concrete, executable programme. There was no compelling necessity for it to do so. It had no access to the governmental process. This exclusion in fact largely determined the Committee's agitational approach. It was strategically sufficient for it to assure itself of popular support by concentrating upon and excessively simplifying those issues on which most of the people agreed. Hence its immediate objectives were limited to the restoration of the Belize dollar to parity with the US dollar, preventing the country from joining the proposed West Indies Federation, the attainment of self-government, and the improvement of social and economic conditions.[8]

Concentration on these objectives had the overall effect of calling into question the country's political, economic, and geographical relationship with other political entities. The devaluation and the accompanying rise in prices and unemployment had removed any remaining doubts about the unsuitability of the imperial system as a framework of economic development. But while the leaders were anxious to rid the country of British rule they showed an equal alacrity to invite the American presence. They spoke in glowing terms of their admiration for America and flew the American flag at their rallies at which 'thousands of Hondurans sang . . . with emotional gusto to the strains of "God Bless America" '.[9] In fact, the popularity of the American Consul in Belize was second only to that of the political leaders. They were also prepared to take their grievance against the British government not only to the United Nations and other international agencies, but also to Washington.[10]

The reasons for the overtures to America are complex. It was primarily in consequence of the revolt against British rule: a negative but forceful way of expressing anti-British feelings. As one of the 'Battlefield' orators, Kemp, remarked 'this is a thunder period in which we mean to hurt the Lion's pride'.[11] It was obviously with this objective in mind that while meetings were held on the 'Battlefield' a band invariably played 'God Bless America' from the verandah of the nearby Supreme Court. The pro-American attitude can also be seen as a psychological reaction to the feeling that Britain regarded the country as a distant colonial outpost which could receive scant and shoddy attention because the British had relatively little vested interest in the colony. There was no large European population and, apart from the BEC, the British economic interests were relatively insignificant.

The feeling that the country was considered distant and remote was not without validity. As indicated in the previous chapter, Belize was and is still removed from the much-traversed West Indian route. Prior to the establishment of air communication in the country in 1945, a newly appointed Governor, for example, usually travelled to Jamaica where he embarked on a warship for his destination. His homeward journey was no less exacting. It took him first to either New Orleans or Puerto Barrios in Guatemala by a local ship where he joined a banana boat bound for home. Secondly, the colony was an unattractive assignment for colonial administrators. It was 'always regarded as an official backwater' and 'frequently suffered at the hands of inferior officials'.[12] Most administrators were posted here either in the evening of their careers or at the beginning of them, in which case they were anxious to leave as soon as possible to avoid 'the risk of being left in a political and economic backwater'.[13] Many relinquished senior appointments in preference for comparatively junior ones in the more important colonial territories which offered a more promising career.

This external image of Belize persisted throughout the 1930s and 1940s and the British still appear to view the country, despite the development of modern communications, as an isolated and forlorn place. Indeed, the British government had placed so little premium on the territory that at the Peace Conference in 1919 'there was talk of ceding it to the US'.[14] The proposal was, however, rejected when 'the policy of repaying American loans by the surrender of Crown Colonies was eventually found to be impracticable'.[15]

This strong local feeling of denial and neglect by Britain was matched by the corresponding belief that the country should look to the USA for delivery from its dilemma. The belief which was shared by the politicians and the people alike, especially the Creoles in Belize City, also resulted from other considerations. Because it was nearer and wealthier than Britain, the USA held a strong attraction for those who wished to seek their future elsewhere. There were in fact several cities in the USA in which Belizeans concentrated, and their material success redounded to the USA's advantage at home. Unlike their counterparts in the West Indies, civil servants who were on long vacation went to the United States rather than Britain, for a variety of reasons. One was to visit relatives. Another was that this visit invariably proved less expensive because of the possibility of remunerative employment even though this violated the leave conditions and those of entry into the USA. There was also a high incidence of absentee wives and mothers who had been driven by unemployment to make short visits to the USA where they worked day and night to accumulate some savings in order to return to their families in Belize as quickly as possible. Altogether there was a greater inter-flow of people between Belize and the USA than between the former and Britain. Visiting American businessmen, in pursuit of new investment opportunities, also imparted a feeling of optimism about the country's economic possibilities. This earned them more popularity than their British counterparts who were invariably recruited to fill controlling positions in the

British holdings. The BEC in particular was so impersonally organized that the Belizean employee felt little identification with his expatriate superiors.

The constant flow to Belize of American literature – journals, magazines, newspapers, and films – also contributed to this favourable American image. The ease with which this literature could be obtained was in marked contrast to the difficulty of obtaining comparable material from Britain. The politically minded were therefore able to acquire a more intimate knowledge of American than British politics. In sports, baseball had by 1950 become a strong competitor of cricket as the leading national game. As early as 1935, Governor Burns perspicaciously commented on the colony's American outlook. He wrote:

A very large proportion of the population is Spanish speaking and the influence of the neighbouring republics, with their Spanish cultures, is considerable. Of the English-speaking section of the population a number have worked in Central American republics but do not appear to have acquired a Spanish culture. The whole colony is, however, largely influenced by the comparative proximity of the US as the people as a whole are more American than British in their outlook. This may be due to a limited extent to the cinema, but is more directly attributable to the influence of trade and education. All of the RC priests and nuns, who are responsible for the education of more than half of the total population, are American, and the children of the better classes, who are sent abroad for their education, go more often to the US than to Great Britain. Owing to the lack of frequent direct communication with Great Britain local trade goes naturally to the US.[16]

The contributing influence of the Roman Catholic clerics to this American outlook can hardly be over-estimated. As we have seen, most of the PC leaders, being Catholics, had received an American oriented secondary education at the St John's College. The Jesuits were so wedded to the American education system that they assiduously avoided using the officially recommended British textbooks.[17] (A striking consequence of the use of British and American textbooks in schools is the curious admixture of British and American spelling in the local press and other publications.) Moreover, the Jesuits were the largest homogeneous group of expatriate intellectuals and, through their pastoral activities, were in direct contact with the majority of the population. Their strong sense of vocation, learning, and simple way of life were impressive. It was therefore not unlikely that the people tended to see America through Jesuit eyes.

It was suggested in interviews that the leaders of the Committee merely rode on the popular wave of enthusiasm for America and apart from offending the British had no other motives for fostering the pro-America campaign. The suggestion tends to ignore the leaders' belief that American investments would have stimulated a more self-sustaining process of development.[18] They had attributed the economic setback in the late 1940s partly to the decline of the traditional commercial trade with the US, and were convinced that the Colonial Development Corporation, with 'its notorious failure of the African groundnut venture', could 'not offer us the economic and social assurances that American Point 4 does. For US Point 4 aid, according to President Truman, will strive to raise living standards to bring about economic development in underdeveloped areas of the world whether in British Honduras, in China, in Central Africa or in Alaska.'[19] They were also confident that American companies would offer higher wages to unskilled labourers than either the government or the CDC which they claimed had 'declared the definite policy not to pay higher wages than the low wages paid to government labourers'.[20] Their faith in American intentions, official and private, was probably unequalled by any other colonial territory in political ferment at the time. They also overlooked the fact that private American concerns were in the habit of unexpectedly repatriating their investments from the country once the British had removed the stipulation that capital invested in its colonies could not be withdrawn within ten years. Nor did the opposition of some of these concerns to unionized labour deter the leaders in their demand for the substitution of American for British investments.

As one of the leading advocates of closer economic relationship with the United States, Price was also probably influenced by his close relationship with his multi-millionaire employer, R. S. Turton. The latter not only had extensive business connections in the United States but was also a large shareholder in two American-financed companies, the Wrigley Company and I. T. Williams Company, formidable rivals of the BEC in the chicle and mahogany industries respectively. These business connections often took Price to the United States and he may well have conceived from his visits and the general success of his employer the idea of a more prominent role for American private capital in the economy. His criticism of the 'imperial preferential tariff system' as an 'infliction on the people of British Honduras'[21] indicated his preference for the traditional trade with the USA, and was also an echo of Turton's complaint that the system was favourable to his rival, the BEC. One of Price's associates, his unofficial economic adviser during his first term of office (1957–61), was an American businessman, Ned Davis, who was eventually imprisoned in Belize for embezzling thousands of US dollars entrusted to him for investment in Belize by an American business partner. Price's demand for a greater inflow of American capital, had it received official compliance, would have posed a threat to the British economic interests.

It is likely that Price's anti-British sentiments were influenced by his association with Turton. Despite his wealth and occasional generosity to public causes, Turton, whose formal education was limited, was not awarded the social patronage of the upper stratum of society. He commanded little respect from the colonial officials and as a Legislative Councillor from 1936 to 1948 was a severe critic of the government. Moreover, he had been one of the principal casualties of the devaluation, having been earlier compelled by the administration to retransfer his monetary assets from the USA. Like many other businessmen who had sustained losses he welcomed the PC. It was also believed that he financed the Committee, which, a critic observed 'never rose above suspicions' that it was 'only serving Catholic Action and the whims of a rich man or men'.[22]

Other long-term political considerations might also have influenced Price's pro-American campaign. Closer economic association with the USA would have bolstered his claim that the country's economic and political future lay with the Central American republics and not the West Indian territories. In other words his idea of a Central American destiny was more likely to be realized not through closer identity with Britain and the West Indies but through the USA with its increasing interest in Latin America. An attempt to forge a triangular relationship, with the USA at the base, could have been detected in Price's assertion that the country's 'economy and way of life is interdependent with the USA and with Central America'.[23] The results which he wished to achieve by contrasting Britain's tardiness in fulfilling its moral and financial obligations after the 1931 hurricane with the ready response of relief missions from the USA and the Central American republics appeared to be twofold.[24] The comparison was intended to 'inject an anti-British spirit',[25] as well as to suggest that there existed a bond between the country and its North and Central American neighbours which was once successfully tested in a crisis and ought to be called upon again.[26]

It should, however, be re-emphasized that the pro-American campaign was based more upon anti-British feelings than on the positive desire for closer economic association with the USA. Even among those who gave equal consideration to closer economic ties with the USA there was little evidence of a willingness to submit the country to American control. While it would have been difficult for them to resist the increase of American influence which was likely to accompany economic aid, they did not wish to become 'a pampered protectorate of the rich USA'. Even the old idea, now revived by the more ardent admirers of North America, that the country should seek provincial status from Canada was not encouraged by the Committee. In the first place the idea was Utopian. Secondly, the nationalist leaders did not accept its basic assumption that the country could not survive as an independent political unit. Their slogan was 'Self-Government' and if political association was necessary, then it should be with Central America.

As we have seen in the previous chapter the possibility of this relationship was invariably raised in discussions of the British proposal to federate its West Indian colonies. Completely mistrustful of the British government's intentions, Price warned that a 'halter would be tied around our necks with the loose end tied to the federal capital of the British West Indies' unless the people voiced their 'strongest protest in the most effective way, unceasingly and energetically, that they are a geographic part of Central America'.[27] The Committee therefore urged the imperial government to 'Discontinue at once all endeavours to federate our country into an unpopular proposed political federation of the British West Indies', with the now familiar rider that 'The people do not consider themselves part and parcel of the British West Indies, but rather a part and parcel of Central America on the mainland with whom we have long had existing economic and commercial ties.'[28]

It should not be assumed that the entire leadership shared Price's pro-American outlook to the same extent or believed that the Committee should be relentless in its anti-British feelings. That this assumption could not be made became evident when at the height of the ferment in February 1950 it was announced that Her Royal Highness, Princess Alice, who was to be installed as Chancellor of the University College of the West Indies in Mona, Jamaica, would be paying a visit to Belize. Some of the leaders suggested the singing of 'God Bless America' which had become the 'People's marching song' instead of the British national anthem. Smith, however, led a moderate group which advocated strong agitation without insulting the visitor. 'Kid' Broaster also attempted to counsel moderation at one of his Open Forum meetings. Although one of the 'Battlefield' orators who had voiced publicly anti-colonial and anti-British sentiments long before the PC came into existence, Broaster was less opposed to the British than to the Americans. He could not reconcile his tragic experience of imprisonment for his anti-war activities among the blacks in the USA with the almost suffocating adulation of that country. He therefore attempted to dissuade the supporters of the PC from singing 'God Bless America' during the royal tour. But he only succeeded in incurring the displeasure of Price, and it was the timely intervention of the police that saved him from the wrath of the surging crowd. Broaster not only abandoned his rostrum but disappeared from the political scene for twelve years, returning in 1962 as chairman of the meetings of the NIP. During the incident tear gas was used for the first time to quell a disturbance. This was not a propitious moment for the royal visit which was therefore cancelled.

According to another Open Forum veteran, Kemp, Broaster was 'not the only member of the People's Committee who place British rule ahead of America' since 'Mr Nicholas Pollard wrote in *The Daily Clarion*, in answer to a rumour of disloyalty against Mr George Price and himself that for him loyalty to British Honduras was first and England second.'[29] There was therefore a difference of opinion between Price and his colleagues over the strategy to be adopted towards Britain and the USA almost from the inception of the People's Committee and perhaps more ominously, as Broaster's fate indicated, a growing intolerance of the extreme element towards internal opposition.

A notable feature of the popular movement was its ideology. Leaders of contemporary nationalist movements in those years in addition to, or as a corollary of, being anti-colonial normally professed an interest in a set of radical principles, usually socialism. But the Belizean leaders were not ideologically oriented in this direction. Not only in 1950, but throughout the period of decolonization one would look in vain for a socialist-oriented politician. In fact, the nationalist leaders, as became increasingly evident, were unmistakably opposed to 'leftist' ideologies. The strong Catholic element within the Committee showed no desire to betray its religious teachings.

From the ideological standpoint, therefore, there was little basis for Governor Garvey's fear that the leaders were creating 'the atmosphere in which anarchy and Communism finally flourish'.[30] Perhaps the fear arose partly from the suspicion that some of the leaders were in contact with Guatemala which had undergone in 1944 a rather deep-seated social revolution and whose government was labour-leftist and nationalistic, with a determined programme for fundamental reform. Nevertheless, it would have been odd, if not inconsistent, for the leaders simultaneously to advocate closer relationship with the USA and indulge in communist activities. The leaders' dislike of Britain and colonialism was based not upon a Marxist interpretation of history but upon their own understanding and experience of colonial rule. For example, they opposed the BEC because of its firm control of the forestry industry and hostility to unionized labour, and not from an ideological conviction that a private enterprise economy dominated by foreign interests was basically inimical to the interest of the country. Such ideological considerations would have demanded an opposition also to the American concerns. The leaders certainly adopted a strong stand against the British but they were not unique by colonial standards.

## The campaign

The campaign confirmed that the PC was the product of a political ferment. The leaders employed almost every recognized technique of agitation: public meetings, demonstrations and deputations to Government House, petitions to the Secretary of State for the Colonies and to the United Nations, and press campaigns. Within six weeks of its formation the Committee submitted three petitions to the British Colonial Office. That they saw in the arbitrary manner in which devaluation was effected a constitutional conflict between their country and the imperial government was one of two recurring themes in the petitions. The other was that the control of currency and trade had created new conflict of interests not only between the colony and Britain but also between different socio-economic groups, the exporters and the labourers in the colony. These two arguments were not exclusive but reinforcing.

The leaders contended that both sets of conflicts could be resolved by increasing political autonomy to Belize. It was not only that the leaders lacked the appropriate ideological perspective to recognize that a process of constitutional decolonization did not necessarily imply national control in economic and financial matters. They had also emerged in a period in which self-proclaimed socialist leaders in other colonies also believed that underdevelopment was primarily a consequence of politics rather than economics and that it was only necessary to accept Kwame Nkrumah's injunction, 'Seek ye first the political kingdom and all things will be added unto it.'

The petitions struck a responsive chord throughout the Caribbean and also in Britain. The *Jamaica Gleaner* in an editorial observed that 'The [first] petition. . .is a document of considerable interest and significance. It strongly marks the nature of the stress in colonial societies at the present time.'[31] Even the pro-imperial London *Daily Express* which had despatched a journalist to the colony within weeks of the first petition was constrained to remark that the situation was 'A story to make Britons ashamed.'[32] There was no doubt the PC recognized the value of international support. In July, Price visited the United States and made personal contacts in the United Nations. On his return he reported that the PC's case was presented to the Trusteeship Council and to the Human Rights Commission which had promised to take it to the appropriate committee of the General Assembly. Price had also seized the opportunity of his visit to appeal to the Pan-American Union Secretariat in Washington and was no doubt grateful to learn that at a recent conference in Havana a commission of the union drafted a series of resolutions against the existence of colonies in the Western Hemisphere.[33]

The campaign within Belize itself took the form of public meetings and demonstrations. Not infrequently these meetings were hastily but successfully arranged at any time of the day because the Committee had in the unemployed a large, willing and captive audience. The meetings did not always materialize as official permission was at times withheld because of the increasing acts of intimidation and molestation of prominent citizens opposed to the movement and the tenor of certain speeches. Rather than comply with the Governor's conditions that names of speakers and subjects should be submitted for government's approval and that there be no music,[34] the PC held no public meetings for about five of the nine months of its existence. The leaders interpreted these conditions as an attempt to frustrate the Committee's activities. Nonetheless they cannot escape a measure of responsibility for the ban. One mid-day demonstration in March 1950 culminated in a disturbance and violence, and if the leaders were not the instigators they were not reluctant witnesses, despite their earlier warning to their supporters not to give a 'pretext or shadow of a chance to make us appear to the democratic world as blood-thirsty, lawless, race-hating mobs'.[35]

Whatever may have been their advice to their supporters, the PC leaders did not spare those sections of the Belize community that gave legitimacy to the colonial political system. The leaders opposed the traditional pattern of celebrating the Battle of St George's Cay which commemorated the victory against the Spanish invaders in 1798 and whose political significance to the Belizean Creoles, it will be recalled, had developed into a controversy during the 'Native First' campaign in the 1930s and 1940s. The annual celebration on 10 September was jointly sponsored by the Belize City Council and the Loyal and Patriotic Order of the Baymen, a Creole-dominated organization comprised mainly of ex-servicemen and pensioners who had an abiding faith in the country's British colonial connection. One of the traditional highlights of the celebration was the City Council President's Address of Loyalty to the imperial sovereign. The Governor would then reply in suitable terms with the expected promise of increased financial assistance from the British government. The new politicians now demanded that the Address be shorn of pleasantries and the 'usual nice-nicey loyalty stuff'.[36] They were too militant and popular not to claim that the traditional 'plea for development struck the type of subservient note long abandoned by the people of British Honduras'.[37]

To the City Fathers the suggestion that the Address 'be a clear, unmistakable, and honest declaration of the grievances of the people of British Honduras'[38] was treasonable. They could find little justification in the prevailing economic difficulties for a departure from the conventional Address and proceeded to observe the celebration in the usual manner. To demonstrate their anti-British feeling and their dissatisfaction with the official celebration, the PC held its own. The two celebrations have persisted, with the one having its origin in the nationalist movement becoming the official one in 1961.[39]

Because of the protracted ban on public meetings the PC relied heavily on its press campaign, and in this respect was singularly fortunate. It found a ready ally in the *Belize Billboard* whose managing and news editors were Goldson and Richardson respectively. The Committee was therefore spared the financial and organizational problem of establishing its own medium. The other services it rendered the PC and subsequently the PUP until the leadership split in the latter organization in 1956 were inestimable. It was in fact as much a party organ as a newspaper. The columns reported extensively the near-seditious speeches of the politicians, and in its editorials fanned the flames of discontent to such an extent that the indictment of Goldson and Richardson on charges of seditious intention in September 1950 and November 1951 had long been foreseen.

In fostering nationalist pride and sentiment, the PC did not rely solely on the denunciation of colonialism. It also took the positive step of introducing new symbols. At the suggestion of Richardson and Goldson the patriotic song 'Land of the Gods' written and composed by two Belizeans, Samuel Haynes and Dr Selwyn Young, who were living in the United States, was given pride of place as the Committee's main rallying song ('God Bless America' also being one) and it has been adopted by the ruling PUP as the proposed national anthem. The adoption of a blue flag with a white centre containing the coat of arms of the country as the movement's flag has since been attributed to Price who claims that it was the ancient flag of the settlement and also wishes it to be the national flag.

The major opposition party, the NIP, objected to a national adoption of the party's flag on several grounds. It viewed the adoption as an attempt to identify the nation with a single party. Perhaps more disturbing to the opposition was that it saw little that was distinctive and national in these colours which are also the national colours of Guatemala. On the contrary, the opposition party interpreted Price's dedication to them as a manifestation of his wish for a Central American destiny for the emerging nation. What became a source of disputes and still remains so was a source of unity among the leadership in 1950. All the leaders enthusiastically accepted the symbols in their attempt to destroy the psychologically crippling effects of the colonial system and to promote a national consciousness.

### Reaction to the Committee

Reaction to the PC came from various quarters and mainly in the form of opposition. A notable exception was the local business community whose reaction was mixed. Not unexpectedly, the merchants did not accept the PC's charge that they were the principal beneficiaries of the devaluation. Few admitted that they had raised the prices of their existing stock or foodstuffs. All of them pointed out that they were no longer free to import foodstuffs from the cheapest and most convenient source which was the United States. At the same time the merchants recognized that their interest could be best served by supporting the PC in its anti-colonial campaign. For within twelve days of the devaluation, the Governor suddenly ordered that price control be extended to practically everything sold in the shops. The order was to take effect within the next four days, by which time the merchants were to hand in to the government a list of their full stock on hand, complete with the imported costs. In this way, together with a series of subsidization measures which had been earlier announced, the Governor hoped to contain the rise in the cost of living. While the Chamber of Commerce had originally pledged to co-operate with the government's corrective measures, and in fact was represented on an advisory committee which the Governor had appointed to discuss such matters as price control, the merchants evidently did not bargain for a drastic extension of price control. In fact they contended that immediate wage increases throughout the colony rather than price control were the best way to offset the devaluation effects. Their solution to the problem was not the only respect in which they shared the sentiments of the People's Committee. Since the Governor had ignored the advisory committee, the merchants agreed that the measure was 'dictatorial, undemocratic, Stalinistic and Hitleristic' and expressed what the *Belize Billboard* regarded as their 'rightful indignation' that such 'totalitarian high handedness should be taking place in this enlightened democratic age'.[40] The Governor's measures had assured the PC of an ally, which the organization had few reservations about embracing. In the first place, as we pointed out, the Committee was neither left wing nor doctrinnaire but rather favourably predisposed to private enterprise. Furthermore as a nationalist movement bent on establishing its own legitimacy it characteristically drew its support from wherever this could be found.

The principal and most obvious opponent of the Committee was the colonial administration. This opposition was however a mixture of aggression and conciliation. No one expected the Governor and his officials to countenance the new political spectacle in silence. But although political meetings were banned, countering the campaign was not easy. In the first place the lack of legislative support for the devaluation measures had placed the Governor on the defensive. Furthermore his price control measures had lost him the confidence of a strategic socio-economic group, the merchants. In fact, evidently anxious to stem the alienation of the business community the Governor, acting on a resolution from the merchants, eventually postponed the extension of price control for two weeks, during which period he negotiated with them. Thirdly, the unimpressive record of the colonial administration was stark and naked. The Governor made little attempt to disprove the PC's charges of imperial neglect but implied in his conciliatory speeches[41] and correspondence to the Colonial Office that the public outcry was justified. In a covering despatch to his draft Development Plan in early 1950 the Governor stated

I have said in the Preface [of the plan] that it is a prime duty of the people of British Honduras to ask for more money...There are other considerations which should be taken into account, not the least of which is the unique position of the colony in relation to the Central American Republics. British Honduras is the shop window into which they gaze to see the product of British colonialism. What they see there should do Great Britain credit; what they find there should answer Guatemala's constant claim that the country in her hands could do better, and what they assimilate there should be the knowledge that our achievements are as high as our intentions.[42]

The British government responded immediately with a grant of over $2 million to be expended on roads, social services, agricultural development and building construction. But while the Governor claimed that no other country 'has given such substantial help to so relatively small a population in so short a time',[43] the PC leaders rejoined that 'the grant was too little and made available too late'.[44] In fact apart from the price subsidy to essential foodstuffs very little was actually done to alleviate the economic depression. The CDC programme on which most of the official hopes were pinned was destined to be a failure, its only significant accomplishment being the erection of the Fort George Hotel. So long as the economic crisis persisted the PC leaders had little difficulty in embarrassing the government.

It was not only in his reference to Guatemala in his despatch to his superiors that the Governor indicated that financial assistance was being governed by political considerations. He also made this clear in his reply to the Presidential Address commemorating the Battle of St George's Cay:

It is because of this programme of development which has been approved that I have greater confidence in the future today than I had when I spoke to you last year. I know that there will be plenty of people who will tell you that I am talking glibly and that all I wish to do is to lull you to sleep with sweet words. But facts are facts: and I ask you to remember what I have said to you today when people try to persuade you that Great Britain does nothing to help British Honduras in its present difficulties and incite you to disloyalty – to insult the Union Jack which stands for British justice and fair play and to refuse to sing God Save the King which stands for loyalty to King and country.[45]

The proposed visit of Princess Alice was obviously intended to be part of the political response. But, as we shall see, much more than a royal visit was necessary to stem the nationalist tide. Had the visit materialized it would only have served to steel the resolve of the loyal element within the local population. The stress and strain within the society was in fact revealed more by the criticisms of various sections of the local population than by the administration's reaction to the movement. Because of their anti-British attitude the nationalist leaders received little support among those inhabitants of United Kingdom origin and the local whites. The most vocal opposition to the growing anti-British sentiments came, however, from the better-off Creoles who felt a kindred spirit with the British. Many recalled with pride their Scottish or English (and West Indian) ancestry,[46] and would have challenged Governor Burns' claim that 'the people as a whole are more American than British in their outlook'. It was their British outlook that lent them distinction and tradition in a country with a sizeable Latin population, hemmed in by Latin American republics. It was not surprising therefore that they resented the Committee's attempt 'to discredit British prestige and to alienate the affections of the people from the British way of life'.[47]

That the attempt was being made by a Catholic-dominated organization added to their apprehension. They 'noticed the decided one-sidedness of the membership of the People's Committee',[48] and believed the Committee's real motive to be the promotion of Catholic and Latin interests. They contended for example, that the Committee's opposition to federation was motivated by a 'genuine fear that the predominance of the Catholics and the growing spectre of Latin influence will be threatened by the Protestant and non-Latin British West Indies'. This was at least one conclusion that they drew from Price's persistent claim that 'the country's way of life was interdependent with Central America'.

The opposition did not hesitate to charge the American Jesuits with complicity. A critic who identified himself as 'Protestant', in a letter to

*The Daily Clarion*, accused the Committee leaders of being 'the tools of a sinister organization in our midst which is exerting every effort to create anti-British sentiments in the colony'.[49] In a more pointed reference to the Catholic Church in general and the Jesuits in particular he stated, 'The fullest freedom is enjoyed under the British flag and this is anathema to the masters of the Billboard and the People's Committee. The cry of Communism is raised time and again but the other totalitarianism is the greater of the two evils.'[50] In the next issue of the paper Price refuted the charge and claimed that 'Protestant' was 'protesting against imaginary creatures of his sinister imagination'.[51] But because he was more than any other leader identified with the Jesuits, having studied for the priesthood and being in close contact with the priests, Price's retort had the effect of confirming the belief. His 'anxiety to answer' was interpreted as 'a betrayal of his stricken conscience'.[52]

While the Catholic Church did not openly identify itself with the PC, its racial composition and the activities of some of its organizations, particularly the Catholic Social Action and the St John's Alumni Association, encouraged the belief that if the Jesuits did not foster the Committee's anti-British campaign and Price's Latin aspirations they at least welcomed them. As we have seen, the church's pastoral activities were mainly among the Mestizos and Indians who lacked the cultural characteristics valued in the colonial society. Through its identity with the Mestizo complex the prestige of the Roman Catholic Church suffered. When the entrenched position of Roman Catholicism in the neighbouring republics was added to these considerations of prestige and cultural composition, it was not unnatural for the Jesuits to believe that the future of their denomination would be more assured in a Central American than in a West Indian environment. Their Secondary boys' school, St John's College, had attracted students from Guatemala, El Salvador, Nicaragua, Honduras and Merida in Mexico, and it is probably not without political significance that in 1952 the present campus was named after a Guatemalan poet, Rafael Landivar, SJ. The Jesuits did not welcome the participation of Belize in the University College of the West Indies which was established in 1948, and when in the following year a visiting lecturer to the University, Professor Robert Peers of Nottingham University, advocated birth control as a solution to the population density in the Caribbean the University fell into complete disfavour. The Superior of the Jesuit Mission, Father John Knopp, took the unusual step of advertising his sermon in which he accused the University of introducing a 'new order'. Observing that 'secularism has set foot on the shores of the colony', he stated that 'the years will prove whether we are equal to the task of maintaining the pattern of life which has hitherto been our pride, our privilege and our saving grace'.[53]

The similarity of views between the Jesuits and the PC leaders on the country's attitude to Central America and the West Indies was no coincidence as far as the opposition was concerned. It contended that the Jesuits had been promulgating these ideas 'before devaluation',[54] and pointed to the activities of the Catholic Social Action and the St John's Alumni Association in the 1940s. More specifically it recalled the claim by the President of the Association, Edgar Gegg, in 1947 that Catholics were best qualified to assume the political leadership of the country and that the immigration laws were not sufficiently restrictive.[55] Indeed, Gegg had openly identified himself with the PC as a member of at least one of the Committee's deputations to the Governor.

The critics of the Committee, recognizing the close relationship between federation and immigration, now began to interpret such references to the immigration laws in racial as well as cultural and religious terms. In an exchange of press correspondence a 'Creole' reprimanded the 'Loyalists' for saying that 'Mr Price and the People's Committee aim at self-government. Has he not heard them say that we are not West Indians but Central Americans?...In short, they do not want in the colony any more "Creoles" (meaning black and coloured British subjects) who it seems in their opinion are interlopers...and hence Mr Price's objection to the celebration of our Day.' In an obvious reference to the Creole members of the Committee he ended his letter, 'It is a pity that so many Creoles (including the Editor of the Belize Billboard) are so myopic as not to see what is staring us in the face.'[56]

While the claim that the Jesuits were the political leaders' mentor should not be discounted, it does not adequately explain the growing prominence of Catholics in the country's political life. This was also the consequence of the Church's increasing numerical strength and the educational opportunities which St John's College offered. In 1946, 59.5 per cent of the population were Catholics, 21.0 per cent Anglicans and 14.3 per cent Methodists,[57] and of the five secondary schools (all denominational) two were Catholic. Of the 273 secondary school boys[58] in 1946, 54.5 per cent[59] were attending St John's College. This high proportion of Catholic students was bound to be reflected sooner or later in the political field. With the exception of Harrison Courtenay who was the leader of the National Party from 1951 to 1953, the leaders of the five political parties formed between 1950 and 1961 were Catholics and three of them, Price, Pollard and Herbert Fuller, alumni of St John's College.

In so far as religion was a factor in the political process there was greater group solidarity among the Catholics than the Protestants. The opposition was in fact not organized, its criticisms being largely the result of individual personal efforts. The slowness of the critics to appreciate the value of concerted action was however more indicative of their social experience than their religious beliefs. Not only were they predominantly Creole and Protestant, but for the most part lawyers, retired civil servants and teachers oriented towards personal achievements. The political system also encouraged this orientation. Although the electoral candidate may have been sponsored by a political group in the 1930s and 1940s he was, like colonial politicians elsewhere, judged by his personal influence and debating skill rather than by his policy.

This lack of collective action reduced the impact of the opposition. Nor was its only medium, *The Daily Clarion*, an asset. The paper's political stand was at best ambivalent as it strove to be neutral while obviously sympathetic to the opposition. One of its critics was even less charitable in his opinion. He wrote,

One of your correspondents maintained that decent newspapers give the news and offer both sides of any question, reserving the personal opinion for editorials. This of course is the old fashioned concept of a decent newspaper. Today the efforts of all progressive newspapers are bent on moulding Public Opinion and such a trend is seen throughout its pages – in articles, letters, as well as editorials. But your paper lacks even a personal opinion of the editor.[60]

Above all, the opposition was unable to attract working-class support because it did not identify with the social and economic problems of this group. These disabilities were too pressing not to impinge upon racial, religious and cultural considerations, and it is therefore not surprising that the working class tended to support the People's Committee.

*The dissolution of the People's Committee*

Formed in response to a specific event the PC was organizationally ill-equipped to consolidate its gains. It was mainly to correct this deficiency that about this time in other colonial territories congresses were giving way to political parties. As Hodgkin observed of Africa, 'A new generation of post-war politicians was emerging who had studied the techniques of modern party organization in Europe and the USA, and were dissatisfied with what seemed to be the old fashioned agitational methods.'[61] It is significant that the first open suggestion for a political party came from Richardson who had been on a Colonial Office sponsored course in the United Kingdom when the political upheaval began. Writing to his newspaper a few weeks before returning home in August

1950, he stated, 'The day of the Battlefield meeting is past. Proper political machinery must be set up and paid for. . .It is a sad commentary that no responsible body in British Honduras has so far issued a programme reflecting British Honduras' political and economic expectations.'[62]

Some of the PC critics also recognized the organizational defects and questioned the leaders' claim to universalism and to be speaking on behalf of the whole country. More specifically, Kemp, who gradually became disenchanted with the PC because of Price's personal ascendancy within it and the party's intolerance with, and extreme reaction to, Broaster's opposition to the Committee's pro-American sentiments, openly reproached the Committee of being undemocratically constituted. 'What had appeared as a hasty combination to arrange for protest meetings and demonstrations of protest against devaluation is now used as a medium to foist a perpetual standing People's Committee on the people of the Colony', he said. 'It is time', he continued, 'for the People's committee to cease foisting itself as a Committee of the people, if the leaders are not prepared to let the people select a People's Committee when one is needed.'[63] The formation of a political party seemed to be the most effective answer to the criticism.

The local consitutional commission which was set up in 1948 also had a precipitant influence on the formation of a party. A more internally structured organization was necessary to exploit any real opportunities of political power which the commission might offer. If these opportunities were not forthcoming then the party would be more justified. As the *Belize Billboard* pointed out, the agitation for further constitutional advance would then be intensified, and this 'demands a united national front, a national party supported in ideology and with finance by the citizens of the country'.[64] Finally, the leaders considered a political party necessary to acquire control of municipal affairs, and the imminence of the Belize Town Board elections in November 1950 most likely hastened the birth of the People's United Party.[65]

On 29 September 1950, the PUP replaced the PC. Smith was elected Leader, Richardson, who had a few weeks earlier returned from Britain, became the Chairman, Price was the Secretary and Goldson the Assistant Secretary. Although the PC had enjoyed a brief existence it had dramatically brought to thousands in Belize City, if not in other parts of the colony, a new awareness of their political environment. No longer could it be claimed that 'Politics was still the business of the few.'[66] But it was precisely because of the changing situation, in particular the opening of the political process to a cross-section of the population, that the established professional middle-class Creoles were upset. After all, as a social group they had been attracted to politics because it contributed to the rigidity of the system of social stratification. Put differently, they had entered politics to advance their overall social class and status within the society. The business component of the Belize elite which historically dominated the political process was much more flexible or accommodating in its response to the political change. Members of the group had entered politics not for its prestige but because it served their economic interests. As we have seen, the rise of the People's Committee did not place their interest in jeopardy. On the contrary, the PC's views on the desirability of a private enterprise economy and the need to promote closer economic ties with the USA were in harmony with those of the Belize businessmen.

As we observed at the beginning of this section the normal process of decolonization was however not free of complications. It had accentuated the problem of the country's future external orientation. The differing pulls of possible Latin American association and union with the West Indies and the British Commonwealth were symptomatic of the racial, cultural and religious cleavages within the society. Significantly, the differing orientations did not only exist between the PC and its opponents. It also existed within the leadership of the Committee, but remained latent and perhaps also unrecognized or unacknowledged. With the possible exception of Price, none of the PC leaders seemed to have entered politics with a clear and precise conception of the country's future relationship with the Central American republics. Nor was this conception necessary once the leaders were preoccupied with attacking the colonial system and gaining political power. How different and divisive were their views became evident when their eventual accommodation in the colonial political system forced them to rely upon their own internal resources for unity and to define more precisely their personal attitudes towards Britain, the West Indies and Central America.

# 5
# Political conflict: scope and dimensions

An agreement on political goals between the PUP and the local groups opposed to it was prejudiced even before the latter organized into political parties. Little mutual tolerance was possible once the devaluation issue had been transformed into a conflict over the nature of the society and its future external orientation. Moreover, like the PUP, the opposition parties were the outcome of crises that were associated in one way or another with the basic conflict. Neither these opposition parties nor the PUP showed any desire to overcome the circumstances of their origin until the colonial government, which remained deeply involved as an opponent of the PUP, brought the conflict to a head by removing the PUP leader, Price, from the government for consorting with a Guatemalan Minister during an official visit to London. The scope and dimensions of the conflict will be analysed in this chapter, while its climax and resolution will be the subject of the next chapter.

## The protagonists

The PUP lost no time in establishing a strong internal organization, cementing its relationship with the GWU and preparing for the municipal election in Belize City. The party was to be governed at various levels. There were to be district executive committees controlled by a central executive committee which in turn was under the supreme authority of the annual convention of delegates appointed by members throughout the country.[1] Although the district executive committees were formed, the PUP continued to look to the GWU to perform the organizational task in the outdistricts, especially when Pollard became the full-time President and organizer of the latter organization in July 1950.[2]

Within two days of its inauguration and before any other political aspirant, the PUP announced the names of six candidates to contest the nine seats in the City Council elections in November.[3] The principal leaders, Price, Goldson, Richardson and Smith, were among the party nominees, the other two being Henry Middleton, Secretary of the GWU,

146

and Cammy Gabb, a member of the party's central executive. With the exception of Middleton, the party candidates were elected, and this gave the party a majority in the Council. The significance of the party's victory did not lie so much in the number of seats won, but in the fact that the party polled 48.7 per cent[4] of the votes under a restricted and privileged income, tenancy and property franchise that was more advantageous to the middle-class Creole professional and business groups that had dominated the Council for decades.

Yet the four representatives of this social class in the City Council, E. O. B. Barrow, a retired District Commissioner, Herbert Fuller, a commission agent and former president of the City Council, Lionel Francis, a university graduate and leader of the Universal Negro Improvement Association, and L. Bracket, a retired primary school headmaster, worked to deny the PUP councillors their legitimacy. The City Council had functioned for forty-six years without its walls being decorated with the portrait of a British monarch or the subject being broached. On July 10 1951 which was within a year of the PUP victory, and about the time of the beginning of the preparation for the annual celebration of the Battle of St George's Cay in September, the opposition councillors moved a resolution to hang the King's portrait in City Hall.[5] This placed the PUP councillors in a dilemma. To support the motion was to invite discredit in the eyes of their followers and the accusation that they had ceased to be uncompromising in their anti-British stand. On the other hand, outright rejection of the motion would have provided the anti-PUP elements with the excuse for seeking a dissolution of the Council. In an attempt to escape the trap the PUP councillors, being in a majority, successfully put forward an amendment that the résolution be not considered until their various requests for economic and political reforms were met.[6]

As far as the opposition was concerned the PUP councillors' decision to shelve the issue was adequate grounds for getting rid of them. Furthermore the PUP councillors had within a week of this incident moved a motion to omit the customary address of loyalty to the King from the Battle of St George's Cay celebration. Accordingly, H. W. Beaumont, a retired Colonial Postmaster, organized a petition in July 1951 urging the Governor to dissolve the Council.[7] Since the Legislative Council was drawn from the same social group of Creoles the petition was assured of parliamentary approval.[8] To complete compliance with the petitioner's request, the Governor restored the middle-class Creoles to their former position by establishing an interim City Council under the Presidency of Arthur Wolffsohn, the retired Colonial Secretary.[9]

Whether they believed that the PUP would be ephemeral or felt secure in their close relationship with the colonial administration, the anti-PUP groups did not coalesce into a political party, the National Party (NP), until they had manoeuvred the PUP into a conflict with the Governor. Except for its urban orientation the NP which was formed in late August 1951[10] had little in common with the PUP. Its social composition, organizational structure and relationship with its followers were different. The leaders were more full-blooded Creoles and belonged to an earlier generation that was socially and professionally well established in Belize City. Harrison Courtenay, who held several government offices, was the leader. In addition to being a Legislative and Executive Councillor he was also the country's representative to the University College of the West Indies. As we observed in an earlier chapter, he was also one of the two delegates of the Legislative Council to the British Caribbean Standing Closer Association Committee. In December 1949, on the eve of the political outburst, he had succeeded the Attorney General, Harold J. Hughes, who had fallen ill and had retired to Britain, as Chairman of the Commission of Inquiry on Constitutional Reform, which reported in 1952.[11] One of the vice-presidents was Herbert Fuller who, in addition to being a Legislative Councillor, and a member and former President of the City Council, had served on the constitutional commission. H. W. Beaumont and Mrs V. Seay, MBE, a matron, leader of the Black Cross and a recently appointed member of the interim City Council, were the other vice-presidents. L. A. Francis and E. O. B. Barrow were the Chairman and Secretary respectively, while Volunteer Force Captain M. S. Metzgen, OBE, a retired internal revenue officer and President of the Loyal and Patriotic Order of the Baymen, was the Treasurer.[12]

Perhaps these Creole leaders were tardy in forming a political party because the Courtenay Commission had already safeguarded the old structure of political influence. In addition to Courtenay and Fuller, the Commission consisted of three other local officials: C. M. Staine, a nominated member of the Legislative Council, Karl Wade, a university graduate, an elected member of the Legislative Council and at the time of his appointment in 1948, President of the Belize City Council, and James Waight, a government surveyor. The Commission set the tone of its recommendations in its historical survey of political and constitutional development. It lauded the country's British colonial institutions which it urged should not be too readily discarded.[13]

When it is recalled that the Chairman of the Commission, Harrison Courtenay, was an outstanding critic of the colonial government and had initiated the demand for constitutional reform in 1947, the cautious sentiments of the Commission seem strange. But the situation was changing and it was against the emergent group of nationalist politicians rather than the colonial oligarchy that the old Creole elite had to safeguard its influence. The Commission, therefore, had no compunction in advancing the well-known imperial argument that self-government was not necessarily an acceptable substitute for good government. Predictably, the Commission essayed that for there to be good government, 'Reliance must be placed on the general good sense of those who are in advance of the majority in political understanding.'[14]

The Commission was not only concerned with devising a constitution to the advantage of the old Creole-educated elite. It was equally concerned in the constitution-making process with the implications of the Latin orientation of some of the PUP leaders for the Creoles as a cultural group. It claimed that the colony was enjoying a 'stable government', 'tranquillity', 'rule of law', 'a just administration' and an 'upright judiciary'. The claim was more an argument against a rapid pace of decolonization or, as the Commission put it, 'the premature extension of political responsibility. . . as in other Colonies'.[15] Implicit in the claim was the comparison between the social and political institutions in Belize and the Central American republics. The Commission was also suggesting that the political culture of the Creoles was likely to be undermined in the event of a Latin ascendancy during the process of decolonization. It went to some length to point out that illiteracy was highest among the Latin peasantry and that their political organizations were rudimentary and different from those of the Creoles.[16] The conditions, the Commission concluded, were

sufficient to show the need for caution in planning constitutional advance. It should be clear that the advance in general and political education has not been uniform among all the races which comprise the Colony's population, and that the lack of balance arising from the long lead which the largest group [the Creoles] enjoys over the minorities calls for the establishment of a system which, while meeting the legitimate aspirations of the one does no violence to the interests of the other.[17]

Against this analysis of the overall motives of the Commission the specific proposals and their intended impact upon the struggle for power between the old elite and emergent nationalist politicians can be discussed. The new Legislative Council was to be composed of fifteen unofficial members as against three official members and a non-voting President who was either a member or someone outside the Council. Four of the fifteen unofficial members were to be nominated and the other eleven were to be elected.[18] The Belize District was to elect three members, and each of the other five districts, Orange Walk, Corozal, Stann Creek, Cayo, and Toledo, was to elect one. These five districts were also to be combined into one constituency to elect three legislators for the colony as a whole. Designed to perpetuate the old structure of political influence, the Commission also proposed that the Creole electorate in the Belize District and the predominantly Mestizo and Indian population in the other districts were to elect their representatives in differing manners.[19] Adult suffrage was to be applied to the whole country, but only the three constituencies – two urban and one rural – in the Belize District were to exercise a direct franchise.[20] Each of the other five districts was to elect this representative by an Electoral College comprised of the members of the District Town Board and the village councils. The members of these local authorities were, however, to be elected by a direct vote.[21]

The Commission claimed that the purpose of this two-stage process of district representation was to make the local political institutions pivotal to the working of the overall political process. Indeed, the Commission held tenaciously to the British political notion of the role and purpose of local government:

We attach the greatest importance to the development of efficient organs of local government. A sound and democratic system of local government is, in our opinion, the best foundation on which to build a solid democratic central structure. If local government is democratic and we can through it ensure that that the principles of democracy are cherished, we need have little fear that its principles will not be cherished at the centre also. Furthermore, it is through local government that the widest possible opportunities will be provided for the majority of the people to make their contribution to the common weal by active participation in the processes of government.[22]

But the real aim of the proposal was not to raise local horizons beyond the village and the town or even to lay the foundation for a nationally integrated local government system that would be a training ground for national leaders as the Anglo-Saxon notion of local government purports to achieve.[23] Rather the election of the district representatives in two stages was an attempt to minimize the impact of the PUP leaders on the rural population. Moreover, in so far as it encouraged parochialism, the indirect franchise was likely to produce diffident Mestizo and Indian representatives who would be prepared to rely 'on the general good sense of those who are in advance of the majority in their political understanding'.

Much more ingenious was the provision for three additional members of the Legislature to be elected by the direct vote of all the outdistrict voters. While the Belize District was excluded, the proposal favoured the politicians who were national figures, and therefore the urban-based Creoles, since none of the outdistricts had produced such leaders. The Commission was, however, not satisfied with these safeguards. It was required by its terms of reference to report on the qualifications for registration of voters, since the 1947 parliamentary delegation to the Colonial Office which, it must be constantly remembered, was led by Harrison Courtenay, had strongly urged the introduction of universal adult suffrage without a literacy qualification.[24] While the Commission recommended adult suffrage, it retained the literacy qualification. Furthermore it transformed the qualification into a test in order to 'minimise the inherent dangers of a wide and too rapid extension of the franchise before the development of that full sense of political responsibility, which is the only true bulwark against the charlatan and the demagogue'.[25] The voter was required not only to sign but also to fill the registration form in the presence of the registration officer or the Justice of the Peace. As the Commission admitted, it expected that only those illiterates who were 'possessed...of character and interest' would 'take the trouble of learning from a copy to fill out his claim form for registration'.[26] It was only of this type of citizen that 'any country can be proud, and he would justly earn and deserve the vote. To insist on less than we have recommended is to ignore the lessons to be learnt from the countries around, to risk similar disastrous experiences and make a mockery of the ballot box.'[27]

Still fearing that the Latin peasantry would be suborned by the nationalist politicians the Commission safeguarded the influence of the Creole elite by reconstituting the Executive Council.[28] This Council was to consist of four ex-officio members, including the Governor as Chairman, two nominated and four elected unofficial members of the Legislative Council elected by this body as a whole. This placed the four ex-officio members and the two nominated unofficial members from the Legislative Council in the majority. The Commission also proposed that members of the Executive Council be given the opportunity to participate in the work of government as quasi-ministers. This proposal was intended to transfer the executive government, at any rate as far as it concerned domestic affairs, from the Governor to the Executive Council which was to be responsible to the Legislative Council. But the Commission immediately nullified this recommendation by leaving the Governor's reserve power virtually intact[29] although its Chairman had crusaded during the 1940s for the abolition of this power. Altogether, the constitutional provisions constituted a standstill policy which imputed a second-class status to the outdistricts and the unlettered population. This policy was to last for five years, as the Commission was of the opinion that this was the minimum period in which its gratuitous recommendation could be tested.[30]

One begins to understand why the NP was organizationally ill-designed to close the gap between its leaders and the ordinary people and between the urban and the outdistrict communities. The party made little pretence to effective organization even in Belize City. The enlisting of members was usually associated with a political crisis or an election, national or municipal, after which the party organization reverted to relative inactivity. This fitful method of recruitment produced a rather uninspired kind of participation in the party's activities which was in marked contrast with the PUP.[31]

In the outdistricts where the party organization was virtually non-existent the NP leaders relied mainly upon infrequent coverage by *The Daily Clarion* and the *Belize Independent* for its communication with the rural population. Apart from the inability of the vast majority of the Latin peasantry to buy or read newspapers,[32] this method of communication was less effective than the face-to-face campaign which the GWU district organizers carried out on behalf of the PUP.[33]

For two reasons it is hardly likely that the British government would have placed the constitution-making process in local hands had it foreseen the political ferment. First, the idea of constitutional reform had taken five years from the time it was initially mooted until the time it was transformed into a firm proposal. Second, since the Commission had been instructed by the terms of reference to report to the Governor, the latter felt obliged to refer the report to a Select Committee of Unofficial Members of the Legislative Council.[34] The establishment of the Select Committee entailed further delay without the prospect of this body recommending fundamental changes since the unofficial members were for the most part the Creole elite with an interest in maintaining the *status quo*.

The Committee's most noteworthy modification was the elimination of the literacy test in the general election and the retention of the income and property franchise for municipal elections.[35] For once the chairman of the Commission was made to appear as a liberal. Harrison Courtenay, in the parliamentary debate, argued that there was no logic and little wisdom in granting universal adult suffrage in the case of the national government and depriving those who were managing the towns of that privilege.[36] In July 1952, more than a year after the Courtenay constitutional committee had reported, the Legislative Council approved the modified proposals.

Most of the Commission's proposals probably carried little weight with the British government. Although there was a precedent in other colonies[37] for a mixed voting system, the British government was generally prejudiced in favour of an undifferentiated system so long as there were no traditional institutions, such as chieftancy, and British settler interest to protect. Although the District Commissioner system existed the British government did not think that control of the Indians required a special method of colonial administration beyond the Alcalde system, which was essentially Spanish in origin.[38] The District Commissioner system was, however, free of the assumptions of indirect rule and therefore the entire issue of representation did not pose a problem of constitutional change for the British government. Thus the Colonial Office rejected the proposal that the district representatives should be elected by electoral colleges, which was indeed a variant of indirect rule, and ordered the extension of the direct vote to these constituencies.[39] Nor did it accept the proposal for the voter to complete his registration form in the presence of the registration officer or a Justice of the Peace. The British government also put an end to the existing income and property qualifications for membership of the Legislative Council, thereby making every voter eligible for this high office. It did not uphold the proposed distinction between representatives elected by the constituencies and those elected for the colony as a whole. The Legislative Council was to consist of three official members, nine instead of eleven elected members, three as against four nominated members, and an appointed Speaker from outside to preside over it. Its life was reduced from five to the existing three years. The Colonial Office also stated that the proposal to make the Executive Council responsible to the Legislative Council was premature. It expressed a similar view on another proposal to have the Legislative Council elect the leader of the Executive Council. In short there was not to be even the semblance of doubt that the Governor's powers were unqualified. These changes were announced in January 1953,[40] almost two years after the Courtenay Commission had completed its report and, as the Colonial Office estimated, the revised constitution would take another year before it could be implemented.[41]

The changes relating to the franchise and representation favoured the PUP. But these modifications should not be mistaken as a gift from the British government. In the first place they were largely the product of sustained PUP pressure. The party's Leader, Smith, had opposed the original proposals in the Legislative Council.[42] He had also taken opportunity of his visit to the Festival of Britain in July 1951, as one of the Legislative Council representatives, to present to the Colonial Office a petition for a more advanced constitution.[43] A nation-wide strike called in October 1952 by the GWU and in which the manual government employees participated was the high point of the PUP counter-pressure on the colonial government.[44] Indeed, the strike demonstrated that the attempt to stifle the ascendancy of the PUP required much more than the establishment of a buffer electoral institution.

Secondly, the constitutional modification could not have been a gift, since the NP's negligible influence had thrown the burden of opposing the PUP onto the colonial administration. The defensive attitude which the Governor had adopted in the first few months of the political ferment in 1950 gave way to an offensive and belligerent approach. Government pressure was exerted upon the two PUP allies, the GWU and the *Belize Billboard*, to alter their relationship with the party. In October 1950, government communiques and advertisements were withheld from the newspaper.[45] The boycott did not only deny the *Belize Billboard* access to reliable information but dealt it a serious financial blow.[46] The government also denied the *Belize Billboard* the services of both its editors, Richardson and Goldson, when they were sentenced to imprisonment for eighteen months on charges of sedition against the Governor in 1951.[47] It also attempted to discourage the GWU from supporting the party. In a letter to the GWU, it discredited the PUP leaders as demogogues interested in their 'own personal and political ambitions... and as tools in the hands of aliens, who, for their own purposes wish to embarrass the British government and to perpetuate a state of discontentment'.[48] The situation, the letter concluded, could only steel the employers in their opposition to labour. This attitude in fact was particularly true in the case of the BEC which continued to deny the workers in its lumber camps the right to join the GWU and placed all kinds of obstacles to the entry of union officials into its veritable domain. In other words, the British government's message to the union was clear and straightforward. If the latter needed to contract a marriage, as its President, Pollard, claimed in 1950, then it was incorrect of the union to conclude that it had 'seen no other possible suitor eligible for such a marriage, except the PUP and the *Belize Billboard*'.[49] There was also the BEC which offered greater prospects as a partner.

This reaction was typical of colonial administrations. As B. C. Roberts has observed about the relationship between trade unions and politics during colonial rule,

Unions have been counselled against forming too close an attachment to political parties [because] this has made their acceptance and recognition by employers more difficult. It is hard enough in any circumstances to persuade employers, who have been used to determining conditions of employment without interference to accept willingly an obligation to bargain with a newly developed union. If the union is also engaged in making a political attack on the employer's position in the territory, the hostility it arouses is an additional handicap to its recognition.[50]

He might also have added that the employer becomes more obdurate when he has a close relationship with the colonial administration.

The government, however, reserved most of its offensive for the PUP and employed an array of strategy. In the first place it attempted to exploit the latent divisions within the PUP leadership. Smith's decision to attend the Festival of Britain in 1951 suggested that the difference still existed between Price and himself over the attitude to be adopted towards Britain which was revealed during the abortive visit of Princess Alice in 1950. Whether or not his decision was endorsed by the party, it was inconsistent with the party's avowed anti-British stand. Significantly, it was during Smith's absence that the opposition in the City Council had tested the PUP leaders' loyalty to the British Crown. Smith, who had been the President of the City Council, was the only PUP councillor to whom the Governor offered a seat on the interim council. This was done with indecent haste since the announcement was made while Smith was in transit from London and presumably before he had been consulted. Although Smith publicly spurned the offer on his arrival in Belize in August 1951 by calling for 'an election now'[51] the entire episode had obviously driven a further wedge between the PUP leaders. For within four months of his return Smith resigned from the party over the party's attitude towards Guatemala and Britain. The party had been accused of receiving assistance from Guatemala and he claimed that it made no attempt to disprove the allegation. He unequivocally indicated his preference for a more amicable relationship with Britain and the Commonwealth by adding that the party ought to have flown the British flag along with the party's Blue and White at public meetings in order 'to establish what should be our true identity'.[52]

The relationship between the PUP and Guatemala was the main issue responsible for the government's opposition to the PUP. After all, even if the rise of the nationalist movement had caught the British government unaware, it was not unique in the colonial world. Perhaps the PUP's relationship with Guatemala would not have caused the British government too much apprehension but for the fact that the latter country claimed Belize as its territory and its government became increasingly attractive to left-wing elements after Colonel Jacobo Arbenz became the President in 1951 and expropriated the United Fruit Company lands in 1952.[53] Apart from its own policy to lead Belize to independence within the Commonwealth, the British government was most likely, under pressure from the expatriate economic interests in Belize and the United States, in which the anti-communist wave of hysteria was high,[54] to prevent the spread of Guatemala's communist influence to the territory. The existence of a Guatemala consulate in Belize City added to the British government's resolve to take the relationship between the PUP leaders and Guatemala seriously. In 1949 the Governor had accused the Guatemala consul of complicity in the local distribution of the anti-British leaflet *A Downright Shame* that had been published in Guatemala, although he conceded that his accusation was not supported by definite proof.[55]

A more effective British counter-intelligence presence was obviously needed in Belize. This was acknowledged in the recruitment of Commander John Proud from Britain as the country's first Public Relations Officer in September 1951 and later as Director of Telecommunications and Chief Information Officer.[56] The colonial administration had long needed a Public Relations Officer. *The Daily Clarion*, although favourably predisposed to the colonial administration, was unsuited to the task of making the government measures palpably acceptable to the people. Proud therefore immediately launched a monthly official newspaper, *The British Honduran*, which in addition to advancing official policies took issue with the PUP leaders on their positive orientation toward Central America in general and Guatemala in particular. That Proud was less concerned with the PUP anti-colonial stand than with its relationship with Guatemala was obvious in one of his frequent letters to the press: 'Many of the objectives of the original programme of the People's United Party would commend themselves to a large number of people in the Colony, but the association of the leaders with Guatemala can do nothing else but create a feeling of mistrust in their ultimate objectives.'[57] He accused Price of 'lending himself to a foreign power' and argued that independence could only mean economic absorption by Guatemala.[58] Proud also confirmed that the British concern for the fate of Belize was compounded by the pro-Communist government in Guatemala. He deemed the Guatemala government's treatment of the United Fruit Company as 'suicidal'.[59]

The PUP leaders did not share this view of Guatemala. Goldson, who was a guest of the Newspaper Association in Guatemala in 1951, was impressed with the country. In a famous article, 'Seven Days of Freedom', he described conditions in that country in a way that was calculated to earn the envy of Belizeans.[60] Price rejected Proud's assumption that an independent Belize would be too small to prevent economic and political absorption by Guatemala.[61] In any case he did not see the need for the concern. For one thing he had supreme confidence in the United Nations' capacity and willingness to guarantee the independence of new nations.[62] For another, Price could also have reasonably argued that the country would look to Britain for protection since the party had adopted (though somewhat airily) at its first annual convention, a policy of self-government within the Commonwealth.[63] At the same time, however, Price envisioned a relationship between Belize and the Central American republics which if it did not necessarily entail the country's economic and political incorporation by Guatemala would certainly have called into question the right of the British government to intervene, or at least its wisdom in doing so, in the case of such eventuality. In a message to the PUP supporters on what the party called the National Day (celebration of the Battle of St George's Cay) on 10 September 1952, Price had said:

In your very backyards, you can see a new confederation of nations rising potentially great, rich and powerful. By geography you belong to it. By trade and commerce, your future prosperity depends on it. By culture and way of life, you can have a great share in endowing it. This confederation of democratic nations that will be fast becoming an influential sphere of world politics under the United Nations is the Confederation of Central American Countries.

You are working and suffering and sacrificing your energies for the just cause of asserting and attaining your rights under God, which no individual or collectivity or state can take away from you.[64]

Price's clear ideas about the country's relationship with Central America, coupled with his view that the 'so called Guatemalan dispute' was a matter between Guatemala and Britain,[65] encouraged the colonial administration to accuse him of wide-ranging affiliations with Guatemala.

These accusations were hurled with varying degrees of intensity for nearly four years before the British government decided to undertake a judicial enquiry. It appointed Sir Reginald Sharpe, a British lawyer, 'to investigate and report upon allegations brought to his notice by the Government of British Honduras of contacts between the People's United Party or its members on the one hand, and authorities, organizations or persons in Guatemala or their representatives in British Honduras on the other hand'.[66] The investigation was by no means solely a response to the growing concern over the activities of the PUP. After all, the charges against the PUP were expected to be more frantic and the cries louder around the time the Commissioner was appointed because the national election under the new constitution was to be held the following month, April 1954. Furthermore, if the British government was concerned with these charges alone, Smith's resignation in 1951, and his accompanying disclosures about the PUP's relationship with Guatemala, would have been a more propitious moment to carry out the investigation. What undoubtedly did have a strong bearing on this seemingly late investigation was the British government's experience with the leftist government of the People's Progressive Party (PPP) in Guyana in 1953. The British had revoked the constitution of that colony on the grounds that the PPP was Marxist.[67] Given the possibility of ideological contamination of the PUP leaders in their alleged contacts with Guatemala, the British government was prepared to risk the charge of intervening prematurely in the party affairs. In this connection the holding of the enquiry one month before the general election was not simply a desperate attempt to undermine the PUP's electoral prospects. It was rather inspired by the British government's accepting a PUP victory as a distinct possibility. Moreover, since this basic problem had already led to the resignation in 1951 of the party leader, Smith, its exploitation offered the colonial administration its only real hope of further dividing the PUP leaders in the post-election period.

It could be argued that the enquiry was not only predicated on a possible PUP victory but also made it virtually certain. The claim that the party was linked with the communists in Guatemala, which Governor Renison openly voiced to the press in London[68] on the eve of the enquiry, provided the PUP leaders with the excuse to identify themselves with their Jesuit sympathizers as part of their rebuttal of the specific allegation and also to claim that their election programme was based on the principles of social justice. To the colonial administration this was no less discomforting than the PUP relationship with Guatemala. For its charge that the PUP leaders 'are tools in the hands of aliens' was perhaps more a reference to the influence which the Jesuits exerted on the PUP leaders than to the activities of Guatemala. With confidence bordering on derision the PUP leaders not only welcomed the investigation along these lines but suggested in a letter to the Colonial Secretary that the now discredited Senator McCarthy would be a more suitable investigator than the British jurist.[69]

One of the preliminary but significant observations made by Sir Reginald Sharpe was that the allegations were at no time formulated before him in any precise form by the Attorney General. It was therefore left to him to put forward the following as a fair statement of the allegations:

(1) That early in 1950 George Price, the Secretary of the People's United Party, was sending to the Guatemalan Consul in Belize written copies of speeches made by him (George Price) in Belize;

(2) That during the public holiday on the 10th September, 1951 a truck took

part in a procession through the streets of Belize, which truck was decorated with flags of the People's United Party which had been sent to the said Party from Guatemala;

(3) That in the latter part of October, 1951, George Price, the Secretary of the People's United Party, was having or seeking to have, secret meetings in Belize with the Guatemalan Consul here;

(4) That in the autumn of 1951, George Price, the Secretary of the People's United Party, received from the Guatemalan Consul in Belize the sum of $500.00

   (a) to cover, or as a contribution towards the cost of the defence of Leigh Richardson and three others who at or about that time stood their trial in the Supreme Court of British Honduras for sedition; and/or

   (b) to pay the fine of $100 imposed upon Armando Diaz another of the accused;

(5) That between the 14th and the 22nd September 1951, Philip Goldson, the Assistant Secretary of the People's United Party, had an interview in Guatemala City with the President of Guatemala, and a discussion with the Guatemalan Foreign Minister on the subject of obtaining from Guatemala a supply of newsprint for the *Belize Billboard*.

(6) That on the 28th November 1951, there was broadcast from the Government Broadcasting Station in Guatemala City an anti-British speech or talk, the material for the same having been supplied to the said Broadcasting Station by the People's United party;

(7) That on or about the 20th October 1952, leading officials and members of the People's United Party attended a social party given by the Guatemalan Consul in Belize;

(8) That on or about the 7th December 1952, the People's United Party caused a document containing a statement of its policy to be secretly conveyed to the Guatemalan Government; and

(9) That Leigh Richardson, the leader of the People's United Party, took the occasion of a visit which he paid to Guatemala for domestic reasons in January and February, 1953, to see the Foreign Minister of Guatemala –

   (a) in order to secure his help in implementing urgently a promise previously made by the Guatemalan Consul in Belize that between five and six thousand dollars would be given to the People's United Party for the newspaper which was its official voice;

   (b) in order to ask him not to change the Guatemalan Consul in Belize (whose recall the British Minister was demanding) unless the person replacing him was one who could be trusted by the People's United Party; and

   (c) in order to obtain from him certain political information.[70]

While the Commissioner could not substantiate some of the allegations he found the majority of them to be true. These included Price's receipt of

$500 BH from the Guatemalan Consul in Belize City in 1951 in connection with the cost of the defence of Richardson, Goldson and three others, and his arranging for the secret conveyance to the Guatemalan government of documents referring to that Government's promised assistance of printing material for the plant which printed the *Belize Billboard*. Sharpe was also satisfied that Goldson's interview with the Guatemalan President in 1951 was something more than a momentary and formal handshaking, and that the editor also discussed with a Guatemalan minister the subject of obtaining from Guatemala a supply of newsprint for the *Belize Billboard*. In his view, Richardson was also a party to the newspaper transactions and also acted as an intermediary between Price and the Guatemalan authorities during his visit to Guatemala in 1953.

The report, however, did not amount to a total and unqualified condemnation of the PUP leaders. Apart from the Commissioner's inability to substantiate a few of the allegations, those that he had established were hedged with doubt. For example, while he was satisfied that Price had received $500 BH, he was not able to say from what source in Guatemala it came; nor whether it was used exclusively in payment of costs or whether it was used in part to pay the fine imposed upon one of the other accused, Armando Diaz. He attributed his lack of certitude to the colonial government having in its principal political target, George Price, a 'definitely untruthful' and 'evasive' witness whose manner 'was far from reassuring'.[71]

By leaving many of the activities of the PUP leaders in obscurity the report fell short of the expectations of the critics of the leaders. Indeed, the enquiry was more noted for its exposure of the activities of Commander Proud, then Director of Information and Telecommunications, than those of the PUP leaders. If many Belizeans suspected the subterranean relationship between the PUP leaders and the Guatemalan authorities few could have imagined before the enquiry the extent to which Proud was involved in the political process and the means by which this was accomplished. It became clear from his evidence that the Commander's duties were more varied than his office suggested. It transpired that he tampered with documents addressed to a Guatemalan official, Sr José Garcia, and prompted the opponents of the PUP, including Smith, to form a third party which was still-born.[72] This was no less reprehensible in the popular view than the PUP's affiliation with Guatemala.

It cannot be over-emphasized that almost every action of the colonial administration pointed to its dislike for the PUP. Not only did it take two years to modify the Courtenay constitution but also denied the PUP an electoral opportunity in 1951 by extending the life of the 1948 Legislative

2. The Honourable Sir Harrison Courtenay, K.B.E., Q.C., LL.D.

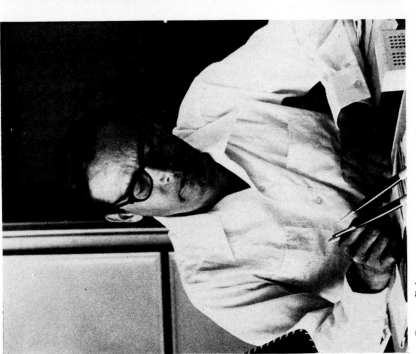

1. George Price

4. Nicholas Pollard

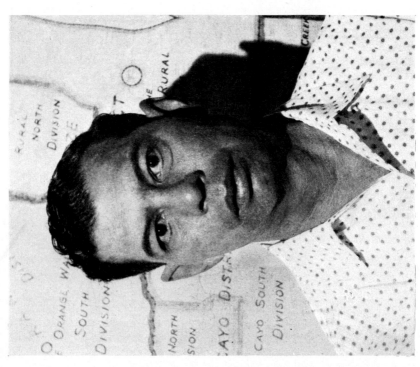

3. Herbert Fuller

6. The Honourable Dean Lindo

5. Philip Goldson

7. Price being given a hero's welcome in Belize on his return from London in December 1957

8. The Assembly Building, Belmopan

Council for two years and further renewing it for another year in 1953.[73] Unwittingly, however, this procrastination proved to be of more disservice to the NP than the PUP leaders. It encouraged the former to cling to the view that the country's political life could stand still indefinitely. Worse, these leaders spent the three years buttressing their declining influence rather than preparing for the new realities. Accordingly, as we have seen, they sought to deny their defeat in municipal politics in 1951 by successfully urging the Governor to dissolve the City Council in retaliation to the PUP refusal to hang the portrait of the King in the City Hall. The appointment of the interim council of old City Fathers further distorted or refracted the middle-class Creole's perception of the general conflict situation. They made little attempt to infuse the party with new ideas and close the generation gap between themselves and the PUP leaders. In March 1952, when another city council election was held, the average age of the NP candidates was fifty-five, which was about twenty years above that of the PUP candidates.[74] The NP won four of the nine seats, and with the support of two independents, continued to control the City Council. But this control further postponed its acceptance of the harsh political realities. Its leaders conveniently overlooked the fact that the returning officer, H. W. Beaumont, who was implacably opposed to the PUP, having organized the petition to dissolve the PUP city council in 1951, rejected the nomination of Richardson and Goldson because they were then serving prison sentences.[75] In their euphoria the NP leaders also ignored the fact that Price topped the polls with a greater number of votes than in 1950 and all the NP candidates who had been elected in 1950 were returned with a reduced vote even though the electorate had increased.[76]

The NP gains, therefore, really represented the last struggle of the old middle-class group. In fact the Legislative Council had deferred to the PUP opposition to Belize joining the proposed West Indies Federation by indefinitely postponing a decision on the issue in June 1952. Introducing his resolution, Fuller conceded that the majority of Belizeans 'are at the moment against Political Federation with the other British West Indian colonies'.[77] This admission could be seen as marking the beginning of the end of their long-standing political hegemony. Their ultimate test as a political force came in the 1954 general election.

## PUP ascendancy

The main election issues were the country's relationship with Britain and its future regional association with the West Indies and Central America. It would however be superfluous to discuss these issues since they were analysed in the previous chapter. Instead, this section will be concerned with three aspects of the election – the electorate, the candidates and the results – the purpose being to show how the differing social composition of the essentially Creole leadership of the PUP and the NP was institutionalized, and the way in which the PUP brought the outdistricts into, and gave the mass of people in Belize City a firmer hold on the national political process.

Perhaps the most outstanding feature of the electorate was the correction of the imbalance in its geographical and cultural distribution. Under the old franchise Belize District provided 70 per cent of the 1,772 voters in the 1948 election.[78] Of the 21,000 voters in 1954 only 53.4 per cent was registered in the four Belize District constituencies, Belize North, Belize South, Belize West, and Belize Rural. Belize City itself, which consisted of the first three constituencies in the Belize District, actually accounted for 43.4 per cent of the votes.[79]

Considering the literacy qualification and the limited political consciousness of the outdistrict population the introduction of adult suffrage does not adequately explain the phenomenal increase of the non-urban electorate. The number of spoilt votes was negligible[80] and it is evident that the PUP had spared no effort to teach the illiterate to write his name and to acquaint himself with the voting procedure. The PUP organization must have been substantial in view of certain considerations. First of all it should be recalled that the onus of registration rested with the voter. Second he had to seek out a Justice of the Peace, of whom there were fifty-two in a population of some 70,000, and the jurisdiction of some was limited to one district.[81] In addition, most of the Justices of the Peace were in Belize City and in any case in the remote areas of the country the voter did not have ready access to such an official. Since the Justice of the Peace would also have been a member of the rural elite and closely associated with the colonial administration, the possibility of his being unco-operative with the PUP campaigners cannot be discounted. In this connection the arrangement whereby the GWU was responsible for the outdistrict organization enabled the urban-based PUP leaders to overcome the difficulties of 'grass root' campaigns. In any case if the registration problem had forced these leaders to concentrate their campaign either in the Belize City area or the outdistricts, the latter was a better choice from the standpoint that these, together with the Belize Rural constituency, were returning six of the nine elected members to the Legislative Assembly. Moreover, the opposition in these areas was less formidable than in Belize City, as the NP contested only four of the six non-urban constituencies.

Altogether the NP contested six of the nine constituencies; the other two being Belize South and Belize West.[82] Its main reason for not contesting Belize North was obvious: it did not wish to prejudice the chances of the defected PUP leader, Smith, an independent candidate, who was running in his constituency against his erstwhile colleague, Price. Being more confident, the PUP–GWU contested all nine seats. The party selected its leaders, Price, Richardson, Goldson, and Herman Jex, who had succeeded Pollard as the GWU President in April 1953,[83] for the four Belize District constituencies while the GWU selected the candidates for the five outdistrict constituencies.

Like the three PUP leaders, four of the GWU candidates and its President were in their twenties or early thirties, but their educational and occupational attainments were not as high. All of them had risen from the rank of junior employees either of a timber merchant or of the Sharpe Citrus Company or of the BEC. These differences between the PUP leaders and the GWU candidates, were, however, overshadowed by the disparity between themselves and the NP candidates. The difference was not only social and occupational but also in terms of generation and to some extent of origin. Fuller, who had succeeded Harrison Courtenay as the NP Leader in September 1953, and was the youngest of his group, was forty-two years of age. C. J. Benguche, the only other Belizean and a Carib, was a retired civil servant and a planter who was an outgoing Legislative Councillor for his home-town, Stann Creek. William George, an expatriate Eurasian, was a retired medical doctor and a landowner who was likewise seeking re-election in the Orange Walk District in which he worked. Lionel Francis, as we observed, was a Trinidadian. Sidney McKinstry, a white Barbadian, was a retired Attorney General, and Manfred Wilson, a Guyanese primary school teacher and sanitary inspector, was a merchant and a commission agent.[84]

Although the majority of these candidates were businessmen they were primarily representatives of the educated elite rather than the old ruling commercial and landowning group. But if the NP candidates could claim to be better qualified to undertake the proposed quasi-ministerial responsibilities the alien origin of the four candidates was, within a nationalist context, a political liability. Moreover, in view of the unpopularity of federation, the West Indian origin of three of them further reduced the party's chances of victory. It stood out against the fact that at least McKinistry and Dr George were long-standing residents in retirement who could therefore claim the country by adoption.

The recruitment by the NP of candidates who belonged to the constituency or had long association with it was one of the few characteristics which they tended to share with the PUP–GWU candidates. Their common cultural origin was another, as only one of them, Enrique Depaz, was a Mestizo. Thus, the election could and did significantly change the social but not the cultural composition of the Legislative Assembly.

On 28 April 1954, 70 per cent of the registered electorate voted in the country's first national election by adult suffrage.[85] The PUP won eight of the nine seats and received 65 per cent of the total votes. These votes were almost twice the combined total of its opponents (which included five independents), and more than twice the amount obtained by the NP in the six constituencies it contested. In fact apart from the leader, Fuller, who was narrowly defeated by Goldson, none of the NP candidates proved a formidable opponent. As was to be expected, the four successful GWU candidates in the outdistricts won by larger margins than their PUP colleagues in Belize City. The constituency lost by the PUP was Toledo District where the subsistence economy and the difficulties of communication did not facilitate trade unionism. The successful candidate, C. E. Westby, was a resident farmer and an independent candidate who had represented the constituency since 1948. No less than the victories in the other constituencies, the PUP–GWU defeat in Toledo underwrote the importance of party organization in this new era of popular politics.

### The PUP split

With its defeat the NP became inactive and did not stir until the next election in March 1957. There was therefore little inter-party politics between the two elections. Instead the period was dominated by factionalism within the PUP. This culminated in Richardson and Goldson breaking away from the party in September 1956 to form the Honduran Independence Party (HIP).[86] The split can be seen at least in part as an outcome of the government pressures which had been exerted on the PUP. In addition to contributing to Smith's departure in 1951, these pressures had placed a strain on the unity of the PUP leaders. Furthermore, as Smith indicated in his statement of resignation, the difference among the PUP leaders went beyond the tactical problem of how extreme and uncompromising they should be in their opposition to the government and centred on the party's relationship with Guatemala and the West Indies.

As the portent of the party split could have been observed in Smith's departure in 1951, it is useful to examine the distribution of power and influence among the leaders and the nature of their differences from that time onwards. To begin with, the three elements within the party that were crucial to the resolution of leadership conflicts should be identified. The first element was the party rank-and-file in Belize City where the party machine operated almost exclusively until the split in 1956. The second was the Central Party Council which determined party policy and consisted of about eighteen of the top-ranking party officials. The third and most recent element was the parliamentary group which the 1954 election created and whose membership overlapped with that of the central party executive.

The leadership struggle which had begun between Smith and Price during the PC's brief existence was not resolved when the former was elected as Leader of the PUP. Instead the struggle all but reached its climax when Richardson and Goldson as editors of the *Belize Billboard* were charged with seditious libel against the Governor in November 1950. They had asked the Governor for a detailed statement of the expenditure of the $2,000,000 which the British government, according to the Governor in his Battle of St George's Cay day speech, had granted the colony. Not being favoured with a reply the editors proceeded to criticize the Governor and to suggest incriminating reasons for his lack of response.[87] They were, however, advised by their Jamaican lawyer, Mr Nethersole, that they had no legal grounds on which to stand because the relevant ordinance made almost every criticism of the Governor an offence.[88] Furthermore the official deposition which the government eventually tendered attested to the proper expenditure of the amount. Recognizing that his colleagues were in a legally indefensible position, Smith used his influence as a Legislative Councillor and party Leader to initiate negotiations for a settlement of the charge between the Governor and the two editors.[89] This involved a written retraction of the accusation by the two editors in return for which the Governor promised, as a gesture of his goodwill, to end the government's advertising boycott of the *Belize Billboard*.[90]

The editors' decision to withdraw their accusations had been reluctantly sanctioned by Price. In his view Richardson and Goldson, together with Smith, were compromising the party's militancy.[91] Worse, the editors incurred Price's full wrath when they compounded their demeanour by accepting the Governor's amendments to their letter. In Price's opinion, the amendments rendered the letter more apologetic and contrite than explanatory.[92]

In their attempt to resolve their differences Smith and Price may well have ignored the Central Party Council. The Council took the view that the negotiation was more a personal than a party affair and should therefore be left to the editors. Largely because of the Council's attitude and also because the party was essentially a popular front the PUP leaders referred their dispute to a general meeting of the three hundred or so party members.[93] In addition to the four party leaders, at least another had been involved in the settlement. This was Pollard who undertook to defend Richardson and Goldson at the meeting. Price therefore stood alone in his condemnation of the settlement which he deemed 'dishonourable'.[94] The general meeting was however too divided conclusively to uphold or condemn the settlement.

This account of the settlement suggests several important conclusions about the source of party power, its distribution among the leaders, and the differing impact of the government pressures upon each of them, and upon the relationship between the *Belize Billboard*, the PUP and the GWU which formed the veritable political triumvirate. First it showed the timidity of the Central Party Council about exerting a positive influence upon the leaders. This fear stemmed from the insignificant stature of the individual member[95] and his uncertainty of the outcome of the leadership struggle. Second, and as a result of the first, the strength of the rival leaders depended more upon mass support than their executive colleagues. Price was the only leader whose militancy seemed unaffected by the official pressures and his uncompromising stand drew considerable support and admiration from the party members. Indeed, considering that his view was in the minority among his colleagues, the inconclusive meeting was a personal triumph.

By being on the same side of the dispute, Richardson, Goldson, and Pollard brought home to Price, if not the PUP itself, the disadvantages of the party not having control over the two organizations, the *Belize Billboard* and the GWU. As Goldson pointed out after his 'trial', the party, the union and the newspaper were 'separate and independent sections of the same movement'.[96] Not unexpectedly the *Belize Billboard* favoured the viewpoints of its editors. In consequence, much more than his colleagues Price had to look to the party for his source of strength. Finally, the incident raised for Richardson and Goldson the problem of resolving their apparently conflicting roles as party leaders and editors. In the final analysis, the newspaper was an independent business enterprise which Richardson and Goldson had acquired from its original owner Nicolas Valdes, a Cuban national, in 1950, when the colonial authorities threatened the latter with expulsion for the newspaper's attack on them.[97] As owners and editors of the newspaper, Goldson and Richardson, by settling the sedition charge had reserved the right to act in a manner that did not prejudice their means of livelihood. Moreover, the newspaper was not more indebted to the party than the latter was to it.

Identification with the party was financially as much a liability as an asset. For if the political association of the newspaper with the party resulted in more sales, it had also led to the advertising boycott of the government and the British section of the commercial community.[98]

Nevertheless, Richardson and Goldson recognized the importance of the opinion of the party rank-and-file and they set out to disprove Price's suggestion that they were moderates. Thus they exercised little restraint in their newspaper or speeches. Soon they were again in conflict with the law for Goldson's article 'Seven Days of Freedom' which we observed was a report on his visit to Guatemala in September 1951. The article was deemed seditious and on this occasion neither he nor his editorial colleague, Richardson, sought to circumvent the course of justice. Both were sentenced, as we have also seen, to eighteen months' imprisonment in September 1951.

There is little doubt that underlying Goldson's glowing account of life in Guatemala and the accompanying denunciation of conditions in Belize was an attempt to retrieve his anti-colonial image rather than to commit the country to the Central American political orbit. In Smith's view, however, whatever benefits the relationship with Guatemala was bringing the party in its psychological warfare with the colonial administration, his colleagues were encouraging Guatemala's territorial ambitions and therefore undermining the dominant Creole culture. As a Creole this was more unacceptable to him than the manifest evils of British colonialism and so also ought it to be, in his view, to Richardson and Goldson who were also explicitly Creole in culture and orientation. In other words in Smith's view, Goldson and Richardson should have seen him as their natural ally, not Price who was a Creole on his paternal side but of a Mayan mother and whose Latin orientation was probably reinforced by his studies in Guatemala.

The basic issue which polarized Smith and Price, then, was their different conception of the future of Belize. One conceived of social and political change in a British framework, the other within the Latin. The nature of this difference should be emphasized if only to guard against the conclusion that Smith's outlook was in all respects similar to that of the NP leaders. The opposition was not only against a change in the country's British orientation but indicated wariness of too rapid a social and political change. While Smith's difference with the NP leaders was not fundamental, it was nevertheless significant. Thus when he resigned from the PUP he did not join the NP although the latter party indirectly supported his candidature against Price in the 1954 election by not contesting the constituency.

Smith's resignation again demonstrated the importance of the masses in the leadership struggle. Within two weeks of the imprisonment of Goldson and Richardson, he called upon the Central Party Council to recommit the party to self-government within the Commonwealth.[99] In a sense he was challenging Price to vindicate himself on the Guatemala issue. The Central Party Council once more recoiled from a decision and referred the resolution to a general meeting of the party which rejected it.[100] Smith's success at the Belize City Council election in 1952 as an independent candidate suggested that he still retained a measure of popular support. But the era of mass politics which he had done so much to inaugurate offered little permanent accommodation to the non-party politician. As we indicated, he lost as an independent candidate to Price at the 1954 election. Earlier his pride had received a more serious wound. The *Belize Billboard*, which Lindbergh Goldson managed and edited while his brother Philip and Richardson were in prison, had declared its support for Smith in the issue in which it reported the resignation.[101] The interim editor, however, switched the newspaper's support within three days to the PUP, presumably on the instruction of the two imprisoned leaders.[102] It was also an indication of his negligible influence within the PUP that only two of the Central Party Councillors, Cameron Gabb and Mervyn Hulse, resigned with him.[103] Bereft of support, Smith faded from the political scene and finally left the country for the USA in 1955 after giving evidence to the Sharpe Commission.[104]

Since the party machinery had assigned to the urban rank-and-file a decisive role in the leadership rivalry it becomes necessary to explain their support for Price's Central American sentiments and his efforts to regenerate the Mayan cultural heritage. After all, as Creoles the rank-and-file were likely to be worse-off socially in the event of closer association with Guatemala. For this reason alone their support for Price could not be automatic.

The answer lies in Price's charismatic appeal and ability to represent both his British and Latin sentiments in a nationalist context. The dispute over the origin of the new name of the country, Belize, illustrates the point. Citing Garcia Bauer, Price claimed that the name originated from the Mayan word Belikin.[105] This contradicted the time-honoured view that the name is a corruption of the surname of a British buccaneer, Wallace.[106] Price's aim was not only to obliterate the colonial past; the new interpretation also signified his belief that the identity of the country is rooted in the ancestry of the indigenous Mayas of Central America. This belief could be made to also appeal as much to the nationalist-minded within the Creole complex as to the Mestizo element. For if it reminds the latter of its cultural affinity with the other Central American countries it also gives Belize autochthonous claim to power.

Despite Smith's resignation the distribution of popular influence within the party remained distorted since Richardson was elected leader although the *Belize Billboard* acknowledged Price as 'the most forceful political personality in the country'.[107] In fact Goldson and Richardson, after their release from prison, had become noticeably restrained in their criticism of the colonial government and in their comments on Guatemala. No doubt they had sufficient time to ponder the legal and financial implications of their attacks on the government. It is significant in this respect that at the parade in honour of their release from prison, Goldson spoke on the conditions of the press in Belize. Implying that under the law criticism of the government was a risky and even self-defeating affair, he informed his audience that Richardson and himself, upon release from prison, had been bonded for the next two years in the sum of $1,500 each.[108] Furthermore, a week before his release from prison, his brother, Lindbergh, the acting editor of the *Belize Billboard*, was arraigned in Court and bonded in the sum of $500 for nine months. The three available editors of the *Billboard* were therefore together bonded in the sum of $3,500 which Goldson observed they personally had to pay if at any time they should 'publish anything disagreeable to Government'.[109]

The pressure which the colonial government was exerting was having its effect. By stifling the *Belize Billboard* it was separating Goldson and Richardson from Price. The two former leaders evidently saw no reason to jeopardize their future merely to advance the aims of the party and more specifically to provide Price with a radical platform while he remained untouched by the law. But their retreat to a more moderate position had less popular appeal than Price's unabated extremism.

The distortion within the party hierarchy was further compounded when in June 1954 Richardson, Goldson, Price and Jex were appointed to the Executive Council which also included the Governor, the Colonial Secretary, the Financial Secretary, the Attorney General and two nominated members from the Legislative Assembly, J. W. MacMillan and Salvador Espat, who had also been members of the old Executive Council.[110] Within four months of their appointment, Richardson, Goldson and Jex accompanied the Governor and Espat to London to negotiate financial assistance and more political responsibility for the elected members of the Executive Council.[111] The interaction between the PUP delegates and their hosts in London produced an identity of interests that went beyond the PUP's pledge to co-operate with the administration. The colonial government received $5 million in aid which

Richardson saw as 'a *bond*' (author's italics) between Belize and Britain and of which most was to be spent on creating 'a proper climate for the attraction of foreign investment' and preparing for self-government.[112] Goldson was no less effusive than Richardson in his account of the negotiations. He commented at length on the British government's decision to introduce the Membership System which was largely a matter of transferring executive functions in an 'orderly' way and ensuring continuity in colonial administration. Former colonial officials with whom he dined were no longer the devil incarnate. He described one of them as 'an outstanding fighter for the rights of colonial people and...one of the greatest friends our country has in England'. The other PUP representative, Jex, was euphoric about the visit. Before his rise to prominence in trade unionism and politics he was an hourly paid employee in the BEC sawmill.[113] Recognizing that he was the President of the GWU, the British government arranged for him to be a guest of the Directors of the BEC which included a former Governor of Belize, Sir John Hunter.[114] As far as Jex was concerned, while the political battle with the British government may not have been won, the industrial strife with the BEC was virtually over. The government and the company, he reported, were 'to start off on a new basis'.[115] Altogether, Richardson, Goldson and Jex had begun to behave as if the party was in power when it was not even in office. For the PUP Executive Council members constituted a minority in this body. Furthermore they had not been entrusted with responsibility for individual departments. This was not done until the Membership System was introduced on 1 January 1955 which they hailed as a significant constitutional advance.[116] Given their unqualified co-operation with the colonial administration it was not surprising that Richardson was appointed the Member for Natural Resources, Goldson became the Member for Social Services, and Jex undertook to be the Member for Public Utilities.

The relationship between these three PUP leaders and the colonial administration was in marked contrast to that between Price and the latter. In the first place Price declined membership of the Executive Council delegation to London in October 1954 on the grounds that one of the three principal PUP leaders should remain in Belize.[117] But no sooner had the delegation left for London than he accompanied his employer, Turton, to the USA only to return about three weeks after the delegation.[118] Claiming that his services in Turton's business could not be spared,[119] he kept his peripheral role intact by electing to be the junior and part-time Associate Member of Natural Resources in January 1955.[120] In general, he appeared oblivious to the party's change in circumstance. His political style remained unaffected by it, as he continued his campaign chiefly among the ordinary Creole women in the market square in Belize City and among the peasants in the outdistricts whenever his business commitments permitted. The campaign in the outdistricts was to pay handsome dividends after the split in the party in 1956 resulted in his loss of support of the GWU which had provided the voters for the party in 1954.

Price's employment as Turton's secretary does not adequately explain his disinterest in a more senior post in the colonial administration. Indeed his explanation ceased to be valid as a result of Turton's death in 1955. Price was retrenched and decided to be President of the City Council rather than a full-time member of the government.[121] The overriding reason was his unwillingness to participate in the working of the British colonial system even to the point of being deafeningly silent in the Legislative Assembly.[122]

Price extended his disassociation from the colonial administration to the actions of his PUP colleagues although they were still in agreement on such important issues as economic policies for the country. Richardson's idea that the primary role of a government was to create conditions favourable for the penetration and consolidation of private foreign enterprises accorded with the views that Price had been expressing from the inception of the movement. Their views however differed in one significant respect. One looked to Britain and the other to the USA to be the chief donor government and source of private capital. Ideologically, the difference was irrelevant. From the standpoint of the country's orientation to external political entities the difference was, however, important, at least as far as Price was concerned. Apart for his dislike for Britain, he saw that collaboration with that country would inexorably draw Belize into the proposed West Indies Federation.

Price should be credited for his unflinching perspicacity. While he remained aloof from the government, Richardson and Goldson became more enwrapped in it. They worked energetically to overcome the social and economic problems of the country within the prescribed colonial framework.[123] Notwithstanding the apparent harmony with the colonial administrators or perhaps because of it, their uncomfortable education of office considerably influenced their outlook on the country's regional orientation. Richardson, in particular, acquired a new perspective of the country's problems from participating in regional economic and Standing Federation Conferences in the West Indies and Britain. He was convinced, for example, that the country was benefiting from its membership of the West Indies Regional Economic Committee which had been set up in 1951 by a resolution of the 1947 Montego Bay Federation Conference, because, as he put it, 'it was felt to be some ordered way of conducting the economic life of the region'.[124] But by merely conceding that there were merits in the economic ties with the West Indies, Richardson re-opened the federation debate which had subsided when the Legislative Council had agreed to postpone a decision on the issue indefinitely in 1952 and died when the PUP won the 1954 election. Drawing their strength from their new role Richardson and Goldson became more alienated from Price. Under pressure from Price to clarify his stand Richardson upheld the economic ties with the West Indies by claiming that there 'was much to gain from economic collaboration with the West Indies'.[125] Furthermore he was predisposed to Belize joining an independent federation, which he now saw as mutually beneficial to all colonial territories in the region.[126] He recognized that a 'cut and dried' decision would require careful consideration but in the meantime he urged that Belize 'should not destroy every possibility of a political union with the West Indies'.[127]

This reversal of the party's opposition to the West Indies Federation could only have prevailed if the issue was debated either by the Central Party Council or the party parliamentary group. For, as subsequent events proved, Richardson and Goldson controlled the votes of these two groups. Several considerations, however, favoured a public debate. First, it was by now the established practice to submit party differences to a general party meeting. Second, because of its composition the parliamentary group was not a *bona fide* section of the party. The majority of its members were rural-based and, because the PUP was still predominantly an urban affair, were considered outsiders.

The general meeting which reviewed the party federation policy in March 1956 was significant for its reference to racial and cultural division in Belize politics.[128] The party had always brushed aside the issue as irrelevant and condemned those who raised it as disruptive. It was not only the middle-class Creoles who had accused the organization of racial bias against the Creoles and claimed that this was not unrelated to the Catholic domination of the movement. Charges were also made by the early sympathizers of the movement such as Kemp who, from the time he was an advocate of the 'Native First' policy in the 1940s, had remained racially conscious and impeccably consistent in his almost self-appointed role as the guardian of the ordinary black man's dignity and interests. In 1951, when the GWU dismissed the last of its old guard, Henry Middleton, from the secretaryship, Kemp and his associate, 'Negro Boy', claimed that this was a conspiracy to get rid of black officials who were non-Catholic.[129]

It was Richardson who invariably ran to the defence of the GWU and the PUP. He vowed in 1951 that Kemp and 'Negro Boy'

will not get away with their spewing of race hatred. It just isn't true that there are officials in the GWU aiming at getting rid of black officials. The GWU and the PUP Executive Councils are comprised of people of the different racial strains which inhabit British Honduras. The people are elected strictly on the basis of estimated worth or else how could the situation arise in which the dismissed general secretary is replaced by another as dark as himself. In any event when people drag in race or creed into an argument to try to win their point it means they have no topic left and must appeal to ignorance.[130]

Ironically, it was Richardson who acknowledged the divisiveness of first culture and then race within the party. On the alternative idea of political association with Central America he commented:

Now what are the facts about Central American Federation? First of all, the Central Americans themselves had a loose kind of federation and dissolved it when they found that for some reason or another, though they spoke the same language and were the same people with similar background and economic and social circumstances and were inhabitants of the same land mass, they could not get together. They have so far taken no practical step in that direction.[131]

The inference was clear. If a fairly culturally homogeneous community of people could not remain united, then it was difficult to conceive of Belize with its different political tradition and a deviant but sizeable group, the Creole, faring well among them.

Richardson continued to call into question Price's optimism about a Central American destiny for Belize:

Moreover, the Central Americans – and this is most important to us – have never given any indication that they want us as equal partners in any federation. In fact, the only Central American country which has expressed any interest in our affairs is Guatemala which desires to have its claim to British Honduras honoured and British Honduras become a department or district of Guatemala instead of a self-governing country. Just last week in the opening of the new Assembly their President Castillo Armas told the members he would continue to press for the handing over of British Honduras to Guatemala.

Then too, if one keeps abreast of both Central America and British West Indian developments, he would learn that right now the Central Americans are busy by-passing us here in Belize and doing their best to develop economic and cultural relations with these same West Indians whom some people would have us despise.[132]

Concluding his lengthy defence of his position, Richardson argued that

Price's political sentiments were not only inconsistent with the regional economic realities but destructive of Belize economic well-being:

> There is no doubt that the Central American countries are going out to get West Indian trade and are now giving us stiff competition in timber though our timber is superior to theirs. Just last year I had to intercede with the Jamaican Government to adjust the conditions in the Jamaican timber market so that we would not suffer too much from unfair competition.[133]

However impressive were his economic arguments, Richardson, in tempering Price's optimism about a Central American destiny for Belize, was not necessarily advancing his own case for federation with the West Indies precisely because the latter territories were in the same position as the Central American states. The federal idea had so far undergone nine painful years of gestation and its birth was still another two years away. Moreover, membership of the West Indies Federation would not have solved the country's cultural problem. The only effect would have been the retention of its Mestizo population as the deviant cultural group.

This difference over regional orientation could no more be resolved between Richardson and Price than it had between the latter and Smith once the protagonists viewed it through differing cultural spectacles. Indeed, as the split became imminent Richardson and Goldson acknowledged the divisiveness of race and culture within the party leadership in a more pointed manner.

> We are now dancing a political samba [*sic*] it seems. When six years ago the people rose up against colonialism there were certain persons who felt that the logical leaders ought to be the Latins among us and so they led until one thing or another swept Creole leaders into the forefront. Certain Latins have never forgotten that and have been scheming since to uproot the Creole leaders. This newspaper [the *Belize Billboard*] will always oppose anybody who thinks with his skin. To us creed, race or colour means nothing in politics, and any attempt to create a particular pigment for instance is abominable. Attempts may yet be made to re-establish the Alumni Party, the political party formed some years ago among fellows of a certain complexion from a certain secondary school. This we regard as an insult to the intelligence of the electorate.[134]

Although Richardson and Goldson stressed race and culture, it appears that the basis of the leadership division within the party included social status and class. Their reference to the Alumni Party and 'fellows... from a certain secondary school' supports the plausibility of this argument. It was clear that they were referring to St John's College whose prestige and influence remained substantial from several standpoints. In the first place it produced the business elite and to a lesser extent the professional elite, from among the Latin and Creole population respectively, and continued to attract the sons of these more established groups. Those Creoles who were Alumni and in some cases also Catholic were however less dependent for their advancement than the Latins on this group affiliation because within the social structure of the colonial society they had not only greater latitude of choice in their social and cultural alignments but also other sets of group affiliations that were more prestigious. Earlier in the study we have indicated that the results of the 'cross-cutting membership' of the Creoles were complex. In one situation, they may have acted as Alumni, aligning themselves with the members of this social group; in another context they may have acted as a cultural group and aligned themselves with the lower stratum of Creole elite or even the bulk of the Creole population in latent opposition to the Latin, or at least acted with indifference to the implications of their actions for the Mestizos.

The Latin elite on the other hand, with fewer sets of group affiliations to exploit, drew their solidarity and group corporateness almost entirely from their various Catholic institutions and tended to be more socially exclusive than the Creole. This situation obviously imposed limits on the acceptance of those who were not Alumni of St John's College, or who were newcomers to the Catholic faith, or for that matter who lacked the other social characteristics of this segment of the elite in the society. All of these considerations more or less applied to Goldson and Richardson who therefore did not satisfy the eligibility requirements for the ruling-class status as far as the Latin elite was concerned. Nor could they easily meet the requirements set by the upper level of the Creole elite. On the other hand there were several Creoles who were not necessarily Alumni of St John's College or Catholics but who by virtue of their occupation, prestige and social rank could have carried weight with the Latin elite had they decided that affiliations with such groups as the PUP would serve their ends. The possibility of such a situation was enhanced by the tendency of the Latin elite to remain behind the political scene. This tendency was part of a vicious circle. The Latin elite had not been encouraged to become actively involved in politics because they were considered by the colonial administration to be untutored in the norms and procedures of central colonial government. This had a debilitating effect on this group and functioned as a sort of self-fulfilling prophecy for the colonial government and the Creole elite: the latter, as the Courtenay Commission stressed, was cognizant of the strategic function that it performed in the Crown colony period[135] and continued to assert its eligibility for this role in the decolonizing process. In this connection, it is noteworthy that it was the rural or outdistrict counterpart of the urban Latin elite that was more inclined to engage in active party politics. Few of them, however, had penetrated the inner core of the PUP national leadership at the time of the PUP split. It may be argued that this was because the difficulties of transportation and communication, and the absence of strong party branches in the outdistricts, prevented the rural-based Latin elite from establishing strong links with the national leadership. But although the geographical and institutional situation changed, the vicious circle has never been completely broken or reversed, although it has sustained some impressive cracks and revolves with less velocity.

This line of argument is borne out by the fact that as the PUP established its legitimacy and became the main viable alternative to the colonial attachment many Creoles, in order to retain their influence and rank within the society, easily assumed leadership roles in the party at a time when its Latin orientation was still very much pronounced. In a word, certain sections of the Creole elite exploited now one and now another set of affiliations, depending upon the potentialities of the situation. Indeed, this was precisely what Richardson and Goldson had done in becoming immersed in the colonial administration. Their problem was that it was too late in the colonial era for there to be much potential in this association to exploit. The entire situation was essentially too dynamic for the society to be frozen and rigidly categorized as 'plural', based on the differentiation in the ethnic and cultural structure, or as 'proletarian', based on differentiation in the class structure. Each framework by itself is of limited value because it necessarily excludes factors that cannot be subsumed in its particular scheme. One ignores the fact that the cross-cutting alignments enabled several segments of the Creole population, including the common man, to identify themselves at different times, in different forms, and at different levels with the various Latin elements in the PUP and thereby justify the party's claim to be national and based on the masses; the other does not fully recognize the importance of ethnic and cultural affiliations as a basis of political divisions.

The immediate occasion for the split was Pollard's suspension from the secretaryship of the GWU in July 1956, for alleged peculation.[136] A discussion of the union split belongs to the next section. Here it should be observed that because of the close relationship between the party and the union a dissension in one was bound to have a similar effect in the other. Goldson and Richardson immediately supported the expulsion of Pollard who was assured of Price's support for at least two reasons. In the first place Pollard was first and foremost a trade unionist and unalterably opposed to federation because of his belief that it would result in an influx of West Indians who would deprive Belizeans of their jobs. He had therefore stood behind Price in the party's latest debate on federation and was receiving reciprocal support from Price in his dispute with the union.[137] But in condoning Pollard's action Price was also looking ahead to the general election in early 1957. Pollard was an electoral asset in several respects. He was a dynamic and effective speaker and more known than any other activist in the outdistricts. Furthermore he retained the support of the workers in two principal areas, Belize City and Stann Creek, which became the nucleus of the Christian Democratic Union (CDU) which he formed after his expulsion from the GWU in July 1956.[138]

The PUP leadership crisis had developed on the eve of the party's annual conference in September. It was therefore simply a matter of time before Price emerged the victor. The unpopularity of federation was not the only factor on which this prediction could have been based. The party rank-and-file had responded readily to a PUP petition to the Governor to remove Richardson and Goldson from office on the ground that 'they have completely changed the political platform on which they were elected'.[139] This reckoning of political influence in terms of active mass support was the underlying cause of Price's success. To have reckoned it in terms of the party organs was illusory because of their minimal role in the leadership struggle in the past. Thus it was of no avail to Richardson and Goldson that, together with the ten officials who supported them, they constituted the majority of both the legislative and the municipal groups as well as the party Central Council. The twelve leaders therefore acknowledged the odds against them by jointly submitting their resignation at the opening session of the conference on 27 September 1956, claiming that Price had 'packed the People's United Party with his personal supporters and paid their dues there in an attempt to achieve control of the conventions and councils of the Party'.[140] Perhaps the only significance of this alignment was the expression of racial and cultural solidarity of the group. Of the five trade unionists in the Assembly, the four Creoles supported Richardson and Goldson.

In reckoning their political influence Richardson and Goldson also miscalculated by placing a high value on their office in the government. They claimed that 'it was not [their] wish to be diverted' from fulfilling their government responsibility to conduct 'a mere struggle with Price for the personal control of the People's United Party'.[141] Indeed this statement betrayed their lack of appreciation of the importance of political parties to colonial politicians in their rivalry for political hegemony. To regard their position in the government as more important was not only illusory but also short-sighted in view of the general election which was to be held before April 1957. In this brief period of six months no newly formed party, as they were to discover as leaders of the Honduran Independence Party (HIP), could have appealed to the electorate. Like the NP leaders these two leaders had to recognize that the maintenance, still more the expansion, of the elite's political influence in the decolonizing period had become increasingly dependent not upon the ability to work the government institutions but upon mass support.

### The GWU split

Although the GWU was a clear example of political unionism its relationship with the PUP, however, rules out generalization because the situations in the outdistricts and in the national centre differed. As we have seen, the outdistricts' trade union apparatus developed, in the absence of local party organizations, into a political machine. At the centre, however, both the party and the union were divided within themselves over the extent to which the PUP leaders should have control of the union. Assured of the union's general support Price was indifferent to its internal management and in fact declined re-election to the Presidency and to the Executive Council in 1953.[142] Richardson and Goldson on the other hand argued for a tight rein in order to prevent Pollard, the General Secretary, from dominating his less able trade union colleagues. Thus while Price withdrew, in order 'to give much more time and energy to the purely political side of the movement',[143] Richardson resigned from the Executive Council in the same year, 1953, and later from the union, critical of Pollard's methods.[144] Goldson, however, continued as Assistant General Secretary until Labour was added to his quasi-ministerial portfolio in September 1955.

For their part the trade unionists viewed the union–party tie in terms of its value to their careers. Almost all of them stood to benefit from an interpenetration of the PUP and the union. They welcomed Richardson's and Goldson's protective influence, and also looked to the high status and income accorded to members of the Legislative Assembly and the Belize City Council. Pollard was the least favoured of the beneficiaries. He was born of (Spanish) Honduran parentage, a mixture of Negro and Mestizo, in Mexico, and although brought up in Belize he was an alien. This legal disability to contest elections rendered politics an impracticable goal. Nor could his passion for trade unionism, which pre-dated the nationalist movement, readily enable him to gain political advantage through collective bargaining. It is therefore not insignificant that his first major conflict with Richardson and Goldson was over the settlement of the politically inspired general strike in 1952. Pollard's insistence on prompt negotiations was, arguably, not wholly inspired by his trade union ideals. An equally important consideration was the doubtful financial value of the strike. This arrangement whereby the worker expressed his allegiance primarily by striking and voting in political elections rather than paying dues contributed to the union's, and therefore its officers' financial insecurity.

The financial aspect of unionism should be further analysed because of the frequent charges of irregularity proffered against union officials. The impression can be easily gained that the GWU treasury was perpetually empty because of sharp practices. The reverse is however nearer to the truth. Apart from the fact that they were not organized primarily for financial purposes, the workers' low income, seasonal employment in the three major industries – sugar, citrus and forestry – and ultimate dependence upon the weather were basically responsible for the union's small due-paying membership.[145] Another important factor was the preponderance of self-employed farmers in the sugar industry which emerged in the 1950s as the principal industry. Moreover, as this industry expanded it attracted a large number of in-transit Mexican cane-farmers who lacked a strong commitment to unionism in Belize.

In these circumstances the GWU officials had to make their salaries as the opportunity arose. Indeed, the solvency of the union depended on its international affiliations[146] with the British Trade Union Congress and the Organization Regional Inter-Americana de Trabajadores (ORIT). The cause of the union's financial problem was not only lack of income but also bad administration. It launched several ill-conceived ventures. Its news-sheet, *Social Justice*, merely duplicated the *Belize Billboard* labour columns and within six weeks of its birth suffered a severe financial loss. The union also operated an unprofitable lottery in 1950 in an attempt to augment its income.[147]

To the extent that the close association between the union and the PUP contributed to the former's financial instability, Pollard resisted it. Above all, however, by enhancing the stature of the other trade unionists the relationship threatened his leadership role. Constantly arraigned before the Executive Council for administrative and financial irregularities Pollard found it difficult to reconcile the Executive Councillors' constraint with his superior intellect and organizing ability.

If the factional alignments cut across the union–party line, the joint participation of these two organizations in the colonial administration deepened the rift between Pollard and the three senior quasi-ministers of the government, Richardson, Goldson and Jex. The role of these three members demanded a less sectarian view of industrial relations, and this invariably conflicted with the aspirations of the GWU. To be sure, labour benefited from participating in the government. Employer's opposition to unionism was easier to overcome, the check-off system was introduced, with the attendant auditing of union accounts at first by anyone and then by the government auditor alone, the registration of unions became compulsory, labour legislation was reformed and greater co-operation between the GWU and the Labour Department was achieved.[148] But the promises of higher wages and employment remained unfulfilled. More specifically, the government, faced in 1955 with a decline in revenue and the hurricane 'Janet' which resulted in damages totalling $4 million, refused a wage increase to its manual employees.[149] Indeed, Richardson and Goldson, as members for Natural Resources and Social Services respectively, were developing an apparent identity of interest with the dominant expatriate industrial concerns. The *Belize Billboard* rebuked the union leaders for their expectancy of early wage increases. In fact, the editorial was a far cry from the sentiments expressed in 1952 when Richardson and Goldson spearheaded the GWU's strike:

We don't know where people in this country ever got the idea from that the government in British Honduras is obliged to find work for everybody at the highest possible wages...The brutal fact is that no government can find work for all the people who wish it. A government can find work for those whom it can usefully employ in providing services that private capital will not provide. In every country, too, there exists some unemployment. Often brought on by government shackling of private industry, admittedly. The case in B.H. would seem to be that private industry is shackling itself and that too many people who can do something about the situation are standing by demanding that the government do something.[150]

In pointing out that the expatriate interests which were being spared government pressure were British- and West Indian-owned and one of their representatives, H. T. A. Bowman, a citrus planter, was the Associate Member for Natural Resources, Pollard cemented his alliance with Price. In relating such statements to Richardson's and Goldson's West Indian sympathies Price and Pollard proved to the worker-voter that his loyalty to one of them involved support of the other. This argument eventually produced the slogan: 'Price for politics and Pollard for unionism.'

The pattern of the power struggle in the union closely followed that in the PUP. The two union factions controlled different components of the organizational structure. Through their parliamentary relationship with the GWU Assemblymen, Richardson and Goldson exerted considerable influence in the Executive Council and the General Council whose membership was largely coterminous. The General Council reported to a biennial National Congress with which Pollard was popular.[151] Since the district branches were countrywide the Congress was much more representative of the population than the PUP annual convention. But precisely because they were widely dispersed, the union members were not in a strategic position to obtain the same measure of influence in the leadership struggle as had been assigned to the urban rank-and-file in the PUP conflict. They, however, established their supremacy and Pollard's popularity at the eleventh National Congress in 1955 when the Executive Council urged that the Secretary be replaced. Price forestalled the attempt by pleading for unity in the wake of a breakaway threat by the delegates of the Belize Sawmill and the Vogue commercial store if Pollard was not re-elected.[152] Neither Price's intervention nor the denouncing of an attempt to limit the Secretary's powers encouraged Pollard to be more amenable to the Executive Council's decisions. The delicate truce was therefore bound to be broken sooner or later.

The occasion arose in January 1956, when Pollard was alleged to have misused funds which an American union, the International Brotherhood of Sleeping Car Porters, had donated to the 'Janet' hurricane fund in 1955.[153] Pollard was suspended after a junior staff member reported the incident to the police, almost six months later. As principal financial officers, Jex, the President, and Albert Arzu, the Trustee, were convicted jointly with Pollard of fraudulent conversion of an amount from the same fund to the use of the GWU.[154] A criminal charge was also instituted against the union administrator, George Gardiner, for misuse of funds.[155] Those who were not involved in these irregularities feared the loss of influence and status that would result from a union split and its estrangement from the PUP.

Pollard's subsequent resignation in July 1956 was therefore a pyrrhic victory for Richardson, Goldson and Jex. As the outcome of the Congress indicated, the personal influence of these three leaders in the local branches was negligible. Moreover, the membership had fallen with the decline in political activity after the 1954 election.[156] The union was therefore of little electoral value in 1957, and in fact three GWU Assemblymen, Jex, Joe Chin and George Flowers, sought re-election as HIP candidates. Finally, after the 1957 election the remaining members tended to support the CDU because of its association with the victorious PUP.

*Price's hegemony: 1957 general election*

As in the previous election a PUP victory could have been foreseen. In the first place, the party alone had a clear policy. It was resolutely against federation, and independence as a Central American republic remained its goal, although this was vaguely expressed in the party election manifesto.[157] Apart from the popularity of the party's anti-federation stand, the constancy and purposiveness of its unrivalled leader, Price, was impressive. He succeeded in making the Federation the main issue by stigmatizing Richardson and Goldson for having repudiated popular sentiment on the subject, especially at a time when the Federation was becoming more of a reality.[158] He called on the electorate to pronounce upon his erstwhile colleagues. Pushed on the defensive Richardson and Goldson became preoccupied with vindicating themselves by pointing to their record in office.[159] At times they launched a counter-offensive by challenging Price to clarify his own position on the Guatemala issue. But this demand was not wholly convincing because the HIP leaders had been parties to relationship between the PUP and Guatemala. Furthermore since the Sharpe enquiry and the subsequent vindication of the PUP in the 1954 election the issue had worn thin. Like the HIP, the other opposition party, the NP, dared not come out unequivocally for federation. In consequence, the PUP could and effectively did point out that their opponents did not know what they wanted.

Secondly, the PUP organization was superior in Belize City where the machinery of all the parties was concentrated. In the outdistricts the PUP also retained the advantage which it had derived from its links with GWU. The breakdown of the GWU created an organizational void in these areas which could only be filled in this short period by the political leaders' personal influence and their judicious influence of candidates. The style of Price's leadership was the most militant and personal, and he alone could claim affinity with the predominantly outdistrict Mestizo population. Moreover, the defection of all the GWU Assemblymen, except Depaz, from the PUP to the newly formed opposition party, gave Price a freedom in the selection of his candidates and therefore a greater opportunity to take account of the cultural factor in party politics. The extent to which his party nominations were determined by the prospect of both local and cultural support is measured by the fact that except in the four constituencies in the Belize District none of the candidates was a Creole. Those in Corozal, Orange Walk, and Cayo were resident Mestizos, and in Stann Creek and Toledo, Caribs. On the other hand, none of the candidates of the opposition parties was a Mestizo.

These three factors – a clear policy, a better organization and the appeal to cultural and local sentiment – combined to give the PUP all nine seats. The third factor rendered the Legislative Assemblymen much more representative of the general population without, however, impinging on the leading roles of the urban Creoles within it. Although the out-district legislators' social and educational attainments were an improvement on those of the GWU Assemblymen they were still below their urban Creole colleagues. Of the four new outdistrict representatives, Santiago Ricalde (Corozal) was a mason, Victor Orellana (Orange Walk), a retired senior civil servant and businessman, and Denbigh Jeffery (Belize time-keeper, and Faustino Zuniga (Toledo), a former primary school teacher and the local court interpreter. Price who became the Member for Natural Resources therefore recommended Albert Cattouse (Belize West), a retired senior civil servant and businessman, and Denbigh Jeffery (Belize South), a former manager of an expatriate mahogany company, to be the Member for Social Services and the Member for Public Utilities, respectively, while Louis Sylvestre (Belize Rural), who was educated at St John's College and in Jamaica, became the Associate Member for Natural Resources.[160]

Perhaps the most significant feature of the election results was the low poll. Of the slightly increased electorate of 22,000 only 53 per cent voted as against 70 per cent in 1954.[161] A breakdown of this figure on an urban-outdistrict basis shows that the proportion of the electorate which voted in the three Belize City constituencies was reduced from 74.1 per cent in 1954 to 55.8 per cent, and in the outdistricts, including the Belize Rural constituency, from 65.1 per cent to 50.3 per cent. This low participation was also recorded in every constituency irrespective of its location.

Two reasons can be given for the lack of urban interest in the election. First, there was the tendency for the middle-class Creoles to regard the election as a continuation of the internecine PUP struggle in which they should not be involved. Indeed, the personal vilification that persisted after the split depressed the electoral scene and gave rise to genuine concern for the future of party politics. To a considerable extent, however, the middle-class Creoles were rationalizing their feeling of ineffectiveness. Their main party, the NP, inspired little confidence. It again contested only six of the nine seats under the leadership of Fuller and did not oppose Price in the Belize North constituency. Since Fuller was one of the least discredited NP leaders a more positive outlook by the party may have turned his narrow defeat by two votes into a victory over the less known PUP candidate, Denbigh Jeffery.

The second reason for the low poll in Belize City was a consequence of the first. A large number of PUP supporters had either been driven by the split into neutrality or simply did not vote because they were certain of the PUP victory. In fact, the more popular the candidate, the greater was the tendency for the poll to decline, compared with 1954. This explains the sharp drop in votes cast in Price's constituency from 75.4 per cent to 55.6 per cent.

This second reason for the reduced participation of the electorate in Belize City also accounts for a similar state of affairs in the outdistricts. Another reason for the low poll in these areas was the organizational weakness of the parties. A comparison between the two constituencies, Toledo and Corozal, with the lowest and highest polls in the election respectively, demonstrates the correlation between the state of party organization and the level of participation. As we observed, the remote location and subsistence economy of Toledo had posed an organizational problem from the outset of the nationalist movement. Of the 1,371 voters only 46.6 per cent voted. In Corozal, on the other hand, a new local party, the Corozal United Party, which was formed in October 1956[162] had not only filled the organizational void created by the breakdown of the GWU but had entered an alliance with the PUP. By no means the most politically conscious outdistrict constituency, it recorded the highest poll, of 63.4 per cent, in the country.

Another striking feature of the elections was the decline of the PUP poll from 65 per cent in 1954 to 59 per cent although the party won all nine seats. Moreover, two of these, Belize South and Toledo, were won on minority votes. Here was a lesson for the two opposition parties: the electorate, ranging from 1,100 in Toledo to 3,500 in Belize West, was too small to accommodate three parties. Their common approach and outlook was however not sufficient to overcome the personality and other differences between their leaders. The NP leaders felt that in paying the penalty for supporting Price, Richardson and Goldson should be unaided. The HIP leaders in turn had recoiled from the idea of an electoral alliance because they did not wish to be tainted with the past failure of the NP. Now that the election was over there was little point to their separate existence. Yet more than a year elapsed before a national crisis brought them together and at the same time turned Price into both a hero and a frustrated leader.

*Price's hegemony: PUP–CDU relationship*

The only founding leader who had not been eliminated from the PUP and who therefore placed a qualification on the claim that Price was an unrivalled leader, was Pollard. This qualification was however more apparent than real. Price dominated their seemingly intimate relationship through his party's control of the CDU. Both the PUP and the CDU functioned in the same office and shared *The Belize Times*, which the CDU had launched as its industrial organ in September 1956 although it was more the voice of the PUP, which had lost the support of the *Belize Billboard* after the party split. More important, the PUP leaders penetrated the CDU Executive Council in the same manner in which they had penetrated the GWU before the split. Cattouse, the party Treasurer and formerly the GWU Vice-President, became the President; Lucas Marin, a mercantile clerk and party activist, was the Vice-President; Pollard was the General Secretary; Leonard Jones, a stevedore and a militant party supporter who had taken responsibility for the petition to remove Richardson and Goldson from office, was Assistant Secretary; and Louis Sylvestre, who was being groomed for the Legislative Assembly, was the Recording Secretary.

Pollard was as chary of this intermingling of union and party roles as in the past. But given the paucity of able trade unionists he could do no more than regulate the tenure of the political officeholders. The GWU rules which the new union adopted were amended to prevent members of the Legislative Assembly from remaining union officials. Although this rule was not rigidly enforced Cattouse relinquished the Presidency on becoming the Member for Social Services. Several other amendments were designed to secure the independence of the union and of Pollard within it. The regular payment of dues was stipulated in order to reduce the union's dependence on non-union support. In assuming the authority to issue directives to the Treasurer subject to the approval of the Executive Council Pollard clarified his role as the chief executive officer. The Executive Council whose actual role in determining policy was superior to that of the Congress lost its disciplinary powers to a membership meeting of the Belize (urban) workers. The latter could expel the national union officials and their right to appeal was to Congress alone.[163]

The political environment, however, reduced the effectiveness of these safeguards against the spread and consolidation of PUP influence. Apart from the politician's dual officeholding, the distinction between the union and the party was blurred by shared goals and strategies. Their electoral alliance in 1957 was inspired by mutual opposition to other political parties, the colonial administration and the British and West Indian business interests. The CDU's support however was not as vital to the PUP's success as the GWU's in 1954. The CDU provided only two candidates: McKoy, the organizing Secretary in Stann Creek, and Victor

Orellana, a PUP supporter who had helped to form the CDU branch in Orange Walk. Once the election was won Pollard was overpowered by the PUP's influence. It was only a matter of time for him to break with Price and remove the last semblance of doubt about the latter's supremacy within the party and position as the major force in the country's political life.

# 6

# The conflict: the climax and resolution

*The climax*

*The London incident* If the first colonial administration in which the PUP participated ended with a repudiation of Richardson's and Goldson's West Indian sympathies, the second began with a renewed suspicion of Price's Guatemala leanings. To some extent this suspicion had been revived by a renewal of discussions towards a settlement between Britain and Guatemala[1] in March 1957, the same month as the PUP's electoral victory. According to Guatemala, the British government favoured some form of economic integration between Guatemala and Belize. This was to be the first step in the formation of a Central American Federation in which Belize would be an independent republic.[2] If Belize was to be sovereign indeed, then Guatemala was conceding its sacred territorial claim. For its part the British government was indicating that the integration of Belize into the Central American economy should be the objective of the country's future development. To this extent it was responding positively to both the unpopularity of the West Indies Federation in Belize and to the proposition that an independent Belize would not be economically viable outside of an economic grouping.

The reopening of negotiations between Britain and Guatemala left Price free to pursue his notion of a Central American destiny without having either to side with Britain in repudiating the Guatemalan claim or uphold the Guatemala viewpoint. There was however a general uneasiness among Price's opponents because of his contact with the Organization of the Central American States (ODECA). This was a regional economic organization which had been formed in 1952.[3] From the standpoint of close regional economic co-operation the choice of organization was eminently sound. It was however from the political standpoint that the apprehension of Price's opponents seemed well-founded. In 1955, ODECA pronounced the reincorporation of 'Belice' to be a Central American question, and pledged to 'incorporate Belice in the movement of economic integration of Central America at a conference in Argentina just before the election in British Honduras in 1957'.[4] Although the declaration was

187

not new, it intensified suspicion among the opposition parties that Price was secretly negotiating a settlement through the Central American organization rather than in conjunction with the British government.

Price's style of conducting public affairs was certainly not calculated to confound these suspicions. Both the nature of his visits abroad and his return to the country, the last leg of which was invariably by land through one of the border routes from Guatemala or Mexico, were shrouded in secrecy. This generated rumours about his activities abroad to such an extent that he felt impelled on one occasion to explain to the Legislative Assembly his visit to Guatemala on a return journey from the United States.[5]

It was in this atmosphere of suspicion that Price, together with five other Executive Council members, departed for London in November 1957 to attend a financial and constitutional conference. The other members were the Governor, the Financial Secretary, two PUP Assemblymen, Cattouse and Jeffery, and Henry Bowman, a nominated Assemblyman and Associate Member for Public Utilities. Within a few days of their arrival Price invited his three unofficial colleagues, Cattouse, Jeffery and Bowman, to a luncheon given by the Guatemalan Minister, Jorge Garcia Granados, at which the 'Belice' problem was discussed.[6] While there has been disagreement about the details of the discussion, the gist of it was Guatemala's willingness to assume financial responsibility for Belize if the invitees would agree to the colony severing its connection with the British Crown and entering into some form of association with Guatemala which would include the latter's control over the external affairs of Belize.[7] More specifically, the delegates were to use their popularity to have the idea accepted. After a period of years a plebiscite was to be held to determine the exact form in which Belize wished to continue the relationship. The minimum form that Guatemala expected Belize to adopt was associated status with it since that would obviate all the difficulties (of negotiation, foregone development possibilities etc.) faced by independent newcomers seeking entry into an ongoing regional organization such as ODECA. If the delegates did not accept the proposals Guatemala would close its frontiers with Belize and all economic contact between the two countries would cease. These proposals were to be energetically pursued if the unofficial members were dissatisfied with the outcome of their mission to London. Alarmed by the magnitude of the implications, Jeffery reported the discussion to the British authorities. The Secretary of State Mr Alan Lennox Boyd, obviously irritated that the negotiations had been disingenuously carried on under the nose of the Colonial Office, denounced Price's 'lack of good faith and candour',[8] and broke off the negotiations when he established that in addition to the luncheon, Price had been engaged in private discussions, which did not include his colleagues, with the Guatemalan Minister.

*The repercussions*   Price was immediately sent home to be dismissed from his quasi-ministerial office and the Executive Council.[9] He was further castigated by Governor Thornley, both in the Legislative Assembly and in a radio broadcast, for being prepared in certain eventualities to hand over the country to the Guatemalan Republic 'lock, stock and barrel'.[10] The Governor reacted further by summoning in December a British frigate HMS *Ulster*, which had arrived unheralded in Jamaica a few days earlier.

What the British government had done in effect was to invite Price's countrymen to rally to his support. It was less than a year since they had reaffirmed their confidence in his leadership, although as Waddell noted, since the election had been won on the policy of 'No Federation' with the West Indies, Price's victory could not be truly construed as the voter's support for his pro-Guatemalan outlook.[11] Nonetheless, the British government had contributed to Price's popularity by overworking the Guatemala issue and making no secret of its desire to be rid of him. The disarray in which the London conference ended, and Price's subsequent dismissal from office, was seen by his supporters as the latest attempt to isolate him from them.

This entire incident was instructive of Price's personal leadership and far-reaching in its consequences for the party process. No-one within the party hierarchy seemed to know the precise relationship between Price and the Guatemala government and his colleagues were perhaps more surprised by the disclosure than was the suspecting opposition. Price's personal control was in a sense a natural outgrowth of the leadership struggle; it had generated a deep loyalty not only to his policy but also his person. It is not insignificant in this connection that his confidence was breached by Jeffery,[12] the newcomer, rather than Cattouse, a long-standing party member and Deputy Leader. Another factor in Price's personal influence was the indebtedness of the new PUP Assemblymen to him for an important source of influence and income. As we have seen, their social and occupational circumstances were exceedingly humble.

The manner in which Price handled the crisis on his return confirmed the development of the party as his *bona fide* machine. Given a hero's welcome at the airport, he kept in play the supportive role of the masses by holding a public meeting on the same night of his return.[13] This was before he reported to the party executive council, and as events developed he persisted with his characteristic tendency of relegating his colleagues to a minor role. He eventually broke his promise to them not to put the Guatemalan proposals to the public until the party executive council had formally considered them.[14] In terms of our argument that the low stature of his colleagues contributed to Price's personal hold on the party, it is significant that Pollard, the leading trade unionist, and Depaz, who had succeeded Price as the Member of Natural Resources, alone objected to the scant treatment. The outcome was Pollard's expulsion from the party and Depaz's resignation in March 1958.[15]

The reason for Pollard's protest was more complex than the above analysis suggests. He was desirous of ending his alien status and becoming a naturalized British subject. His claim that the London incident convinced him that 'Price is committed heart and soul and body to continue preaching the doctrine of political association with Guatemala'[16] was therefore not entirely in the nature of a discovery. Since the 1956 split, which had rekindled his political ambitions, he had been doing his best – which included serving on the Central Committee for Princess Margaret's visit to the country in early 1958[17] – to demonstrate to the colonial authorities that he was as loyal as any of Her Majesty's subjects. To have continued his association with the discredited Price was to prejudice his chances of obtaining citizenship. Indeed, the long years of association seemed to have been of little political value to Pollard who claimed that Price after winning the election seemed disinclined to intervene on his behalf.[18]

The difference then between Price and Pollard was to a large extent personal. This was reflected in the rudimentary structure of the high-sounding Democratic Agricultural Labour Party (renamed the Christian Democratic Party) which Pollard formed in August 1958.[19] It served mainly as the political platform for his attacks against Price, the futility of which was seen in the party's complete annihilation in the 1961 general election and its absorption by the other opposition party soon after.

Yet, more in desperation than hope, the colonial administration supported Pollard's attack on Price. It had been forced to the conclusion that the PUP leader could not be broken by parliamentary means. In the first place the organized opposition was still too feeble and nascent to cause his electoral defeat. For example, in November 1958, eleven months after Price was shorn of his office, his party won twenty-nine out of thirty-three seats in seven municipalities and he became the Mayor of Belize City.[20] This weakness explains the colonial administration's persistence with the 1957 Legislative Assembly which contained at least two PUP dissidents. Alternatively it could have replaced the Legislative Assembly with an interim administration of nominated legislators, as it had done when it dissolved the Belize City Council in 1951. But this would have sealed the political fate of a large number of opposition leaders.

Secondly, its own efforts to eliminate Price as the major political force were unsuccessful. An attempt to have him convicted in 1958 on a sedition charge for an uncomplimentary suggestion about the manner in which Princess Margaret should be welcomed failed.[21] Nor did Price's dismissal from office mean an end to his influence on government policy as the government may have hoped. He continued to exert considerable influence in the Executive Council through his two remaining party colleagues, Cattouse and Sylvestre, in this forum. In fact his anomalous relationship with the government enabled him to speak authoritatively (and invariably to the embarrassment of the colonial officials) in the Legislative Assembly, of which he was the Deputy Speaker.

At the same time, however, the defection of Jeffery and Depaz had reduced Price to the leader of a minority group of seven in the fifteen-member Legislative Assembly. That nine of them, including some of his colleagues, were committed in advance of debates by virtue of their membership of the Executive Council added to his frustration and turned him into a back-bencher.[22] Furthermore the party's extra-parliamentary organizational strength was also weakened by the dissensions and pressures of the colonial administration. Price had gained control of the CDU when Pollard defected, and he entrusted the secretaryship of the union to Norman Lainfiesta who was neither a trade unionist nor a politician.[23] Furthermore, Lainfiesta was no more amenable than Pollard to the politicians' control of the union. Price's preoccupation with his own political future enabled Lainfiesta to purge the union leadership of the former's supporters. Price finally lost his main link with the union when Lucas Marin, who had succeeded Cattouse as President of the union and was elected to the Belize City Council in 1958, departed from the PUP.[24] By itself the party's loss of union support was not critical because of the financial hold which the former had over the latter. The party withdrew its subsidies to the union and this forced the latter into a rivalry with the other unions for membership and for the support of the main regional international organization, ORIT, in order to bolster its financial position. As a consequence jurisdictional conflicts in which ORIT was called upon to mediate were rife, and this lowered the stature of unionism both in the eyes of the employer and the labourer.[25] Far from heaping further troubles on the PUP during the political crisis the CDU slowly sank into oblivion as its members first became inactive and then withdrew to await the emergence of new trade unions, which occurred in the early 1960s. Nonetheless, it is important to note that during the political crisis the PUP for the first time in its history was bereft of trade union support.

Perhaps of greater concern to Price was the impact of the political developments on the Catholic hierarchy. The Church, it should be recalled, did not officially support the PUP, and it is likely that the political events stimulated a variety of responses among the Jesuits. Some felt that the lean period which the party and its leader were undergoing required the open support of the Church. After all Price had more than a tenuous affinity with the Jesuits. He had studied for the priesthood and still possessed, as we have seen in his opposition to federation, a jesuitical singleness of purpose, and was unflinchingly committed to his goals. As Pollard claimed 'from personal knowledge' after his expulsion from the party in 1958, 'one or two priests have supported Price, and some still like him personally for his seeming personal piety'.[26] Some of the other Jesuits felt uncomfortable with the close affinity between their colleagues and the PUP.[27] For one thing the opposition parties and groups did not discriminate in their increasing condemnation of the close relationship. This threatened to mar the image of the entire religious order and the Diocese during the current crisis. Secondly, however favourable were the political changes to the Catholic Church, the Jesuits were still seen as an alien group. Their open involvement in the crisis could be less justified than that of their Protestant counterparts and rendered them more vulnerable to pressures from the colonial administration which recognized few limits in its attempt to dislodge Price. Long-term considerations also suggested a cautious response to the new political developments. Given the manner in which Price had systematically disposed of colleagues as he grew in confidence and popularity, it was reasonable to assume that the Church's role as a convenient political lever would diminish should the PUP survive the crisis and consolidate its own legitimacy if and when it became the government. It is possible that the principle of reciprocity which was implicit in the relationship would not then work to the advantage of the church, particularly in the sensitive field of education. Even if it did redound to the Church's benefit a measure of disengagement from the 'Establishment' was probably desirable in so far as the Church's identification with the ruling stratum would not necessarily be in the interest of its pastoral work. If these long-term considerations were valid, then the crisis was the opportune moment to alter the relationship with the PUP and its leaders.

From Price's point of view, a part of the problem was that he could not look forward to an early election to determine the extent of his losses and to try to redeem them, as one was not due before 1960. Furthermore, the colonial administration could have re-employed the technique of extending the life of the Assembly indefinitely, as it had done in the case of the Legislative Council in the early 1950s, and thereby prolonged the uncertainties of Price's political future. Indeed, subsequent to the London incident, the British government adopted a 'wait and see' attitude to the wider issue of constitutional decolonization.[28] The talks in London had been broken off before discussions reached constitutional matters. Within two months of the debacle however, in January 1958, a reconstituted delegation returned to London to resume discussion with the Colonial Office.[29] Although the PUP Deputy Leader, Cattouse, attended the conference in his capacity as a member of the Executive Council, this was the first delegation since the PUP's ascendancy that the party had been deprived of a leading role. On behalf of the PUP, Cattouse submitted to the conference constitutional proposals which called for internal self-government under a ministerial system. The British government was too distrustful of the PUP to accede to these proposals.[30, 31] Instead, the Secretary of State for the Colonies placed the issue in abeyance by deciding that if within a year the Governor recommended constitutional reform, he would send a Constitutional Commissioner to Belize.[32]

It is now possible to understand the acrimony that characterized the parliamentary debates between Price and the Colonial Secretary, T. D. Vickers, the chief colonial representative in the Legislative Assembly, and in particular their claim to be saving the country from each other. For different reasons both were frustrated parliamentary leaders. They drew their strength from contradictory sources of legitimacy. Behind the Colonial Secetary was the largely unrepresentative Legislative Assembly – the other two ex-officio members, the three nominated unofficial members and the two PUP defectors. Behind Price, who continued to call himself Majority Leader in the Legislative Assembly, stood a movement vehement in its loyalty.

That the Colonial Secretary was preoccupied with dislodging Price cannot be over-emphasized. It was in relief that Price bade him farewell in an open letter in 1960. 'You have been a ruthless political adversary of mine',[33] he wrote. A part of the problem was Vickers's relatively long service and the time it had begun. He came to Belize at the height of the crisis (1953) and had been influenced by it. As a participant in the Legislative Assembly he was caught up in a highly partisan atmosphere. Perhaps more than any other colonial official, he realized that but for Price the PUP's opposition to federation could probably have been overcome. Pollard, who was the only other influential party leader, was, since 1957, a comrade-in-arms. After his expulsion from the party however, the colonial strategy of playing upon party leadership ambitions ceased to make sense. The attack on Price had therefore to be direct and personal.

The hostility of the colonial administration no doubt also arose from its disappointment in the social group that constituted the new political elite. The emergence of politicians from the lower class and the outdistricts was unexpected and upsetting. Moreover, these politicians showed no intention of assuming the old symbols and ritual of office. The old political elite of wealthy businessmen, Espat, J. W. MacMillan, H. T. A. Bowman and E. W. M. Bowen, who were retained as parliamentary nominees and Associate Members, therefore appeared to be not only a counterbalancing but a countervailing influence.

Whatever the reasons for the hostility towards Price it encouraged the middle-class Creoles to reaffirm their faith in British protection. With the resumption of the negotiation between Britain and Guatemala, it was hardly likely that Britain could not continue forever to hold on to a possession whose principal leader wanted to sever the connection and which was itself of no strategic or economic value. To this extent the middle-class Creoles had come to realize that sooner or later they would have had to fend for themselves. The London incident also brought home to them the need for their party, the NP, to join forces with the stronger anti-PUP party, the HIP. The HIP also welcomed the merger into the NIP under Fuller's leadership in July 1958 because of its own leadership difficulties.[34] Its Leader, Richardson, had resigned in early 1958 to take up an appointment with a publishing firm in Trinidad. Goldson, the Acting Leader, also wished to devote more time to the *Belize Billboard* which had declined with the popularity of its owners. Thus, while he accepted the secretaryship of the fused party, he eventually resigned the office before the 1961 elections which he did not contest.[35]

It was inevitable that the pattern of organization and the political orientation of the old parties would influence the character of the NIP. Although district branches were formed the party machinery continued to function mainly in Belize City until Goldson became the Leader in late 1961 as a result of Fuller's illness. The social basis of the party membership remained middle class although the old professional group did not monopolize the new hierarchy. There was, however, a growing tendency for the party to perceive the political situation more in a cultural than a class context. This reflected the fact that the break of the HIP leaders with Price had been motivated less by the fear for the social changes that usually accompany the decolonizing process than by the cultural implications of closer Central American ties. As we pointed out in the previous chapter, however, it was not always easy to distinguish class and status considerations from cultural within the party political process since these were still highly correlated.

As can be expected, despite the identity of purpose, the two groups of leaders did not weld instantly. There was, for example, considerable jostling for the party's nomination in the Belize City Council elections a few months later, in December 1958. This led to the expulsion of James Meighan, the Deputy Leader,[36] who was denied nomination and contested the election as an independent candidate. The lack of internal unity was also largely responsible for the resignation of Lindberg Rogers, a city councillor and the party Treasurer in 1960.[37] What were NIP losses became PUP gains. Both Meighan, a retired District Commissioner, and Rogers, a transport owner and mechanic, joined the PUP and provided it with a more ethnically and culturally varied leadership and much-needed ability.

The various factional realignments within the short period of one year, from November 1957 to December 1958, glaringly pointed to the urgent need for the contending forces to formulate a common goal. In fact the general situation had deteriorated to a point where none of the political parties or the colonial administration could 'go it alone'. The PUP was too popular for its leader to be indefinitely excluded from the government. It however had been rudely awakened to the fact that popularity by itself did not confer legitimacy in a colonial society. To achieve effective power it also had to recognize that the constitutional structure consisted of at least two parallel systems, the colonial and the emergent Belize regime. While the structure in the context of decolonization assumed that full constitutional powers would rest ultimately in Belizean hands, it expected in the 1950s that the local political elite would in the meanwhile abide by the British government's policy of self-government within the Commonwealth.

Price eventually acknowledged the British constitutional structure of decolonization when, in the Legislative Assembly within a few weeks of the breakdown of the London conference in November 1957, he supported a parliamentary resolution of loyalty to the British Crown which also repudiated the Guatemalan claim.[38] The constitutional arrangement also required the PUP to recognize at least the main opposition party, the NIP, irrespective of the latter's parliamentary strength and structural viability. Ironically the two main political parties went beyond mere co-existence and presented a united stand against the British government in response to the recommendations of two separate constitutional and economic commissions in 1959. The constitutional commission was in accordance with the British government's promise to review

the constitution on the recommendation of the Governor. The outcome was Sir Hilary Blood's report which, however, was as gloomy
as the time it was written and recognized few of the parties' separate
demands.[39] The common outlook between the parties was reinforced
by the unpopular recommendation of Jack Downie, a senior Economic
Adviser in the British Treasury, that large-scale immigration was a
*sine qua non* for the country's economic development.[40] The reaction of
the political parties of the two reports not only marked the beginning
of the resolution of party conflict but perhaps more important under-
scored the need for a top level conference of all the political elements
that were involved in the wider political conflict, which was eventually
held in London in February 1960.

## The resolution

If our contention is correct that the conflict had reached a deadlock and
none of the protagonists could live alone with the situation indefinitely,
then the Blood and the Downie reports should be seen as the immediate
occasion of the *rapprochement*. Nonetheless, since these reports provide
further insight into the political process and were far-reaching in their
consequences, they deserve detailed examination.

*The Blood constitutional enquiry*   From the outset the constitutional
enquiry was a unifying force. It brought together the two parties, the NIP
and CDP, which were opposed to the PUP. They submitted two joint
proposals,[41] in the obvious attempt to strengthen their position *vis-à-vis*
the PUP. The basic objective of the joint NIP–CDP proposals more or less
matched the demands of the PUP for internal self-government. This was
not surprising. For one thing the conservatism and at times outright
antagonism of the middle-class Creoles to rapid constitutional change had
paid no political dividends. For another, the NIP did not only consist of
these types of leaders but like the CDP had a number of influential PUP
dissidents who were committed to constitutional advance to the extent
that they did not necessarily accept the Guatemalan claim as a complicat-
ing factor. Finally, both the NIP and the CDP had a vested interest in a
constitutional change to a ministerial system within the existing government, for two reasons. Their influence in the Executive Council had been
disproportionately enhanced as a result of two of its three unofficial
members with major portfolios, Depaz and Jeffery, having transferred
their support from the PUP to the CDP and NIP respectively.

The second reason for the NIP–CDP demand for the introduction of a
full ministerial system 'overnight by a stroke of a pen',[42] in Sir Hilary

Blood's words, was a genuine disenchantment with the limited scope of the Membership System. Every submission to the Executive Council had to go through the Colonial Secretary's office. As the Colonial Secretary conceded in the debate of the Blood Report, 'the elected members of the Government with portfolios have responsibility but no authority'.[43]

Beyond sharing the view that the new constitution should confer internal self-government, the PUP and NIP–CDP proposals differed on almost every other important issue. The proposals highlighted once more their differing orientations to outside political entities. The NIP and CDP advocated that the constitutional advance should be within the Commonwealth but were careful to add 'outside the West Indies Federation'.[44] On the other hand the PUP reiterated its request for 'self determination under the United Nations'.[45] It also insisted that no provision denying the place of Belize as part of Central America, or implying an aspiration for an eventual union with any other entity of the Caribbean, should be embodied in a new constitution.[46]

The PUP and the NIP–CDP also held divergent views on the Governor's residual powers, which reflected their mutual deep-seated distrust and also the PUP's lack of confidence in the impartiality of the colonial administration. The NIP–CDP had significantly qualified its demand for full internal self-government with the suggestion that Britain for the time being should retain responsibility, not only for the external, but also internal security of the country on the ground that under modern military conditions it would not be possible for the people of this country to protect themselves from 'internal subversion'.[47]

This consideration grew out of their concern about the statement from the new President of Guatemala, Miguel Ydigoras Fuentes, on the 'Belice' issue in 1958. The President asserted his country's claim with a vigour and in a demonstrable manner that had been unknown in previous regimes.[48] In August 1958, he decreed that 1959, which was the centenary of the Anglo-Guatemala treaty of 1859, be the 'year of the recovery of Belice'.[49] He did not rule out the use of force[50] in the solution of the problem and played upon the cultural and ethnic differences in Belize by appealing to the Latin element in the society for moral support.

Although Price had supported the parliamentary resolution of loyalty to the British Crown in November 1958 and another one in January 1959[51] in the wake of Ydigoras Fuentes' declarations, the NIP and CDP were evidently still maintaining their charge against him of complicity in the Guatemalan claim. To some extent Price had only himself to blame for the persistence of the opposition's concern about his role in the renewed and strident Guatemalan pressures. His support of the various resolutions of loyalty were either preceded by an amendment or accompanied by an attempt to represent the Guatemalan claim as 'merely a political strategy [and] civic pride'.[52] This disarming observation was valid and it may even be argued that the Guatemalan claim should have been ignored as being only a useful diversion for President Ydigoras Fuentes in time of internal pressure.

Far from accepting the view that it was necessary to leave the responsibility of internal security in the Governor's hands, Price argued that he should be relieved of it. Since, as we have seen, the colonial administration spared no effort or method in its attempt to isolate Price from his supporters, it was vulnerable to his charge that the law enforcement agencies had been unleashed upon the PUP and were 'being used as a Colonial instrument of repressing the people's rightful political aspirations'.[53] The police force had come under fire when one of his colleagues, Louis Sylvestre, a Member of the Executive Council and Associate Member for Natural Resources, was arrested and, as Price claimed, treated in a way that did not acknowledge his position of honour and responsibility.[54] To prevent a recurrence the PUP proposed that the new constitution should provide immunity to members of the Assembly from prosecution for their political opinions expressed privately, or at meetings outside the Legislative Assembly, and protect them from being arraigned in court without the consent of the Assembly.[55]

As in the other departments of the government service, the Creoles virtually monopolized the ranks open to Belizeans in the police force. Since the Creoles as a whole were favoured by the colonial social order, the possibility that the police officers were protecting it not only because they were instructed to do so but also out of racial and cultural considerations cannot be discounted. But it would be wrong and misleading to leave the matter there. A part of the problem was that the colonial political system was not structured to accommodate new political institutions that were non-governmental in origin and character – such as mass political parties – without generating friction between government officers and the new type of political functionary. This was particularly true in the case of the outdistricts where the government institutions had historically encountered fewer competing sources of authority and influence.

It is not surprising therefore that the PUP had also severely criticized the district commissioners (later restyled district officers) in connection with their relationship with the town boards[56] whose political character had changed with the introduction in the principal district towns of the elective principle and party politics in 1955. Being accustomed to running the town boards from their inception decades ago, the district commissioners did not respond readily to the change, especially as it produced PUP-controlled boards that were socially heterogeneous and opposed to the old ruling elite. Accordingly, the PUP proposed to Sir Hilary Blood that the district commissioners be divested of their judicial powers and appointed by the Cabinet with the approval of the Assembly.[57]

It was partly to safeguard against such radical changes that the NIP–CDP proposed the creation of an upper chamber of the Legislature which would 'act as a brake on the more extravagant vagaries of the political parties and give the country time to express its views before action was taken inimical to its interests'.[58] The proposal was also intended to provide representation for the middle-class and professional Creoles who supported the NIP and still provided some of its leaders. Having suffered several electoral defeats at the hands of the PUP, members of this group were unwilling to come forward as candidates for elections, but were prepared to accept nomination to the Legislature. But the NIP recognized that the retention of the nominated element in a single-chamber Legislative Assembly would be unpopular and somewhat incompatible with a more advanced constitution.[59] As the only alternative method of retaining a nominated element, the creation of an Upper Chamber was more vital to the NIP than it cared to admit. After all, none of the opposition parties had won a seat in either the 1954 or the 1957 general elections. Furthermore the PUP had swept the municipal elections in December 1958. If this was taken as an index of the parties' popularity in the country as a whole then the NIP–CDP chances of providing a single elected representative at the next general elections were slim. Indeed the two opposition parties being less than a year old were too weak organizationally to prevent another PUP landslide victory in a general election.

These considerations could also have been discerned from the NIP–CDP proposals on the electoral and voting system. In the first place they did not overlook the fact that the opposition parties had polled 30.0 per cent and 37.1 per cent of the total votes in 1954 and 1957 respectively. It was most likely from this quarter that Sir Hilary Blood received the suggestion that proportional representation be introduced.[60] In order to overcome their organizational weakness and because they reasonably believed that a low poll of 52.0 per cent of the registered voters in the 1957 election was due to a large extent to abstention on the part of the anti-PUP elements, the NIP–CDP also recommended compulsory registration and voting.[61] To maximize their chances of success they suggested that voting by proxy and by mail should also be introduced.[62] This suggestion was derived in part from the distances which voters had to travel, and the shifting and seasonal nature of employment throughout the country.

But perhaps more important it was to facilitate voters who, the NIP–CDP observed, 'were compelled for financial reasons to live abroad but who have retained a deep interest in their homeland'.[63] The NIP, more so than the CDP, was catering not so much for the dwindling or stagnant group of Belizeans to be found in the Central American republics but for their Creole supporters who were migrating in increasing numbers to the USA.

Sir Hilary Blood was, however, less concerned with the problems of the NIP and CDP, and for that matter the PUP, than those which the overall situation posed for the British government. As he reverently stated at the outset of his report:

The constitution of a dependent territory is not just a formula to be changed to meet the exigencies of local politics. Any constitutional advance is a conscious act of delegation into local hands of part of the responsibility for dependent people for which the Secretary of State for the Colonies has to account to the parliament and electors in Britain. It is in the end they who decide how dependent territories shall be governed: and, just as they are concerned to see that there shall be colonial constitutional advance, so equally are they concerned that the pace of such advance shall be appropriate to local conditions and that the loosening of control by the United Kingdom Government is not made the occasion of the assumption of control in a dependent territory by one party, nor by one section of the community, to the exclusion of such opportunities for criticism and opposition as are the symptoms of a healthy democratic way of life, and the safeguards against the arbitrary use of power.[64]

It is clear that in Sir Hilary Blood's view constitutional decolonization did not only imply that authority ultimately rested with the British government but also entailed the extension to the colony of a system of parliamentary government on Westminster lines. British constitutional theories and practices were not only to be acquired but must necessarily take the same form as in Great Britain. Little scope must be allowed for them to be moulded in their course of development by social conditions and national aptitudes. Sir Hilary Blood even felt constrained to comment adversely on the small size of the Legislative Chamber and the limited space between the public accommodation and the area in which the members sat. He claimed that members could not debate without being conscious of the near presence of the public audience, while the latter was made to feel it was at a public meeting. 'A projection of the Mother of Parliaments', he declared 'deserves better treatment than this.'[65] It was however the Belizeans who deserved better judgement. Although the proximity which the Chamber offered the public to the legislators was an accident rather than a design, it symbolized the familiarity, intimacy, and the type of communication between the leaders and the led which had developed with the advent of mass political activity on the 'Battlefield'. It was through this kind of relationship that the latent individual protest against colonialism became grouped into a social force and formalized into a line of struggle and way of life for the PUP. It is arguable that the danger which Sir Hilary Blood feared arises only after political power is transferred from the imperial power to the national unit and if it is monopolized by the political elite, as is often the case in the new nations.

If Sir Hilary Blood was concerned with the fact that the Legislative Chamber was not a replica of the British Parliament then it was easy to predict the conclusion which he drew from the absence of a viable two-party system and the non-existence of an elected parliamentary opposition until a feeble one was created by the defection from the PUP of Depaz and Jeffery in 1957 and 1958 respectively. 'This', he observed,

hardly indicates a healthy state of affairs. The essence of the British parliamentary system of government is the existence of two parties, either of which may be called upon by the electorate to form the government of the country. One cannot, of course, expect to find a two-party system functioning on United Kingdom lines from the very start of political developments in a dependent territory, but it must be the goal at which to aim. And until there is some indication of an approach to that goal, constitutional development requires careful handling.[66]

Neither the NIP–CDP nor the PUP could share his views. The NIP–CDP had argued that the fault was not so much with the party system as with the electoral system. Under a proportional system of representation the parties' strength in the country would have been more accurately reflected in the Legislative Assembly. But Sir Hilary Blood rejected this proposal as well as those about compulsory registration and voting on the ground that the onus was with the political parties to stimulate more popular interest in party politics.

For its part, the PUP could not be held responsible for the inept opposition. To delay constitutional advance until a stronger and more viable opposition party emerged was in effect to penalize the PUP for its popularity. Furthermore, Sir Hilary Blood was not being consistent and straightforward. He observed that countries such as Singapore had achieved political independence or were in sight of it, despite their limitation of size and natural resources. He failed to mention however that almost all of these countries had in common with Belize a dominant nationalist party. In fact the 'wind of change' had in the same year, 1959, just begun to blow Tanganyika rapidly to independence, by-passing in the process several stages of constitutional development, despite or because of the virtual existence of a single party, the Tanganyika African National Union (TANU).[67] Yet Sir Hilary Blood insisted that in Belize full internal self-government had to be 'earned – and this is the essential point – in successive steps by revealed capacity for responsible government'.[68]

By 'revealed capacity for responsible government' the Constitutional Commissioner meant several things other than the development of a two-party system. He was also referring to the country's grant-in aid status. Sir Hilary believed that to bring this to an end, which self-government would entail, would be 'disastrous',[69] although his financial counterpart, Jack Downie, was at the time arguing that Treasury control was not the best way for Belizeans to find their footing.[70]

The quality of both political and administrative leadership was another criterion which Sir Hilary Blood used to determine the country's ability to undertake greater responsibility. As we indicated in the Introduction, he was appalled at the low level of formal education of the elected members and lamented the virtual absence of a single member of the professional elite in the Legislative Assembly. On the basis that it was this latter group on which the success of internal self-government largely depended else-where, the Constitutional Commissioner concluded that Belize did not qualify for this major step of constitutional advance.[71] To do so the country had to not only replace the existing political leaders with persons who had had university, professional and technical training but also to provide the civil service with more trained personnel.

These were imposing conditions which were not necessarily being applied to other countries. To refer to Tanganyika again, it lacked a veritable African middle class from which the nationalist politicians could be drawn. Furthermore the Tanganyikan politicians had little experience of operating a political system on a national scale when independence was achieved in 1961. Nor was Tanganyika better served than Belize with local-trained civil service personnel. Two suggestions[72] that the administrative service in Belize be reinforced with experienced expatriate officers from the Central Pool which the Colonial Office created in the mid-1950s[73] to met such contingencies did not materialize. From the inception of the quasi-ministerial system in 1955 nationals were therefore appointed as administrative heads of the quasi-ministries.[74]

The political parties did not dispute Sir Hilary Blood's observation about the dearth of professional and trained personnel. Nonetheless the NIP-CDP felt that Sir Hilary Blood had overstated the problem or even failed to grasp its true nature when he claimed that 'the field from which candidates for election to the Legislature are forthcoming is limited, and the sources from which nominated members can be drawn are by no means wide'.[75]

In their view, the reservoir of professional persons was larger than was apparent to an outsider. The deficiency arose from the withdrawal of most of these people from public life once political influence had begun to elude their grasp with the advent of the PUP. In other words the problem was not so much one of numbers as the reluctance of the middle class to engage in electoral politics. Indeed, since the Creoles provided almost all of the members of the professional elite, the reluctance of this group was likely to persist, irrespective of the extent to which the field was enlarged.

Before the constitutional enquiry, Price had responded to the entire problem of trained personnel in a more critical manner that was designed to put the colonial administration on the defensive. Far from giving assurances to the colonial authorities he took the view that Belizeans were entitled to an explanation from them since the lack of trained personnel was to be attributed to the British imperial system in general and the limited opportunity for post-secondary education in particular. Since he never lost an opportunity to prove that Belize would be better off within the Latin American framework rather than the British Commonwealth, he went on to observe that under the Spanish colonial system a university was established in Peru, even before Harvard or before the University College of the West Indies.[76] It was evident that the PUP did not accept the logic of Sir Hilary Blood's argument, namely that the British colonial system should be prolonged as part of the solution to the problem of qualified personnel.

There was a fourth and final context in which the Constitutional Commissioner assessed the country's suitability for a greater measure of responsibility. This was the Guatemalan claim. He agreed in principle with the joint proposal by the NIP and CDP that the Guatemalan claim should not be allowed to hold up the internal progress indefinitely.[77] At the same time the intensification of the Guatemalan pressure under the Presidency of Ydigoras Fuentes more or less coincided with his visit and left its mark on him. Furthermore he saw as 'danger signals' the PUP's demand for self-government 'under the United Nations' and 'within the geographical framework of Central America'.[78] Nor did he seem to recognize that there was a possible distinction and even incompatibility between the Guatemalan claim and Price's policy of incorporation into ODECA as an independent entity. Thus he concluded, 'I cannot entirely neglect the problem, and in my opinion it must affect the pace at which progress towards internal self-government can be made'.[79]

Of the four considerations – the absence of a two-party system, the country's grant-aided status, the shortage of trained manpower and the limited role of the middle class in the country's affairs, and the Guatemalan claim – he stated that it was the third, the paucity of experienced political leaders, that mostly affected his recommendations. There is no doubt that Sir Hilary Blood strongly believed that until Belize showed more interest in improving the quality of its leadership the British government would be ill-advised to confer a large measure of responsibility upon the country. It would 'be unthinkable to make, at virtually one jump, a change from the present constitution, which itself is only five years old, to that very wide measure of internal self government advocated by the political parties. The men, the women and the experience are simply not yet available.'[80]

It can be reasonably argued, however, that the crucial consideration was not the quality of the leadership but the Guatemalan claim. After all, as he eventually admitted, the internal factors – limited economic and financial capacity, the overwhelming dominance of one party, the nature of the leadership – were 'not entirely peculiar to the British Hondurans' and did not necessarily impede major constitutional advance elsewhere. But the political life of few colonial territories was bedevilled by a territorial claim. Furthermore whereas such a claim usually acts as a unifying force within the threatened colony it had divided Belizeans. Since the role of the dominant PUP was also equivocal, it was not surprising that Sir Hilary Blood should firmly state, 'For the present the Governor must, in the end, still govern.'[81] Accordingly full ministerial government was the maximum advance that he conceded. The single-chamber Legislative Assembly was to be retained with its nominated element. Its elected members were to be increased from nine to eighteen, Belize City being given four constituencies, more or less in direct proportion to its share of the country's population. The nominated members were increased from three to five and, without giving reasons, specific provision was to be made in the constitutional documents for a woman to be one of the nominees. Two of these members were to be nominated by the Governor after consultation with, but not on the advice of, the Leader of the majority party in the Legislative Assembly; one was similarly to be nominated after consultation with the Leader of the minority party or parties if such existed; if not, the nomination of the third member, like that of the fourth and fifth members, was to be entirely at the Governor's discretion. With the replacement of the Financial Secretary by a Finance Minister, the number of ex-officio members in the Legislative Assembly was to be reduced from three to two. Altogether the recommendations were to produce a Legislative Assembly of twenty-five as against the existing total of fifteen. The Executive Council was to consist of six unofficial members, four elected and two nominated from the Legislative Assembly, and the two ex-officio members, the Colonial Secretary and the Attorney General, apart from the Governor as Chairman. All six unofficial members were to have ministerial status, but two were not to have portfolios since Sir Hilary Blood limited the number of portfolios to four. There were also a number of other minor changes in response to the representations made to Sir Hilary Blood, the most noteworthy being a wider system of voting by proxy, or of postal voting. Nonetheless when taken as a whole these recommendations amounted more to a step away from the existing arrangement than one toward internal self-government.[82]

It can be further argued that because of the Guatemalan claim the outcome of the enquiry was predetermined. At times Sir Hilary Blood wrote as if he was under instructions that did not appear in his terms of reference, which were simply 'to inquire into the working of the present constitution of British Honduras and to make recommendations for any changes which may be thought desirable'.[83] He would have 'unhesitatingly welcomed' the proposal for a bicameral legislature 'if I thought the United Kingdom government would in fact now be willing to abrogate for the most part its responsibilities for the internal affairs of this country'.[84] Almost apologetically, he concluded his report with the admission that he was only too well aware that the recommendations which he had made in it for constitutional advances fell very considerably short of the requests and proposals which had been put to him.[85]

Evidently the British government's strategy was to mark time constitutionally and observe the behaviour of the somewhat chastened PUP leader, Price, presumably in the hope that more tangible evidence of his co-operation than his recent professions of loyalty to the Crown would be forthcoming. This was implicit in Sir Hilary Blood's belief that he 'can recommend changes which if worked in a proper spirit of co-operation will pave the way for further advance later'.[86]

The observations of the Colonial Secretary when he moved the Legislative Assembly acceptance of the report of the Constitutional Commissioner support our contention that Sir Hilary Blood had not been necessarily encouraged by the Colonial Office to approach his task with an open mind. The Colonial Secretary claimed in his preamble to the resolution that there were no grounds for supposing that the British government would be prepared to contemplate the establishment of Cabinet government in Belize without the usual preceding period of some years of ministerial government.[87] The resolution itself also clearly stated that the report should be viewed as a means towards achieving 'internal self government within the British Commonwealth'.[88]

In a business-like manner he urged the Legislative Assembly to adopt his resolution on that day, 13 November 1959, for several reasons. First, elections under the existing constitution were due between May and July of the next year, and could be held at that time under a new constitution only if the necessary administrative and legislative machinery were put into action as soon as possible. Second, some members of the government were to leave for London within the next two weeks and were likely to be away for three or four weeks, that is, almost until Christmas. Their absence would delay acceptance of the report. Furthermore, the immediate acceptance of the report would give the delegation to London, including the Deputy Leader of the PUP, Cattouse, the opportunity to discuss the recommendations with the Secretary of State for the Colonies. Finally, the delimitation of the new constituencies entailed a complete revision of all the electoral rolls in early 1960. This could not be accomplished if the report was not accepted early.

In reply, Price easily demolished these arguments and implied that these were not the real reasons for the indecent haste. In the first place, he contended that the preamble to the Colonial Secretary's resolution was unnecessary and even misleading. It assumed that there was an immutable and uniform pattern and also stages of constitutional development towards self-government in the Commonwealth territories.[89] Even if this was the case in theory, it was not so in practice. As he observed, the Commonwealth territories had reached independence by many different ways and at least one colonial territory, Burma, had also achieved this goal outside of the Commonwealth.[90] There should, therefore, be no infallible premise that the recommendations as made by Sir Hilary Blood constituted the only means for Belize to achieve self-government.[91]

Price also could not accept the Colonial Secretary's premise that there were no grounds for supposing that the British government would contemplate proposals other than those put forward by Sir Hilary Blood. This was to predetermine the outcome of the debate and therefore render the whole exercise academic if not meaningless. Indeed, he observed that the Colonial Secretary, by pleading urgency, seemed intent on denying the elected members of the Legislative Assembly the opportunity, which the Governor-in-Council had claimed for itself by modifying three of the provisions, of changing the constitution. The Executive Council had not seen the need to extend the voting by proxy and postal voting or to legislate for compulsory representation by a woman. It had also agreed not to limit the ministries to four as Sir Hilary had recommended but to leave the number open.[92] The PUP Leader insisted that the Legislative Assembly exercise its right to examine the Blood Report in its own time. Neither the impending departure of a government delegation to London nor the imminent general election was a sufficient reason for dispensing with a careful consideration of the report. In the first place the delegation was going to London primarily to discuss financial and economic matters. Price also noted that the parliamentary motion to approve the recommendations of the Downie Report which was intended to be the basis of the London discussions had been withdrawn, to his surprise, that very morning from the proceedings of the Legislative Assembly.[93] If the delegation could proceed with its financial discussions without the Legislative Assembly's approval of the Downie Report why did it necessarily require parliamentary approval of the Blood recommendations? Behind this rhetorical question lay Price's unwillingness to lend legitimacy to the efforts of the government delegation which he observed did not truly reflect the composition of the Assembly.[94]

In upholding the privileges of the Legislative Assembly Price's stand was not novel. The precedent was established when the Courtenay constitutional report was presented to the Legislative Council. As we observed in chapter 5, this body did not accept the report then and there but referred it to a Select Committee which made modifications that were debated before the views of the Legislative Council were forwarded to London. It took over two years for the Legislative Council to receive a reply from London and to approve the bill for the relevant ordinance.[95] Meanwhile, elections were postponed indefinitely, to the chagrin of the PUP. If the Legislative Assembly was to act in any other way now, Price argued, it would be failing in its duties to the people of this country.[96]

In confronting the colonial administration with the technique which it had itself employed against the PUP in the early 1950s Price was not merely dispensing poetic justice or protecting the Legislative Assembly from executive pressure. Price had to avoid an open confrontation with the Legislative Assembly at all costs until he had the opportunity to invoke the supportive role of the PUP rank-and-file. As in the case of the West Indies Federation, the legislature was unlikely to fly in the face of public opposition to the report. On the other hand, if this opinion was not forthcoming it could use its majority to dismiss the grounds on which Price was likely to oppose the recommendations. As he reasoned, the Legislative Assembly did not have to be led entirely by public opinion, but should 'take great note of it', and 'be influenced by it'.[97] These considerations were so vital to Price that he modified his forthright Central American stand in order to forestall a debate. He claimed in the debate that 'it should be very plain to all that the political objective of the People's United Party is to achieve self government within the British Commonwealth and ultimately, in accordance with the United Nations Charter'.[98] Although it was as a prelude to 'self determination' that Price now conceived of self-government within the Commonwealth, the statement was also intended to allay the fears of the British government since Sir Hilary Blood was disturbed that the PUP's memorandum 'says nothing about it in the context of the Commonwealth'.[99] In the final analysis it was to the British government and not the Legislative Assembly that he had to be conciliatory if his demands for internal government were to be met. As Pollard pointed out, Price had 'awakened. . . to the fact that to continue a forthright pro-Guatemala policy after Blood's report would be to continue kicking his brains against the British brick wall'.[100]

Fortuitously the annual conventions of all three parties were soon to be held. Surely, Price argued, the conventions should be given an opportunity to 'feel the pulse of popular reaction to his report'.[101] The parliamentary representatives of the two other political parties could not reasonably oppose this argument since they too were disappointed with the report. Yet the CDP representative, Depaz, countered the argument with the suggestion that the executive councils of the three parties were more likely to deal with the report expeditiously and could submit their recommendations to the government before the delegation left for London.[102] The reason for his suggestion was not merely to effect a compromise between the Colonial Secretary's plea for immediate action and Price's view that the public opinion should be determined. It was also an attempt to relegate the mass factor to a minor role since Depaz recognized that the mobilization of mass political pressure was a technique which Price had perfected and successfully employed to outmanoeuvre his opponents. Nonetheless, the Colonial Secretary conceded the merits of Price's arguments and agreed to refer the report to a Select Committee of the Unofficial Members of the Legislative Assembly.[103]

For all practical purposes Price had captured the initiative because the PUP had a majority of two among the unofficial members. Nevertheless, Price refrained from using the majority to override the views of the other members of the Committee or even to take the discussion outside the framework of the Blood constitution. On the contrary, he was extremely conciliatory. Far from pressing the politicization of the District Commissioner system, for example, Price agreed with his colleagues that an impartial, non-political civil service should exist in the country.[104] Nor did Price stand firm against the nominated system. The exclusion of unofficial nominated members from both the Legislative Assembly and the

Executive Council was a matter of principle for him. Nevertheless, he reluctantly agreed that this element should be retained in the Legislative Assembly.[105] However, their appointments were not to be at the discretion of the Governor. The final say should rest with the leaders of the majority and minority parties. This was to take the form of a constitutional convention whereby the Governor would normally be obliged not only to seek, but to accept the advice of these leaders. This practice was also to extend to the Executive Council where the powers of selecting the unofficial members were to reside with the Majority Leader alone. Price was also firmly against the compulsory participation of the nominated members in the Executive Council. The majority party should not be restricted in its choice of unofficial members. Whether or not these included a nominated element would depend largely on the composition and character of the Assembly after an election.[106] This was the most contentious issue. J. W. MacMillan, a nominated member, argued that the PUP should have stuck to its principles and opposed the nominated system; however once the system was allowed to exist it must be preserved through all its stages.[107]

The PUP's compromise could not prevail once the Committee had reported to the Legislative Assembly. For the nominated unofficial members were certain of the support of not only the two PUP dissidents, but also the ex-officio members. Echoing Sir Hilary Blood, the Acting Colonial Secretary asserted that the time had not yet come when the government should dispense with the valuable help of the nominated members, especially as they represented a section of the community which did not normally engage in electoral politics.[108]

There was in any case little point to a struggle over this issue since the Select Committee had recommended that a delegation from the Legislative Assembly should go to London to discuss in detail the recommendations of the Constitutional Commissioner.[109] The NIP in fact had gone a step further earlier in the year. It had suggested to the Secretary of State for the Colonies that an all-party delegation should visit Britain to confer with the British government on the political and economic future of the country.[110] In this suggestion the possibility of a realignment of forces could be foreseen. The CDP leader, Pollard, had argued that the two NIP–CDP Assemblymen should continue to demand the minimum NIP–CDP proposals in the Legislative Assembly. The NIP considered this a 'time-wasting and unconvincing manoeuvre and one most likely to promote between Britain and British Honduras the maximum of ill-will and suspicion'.[111] It preferred to expend its energies in renewing its demand for direct consultation between the political parties and the Colonial

Office. Considerable force was added to this argument when the Downie Report proved to be as controversial as the Blood Report.

*The Downie economic report*    The fact that Downie found it necessary in his examination of the economic situation in Belize to disagree with one of the bases of Sir Hilary Blood's recommendations suggests that the problems with which the two commissioners were concerned were not unrelated. The new politics clearly needed to be serviced by new economic ideas, especially as the economy retained many of the debilitating features which had contributed to the birth of the PUP.[112]

Downie was particularly struck with the small size of the population, first in absolute terms, second, in relation to the size of the country, and finally with the way in which it was widely scattered throughout the country. He considered these aspects of the population the crucial obstacle to the transformation of the economy.[113] The small population meant a tiny local market and also precluded economies of scale in the provision of government and public utility. An effective government organization of the country needed to be only very little expanded to deal with twice or even three times the population. Without this increase the country would continue to be incapable of supporting the basic services unless it was fortunate to discover mineral resources which would increase the government revenue substantially through royalties. Thus the 'many complaints about the inefficiency of government in general with its alleged dilatoriness [and] the standards of social and public services being low and in some cases deteriorating'[114] which he received did not come as a surprise to him. So also were the representations made to him about the low incomes and living standards of people. He believed that the country could not hope to remedy this situation by adopting the suggestion the PUP put to him. This was that the size of the area to be developed should be used as the yardstick of sustainable economic progress. As he put it, he could not 'accept the conclusions which the PUP derived from this; in particular, the implications that the object of economic policy is to develop unused resources at whatever cost, as an end in itself, as opposed to raising the incomes and living standards of people'.[115] The party's point of view, however, only served to reinforce his conviction that the small size of the population was the fundamental reason for the poverty and lack of economic progress of Belize, since it was incapable of subduing 'a land which is too big and luxuriant for their numbers to handle'.[116]

Downie drew the logical conclusion from this basic argument. The economy would always remain under-developed and undeveloped unless the population was substantially increased to about 300,000 by 1975.[117]

This could not be achieved by the natural increase of the population at its annual rate of 3.7 per cent. Accordingly, an annual immigration intake of seven thousand, or one thousand families, based on the assumption that the reproductive characteristics of the immigrants were the same as those of the existing population, was required. These immigrants were to be primarily agricultural settlers for whom new and concentrated peasant communities were to be established.[118] The recommendation, as Downie acknowledged,[119] was not new; it merely rehearsed the old tune of the Evans Commission of 1948 without the full orchestra. His supporting arguments lacked the thoroughness of those of the Evans Commission. Agriculture, for which the settlers were to be recruited, was cursorily described in three brief paragraphs[120] and treated *en passant* in other parts of the report. Peasant cultivation was to be preferred to plantation agriculture not because of any inherent advantages which it possessed, but simply because Downie had little faith in the ability of governments to run plantations themselves.[121] Equally his economic development plan,[122] which was a concomitant of his immigration scheme, was not put forward with the same certainty and eloquence as that of the Evans Commission.

In fairness to Downie, the idea of massive immigration was the conclusion which he reached, whereas it was the specified starting-point of the Evans Commission. Furthermore, he was proposing a solution to the problems of Belize while the Evans Commission had been concerned with solving the problem of overpopulation in the West Indian island territories and persons displaced as a result of the World War. In other words, since the perspectives of the two reports were different, comparison is probably misleading and the specific answers to the two different problems hardly the same.[123]

If these circumstances were extenuating, the NIP did not consider them an excuse for the recommendation which Downie implied, rather than made, on the likely sources of the immigrants. While he did not specify the sources, he suggested that they should be determined by the provenance of the immigrants.[124] In other words, the immigrants should be procured from countries whose governments were capable and willing to assist the British government in meeting the land settlement cost. The alternative was for the cost[125] to be borne by an international organization since it was beyond the Belize government's means. The first alternative placed West Indians and Central Americans at a disadvantage. It also created the possibility that the immigrants would add to the racial and cultural mosaic of Belize. In fact, on the basis of Downie's demographic projections the immigrants and their children born in Belize were to constitute about one-half of the total population in 1975. Yet he was unperturbed about the sociological implications of his immigration plan: 'As regards the capacity of the British Honduras people to absorb migrants on a large scale without there developing cultural or political strains, I confine myself to the very tentative observation that a marked degree of ethnic fragmentation exists today without the appearance of such strains.'[126] Like so many visiting observers, he did not appreciate that the apparent absence of racial and cultural friction was due to a large extent to the social and occupational distance separating the two major cultural groups. Furthermore, as the ongoing process of political integration which had begun with the rise of the PUP brought the various cultural groups into contact, conflicts arose. Indeed, the NIP with its strong Creole support was concerned that their cultural group was not likely to be augmented with West Indians and that the position of its middle-class elements, already threatened by the political change, would be further undermined.[127]

The concern developed into apprehension when the Colonial Secretary gave some indication of the government's thinking on the matter. The government was considering another community of Mennonites and a community of Dutch displaced persons from Indonesia as the first batch of settlers.[128] To the question of whether West Indian immigrants would be allowed into Belize, he answered at a press conference that public opinion would have to be considered first. This drew a strong protest from the *Belize Billboard*. It felt that the colonial administration was trying to avoid a confrontation with the more popular PUP, even at the risk of being charged with racial discrimination and insensitivity to the animosity that people of African descent were expected to have towards Dutch colonial settlers. As the newspaper indignantly asked,

Why should Dutch refugees and Mennonites be admitted freely into the country while the question of West Indian immigrants being admitted must first be submitted to a public opinion test? This sounds too much like racial discrimination and looks too much like playing up to the racial prejudices which the leader of the PUP has been preaching and advocating for the past few years. We have no objection to the Mennonites, though we do not consider them to be the ideal type of immigrants. We do believe however that we must be careful about admitting Dutch immigrants into the country. We cannot ignore the fact that in South Africa the descendants of Dutch immigrants are carrying out an apartheid policy against the native people with little regard for the rights, desires and aspirations of the people who were the original owners of the country.[129]

Certainly this scant regard for their racial, cultural and social interests

was not what the middle-class Creoles expected from the colonial administration in return for their devotion to the country's colonial attachment.
The disillusion with the colonial administration had once more struck the
middle-class Creoles and was to find expression in the *rapprochement* with
the PUP.

On the whole both Downie and the Colonial Secretary dodged the issue
of the West Indies as a source of immigration. It is more than conceivable
that these officials had sought Sir Hilary Blood's advice on the general
question of where the immigrants were to come from. Blood's colonial
experience was wide and he had served in two of the most overcrowded
British territories, Barbados and Mauritius; the population density of the
former country was one of the highest in the world. Speaking on the
Downie Report to the Royal Commonwealth Society in 1960, he came out
decidedly against West Indian immigrants. They were not, in his opinion,
the right type of people to help in developing natural resources because
they were not 'pioneers', but wanted a settled, organized community with
civilized amenities.[180] Of course this was part of the stereotype image of
West Indians that colonial officials projected to the world. However, the
quiet, but enterprising and industrious manner in which the West Indian
agricultural immigrants from the smaller islands were and still are con-
quering the hinterland of Guyana, contradicts this image. In fact, as we
pointed out earlier in the study, the West Indian agricultural settlers, like
their professional counterpart in Belize City, commanded little admiration
in the 1930s precisely because they accepted the 'frontier' challenges posed
by the virgin lands on which they settled.

Like the colonial administration, Downie seemed less concerned with
the views of the NIP than with those of the PUP. The latter party was
just as opposed to the Downie recommendation although for different
political reasons which were more or less expressed in an economic
context. The PUP was not unappreciative of the need for a larger population. Nevertheless, it rejected Downie's conclusion that the root cause of
the major economic problems was the small size and scattered disposition
of the population.[181] Rather than using size as the starting-point and
conclusion of its argument, the PUP used it as a point of departure. The
size of the country demanded that the solution in terms of economic
policy should be conceived within a broader framework of regional
economic integration and specialization in capital-intensive and mechanized products. Belize was to export these goods in exchange for those goods
which would be more advantageously obtained from abroad. In short,
to the PUP the best prospect of growth still appeared to lie in strengthening
and improving the country's position in regional and international trade

rather than exploiting the relatively large absorptive labour capacity of the country.

But this broader framework of economic development entailed two changes that once more pointed to the ubiquity of the country's multiple orientation to outside political entities. First, membership of the sterling area and the imperial preference system had to end[132] because the PUP thought that it had established trade and payment arrangements which prevented Belize from attracting American capital of which, the party claimed, there were large amounts seeking a home.[133] This idea was linked with the additional suggestion that if it had self-government the country could tap sources of foreign investments which were not then available. The only advantage which Downie saw in the suggestion was that it would result in the fall of the cost of living. This was on condition that Belize revalued its dollar to parity with the US, substituted dollars or gold for sterling as the banking currency, abolished the quota restriction on the import of dollar goods, and returned almost exclusively to the USA as its source of imported goods.[134] Beyond this, he could not see how these changes in trade and payment arrangements, and a free transferability of capital as well as current account between Belize and all other countries, would make any difference to the willingness of American or other capital to come into the country. The foreign investor, he believed, was less interested in the currency *per se* than in the international confidence in it and in his unrestricted ability to withdraw his investments. Furthermore, Downie claimed that neither the country's relationship with the sterling area nor its dependent political status impaired its ability to borrow from other countries or from international institutions on its own credit. Ending his rebuttal on a conservative and somewhat threatening note, he cautioned that the withdrawal from the sterling area might have the repercussion of the country losing its preferential access to the British capital market without any guarantees of compensatory arrangements from the dollar area.[135]

Of course, Downie's arguments were not devoid of enlightened self-interest. The colony's withdrawal from the sterling area would have made the pursuit of one of his ideas difficult. He had accepted arguments put forward that the need for private capital in the agricultural and manu-facturing industries was also important for the future development of the country. Towards this end he suggested the formation of a body of British volunteers, 'friends of British Honduras',[136] as he called them, consisting of senior financiers and businessmen who would attract private investment to Belize under the initiative of the British government. In justifying his recommendation he conceded that American capital had so

far shown more interest in Belize than had British capital, so that formation of such a committee in the United States might seem the most logical
step. But he did not see what the United Kingdom government could do
to promote such a committee in the United States.[137]

Even if Price accepted Downie's recommendation about the need for
massive immigration in principle, the cost of compromising his preference for American capital was too high a price for him to pay. Apart from
preferring American to British investors, it is doubtful whether Price
shared to the same extent Downie's view on the need for and desirability
of greater promotional initiative by the state. He was not comfortable with
Downie's recommendation of setting aside development areas in the
country for agricultural settlement. This required government intervention and development by 'force' and 'compulsion' which Price was certain
would result in increased land tax.[138] He also regretted that Downie had
not recommended more than the existing development concession
arrangements so as to facilitate the flow of private capital.[139] On the whole,
*laissez-faire* dominated Price's thinking. He was not only wedded to
the assumption that private enterprise would show a dynamic initiative of
its own but seemed intent on entrusting crucial aspects of public policy to
the hands of foreign investors. This intention was to be clearly enunciated
in the PUP manifesto for the 1961 general election. It promised a general
economic survey of the country's resources and the resultant preparation
of a Master Plan of Development, preferably by a commercial consulting
firm which would also implement it by trying to procure the necessary
financing.[140] It can therefore be contended that in repeating his demand
for the withdrawal of Belize from the imperial preferential system, Price
was removing a possible obstacle to the pursuit of his notion of economic
development.

This demand was also reinforced by the second change which his
broader framework of economic development entailed. This was the
development of some form of closer economic integration with the neighbouring countries of Central America. From the British government's
standpoint this idea fell into a much more conventional mould. The only
aspect which was foreign to the British colonial experience was the association with non-British territories. Nonetheless, as we have seen, once
it had come to terms with its inability to induce Belize to join the
West Indies Federation, the British government turned to the idea of
closer economic co-operation between Belize and Guatemala. Downie,
however, turned down the PUP suggestion on the ground that it would
not overcome in practicable terms the country's problems of smallness.[141]
He appreciated that in so far as closer economic association with the

Central American countries encouraged Belize to specialize in the production of a few commodities for export to the regional and world markets in order to secure the benefits of economies of scale, it would meet the dictates of the tiny domestic market. But, he argued, this benefit could not sufficiently balance the disadvantages and constraints. First, the communication network was lacking between Belize and the participating members of the proposed Central American Common Market on which the success of Belize relied. Second, the benefits of such an association tended to accrue to the larger, densely populated, developed centres. Downie noted that the provisions of the Agreement on the System of Integrated Central American Industries were intended to prevent a polarization of the benefits of integration, but argued that it was impossible not to suspect that Belize might find itself getting the worst part of the bargain, without the possibility of subsidies from the other members of the regional organization and the free movement of labour to the developing regions. Third, the Agreement was still to be ratified and the high degree of political self-discipline upon which the effectiveness of the guarantees of the integration treaties depended was still a matter of speculation. Fourth, under the rules of the international commercial behaviour contained in the General Agreement on Tariffs and Trade (GATT), the entry of Belize into a Central American Customs Union would 'involve it sacrificing the very solid advantages which it was enjoying from preferential markets in the Commonwealth'.[142]

Whatever were the economic merits of these arguments, they were politically unacceptable to the PUP. In fact, the PUP may even have regarded the report as suspect since it seemed more concerned with presenting the case for the Commonwealth ties than with posing a variety of solutions from which Belize could choose. Even the NIP, which was firmly committed to the Commonwealth, shared this view.[143] The report forcefully brought home to both political parties the futility of dealing with emissaries, however high ranking, from the British government, and sharpened their resolve to obtain the response to their constitutional and economic proposals directly from the highest political source. Accordingly, in an open invitation, the NIP called upon Price to submerge their differences and make joint representation to the Secretary of State for the Colonies.[144]

To the NIP's previous request the Secretary of State for the Colonies had replied that a decision on whether such a conference should be held would be taken after the completion and consideration of the Blood constitutional report and the Downie economic report.[145] There were reasons for supposing that the Secretary of State for the Colonies would respond positively to the renewed request. First, given the reaction in Belize to the reports and in particular the reservations of the otherwise co-operative opposition parties, the Colonial Office could not judge the reports a success. Second, the negative responses had shaken the self-confidence of the colonial officials, including the Governor. Third, the situation within the Executive Council and the Legislative Assembly was becoming untenable. The different party political persuasions of the unofficial members, in particular those with portfolios, were dividing the Executive Council and impairing the work of the colonial administration. Within the Legislative Assembly, Price had resorted, as a matter of routine, to the strategy of demanding that every issue be referred to a Select Committee of unofficial members where his party commanded a majority. This was also delaying the work of the administration. Fourth, there was little point in inviting to London an official delegation which did not include Price. He alone had the authority to commit the PUP on any issue.

The holding of an election, while it may have solved the anomalous situation in the Executive Council and the Legislative Assembly, was not a realistic alternative to a high-level conference on constitutional and economic matters. In fact, there was considerable merit in postponing the elections until a new constitution had been settled. For one thing, the life of the new Assembly under the existing constitution was most likely to be short because of the combined pressures of the NIP and PUP to change the constitution as soon as possible. Under these circumstances, the Assembly would have been reluctant to take far-reaching decisions, especially if they were controversial. Furthermore, its actions may have been in vain since a subsequent government with greater powers under a new constitution would hardly have felt morally committed to them, especially if it had opposed the idea of holding an election under the old constitution. Similarly, the situation was too fluid to be conducive to long-term planning by the colonial officials. This was particularly true in the case of the Financial Secretary who was certain to be replaced by a political appointee whenever the new constitution was introduced. It was therefore not surprising that on his return from the economic and financial conference in London in December 1959, the Governor met the leaders of the three political parties, Price, Fuller and Pollard, in separate meetings to discuss the composition of the Belize delegation to a London conference on constitutional and economic matters in January 1960.[146]

*The United Front*   In presenting a United Front to the British government the PUP and NIP were seeking not only a common goal for the country but also their own legitimacy. The NIP was intent, especially after the colonial government decided to throw most of its weight behind the CDP, on convincing Price that despite its negligible parliamentary representation it was most vital to the welfare of the country. The partial government support, as well as its limited popular appeal, were key factors in the NIP's attempt to prove to the PUP that in the first place it was the only viable opposition party and in the second, it was entitled to the PUP's recognition. As the *Belize Billboard* observed, 'All through the years of bitter political strife the hope had been expressed that at some appropriate time the political parties, leaders and personalities could be united in an effort to secure for the country those things which only a united effort can bring.'[147] What had now occurred was not as unexpected as it may seem but 'a normal development arising out of the establishment of the two-party system in Belize after some ten years of political development'.[148]

Price accepted the NIP's contention for a different reason. The credibility gap between himself and the colonial administration could only have been bridged through his collaboration with political leaders acceptable to the officials. He therefore welcomed not only the NIP suggestions, but also two prominent citizens, Harrison Courtenay and Gilbert Hulse, the former Anglican Archdeacon whose pastoral work had kept him in Mexico during most of the period of political conflict, as Chairman and Secretary respectively of the Working Committee of the United Front in January 1960 and later on as leaders of the delegation to London. Harrison Courtenay's role should be stressed. He was one of the professional Creole elite who had quietly withdrawn from the political maelstrom in 1953 and had successfully reappeared on the political scene as the defence counsel to Price in his sedition trial in 1958. Price appeared eternally grateful to him because, as he admitted in 1959, his trial may have been different but for the fact that he had in his 'defence Attorney, one of the most brilliant lawyers that this country has ever produced'.[149] Harrison Courtenay had also voluntarily come to the legal rescue of Goldson, his first cousin, who had been prosecuted for not revealing the source which enabled him to secure and publish in the *Belize Billboard* the Downie Report which had not been made public at that time.[150] Harrison Courtenay was, therefore, eminently suited to being a political broker and, in fact, took the initiative in bringing together the leaders of the two opposing parties.[151] The logical outcome of his role was his appointment as Speaker to the newly-elected Legislative Assembly in 1961 and as legal adviser to the Belize government in the various rounds of the Anglo-Guatemala negotiations in the 1960s.

The United Front was not as broadly based as it probably should have been. Invitations were extended to a few minor political groups that were based in either Belize City or the outdistricts but which made no pretensions to be national in character. None of them evinced an interest, except the pro-British front which was represented by its leader, Luke Dinsdale Kemp, and James Meighan who, though expelled from the NIP, had not yet joined the PUP. The trade unions, however, were not invited to participate. This was not because the politicians had changed their views about the role of trade unions in the political process, but because these organizations had ceased to be an asset to them. The trade unions were in fact preoccupied with their own fragmentation and weakness. The CDU, for example, was still suffering from the effects of the owner-ship dispute between the PUP and the CDP. With the assistance of ORIT, the GWU and the British Honduras Development Union (BHDU), which had been established in Stann Creek in opposition to the other unions in the citrus industry, were busy negotiating a merger into the British Honduras General Workers' Development Union which material-ized in June 1960.[152]

The notable absentee was Pollard, the CDP leader, who had chosen not to accept the invitation precisely because he recognized the value of the United Front to Price. He remained very sceptical of Price's motives and presented several demands to the United Front as a pre-condition of his participation. These included the group's commitment at the outset to constitutional change within the Commonwealth. While several members shared his sentiment, they could not accede to his request because this was prejudging the outcome of the negotiations.[153] In any case, Pollard could afford to take this stand. His legitimacy was in the final analysis not dependent upon them since he was invited by the British government to attend the conference against the expressed wishes of the two major political parties.[154] It is also worth adding that he was also granted British citizenship.

The Blood constitutional proposals were the basis of the discussion of the Working Committee of the United Front. The Working Committee did not only believe that the Commissioner gave too much weight to the Guatemala problem, but reiterated a NIP–CDP argument that constitu-tional advancement for the country should not be conditional nor depend upon the rejected claims of Guatemala.[155] Indeed it contended that the twin problems of West Indies federation and closer association with Guatemala were so fundamental that they should be the subject of a referendum and a clause setting this forth should be embodied in the constitution. Moreover, the isolation of these problems would clear the way for any differences in the parties' domestic policies to emerge.[156]

The re-introduction of the issue of the West Indies Federation merits comment. Support for the idea had contributed to the downfall of several Creole politicians. As we observed, the NIP and the CDP were careful in their constitutional proposals to Sir Hilary Blood to state categorically that they were seeking 'Self government. . . outside of the West Indies Federation' which had by then become a reality. No-one whom the PUP did not consider almost indispensable would have dared to raise the issue. It is not surprising therefore that the suggestion for a plebiscite on federation with the West Indies or integration with Guatemala came from Harrison Courtenay. Although his stand on the Federation had been partly responsible for his political eclipse he was unshaken in his conviction that the Guatemalan claim should not be seen in isolation from the West Indies Federation and that Belizean membership of the latter would have gone far toward settling the dispute.[157] It was an indication of his value to the Working Committee as a political broker that a resolution endorsing his suggestion was moved and seconded by the leaders of the NIP and the PUP respectively and finally passed unanimously.[158]

The Working Committee also put forward constitutional proposals that were much more radical than the modifications which the Select Committee of the Legislative Assembly made to the Blood report. The proposals took the country to the verge of internal self-government. They also went further than the Blood Report in three significant respects. First, provision was made for a Premier, who obviously was to be the Majority Leader in the Legislative Assembly. Second, the Executive Council was to approximate more to a Cabinet. While the Governor was to remain as President, he was to be relieved of his vote. In his absence, the Premier was to preside at meetings. The distribution of ministerial portfolios was not to continue at the Governor's discretion. Instead, it was mandatory for him to take the advice of the Premier on this issue. Third, while a nominated element was to be retained in the Legislative Assembly, the Working Committee, unlike Sir Hilary Blood, made no specific provision for this element to be represented in the Executive Council.[159] In this respect it agreed with the Select Committee not to accept Sir Hilary Blood's twofold assumption that the normal electoral process would not produce politicians capable of running the administration and that nominated members from the 'well-educated class' were indispensable.

While it demanded more authority for Belize, the constitution was much more a reflection of NIP than PUP thinking. Retention of the nominated element was as sacred to the NIP as it was offensive to the PUP. While the former party would also have preferred the Legislative Assembly to be wholly elected, it was less prepared than the PUP to sacrifice its principles. That the NIP's views prevailed can be attributed to the influence and personality of the Chairman of the Working Committee who, it should be recalled, was the founding President of one of the NIP's precursors, the NP. Another contributory factor was the low profile which Price deliberately maintained. To begin with, the fate of the nominated system was not a life-or-death issue for his party. The retention of the system was not likely to deny the PUP a majority in the Legislative Assembly. It could, therefore, be tolerated until such time as an election enabled the party to regain control of the Legislative Assembly and the constitution making process. This did not seem to be too far off since the Working Committee had decided to insist upon the fixing of a date for the introduction of full internal self-government.[160]

Although the delegation was also to discuss the country's economic future, the Working Committee did not give the subject the same exhaustive consideration. For one thing, it felt that the constitutional problem was much more crucial and immediate. For another, meaningful discussion of the economy would raise financial matters which the Working Committee felt were the concern of the existing government. Indeed, arrangements had been made for separate financial talks between the government members of the delegation and the Colonial Office. Furthermore, the Working Committee had not seen the Development Plan which the government officials also proposed to discuss with the Secretary of State for the Colonies. On the whole, it did not pretend to be sufficiently informed on several aspects of the economy to engage in detailed discussion and was prepared to leave this to the government which the election would produce under a new constitution. Nonetheless, the Committee expressed serious reservations with regard to the Downie Report, especially the recommendation on immigration.[161]

At the London conference, which began on 1 February 1960 and lasted for seventeen days, the only fly in the United Front's ointment was Pollard. Issues which he opposed encountered a rough passage.[162] It was not so much a matter of the British government exploiting the party division as of its being reluctant to ignore any of the viewpoints. At the same time, the British government was vulnerable to the charge of paying attention to Pollard to an extent out of proportion to the strength and influence of his party. The basis of such an accusation was, of course, the support which Pollard was giving to the colonial administration.

In any event, the Secretary of State for the Colonies acquiesced in the proposals of the United Front. This included the creation of the office of First Minister to give full effect to the ministerial system. The Legislative Assembly was to consist of eighteen elected representatives, five nominated unofficial members, two ex-officio members, the Chief (formerly Colonial) Secretary, and the Attorney General. It was to elect from among its number the remaining five unofficial members who were to be members of the Executive Council. This formalized the role of party politics in the constitutional and political process. It was also one of the means by which the power of the Governor was reduced. Another way was that he remained on the Executive Council as Chairman, but without a vote.

A third way was that the Governor was partially relieved of his discretionary powers to appoint the nominated members. He was compelled to consult with the First Minister on the appointment of two of these members, and also with those persons who 'in his judgement can speak for the political points of view of the other parties which had put forward candidates at the general election on the appointment of a third member'. This rather elaborate phraseology was necessary to take care of the likely possibility that none of the opposition parties would win a seat. The Governor retained the decisive voice in the appointment of the other two nominated members although he was expected to seek the advice of both the First Minister and the persons whom he had identified as representing the other parties that had contested the election. On the whole, the United Front had extracted from the British government a wider measure of self-government than Sir Hilary Blood had thought appropriate to the colony's stage of social and economic development and compatible with the responsibility of the Secretary of State for the Colonies.[163]

The term 'extracted' is used advisedly. It should not be assumed that the British government readily conceded to the proposals. As we argued, the tone of Sir Hilary Blood's report suggested that some of his recommendations were predetermined in consultation with the Colonial Office. In any event, the Secretary of State for the Colonies had to give due consideration to Sir Hilary Blood's report which implied that a timetable for further constitutional advance should not be anticipated. This was the stand which he in fact took in response to the United Front's suggestion that full internal self-government should be achieved by 1965. He refused not only to endorse the date, but also to promise that the next stage of constitutional development would be full-internal self-government. The Secretary of State for the Colonies contended that the parties were only then about to sign an agreement involving a major change and it would be some months before the agreement could be translated into action, let alone tested by experience; to agree now to a fixed date for a further advance without experience of the present one was unwise. It would divert the efforts of everyone when these should be concentrated wholly upon making a success of the present arrangement.

Such success would be jeopardized if, as would inevitably be the case should a date for further advance be fixed, the minds of everyone concerned were between the job in hand and another not even defined.[164]

The Secretary of State for the Colonies also did not accept the United Front's idea of separating the issue of constitutional progress from that of regional orientation toward the West Indies and Central America. Perhaps he might have accepted the proposition but for Pollard's threat to withhold his signature from the report unless the constitution expressly committed the country to the Commonwealth and the conference deemed the local usage of the 'Guatemalan imposed name of Belize' improper.[165] A compromise was reached when the participants agreed to affirm, in the preamble to the constitutional ordinance, their desire to remain in and to be part of Her Majesty's Dominions of the Commonwealth.[166] The PUP and the NIP went a step further. In a joint declaration toward the end of the conference, they repudiated the Guatemalan claim. The statement also reaffirmed the two parties' undertaking not to introduce into the Legislative Assembly any measure for political integration with any other country 'without a clear mandate. . . from the electorate at a general election'.[167]

The extent to which Price modified his stand should not be exaggerated. He had not abandoned his Central American aspirations. While membership in the Commonwealth would have precluded any immediate possibility of political association with Central America, it did not, as Waddell points out, stand in the way of economic integration, although it might determine the form.[168] Nor was Price's denunciation of Guatemala at variance with his economic plans. Indeed, he had separated the two issues in order to reiterate that, whatever was his relationship with Guatemala in the 1950s, his goal was the association of his country, as an independent political entity, with the Central American Common Market which had superseded ODECA.

On the economic side advances were also made. Outstanding among the economic decisions was the agreement, in principle, that the central feature of Belize's economic policy should be agricultural development by means of planned immigration. Although never rejected by them, it was the first time that the Belizean politicians endorsed the concept. Less spectacular but of more immediate importance than the acceptance of the immigration policy was the British government's decision to replace the system of annual grants-in-aid with a block grant for four years. This was a response to Downie's criticism that the annual grant promoted neither goodwill, good administration, nor financial sense. As the Secretary of State for the Colonies put it, the change 'should introduce a valuable additional measure of flexibility in the handling of the territory's economic and financial problems, and should be at once a help and challenge to the first Minister of Finance under the new constitution'.[169]

As a whole, the United Front and the London conference were an excellent augury for the next stage of the country's political development. This was not because the British government had conceded a greater measure of responsibility to the elected representatives, but because of the Belizeans involved in the negotiations. It would have required an act of faith in 1950 to foresee Harrison Courtenay, Fuller, Price and Goldson as signatories to a unanimous constitutional report in 1960. Perhaps their realignment had been necessary before concessions were possible.

This cordiality between the PUP and the NIP was not maintained after the London conference. In fact, having achieved its objectives, the United Front was dissolved. Nor did the country's multiple orientation to outside political entities cease to be a party political issue. On the contrary, it has remained a key issue in the penultimate stage of decolonization. At the same time, however, the relationship between the political parties has seldom undergone the same degree of strain as in the years before the United Front. Equally, the conflict between the PUP and the British government has subsided to the point where there is considerable identity of interests. Altogether, United Front and the London conference should be seen as turning-points in the political change of Belize.

PART THREE
# Towards independence, 1961-1974

# 7
## An overview

The aim in this concluding section is to examine our contention that after the London constitutional conference in February 1960 political change in Belize entered a less troubled phase and settled into a definite channel. The years since 1960 have witnessed a consolidation of power by the PUP. In three successive elections – 1961, 1965 and 1969 – the PUP's success was overwhelming. The party won all of the seats, which were doubled from nine to eighteen in 1961, numbered sixteen in the second election and seventeen in the third.[1] Its parliamentary strength was reduced to twelve in the 1974 election, but this has not affected its ability to govern.

The PUP's overwhelming dominance is as much the result of the ineptitude of the opposition parties as of its own strength *per se*. Until the 1974 election, the opposition parties were incapable of any unity, coherence or stability. At no time in the 1960s did they remotely threaten the PUP with displacement. Indeed, the CDP was obliterated in the 1961 election and its remnant absorbed by the NIP which was reduced to a nominated opposition.[2] Although the latter party rallied in the 1965 election to win two seats,[3] it never acquired an image of purposefulness and internal solidarity. Instead the party's successive defeats resulted in a crisis of confidence in its leadership which culminated in a split in November 1969, and the immediate formation of the People's Development Movement (PDM) under the leadership of Dean Lindo.[4] This was self-defeating for it occurred at a time when an election was expected to be called at any moment. Indeed, the PUP did this in December 1969, and had no difficulty in winning although the two opposition parties hurriedly entered into an electoral alliance.

The British government also contributed to the consolidation of the PUP's supremacy. The PUP's demand for a greater degree of constitutional autonomy in 1960 more or less coincided with the British government's resolve to liquidate the residue of its Empire and to develop as a European power. The British government became even more appreciative and supportive of the PUP's political aspirations after the collapse of the

West Indies Federation in 1961;[5] for this outcome added to the British government's determination to reduce its political involvement in the region. The British government established the constitutional basis of an identity of interest with the PUP by introducing a ministerial system of government in 1961.[6] At no point in the subsequent change to internal self-government in 1965 were there substantive differences between the two of them.

Since then the major political question in Belize has been not the taking of independence from the British government, but how to protect it against the Guatemalan claim. As far as the British government is concerned this is a problem for Belizeans to solve and it has expressed its willingness to hold an independence conference whenever the Belize government asks for one.[7] Within Belize, however, the difficulty of solving this problem is recognized and there seems to be a general consensus among the political parties that independence should not be precipitate.[8]

This consensus is however recent. Throughout the 1960s the Guatemalan issue remained an explosive matter in Belize's internal politics, especially when the US government undertook in 1965 to find a solution.[9] The issue became a handy weapon that the political parties hurled back and forth until it tended to obscure some of the real domestic difficulties and to make rational action less easy for anyone. This was particularly true of the opposition elements which refused to attach any sincerity to Price's efforts to obtain independence for the country during the mediation of the claim by the US. Although the NIP was represented at several of the Anglo-Guatemalan conferences from May 1965 onwards,[10] its attitude towards Price remained unchanged. As far as the party was concerned Price's role in the Guatemalan claim in the 1950s had been equivocal and he was incapable of undergoing a change of heart. For example, in May 1967 the *Belize Billboard* charged Price with making secret and surreptitious visits, at least weekly and at dead of night, for almost a year, to the Gallon Jug area near the Guatemalan border. Although a judicial commissioner, Sir Colin MacGregor Knight, whom the government had appointed from Jamaica, cleared Price of the charges, the NIP clung to its views.[11] It was a similar kind of outlook that prompted the predominantly Creole civil service association, the Public Officers Union (POU), to take matters into its hands and call a strike in June 1966[12] when Goldson, the NIP Leader, claimed that the American mediator, Bethuel Webster, favoured at least the *de facto* incorporation of Belize into Guatemala.[13]

It is not too difficult to put the antagonistic outlook of the NIP and the reaction of the POU into their proper perspective; their suggestion of a lack of confidence in the ability of the PUP to prevent the absorption of the country by Guatemala was superficial. There were undertones of the old fear of the submergence of the dominant Creole culture, and resentment of the fact that the professional middle-class Creole leaders continued to be under-represented within the new political elite.[14] The PUP, for example, was never certain of where it stood with the POU, which became very active and militant in response to the overall political change. As early as 1962 the PUP government observed that the Union was behaving as though it 'felt itself embattled; as though the public service was unsure of its closest allies'.[15] This was an oblique suggestion that the civil servants were aligning themselves with the NIP and were probably also suborned by it. Indeed, the strength of the NIP had to be reckoned in terms of the support which it could muster among groups whose services were indispensable to the government. Once it took this into account, the PUP could not afford to take refuge in its overwhelming dominance and ignore the extreme reaction of the NIP. On the contrary it had to be attentive to the criticisms of the opposition and respond to them at great length when circumstances suggested it was wise to do so.

The problems which the PUP have encountered are not only political but also economic. Once its differences with the British government approached resolution and it assumed office, the PUP could not avoid responsibility for the task of trying to bring about rapid economic and social change. In fulfilling this responsibility the PUP has never wavered in its belief in the sanctity of private enterprise or in its belief that heavy foreign capital investment is a prerequisite of economic growth. Furthermore, its policy continues to favour the exploitation of the country's natural resources by corporate American capital. But few sections of the society are satisfied with the benefits which this economic policy has brought them. The country has made important advances in the diversification of commodity exports. The expansion in the production and export of sugar and citrus, which are British- and Canadian-controlled respectively, represents significant steps towards harnessing the agricultural potential of the country.[16] But this has been achieved at the expense of the development of mixed peasant farming. Large-scale commercial sugar production on a plantation basis has resulted in an extreme shortage of land on which to grow food crops and this is gradually squeezing out the small milpero, as the Indian subsistence farmer is called.[17] This militates against the cultivation of long-term crops. It is also producing the type of social order that is found on West Indian plantations in which the small farmer is politically and economically dependent on a foreign-owned sugar company,[18] in this case Belize Sugar Industries Ltd, a subsidiary of Tate and Lyle. The small cane-farmer, or *cañero* as he is called, is committed to mono-crop agriculture. His potential scope increased when the company, after a brief venture into highly mechanized cane production, withdrew from this activity and drew all of its cane inputs for its factories from the farmers. But the peasant cane-farmer lacks the financial means or the technology which would permit him to expand substantially and improve his methods. The plantation arrangement also throws him into conflict with the more established growers over the allocation of licences for cane production, a conflict that is sharpened by the fact that the peasant cane-farmer may also work for his competitor.[19] Altogether, the development of plantation agriculture has given rise to a dissatisfied agro-proletariat that is constantly exerting pressure upon the government for a revision of the conditions of its participation in the industry.[20]

Pressures upon the PUP government also came from the Chamber of Commerce. The alliance between internal and external private enterprise which produced a local class of entrepreneurs and managers who have a vested interest in a continuous inflow and mollification of private investors remains an enduring feature of the economy. The main attraction to foreign capital is the tax concessions which were provided for under the Development Concessions Ordinance of 1960 and which are considered generous by any standards.[21] But the business community claims that concessions are not enough to induce new ventures. It argues that these must be accompanied by an aggressive promotional thrust from the government to ferret out and establish a liaison with the most appropriate interests abroad. Considerable legitimacy was given to this view by a Tripartite Economic Survey Commission, consisting of the Canadian, British and US governments, in 1966. The Commission criticized the government for its lack of dynamism in encouraging new industries. It noted that the government's approach and stated plans for the future were largely passive, relying mainly on some general advertising and general discussions with and entertainment of such prospective investors that might happen to visit because of a chance previous business contact with someone in the country. Furthermore, even when the interest of the foreign investor was arrested, he was confronted with too many legal and administrative obstacles.[22] Such observations encouraged the Chamber of Commerce to abandon the political neutrality which the differing political persuasions of its members dictated and to become one of the more revitalized political groups. It started a weekly medium, *The Reporter*, in 1966 and adopted a posture that was at times uncomfortably reminiscent of the 'forestro-cracy'. It was not surprising that two of its members, Harry Lawrence, a former President, and Paul Rodriques, former Executive Secretary, eventually formed a political party, the Liberal Party, in 1973.[23]

Because it is foreign-controlled and is losing its drive, the economy provides few substantial avenues for the expression of pride and hope. This problem became evident when a black nationalist movement, The United Black Association for Development (UBAD), was formed in 1968.[24] It was founded and led by Evan Hyde, a young middle-class Creole, upon his return the same year from the USA where he received a university education at Dartmouth College with a USA State Department Scholarship. The organization was initially cultural. It stood for the dignity of Afro-Belizeans and the unity of the millions of non-whites in Asia, Africa and the Americas. Such aims implied an attack on white imperialist exploitation of the Third World and were incompatible with the PUP government's fatalistic dependence upon metropolitan capital in general and American capital in particular. It was not very long before UBAD was calling upon the government, in its newspaper *Amandala*, to discard its economic innocence and recognize, at least in principle, that whatever were the problems inherent in the country's small size, under-population and limited resources, the economy would not be radically altered by foreign domination. This was the thinking prevalent in under-developed countries. From the beginning, however, (UBAD), was labelled communist, which is the most effective device to discredit radicalism of any kind in Belize. It was also denounced as racially divisive by the government, the opposition party and the business community. Yet it attracted considerable support among the poorer classes, especially from the slum of Yarborough, the secondary school leavers and some professional people from Belize City and Stann Creek Town. It was largely with the zeal and voluntary efforts of its supporters that UBAD started a breakfast programme for needy children and a bakery in 1969. Both ventures were short-lived, and there was never any possibility that they would survive because they operated more on a charitable than a business basis. The organization also suffered from internal dissension and external pressures, but rallied to become a political party with the same name in 1970. Although the enthusiasm which the movement easily mobilized at the outset was not carried over in its entirety to the political party, its success indicated the extent of the latent forces in Belize waiting to be released.

The economic and political problems are not only internal but also external. The political problem always existed in the form of the Guatemalan claim even though the PUP considered it to be highly exaggerated in the 1950s. The economic problem was emphasized with the diminution of British responsibility in the early 1960s. The PUP pursued its policy of dependence on US investment and aid only to discover that the response was limited. What was once an undying fervour for the US to become a surrogate of British colonial rule quickly turned into disenchantment with the nature of investment proffered. Most of it was in land speculation. The PUP government was constrained to increase the land tax in 1966 to ensure the productive utilization of its most valuable natural resource.[25] Indeed this disillusionment was to some extent mistaken for complacency for which, as we saw, the PUP government has been criticized. The PUP government, however, did not lose all of its hope. It had always recognized that an indirect way of obtaining US assistance was to become an integral part of the Inter-American System, in particular to become a member of the Organization of American States (OAS) and to develop a closer economic relationship with the Central American Common Market (CACM) which the Economic Commission for Latin America (ECLA) had been investigating since 1962 at the request of Guatemala and Britain. Indeed a regional orientation toward Central America remained one of the corner-stones of PUP policy. All that appeared to stand in the way was the Guatemalan claim, and the outcome of the US mediation was therefore awaited with anxious expectation.

The mediator, Bethuel Webster, put forward his proposals in April 1968.[26] These offered Belize a nominal independence which the PUP government and the opposition NIP summarily rejected. As we observed in the Introduction, the prospect of a closer association with Central America was further reduced when at the end of that year ECLA reported that the possibilities of economic co-operation between Belize and the CACM were limited.[27] This drove the PUP government to emphasize its Commonwealth Caribbean ties and to join the newly established Caribbean Free Trade Area (CARIFTA) in 1971.[28] Meanwhile the government recognized that Guatemala was unlikely to yield its stand. It therefore embarked upon a search for a defence guarantee of its territorial sovereignty. But so far no-one has come forward with a plan. This has prevented the PUP government from taking the final step to independence. For it fears that what should be the exhilaration of freedom could well become a smothering at birth.

# 8

# Constitutional advance and imbroglio

Perhaps more than any other issue, the constitutional advance toward self-government confirmed that politics in Belize had entered a less turbulent phase. Of course, there were several outstanding matters that were potentially contentious. One was the pace of constitutional advance and in particular, the necessity for the Governor's residual power. Another was the future of the nominated system and the type of electoral system that would be most appropriate to the multi-racial and multi-cultural society. Finally, there was the Guatemalan claim, notwithstanding the decision of the two main political parties at the London conference to keep it outside the arena of national politics.

## The political and economic context

*The uncomfortable education of office.* The crucial factor in the constitutional change was the relationship between the PUP and the colonial government. At the beginning it was difficult to predict the nature of this relationship. To begin with, Price, as he admitted, had accepted the constitution as an 'expediency [which] had to be done in the circumstances'.[1] Even though he may have decided in advance of the London conference in 1960 to settle for a constitution that was not self-governing, the outcome fell short of his expectations in at least two important respects. The constitution left intact the power of the Governor to act without the advice of the Executive Council and without the prior approval of the Colonial Office in matters he deemed urgent.[2] It also retained the nominated element in the Legislative Assembly.[3] Secondly, only time could have proved whether the London conference had finally closed the door on the incident three years earlier when Price was found discussing the colony's future with the Guatemala embassy officials in London.

It turned out that the colonial authorities and the PUP government were more mutually accommodating than could have been optimistically foreseen at the time of the 1960 agreement. One reason for this was the effect of office on Price's economic and foreign policies. Like most leaders of government, especially those in the developing countries, he had hardly assumed office than he began to travel abroad for economic and diplomatic purposes. A meeting of the Economic Commission of Latin America (ECLA), a United Nations organization, in Chile in 1961, was responsible for his first overseas visit within two months of his taking office. The purpose of the visit was to seek admission to the ECLA as an associate member, and this was fulfilled. Seen in isolation, there was little noteworthy about either the visit or its purpose. The other British colonial governments in the hemisphere, the Federation of the West Indies and what was then British Guiana, had already obtained this status. Seen in the context of the Guatemalan claim and Price's Latin American aspirations, the visit and its successful outcome were of political significance. In the first place the motion was co-sponsored by the British government and the Guatemala government.[4] This was a diplomatic coup for Price who, in his speech to the conference before the vote was taken, said that he would interpret approval of the resolution as 'a step toward independence which the people of [the] country ardently yearn for'.[5] It was a point that he could hardly have over-emphasized, with the result that he triumphantly reported to the Legislative Assembly that with admission to ECLA the country's 'international identity and separateness had been established'.[6] In the second place, he seized the opportunity on his return journey in Peru, Costa Rica, Nicaragua and Guatemala informally to renew acquaintances and forge new ones.[7] Three years had elapsed since he had made an extensive tour of Central America to observe the progress being made towards economic integration and political union of the five Central American States.[8] That tour had also been under different circumstances since he had undertaken it after he was ousted from office. Now on this second visit as First Minister and Minister of Finance he was given the firm assurance that Guatemala, Nicaragua, El Salvador and Honduras were going to present a resolution asking ECLA to make an economic study of Belize to see how this country could fit into the proposed economic integration of Central America when and if the time became opportune.[9] In Guatemala, Ydigoras Fuentes went beyond the assurance given in Chile and invited his guest to 'bring the country into Guatemala as an associate state'.[10] Price politely but firmly rejected the gesture. He reiterated his party's goal of 'eventual independence as a sovereign state on the Central American Mainland'.[11] It was evident that Price and Ydigoras Fuentes interpreted differently the latter's decision to co-sponsor the admission of Belize into ECLA, or at least drew different conclusions from it.

The ECLA conference was, nevertheless, an encouraging start, and the prospects for Price's hemispheric preferences seemed bright indeed. However, these were considerably dimmed by the limited inflow of American private capital, notwithstanding a visit by Price to Canada and the USA in search of investments in 1961.[12] Because it offered limited possibilities, the industrial sector was not expected to attract very much foreign capital, and the only noteworthy investor in the field in the early years of the PUP government was the Hercules Powder Company of Delaware, USA. In 1962, the company established a $5 million plant in the Stann Creek District to produce resin from pine stumps.[13]

It was the country's agricultural potential that the PUP government looked to North American investments to realize. In 1960, the year before the PUP assumed office, generous tax concessions, including a tax holiday period of ten years, were created for new business ventures.[14] The enabling law, the Development Incentives Ordinance, provided the added inducement of exemption from income tax and customs duties for another one to five years for the large-scale commercial production of certain long-term agricultural products. These concessions had a lot to do with the attraction of the Dibrell Brothers Tobacco Company of Virginia and the Canadian firm of Salada Foods Company in 1962.[15] The Tobacco Company placed 1,500 acres of lease land under tobacco cultivation. The Salada Foods Company took over the British Honduras Fruit Company from the Commonwealth Development Corporation in Stann Creek and invested $2 million in a frozen fruit-juice concentrate factory.[16]

Nonetheless, by 1963, two years after the PUP took office, the list of American individual investors and companies which had been granted development concessions gave little indication that Price's expectations would be met. When the investors were not showing a reluctance to invest except in partnership with local interests, they were engaging in land speculation in either tourism or agriculture. As early as 1962, this development was sufficiently disturbing to the government for A. A. Hunter, Minister of Natural Resources, Commerce and Industry, to caution the investors. He repeatedly pointed out that while the government was prepared to encourage and attract private and pioneering investment, it could not tolerate 'land speculators whose fragmentation policies offer no solution but rather add to our already existing problems'.[17] On the contrary it was prepared to pass legislation to control this aspect of land use.[18]

The US government, however, did not prove to be a more prolific source than its private counterpart. This became evident when in October 1961 Hurricane 'Hattie' struck the country, ruining the economy of the southern districts of Stann Creek and also leaving thousands homeless.[19] But the US government fell short of the expectations of the Belize government in its response to the latter's appeal for assistance to finance the programme of reconstruction. In a sombre tone, Price reported to the Legislative Assembly that 'In Washington, the response was most disappointing especially when viewed against the background of destruction and our country's overwhelming need. Despite efforts made, and arguments adduced, we were told that only technical aid could be given by the United States government. Our intention is to pursue the approaches to the United States government in the hope that eventually we shall obtain some more substantial measure of assistance.'[20]

No less disappointing to the Belize government was the United States government's response to its application for a sugar quota. Price had assured the Legislative Assembly in 1958 that a market for the entire production of Belizean sugar could be found in the United States at a price that was substantially higher than the world price and that guaranteed under the Commonwealth agreement.[21] However, he had conveniently ignored the fact that the American embargo on Cuban sugar was largely responsible for the sellers' market which was not likely to persist indefinitely. In consequence, the experience of A. A. Hunter, four years later in 1962, failed to match Price's optimistic expectations. Instead of satisfying the Minister's request for a quota starting with a quantity of 5,000 tons and going up to 30,000 tons, the US government allocated to Belize a fixed quota of 10,000 tons.[22] Evidently with the general idea of bringing down the guaranteed American price to the world price level over a period of years, the US government also offered a price for any surplus that was based on an annual declining percentage of the American price. This offer occurred at the most inopportune moment. For the PUP government was at that time negotiating the expansion of the industry with Tate and Lyle which was interested in acquiring the Corozal Sugar Factory and constructing a modern factory in the Orange Walk District.[23] The government felt that the US decision weakened its bargaining position and it doubted its ability to induce the company to go ahead with the building of the new factory and still more to determine its location.

On the whole, the disillusionment with the USA as a source of financial assistance had set in, or perhaps more correctly the PUP government was receiving an uncomfortable education in great expectations. The government acknowledged its misconceptions and miscalculations in several ways. One of these was its call upon local investors in 1963 to support the Development Finance Corporation which it had recently established and not to depend upon foreign investors to do so.[24]

A second way was its decision to take a greater initiative in the financing of development projects.[25] This was a far cry from the PUP election promise in 1961 to contract these and other related activities if possible to a commercial consulting firm which it most likely had envisaged to be American. Implicitly the PUP was admitting that its notion about government was too simplistic. The economic survey was instead undertaken by a United Nations mission in 1962.[26] The mission urged that Belize should take full advantage of its extremely favourable ratio of cultivable land to labour force and specialize in the production of capital-intensive export crops.[27] While this was the original PUP policy, the recommendation underlined the government's disappointment over the limited inflow of American private enterprise. For in practice the mission's recommendations depended on private foreign investment in estate agriculture.

Perhaps the most important way in which the government conceded that its expectations were misplaced was the change in its outlook towards Britain. It suddenly seemed to recognize that there was an umbilical connection with the imperial country which could be profitably exploited to obtain the much-needed aid. Having discovered no significant alternative source of finance and faced with the need to undertake a hurricane rehabilitation programme, the government deepened its dependence on grants-in-aid and other loans from the British government.[28] In 1962 the British government authorized expenditure of $23 million and promised a further $3 million, if that amount was required. Of the $23 million, $4 million was to cover the cost of emergency services. Another $6 million was to assist in the construction of the new capital, Belmopan, which was recommended by the United Kingdom mission that assessed the damage. The remaining $13 million was to pay for the general reconstruction.[29]

The negotiation of the assistance brought home to the PUP government once more the difficulties of attracting financial assistance even from a source that was ultimately responsible for the country's economic and political development. The negotiations kept Price in London for nearly one month, and, as he remarked, were 'hard and time-consuming'.[30]

However necessary, this growing dependence on Britain produced a variety of reactions in Belize. To the NIP, it was a warning that the country should not lightly sever its connections with Britain and the Commonwealth in favour of either Central America or the USA, one of which was incapable of being and the other unwilling to be of financial assistance. Indeed, the NIP Leader, Goldson, claimed that it was no accident that the Salada Foods Company, which had made the largest investment in agriculture so far, was owned by a Commonwealth country.[31] Intent on denying the government any credit, he also claimed that the Hercules Company, although American-owned, 'was brought in here by the Belize Estate, a British Company'.[32] This latter company, he finally observed, was also instrumental in the establishment of Pine Harvesters

Ltd which eventually extended into a combined operation with the Hercules Company in January 1963.[33] Goldson's faith in the Commonwealth ties was reinforced later, in 1963, when Tate and Lyle finally took control of the sugar industry and put it on a plantation basis.[34]

On the other hand, Horace Young, a lawyer and nominated member of the Legislative Assembly, saw little in the British government's response to the overall situation that deserved compliment. He viewed the dependency as the result of British colonialism and observed that the country could hardly maintain its national self-respect by 'depending on someone else's sympathy to balance our budget'.[35] The irony of the situation was that although in 1950 the PUP had burst upon the political scene espousing this very theme, the changed situation suggested that it should strike a different note. It therefore marked the British government's formal approval of its assistance in the old colonial fashion that it formerly denounced. The announcement coincided with the National Day celebration in September 1962, and Price took the opportunity to fly the Union Jack alongside the unofficial national flag. In his address he referred to this unique act by the PUP government as a symbol of the 'good relations which now exist between the United Kingdom and this country'.[36] His doctrinaire outlook towards the British government also gave way to flexibility on the constitutional relationship between the two countries. He agreed that the Governor would soon have to go. But he hastened to add that 'while we get money from the United Kingdom government to balance our budget, we have to live with Governors', and rationalized this predicament by observing that the Governor, Sir Peter Stallard, was 'quite a change from the past'.[37] But for the fact that the ultra-conservative element of the middle-class Creoles knew that they were contrived, such gestures to the British government might have created euphoria among them. Furthermore, this group still expected the Governor to govern and not to preside over the transition to independence, as Price's remarks implied.

*British strategy.* If its fiscal incapacity had compelled the PUP government to accept the decolonizing procedure pursued by the British government, the changes in the European and the colonial worlds contributed to the *rapprochement.* Britain by the early 1960s wanted not only to liquidate the residue of its Empire but to link its own development more closely to Europe. In other words, a shift in emphasis from the Commonwealth to the Common Market could be foreseen. The British government, therefore, saw little justification in persisting with the wait-and-see attitude towards constitutional advance for Belize which it had adopted at the London conference in 1960. It was, therefore, no coincidence that during the negotiations for the hurricane rehabilitation assistance a decision was taken to hold the next constitutional talks in 1963.[38] The message was clear. Belize should be given its independence as soon as possible and seek its future in its hemisphere in a regional grouping of one kind or another. Thus, the British government was unlikely to entertain any idea for associate status which would have left the country's defence and the conduct of its foreign affairs in British hands. Admittedly, the British government was to give this status to the small West Indian territories, but only after it had failed to develop the lean rump of the West Indies Federation into another federation.[39] Belize, on the other hand, had an alternative in closer association with Guatemala and the Central American Common Market which was being explored.[40]

Britain's changing circumstances were therefore largely responsible for the renewal of the Anglo-Guatemala negotiations in April 1962 although the venue (which was changed from the USA to Puerto Rico) lent credence to Ydigoras Fuentes' claim that the parley was part of a deal between Guatemala and America. According to the Guatemalan President, the US government had promised to exert pressure on Britain to settle the dispute in return for using a Guatemalan plantation to train the insurgents for the ill-fated Bay of Pigs episode.[41] These changing circumstances also explain the British government's decision to invite the PUP government to be present at the negotiations.[42]

It is consistent with our argument about the British government's strategy that while it could not ignore the juridical aspects of the claim it was more concerned with economic proposals that would be of mutual interest to Belize and Guatemala. This was the best hope for the easing of tensions since the Guatemalan claim sprang in the final analysis from a real annoyance. As we indicated in previous chapters, the development of the forestry potential of the Peten Department depended upon access to the Atlantic Ocean, which only Belize could provide. Improved transport facilities would also reduce the economic difficulties of linking Belize with her Central American neighbours. The idea that Belize might at length join the Central American Common Market (CACM) was not only consistent with Price's sentiments, but was also likely to appeal to Ydigoras Fuentes. As *The Economist* pointed out, the President 'tends to see economic union as a step to political fusion; although this is not a logic to which all his neighbours subscribe'.[43] The Puerto Rican conference, therefore, agreed that the two high contracting governments would request ECLA to implement its 1961 Chilean resolution by exploring the possibility of closer economic co-operation between Belize and Guatemala with a view to the former joining the Central American Economic Co-operation Committee. It was also decided to establish a tripartite committee of the countries involved. The committee was to give special attention to the improvement of road and port facilities in Belize.[44]

In reopening the negotiations with Guatemala the British government did not run the risk of negative or evasive response from the PUP government. Unlike in the 1950s, when he took the view that Belize was not involved in the dispute, Price for a variety of reasons could no longer side-step the issue. First, although the constitutional conference in 1960 now seemed to have closed the doors on the London incident in 1957, he had to make sure that they were securely locked. Further disagreement with the British government on this issue was likely to jeopardize his most reliable source of financial assistance without necessarily affecting the prospect of further constitutional change.

Second, Guatemala had intensified its campaign. This included the incessant indoctrination of its citizens with the notion that it was their duty to recover the disputed territory. In January 1962 about thirty armed but untrained Guatemalan civilians made an incursion into the border villages of Pueblo Viejo and San Antonio in the Toledo District.[45] This ended in the arrest and sentence to ten years' imprisonment of the leaders, Francisco Sagastume y Ortiz, a young, intelligent and prosperous businessman and politician from the Department of Peten, and Gustavo Rosado Palmer, a Belizean student in Guatemala, in March 1962.[46] There was also the tendency for the Guatemalans to implicate Price and his colleagues in their hoary claim. This ranged from President Ydigoras Fuentes' suggestion, made at a convention of his Redemption Party in June 1960, that he maintained a fifth column in Belize and would invade the country in the event of war in Europe[47] to reports in the Guatemalan official newspaper, *Diario de Centro America*, in 1961 that the President would be invited to visit Belize[48] and that he had been assured by three visiting PUP Assemblymen of the country's desire to be reincorporated into Guatemala as an associated state.[49]

Guatemala's method of pursuing the claim was, as the PUP government admitted, to deter potential foreign investors to the country and hinder economic progress.[50] Even worse, it was producing fear in the people of Belize that when they achieved independence their identity would be lost, their dignity outraged and their country absorbed. Indeed the report of the proposed visit of Ydigoras Fuentes had caused considerable consternation in several quarters in Belize before Price had the chance to explain to the Legislative Assembly that the idea had come from the Consul General of Guatemala in Belize, and had been turned down by the

Executive Council.[51] The attempt to compromise the position of the PUP leaders was also adding to Price's problems of erasing his equivocal past not so much from the minds of the colonial officials as from those of the middle-class Creoles. In this connection it is not surprising that he entrusted the task of making the first public statement on the outcome of the Puerto Rican conference[52] in April 1962 to Harrison Courtenay, who was legal adviser to the Belize ministers and whose credibility among the opposition elements was incomparably greater. Admittedly, Price, who had travelled from London to Puerto Rico, broke his return journey to Belize in Washington to renew his efforts for financial assistance[53] and probably took the view that a report to the country on such a vital issue should not await his return. Nevertheless, Harrison Courtenay's account of the conference was more likely to be unreservedly accepted by the Creoles.

Apart from the need to restore his own credibility, the Guatemalan pressure and its harmful effect made Price more than willing to co-operate with the British government in renewed initiatives to explore the possibilities of some kind of economic association between Guatemala and his country. Although their perspectives were influenced by different considerations the PUP government and the British government found that their interests coincided. This increased the chances of an amicable outcome of the constitutional conference which was to be held in July 1963.

## Internal self-government

*PUP constitutional proposals.* In addition to the identity of interests, the PUP constitutional proposals were sufficiently orthodox to eliminate the possibility of conflict between the PUP and the British government. These proposals called for a Belize Council of Ministers or Cabinet, under a Premier, which would be given general direction and control of the government, and would be collectively responsible to the legislature. The British government, through the Governor, would remain responsible for external affairs and defence. The PUP, however, envisaged an arrangement whereby the Premier was to be kept informed and consulted on these two subjects. This consideration derived most of its importance from the Guatemalan claim. Certain functions such as those connected with the Royal Prerogative, which the Cabinet would be an inappropriate body to discharge, were also to be handled by a Committee of Mercy and Prerogative. The proposals also envisaged a Privy Council which would give advice to the Governor on matters of local importance where local knowledge and experience were essential.[54]

By far the most important proposal was the establishment of a bicameral legislature. One of its features was the retention of the nominated members as Senators in an Upper Chamber. The PUP had compromised its stand on this issue during the constitutional conference in 1960, but had never abandoned its objection in principle to a nominated element in the legislature. Evidently, this reversal of policy required an explanation. The PUP claimed to have adopted the bicameral system because it had been found acceptable in many Western political systems, not only in the Commonwealth but also the United States of America and many Latin American countries. 'Everywhere you find them', Price said, 'and it will be much easier... to fall in with the pattern of development.'[55]

Table 9. *Occupations of the members of the Legislative Assembly, 1961*

| Occupations | Number of members |
| --- | --- |
| Politician | 5 |
| Merchant | 4 |
| Construction contractor | 2 |
| Clerk | 1 |
| Labourer | 1 |
| Valuator | 1 |
| Mechanic | 1 |
| Dairy farmer | 1 |
| Primary school teacher | 1 |
| Housewife | 1 |
| | 18 |

Source: *Government Gazette*, Belize City, 1961

Perhaps a more important reason for the proposal was to be found in the party's inability to attract capable persons to contest elections. This problem was much more acute for the PUP than for the NIP, which had initially raised the issue during the Blood constitutional enquiry.[56] The eighteen PUP candidates who had won the election in 1961 had given their occupations as listed in table 9. These occupational categories were somewhat misleading. Some of the representatives were, for example, retired civil servants. On the other hand, of the four merchants, only one, A. A. Hunter, could claim to be well established. Also, the formal education of some of the representatives could not be deduced from the occupational categories. Finally, there was some attempt on the part of the more able representatives to present a low profile and to project an image of political dedication and commitment, on the assumption that this was more likely to impress the ordinary voter. Hence, the category 'politician' accounted for the largest number of representatives. However, after allowance is made for the problem of establishing a more accurate occupational picture the fact remains that in so far as the PUP recognized high educational attainment as an essential attribute of leadership, it had a problem. It had been unable to attract many members from the predominantly Creole professional class. While the tendency, which had begun in the 1957 election, to recruit parliamentary candidates from their constituencies had its political advantages, it also limited the number of candidates who could have been selected from the intellectual repository of Belize City. It is no accident that the six ministers appointed in 1961 were from Belize City, and that one of them, J. W. MacMillan, was a nominated member[57] even though this was not constitutionally necessary.[58] Equally important, the four persons, including the Governor's two nominees, Young and Evadne Hulse, in whose nomination to the Legislative Assembly the PUP had a voice, were middle-class Creoles and of considerable occupational and social standing in the society. J. W. MacMillan was a local white Creole who owned an established business and had received the OBE; J. N. Meighan who was the other PUP nominee had received the MBE and was a retired District Commissioner;[59] Horace Young was a lawyer and also a former Crown Counsel, and Evadne Hulse was a social worker, a longtime secretary to Archbishop Dunn, and belonged to a family which included a minister of religion and a medical doctor. It is, therefore, not unlikely that after two years as First Minister, Price conceived the Senate primarily as a recruiting agency for able politicians and technocrats who were not interested in electoral politics. In fact, provision was made in his constitutional proposals for ministers to be appointed from the Senate.[60]

*Local response to the constitution-making process.* The NIP showed little enthusiasm for the proposed constitutional advance. For one thing the constitutional change in 1960 was not operating in its favour. Neither the PUP government nor the colonial officials offered concessions to the NIP. The PUP government took the view that since it had won all of the seats there was no parliamentary opposition,[61] although the defeated parties, the NIP and CDP, had chosen Goldson, the NIP leader, as their nominee to the Legislative Assembly. The PUP government considered Goldson's status to be no different from that of the Governor's two nominees, Young and Hulse. Like them, the NIP leader was a nominated member in the minority.[62] At the most his constitutional role was to make representation on behalf of his supporters[63] and certainly did not extend to the right to be consulted. Goldson disputed this.[64] He had assumed the leadership of the NIP after the general election in 1961 as a result of Fuller's illness and eventual death in March of that year. The new leader claimed that his position was much more analogous to that of the PUP nominees, J. W. MacMillan and J. N. Meighan, who had to be considered members of the emergent government. By the same token, he concluded, if the minority parties had gained any elected seats in the Assembly he would have formed part of the opposition.[65]

Goldson's pretensions suffered a further setback when the Governor turned down his request to attend the Puerto Rican conference in April 1962 which Goldson hoped would settle the Guatemalan question.[66] Indeed, far from being able to count on the colonial officials to frustrate the PUP, the NIP now had to face the world of political reality unassisted. As our analysis in the previous chapter indicated, this development could have been foreseen towards the end of the 1950s.[67] The NIP, however, did not bargain for the *rapprochement* and the blurring of the distinction between the colonial officials and the PUP government. Its disappointment and frustration shaded off into outright hostility towards the colonial officials that was perhaps only exceeded by its obstinate antagonism towards the PUP government. For it was not long before Goldson pointedly accused the Chief Secretary of 'beginning to talk like the PUP' and to 'act like it', to the extent of deeming the opposition party 'mischievous and irresponsible' in its handling of the Guatemalan claim.[68]

Essentially, the NIP leaders realized that effective political power was not likely to be theirs. They, therefore, had no wish to assist the PUP in achieving internal self-government. At the same time there was little in the principal provisions of the PUP draft constitution to which the opposition party could have taken objection. The only point on which the NIP was likely to differ was the electoral system. It had advocated proportional representation in 1959 because this electoral system was most likely to increase its parliamentary strength. Now, however, it seemed to have lost interest in the proposal. As we shall see in the next chapter, it was not until 1968, when the Representation of the People's (Amendment) Bill was being considered, that the NIP half-heartedly reopened the issue.

The NIP had therefore to confine its objections to such matters as the basis of party representation at the conference, the manner in which the PUP handled its constitutional proposals, and the PUP's views on the country's ultimate political status preparatory to independence.[69]

The PUP government had recommended to the Secretary of State for the Colonies that the PUP and the NIP be invited to the conference in order to ensure that a cross-section of public opinion was represented.[70] However, the PUP government's main criterion of representation of the two parties was their respective parliamentary strength. This produced four delegates and one adviser for the PUP as against one delegate and one adviser for the NIP.[71] The NIP rejected this proposal as being 'out of proportion' with its party poll of 23 per cent of the vote in the 1961 election.[72] Its leader demanded parity of treatment on the ground that the two opposition parties, the NIP and the CDP, had been given equal representation with the PUP at the London constitutional conference in 1960, and that the NIP had inherited the supporters of the CDP.[73] The PUP contended that the weight and the force of the arguments to be put forward at the conference were unrelated to the number of delegates.[74] This certainly was a weak counter-response. If the number of delegates was not crucial, then the PUP could have conceded equal representation. A much more impressive and realistic argument which the PUP government advanced was that irrespective of the outcome of the constitutional talks, the new constitution had to be acceptable to the Legislative Assembly, which in effect meant the PUP.[75]

The second point of difference was the PUP government's decision to confine the method of soliciting public opinion to appointing a Select Committee of the Legislative Assembly, which was to report within ten days. Goldson questioned the suitability of the Select Committee as a machinery of public consultation and vociferously condemned the PUP government's 'indecent haste' in allotting only ten days for comment.[76] This was ironic. For in 1959 the PUP had objected to the Legislative Assembly being rushed into considering the Blood Report even though the Select Committee had taken more than ten days to submit the report on that occasion.[77]

Price, in defending his government's method of eliciting public opinion, argued that the situation had changed. For one thing, the move to internal self-government was a 'natural, logical sequence of the 1960 constitutional conference'.[78] It was also less controversial than the Blood constitutional proposals which were unwilling to break with the colonial past. Furthermore, the proposed conference had been announced more than a year before, and this was enough time for the parties to canvass and influence public opinion. In any case, it was unnecessary to refer the issue to the political parties since the PUP had received a mandate to seek internal self-government at the general elections in 1961. Price, however, apparently forgot that the party had advanced a similar argument to Sir Hilary Blood in 1959. 'The overwhelming victory [in the municipal elections of December 1958]', the party stated, 'can be considered as a fitting mandate from the vast majority of people to the People's United Party to speak for them on constitutional reform.'[79] Yet the PUP did not accept the consideration of the Blood Report by the Select Committee as being adequate. It went on to suggest that the constitutional proposals be referred by the political parties to the public.[80] Even if the PUP argument about receiving a mandate was valid, it was now proposing at least one change that was contrary to the party's policy and of national importance. This was the retention of the nominated element and its accommodation in the Upper House, the Senate, in a bicameral legislature.

What happened, in effect, was that the PUP, apart from being dominant, viewed the constitutional reform from the standpoint of a government rather than a party. This affected the character of its relationship not only with the NIP, but with its own rank-and-file supporters. Its *rapprochement* with the British government provided a new source of legitimacy and in turn weakened the mass factor as a crucial feature of political change. It was no longer the people's party but the 'Government Party', to which Price referred as having been selected 'to represent us at this conference'.[81] PUP leaders were now ministers who were resorting to the radio to communicate with the electorate. This was less exerting and more economical, especially as Price claimed that ministers were 'very busy carrying out the Hurricane Reconstruction and Development Programme'.[82] The masses were still hearing their leaders' voices without seeing as much of their faces, or having the same degree of opportunity to be intimately involved in the political process, as in the days of the party's struggle for ascendancy. In short, the PUP government did not maintain the same premium on mass-meetings as a direction giver, as a mood tester, as a solidarity builder and as a means of communication between its leaders and followers. Accordingly, it took its 'constitutional proposals to the people for ratification' after these had been considered by the Select Committee.[83] This exercise began about two weeks before the conference and was only achieved by what the PUP government admitted was a 'fast-moving campaign'.[84]

This changing leader–follower relationship was reflected in the representation made to the Select Committee. Apart from the PUP, the Federation of Christian Trade Unions and one of its constituents, the Christian Workers' Union, were the only organizations that appeared before the Committee.[85] As we shall see in the next chapter, both organizations were closely associated with the PUP and it was not surprising that the Committee's hearings took about one and a half hours.[86] Except for the Public Officers Union, no other organization submitted a memorandum.[87] Having boycotted the Committee, the NIP viewed the meagre response as a triumph and evidence of its claim to being influential despite its weak parliamentary position. The PUP, of course, argued that the brevity of the meeting 'proved conclusively' that its supporters 'had full confidence in the ability of their leader to present them [the proposals] to the Committee'.[88] While the differing interpretations of the NIP and the PUP cannot be discounted, the changing nature of the relationship between the PUP leaders and their followers was also dulling the latter's awareness and making them complacent.

Of course, this does not mean that the PUP was irrevocably consigning its mass elements to a passive or merely supportive role. It still conceived the rank-and-file as active agents in the residual political change. This was evident in the PUP government's response to the NIP's third objection to the way in which the constitutional change was being handled. The NIP had observed that since 1960 Price had claimed his political objective to be 'full internal self-government within the Commonwealth and eventual self-government'.[89] As Price admitted, the first part of his objective was redundant since internal self-government could not have been achieved outside of the Commonwealth.[90] In no longer speaking of independence within the Central American framework, Price was either leaving his options open or being tactful. The NIP attempted to commit him to a more specific goal, but only drew the response that the decision about the framework within which independence was to be achieved should be a matter for the people. In other words, because of its new and increasing political status as the government, the PUP was viewing its rank-and-file as an element to be called upon to give direction to change not as a matter of routine, but when it was expedient. In a sense, the party had begun to cease to act as a nationalist movement or a people's party, to become instead a leaders' party – a pitfall that few parties in developing nations have avoided.

On the whole the NIP could not resist the conclusion that there was a sinister connection between the PUP government's railroading of the constitutional proposal and the latter's reluctance to declare its support for independence within the Commonwealth.[91] Its fear that Price had an ulterior motive for leaving the second issue open was by now pathological, and this condition was intensified by the NIP's complete loss of the colonial officials' support to the PUP government and its failure to gain recognition as a parliamentary opposition and representation at the Puerto Rican conference. The NIP's demand for parity of representation at the constitutional conference was as much a desperate attempt to disprove any suggestion of political impotence, as to deny the PUP complete legitimacy as the government. With the PUP roundly opposed to the idea, the NIP decided to boycott the conference.[92]

*The constitutional structure.* The PUP proposals which formed the basis for the discussion at the conference were more or less accepted in their entirety, with one notable exception. This was the control of internal security which, along with defence, external affairs, and the Public Service, remained with the Governor.[93] However, the British government accepted the PUP's suggestion that the decolonization of these responsibilities should begin. Accordingly, the ministers were given an effective voice in the appointment of members of the localized Public Service Commission and, through membership of permanent advisory committees, in defence, internal security and external affairs.[94]

The change to the bicameral legislature[95] and a general election under the new internal self-governing constitution did not take place until March 1965. However, the movement towards the transfer of power began earlier. In January 1964 the Executive Council was replaced by the Cabinet in which there were no colonial officials. The post of Chief Secretary was abolished and the responsibility for those subjects (except the civil service) which had fallen to this office was assumed by the Minister of Internal Affairs and Justice, a newly created appointment. It was, however, not possible for the office of Attorney General to be placed in ministerial hands because the PUP lacked a representative with the requisite professional qualification. Accordingly, the civil servant, a British expatriate, retained the post but his membership in the legislature was discontinued in 1964. More than in any other area of government, the judiciary laid bare the dearth of professionally qualified PUP representatives and the indispensability of the middle-class Creoles who monopolized the legal profession. For the transfer of power within the legal section of the judiciary necessitated not only the replacement of a civil servant by a politician for the post of Attorney General, but also the creation of the post of Director of Public Prosecutions.[96]

The PUP's problem in attracting members of the predominantly Creole professional class and capable people from other prestigious occupations cannot be over-emphasized. Price admitted the party's difficulty of attracting 'a top professional man, a top technical man, a top businessman into the Cabinet' when he allowed A. A. Hunter, the Minister for Natural Resources, Commerce and Industry, to continue as Director of Brodie and Company Ltd and to retain his monthly allowance from this office.[97] Price also used the Senate to co-opt professionally qualified persons into the government as non-party members presumably in the expectation that they would eventually become party members through the normal process of interaction. In 1965, two bright young Creole men were recruited to the Senate. One was Vernon Leslie, the locally born Resident Tutor of the University of the West Indies, who was the Governor's nominee. The other was Vernon Courtenay, a lawyer and a son of Sir Harrison Courtenay, who was appointed Vice-President. Another Creole lawyer, E. W. Francis, was appointed President. It was not until Vernon Courtenay was appointed Attorney General in 1969 that the transfer of power in the judiciary was complete. However, the fact that he was permitted to continue his private practice in his father's law firm until he successfully contested a seat later in that year as a PUP candidate further demonstrated the extent to which the dearth of professionally qualified persons created a constitutional anomaly.

Since the constitutional advance in 1965 there has been no further reorganization. As we have indicated, the delay is due to the unsettled Guatemalan claim. As early as 1967, the PUP government stated in an address to the United Nations Trusteeship Committee that it could not 'imagine anything more injurious and unhelpful than that Belize should proceed to independence with the Guatemalan claim still remaining to be settled'.[98] Indeed, although the decision to hold the constitutional conference in 1963 had been announced at the Puerto Rican conference in 1962,[99] the Guatemalan government protested against the grant of internal government in a more dramatic form than hitherto. It reduced its relations with Britain to consular level and caused apprehension in the colony by building up its troops on its border with Belize.[100] At the same time, however, the PUP government was hopeful that the American mediator would produce a solution which would give Belize its independence and still leave the new nation in peaceful relationship with its neighbour. For it could be argued that despite its show of force, the Guatemalan government was asserting its case for sovereignty more as a political bargaining counter than a serious claim.[101] The PUP government, therefore, proceeded to plan for independence, establishing a Joint Select Committee of the House of Representatives and the Senate in April 1968 to consider the draft terms of an independence constitution.[102] In the next section are discussed the constitutional proposals that were put forward.

## The imbroglio

*Proposals for an independence constitution.* Because it is seen by political parties and other organizations as the last major opportunity to gain or safeguard their respective positions, the formulation of an independence constitution is usually the occasion for intense bargaining and rivalry within the society. In Belize the competition was expected to be between the PUP and the NIP. For one thing, the legitimacy of the NIP had been strengthened in the 1965 election under the new constitution. The party won two seats, one of them by Goldson. This gave him an undisputed claim to being Leader of the Opposition. His status was further acknowledged when the opposition was invited to join the ruling PUP in talks with the British government and the Guatemalan government in London in July 1965.[103] The NIP victory also ended the PUP monopoly of the elected representation without, of course, reducing its overwhelming dominance. For another thing, in its 1965 election manifesto the PUP had developed its political objective from simply 'eventual self-government' to 'independence and prosperity within the Central American orbit, within the Commonwealth of Nations and under the protection of the United Nations'.[104] While this may partly have been a reflection of the country's multiple orientation to its Central American neighbours, the West Indies and Britain, the objective remained unclear and contentious.

The PUP was, however, more specific about the country's status in its preamble to the resolution which established the Joint Select Constitutional Committee of the National Assembly. It categorically claimed that the 'will of the people [is] for independence within the Commonwealth' and that the government had been given a mandate 'to attain this objective'.[105] This exclusive commitment to the Commonwealth did not necessarily defuse an explosive issue since the PUP could have argued later that it did not exhaust its mandate. Nor did this option take care of all the NIP's reservations about independence. Goldson made this known to the Committee at its first meeting. The presence at the meeting of the opposition should not, he stated, be misinterpreted; it 'in no way commits the opposition to independence before a general election or before the Mediator in the Anglo-Guatemala dispute has submitted his proposals, and these have been dealt with in a referendum, if necessary',[106] as was agreed between himself as Leader of the Opposition and the Premier in August 1967.

The participation of the opposition party was, however, short-lived. At the second meeting, Goldson and his colleague, Senator Hassock, withdrew on three grounds. One was that the PUP had pre-empted the work of the Select Committee by requesting the government to call for a constitutional conference with the British government in June or July 1968. The second reason was that the NIP had learnt that the government had already drafted an independence constitution which it circulated to the PUP representatives and was, therefore, not acting in good faith.[107] Finally, the two opposition leaders observed that there were demonstrations against the Webster mediation proposals and of 'no confidence' in the government's handling of the Guatemalan issue.[108]

The third reason was so flimsy that it seemed that the opposition had decided from the outset to boycott the Committee. The NIP was too aware of its numerical weakness not to view its participation as lending legitimacy to an exercise which was unlikely to result in adjustments in its favour. It certainly viewed the ruling party's commitment to the Commonwealth not as a concession to the demands of the opposition but the result of enlightened economic self-interest. As we indicated in the previous chapter, the NIP also calculated its impact on the government in terms not so much of its own contribution, but of its relationship with those occupational and economic groups which were strategically important to the government and the economy. These groups were capable of putting such a strain on the new country's institutional arrangements as to compel acceptance or serious consideration of their views on the constitutional structure. The NIP, therefore, saw it as a better strategy to support the POU's proposals which were likely to be similar to its own in spirit and in letter. Indeed, in its memorandum to the Committee the POU suggested that there be no change in the British parliamentary system which it believed protected the civil service from the whims and caprices of those in political power.[109]

Another influential group which justified the NIP's strategy was the Chamber of Commerce. Like the POU, this organization was concerned with the constitutional constraints on the exercise of political power. It, however, took the opposite view that the constraints within the British parliamentary system were not adequate for a situation in which the government was virtually unopposed and its leader supreme. As its medium, *The Reporter*, put it, the Cabinet system of government 'has to be responsive to the desires of the Premier', who, with his overwhelming majority, 'can get...whatever he wants...without having to bother about whether his National Assembly approves or not'.[110] Accordingly, the Chamber of Commerce recommended a constitutional structure modelled on the US system of government.[111] It, however, proposed that the Heads of the State and the Government were not to reside in the same person and that the latter incumbent was not to hold office for more than two consecutive terms (this did not preclude his serving on any subsequent occasions). The Chamber of Commerce had recommended the US system of government not only because the latter was supposed to provide for the separation of powers and checks and balances between the executive, the legislature and the judiciary, but also because the political values of the business community were influenced to a considerable extent by its close commercial connections with the USA. This was in sharp contradiction to the civil servants who retained a strong attachment to the colonial political traditions.

Apart from these two groups, no other influential persons or organizations such as the Guild of University Graduates, or individual members of the Bar Association who were likely to share the NIP values on one issue or another pertaining to the independence constitution, responded positively to the Committee's specific invitation to submit oral or written evidence. As one of the Committee members, Santiago Peredomo, the representative for Cayo South, remarked, from 'the trend of replies it seemed that they were not much concerned'.[112] It seemed that the forces which had repelled influential and professional persons from active participation remained immeasurably stronger than those which attracted. This evidently was a matter of concern for the PUP which was looking as much to the higher occupational and economic status groups as to any other for its legitimacy as a government.

As a result of the NIP boycott and the limited response from the more prestigious and national organizations, the constitution-making process turned out to be more or less a PUP affair. This, however, did not detract from its importance. The exercise confirmed that the nature of the relationship between the PUP leaders and their rank-and-file supporters in general was changing. To the extent that a close relationship existed, it revealed that the predominantly Latin outdistricts were replacing Belize City as the main focus of mass interest in the PUP. Several factors may have been responsible for these changes. As we suggested the party was seeing itself primarily as a government. Another factor may have been the location of the PUP central organization in Belize City. This national organization probably overshadowed or even pre-empted the work of its branches and ancillary organizations in this part of the country. Thirdly, the change probably indicated the development of a structured organization within the ancillary groups themselves. Whatever the cause, the PUP seemed incapable of generating the same enthusiasm and response among its urban supporters to its proposed independence constitution as it had done on other crucial issues in the past. The greatest response to, and interest in the enquiry was in the outdistricts. The experience of the Committee was the opposite to that of the Courtenay Commission which found in 1949 that 'most of the persons who attended our meetings were merely onlookers, and the few persons who gave evidence did so with much reluctance and only after considerable encouragement from the Commissioner. In most instances the meeting was in the nature of a seminar.'[113]

The second standpoint from which the constitutional enquiry was important related to the heterogeneity of interests within the PUP as against those of the NIP. The PUP fragmented into distinct categories, each defining its relationship to the constitution-making process in terms of its position and political values within the society. As we indicated, social divisions among the leadership had begun to emerge with the recruitment of the professionally qualified Creoles into the party. This again was manifested in the Committee. It was not surprising that it was Vernon Courtenay, the lawyer and senator, who had suggested that various influential organizations and persons with a strong professional bias not only be specifically invited, but also 'spurred on to give their views and recommendations to the Committee'.[114] It was even less surprising that it was Peredomo who observed that these organizations and persons had failed to heed the call and therefore did not seem interested. The tenor of the latter's remarks seemed to imply that, despite or because of the party leadership still being predominantly Creole, the PUP was wasting its time in trying to obtain the support of the middle-class Creoles.

It was this Creole element within the PUP that was largely responsible for the drafting of the PUP proposals, and they showed no signs of betraying their constitutional heritage. Indeed, Rogers, who was, and still is, the Minister of Internal Affairs and is also the Deputy Premier, demonstrated the Creole attachment to the country's constitutional origin as early as 1962. He upheld the country's 'Parliamentary System of Government' as one of its cultural virtues which would 'be the envy' of the two Latin countries, Guatemala and Mexico, that were claiming Belize.[115] The two key figures who were involved in the constitution-making process were even more committed to the retention of the system of government along the Westminster lines. These were Harrison Courtenay and his son, Vernon, who were two of the three lawyers associated with the government. The senior Courtenay, who had played a crucial role in the three previous constitutional changes during the period of decolonization, was the Constitutional Adviser to the Committee. The younger Courtenay was by then in line for the position of Attorney General.

The main proposals came from the PUP national executive in broad outline and were fairly orthodox.[116] They were not dissimilar in principle and actual provisions on such subjects as fundamental rights, citizenship, the judiciary and the public service, to those proposed by most Commonwealth West Indian territories. The PUP clearly preferred to remain within the Commonwealth. It however had an open mind on whether the constitution should confer dominion or republican status, although the spokesmen, who included two ministers of government, seemed to envisage the retention of the monarchy as the Head of State at least at the outset.

Underlying these proposals was the assumption that a fairly well-integrated society existed in which communalism and parochialism were being rapidly replaced by a rising national spirit.

Unlike the proposals of the national party executive, those of the various groups within it suggested that a common political identity of purpose was still a long way from being achieved. The underdeveloped state of this identity could be attributed to varied cultural, regional and socio-economic factors that differentiated the Belizean population in general and the PUP groups in particular. The two principal party groups in Belize City, the United Women's Group and the Men's Marshalls Group, specifically supported the idea of independence within the Commonwealth. The former organization believed that this 'was the only way to curb Guatemala's unfounded claim'.[117] This was essentially a Creole view. It was shared by five individuals from Belize City each of whom submitted evidence but was not necessarily associated with the views shared by the PUP.[118] A similar outlook was also evident among the Caribs in Stann Creek who tended to identify with the political values of the Creoles.[119] It was, however, not pronounced in the predominantly Latin communities except among the sugar-cane growers in the northern districts of Orange Walk and Corozal.[120] The reason for this economic group positively supporting the idea of remaining within the Commonwealth was obvious: the sugar industry depended upon Commonwealth preferences which the farmers did not wish to be placed in jeopardy. As the President of the Cane Farmer's Association, a primary school teacher in Orange Walk, stated, 'an Independent Belize within the Commonwealth should safeguard the present sugar arrangements with the Commonwealth'.[121] The Cane Farmers' Association was controlled by the large-scale and wealthy farmers. But it is not unlikely that the economic considerations also dominated the thinking of the peasant cane-farmers on this issue.

This, however, was perhaps the only important subject on which there was an identity of interests between the rural Indians and Mestizos and the urban Creoles, and even then, it should be emphasized, the common outlook was based on differing considerations, one economic and the other cultural. The Latin element was however unwilling to further dilute its political values and preference for a closer political identity with Central America. While the PUP group in Belize City seemed to share the national party executive's proposals for the retention of a cabinet system of government under a monarchy, the Mestizo leaders in the north strongly favoured the immediate introduction of a presidential system. Mateo Ayuso, who was one of the leaders of the Cane Farmers' Association, felt that the 'Republic System was most suitable for the country' and that the people 'should elect their Congress, then elect their President'.[122]

The idea of a President who was both Head of State and Head of the Government directly responsible to the electorate was put forward with even greater force by the elected parliamentary and Town Board representatives from the north. Their views indicated that their political values were non-British and more specifically hemispheric, looking to the USA and Latin America. To the extent that the national PUP organization and other organizations and persons in Belize City thought of a republican system of government, they riveted their attention on the various modes of this system within the Commonwealth. It was not even necessary to look outside the north for confirmation of our argument that the differing cultural values of the Creoles and Mestizos ran along political lines. William Gegg (the brother of Edgar) remained firmly attached to his British connection and was a member of the small white Creole community in Corozal. He urged the Committee to 'adhere to the monarchy system' and to continue to look to Britain for military protection after independence.[123]

Since cultural and regional differences were more or less coterminous, the latter were certain to be asserted even at the expense of the process of national integration. Thus Florencio Marin, the representative for Corozal South, suggested to the Committee the creation of regional military forces that were independent of each other but responsible to the appropriate minister. Belize City 'was to retain *its* [emphasis mine] Volunteer Guard and Police Force'[124] and Corozal and Orange Walk, the new capital, Belmopan, and Cayo, and Stann Creek and Punta Gorda were to be combined into three pairs of regions for military purposes.[125] The outdistricts were also evidently not satisfied with the local government changes which the PUP government had introduced in 1963. These did not affect the highly centralized features of the system since they were confined to the introduction of wholly elective Town Boards and adult suffrage to bring them in line with the Belize City Council.[126] The Corozal branch of the PUP, therefore, took the opportunity to propose a 'large measure of self-government for the districts'.[127]

These proposals reflected the dissatisfaction of the outdistrict representatives with the centralized character of the party and their inability to penetrate the national Creole leadership both of the party and the government. The problem of the outdistrict representatives was as much social as it was cultural and geographic in so far as the professional middle-class Creoles were trickling into positions of influence and power. If these outdistrict representatives could not effect a change in the power distribution then their goal was to curb the consolidation of the Creole middle class in the upper ranks of the government. Accordingly, the PUP groups in the outdistricts unanimously demanded the abolition of the Senate.[128] This was an issue on which both the national party organization and the groups in Belize City had been silent in their submissions to the Committee, presumably because they expected the institution to be retained. The Men's Marshalls group was much more concerned with the problem of national unity which it believed should be built around such symbols as the flag, the new name of the country and the anthem. The group recommended that provision for the pledge of allegiance to the flag and the anthem should be included in the constitution and non-compliance be deemed a criminal offence.[129] While, in insisting that these injunctions be enshrined in the constitution, the PUP group may have specifically had in mind the possibility of disloyalty among the anti-PUP elements it was not inconceivable that this would have existed among disaffected groups within the PUP.

*The Webster mediation.* Even before the Constitutional Committee held its first public hearing in May 1968 it was overtaken by the publication of the Webster mediation proposals in April.[130] It had taken the mediator almost three years to conclude his investigation. A discussion of the events that transpired during this period, the proposals themselves and the immediate reaction to them in Belize are important to an understanding of the PUP Government's unwillingness to take the final constitutional step to independence.

After the Puerto Rican conference in April 1962, Belize was not represented at the Anglo-Guatemalan talks[131] until May 1965 when representatives of the government and opposition met officials of Britain and Guatemala in Miami.[132] Two months later, in July, there was another meeting in London where it was decided to have a tripartite mediation and to request the United States and possibly a Scandinavian and an African, Asian or South American country to be the members.[133] In a rare show of unity the Belize delegates insisted that the US alone should not mediate because it was involved militarily, economically and politically in Guatemala.[134] It came as a surprise to the opposition to learn for the first time from a Voice of America broadcast in November 1965 that the United States, at the request of Britain and Guatemala, had agreed to act as sole mediator in the dispute and that Bethuel Webster was attending a conference in Washington with British, Guatemala and Belize officials to receive his terms of reference.[135]

As far as the opposition was concerned this was not an auspicious and reassuring start. It was being reminded at the outset that although its leaders were consulted, Belize's colonial status, small size and population, weak international voice and economy militated against due recognition of its view. Price also shared these misgivings and seemed to have accepted a single mediator as a *fait accompli*. In a letter to Goldson in August 1967, he reminded him that they had 'realized that mediation was a most difficult undertaking and that its chances of success were slim'.[136] A year earlier, in June 1966, Price had also been reminded that the success or failure of the mediation depended not only on the predisposition of the high contracting parties, but also on that of the opposition party. In that month representatives of the British government and the Belize government met in London to discuss matters which Webster proposed to include in his report. Within days of the conference and before the Belize delegates returned home the *Daily Mirror* in Trinidad reported that 'Britain wants to quit British Honduras and in effect hand the colony over to Guatemala as soon as possible.'[137] Goldson confirmed this claim on his return and revealed, in the form of thirteen points, the details of the mediator's proposals at a public party rally.[138] In response the PUP government claimed that the article was false and that Goldson's memory had played him false since the delegates were not allowed to make notes at the meeting. Despite the refutation, there were demonstrations and attacks on government buildings which were quelled by a nightly curfew.[139]

It was clear that even if Price's reservations about the outcome of the mediation proved to be without foundation, the chances of the proposals being accepted by the opposition elements would be slender. Indeed, the NIP maintained the pressure upon the PUP, probably at the expense of the PUP government's bargaining position in the mediation, by taking its case to the United Nations Trusteeship Committee[140] and forcing the PUP government to also present its case to the Committee.[141] The latter could not have responded otherwise without inviting from the NIP charges of complicity in the mediation. At the same time it took steps to handle amicably the mediator's proposals when these were made available. As indicated earlier, in August 1967, Price reached agreement with Goldson to discuss the proposals with him before either Leader had taken them to the public, in the event that there were matters in them that were controversial between the parties. In the case of disagreement the proposals were to become the subject of a referendum. This would be unnecessary if the proposals were unacceptable to both parties as they would then be rejected outright.[142]

The mediator presented his proposals in the form of a draft treaty and in the first of seventeen articles conceded sovereignty to the colony. He envisaged that not later than the end of 1970 'sole responsibility for and the right to exercise all and any powers, both internal and external, of government administration, legislation, and jurisdiction shall vest in Belize'.[143] However, the sovereignty was at once rendered nominal by the co-operative aspects of the treaty and the wide powers conferred on a Joint Authority of Belize and Guatemala in its administering of them.[144]

The plan placed the defence, foreign affairs and, to a certain extent, the economy of Belize under Guatemalan control after independence.[145] The normal channel of communication to international bodies by the Belize government was to be through the Guatemalan government. The two governments were to consult on matters of external defence but this was tantamount to Belize being subjected to the dictates of Guatemala. Even the provision of internal security in Belize, a responsibility expected with independence, was to be the subject of consultation and co-operation. Belize was to accept a customs union with its neighbour which was to be allowed free access to its Caribbean ports and territorial waters. It was to be rewarded with Guatemala's support for its entry into the Central American community and into the Inter-American community and in particular into the Organization of American States and the inter-American Development Bank.[146]

In sum, the proposals exclusively committed Belize to a hemispheric destiny as a satellite or department of Guatemala. Nowhere in the document was it stated that the Guatemalan claim was revoked. Nor was Belize explicitly given the right to seek membership of the Commonwealth, the United Nations or international bodies outside of the Inter-American system. It was, in short, denied the prerogative of an independent state to choose or reorder at least some of the priorities of its future. As Price put it, the 'treaty predetermines the choice for us in many of these fields'.[147]

With regard to the country's internal politics, the proposals also made few concessions to the dominant traditional social values. For example, degrees granted from outside Belize or Guatemala were excluded from the reciprocal recognition of educational qualifications.[148] This undermined the dominant British orientation of the educational system in Belize and, in the absence of post-secondary facilities, virtually decreed Guatemala as the new centre of higher learning for Belizeans.

As the mediator could not have been unaware of the cultural factor in Belizean politics, his proposals should be seen as an outright attempt to end the country's artificiality as a British enclave within the Latin environment and render its connections with the Commonwealth Caribbean tenuous. No allowance was made for the development of a distinctive Belizean culture deriving its strength and character from the contributions of the two principal cultural groups. As we mentioned, the proposals were not discursive and perhaps the mediator considered this viewpoint only to reject it as idealistic. Moreover, the gradual process of developing a common culture would necessarily be set against the political disposition of both the high contracting parties, Britain and Guatemala, for a quick solution.

In placing the economic, political and military life of Belize under Guatemalan control, the mediator had evidently conceived his task as being more than the reconciliation of Belize's aspiration for political independence with some form of economic co-operation which guaranteed Guatemala unrestricted access to the sea-ports in Belize and enabled the latter country to participate in the Central American union. The proposals confirmed that the problem had over the years assumed new dimensions that were linked to Guatemala's internal problems of communist insurgents and to the emergence of revolutionary Cuba. In the address of 1 January 1962, in which he claimed to have been promised American support in the dispute with Britain, the President of Guatemala charged that Guatemala had begun to 'receive exports of the Cuban revolution' and spoke of the need 'to free our territory of trouble-makers, guerrilleros, terrorists, conspirators, all spurred on by money arriving from Cuba'.[149] The fact that Ernesto Che Guevara had lived in Guatemala during the Arbenz regime, which he actively supported, probably reinforced Ydigoras Fuentes' conviction about Cuban communist infiltration into Guatemala. With the unsuccessful American invasion of the Bay of Pigs, the problem of communist infiltration had become an even more critical issue for Guatemala.[150] A solution could not ignore the fact that Belize was of strategic value since it is for all practical purposes the north-eastern border of Guatemala and an ideal beach-head which provides easy access to the hinterland department of Peten. The Guatemala government could hardly be in doubt about the PUP government's ideological support. However, it recognized that with all the political will in the world, an independent Belize would be too small and weak to safeguard effectively its borders from communist infiltration. It is in this wider context that the mediator's proposals should be seen.

The proposals were presented to the representatives of the PUP government and the opposition at a meeting with the British government in Washington on 26 April 1968. Price laid them in the House of Representatives on 29 April with the information that they had the 'full support and backing of the US government'.[151] The response of the opposition party was quick and unrestrained. Within ten hours of the proposals being made public, and without prior consultation with the ruling party as the agreement between Price and Goldson had envisaged, Goldson announced at a public meeting that his National Executive Council had rejected the proposals which did not differ in substance from those he had disclosed in June 1966.[152] Indeed, the proposals vindicated his stand in 1966 and encouraged him to totally disregard his agreement with Price and repeat the series of demonstrations and protests in mobilizing support for his party's decision. The proposals in fact ran into equally swift and angry opposition from a variety of organizations including the PUP-controlled Town Boards. The Guild of University Graduates deplored 'the callous attempt of the British government to relegate its responsibility to safeguard the sovereignty of our people and to condone the blatant attempt on the part of the US to gain a direct foothold in the control and conduct of our national affairs'.[153] The POU also reserved its most vitriolic attack for these two governments. It viewed with 'horror' and 'gravest misgivings' the 'immoral and unashamed betrayal of trust' which it was proposed the British government should 'perpetuate upon the people of British Honduras with the obvious acquiescence, indeed encouragement of the United States'.[154] Although the POU regarded the proposals as matters of national importance transcending party political connotations, it went on to 'question the part played by our own government in the whole sordid affair'.[155]

The PUP government instead of initiating firm, positive reaction had indeed allowed itself to be put in the position of reacting to the offensive of the opposition party and other organizations within the society. At best its strategy seemed to be limited to reacting to public opinion on a purely tactical basis. It was not until five days later, on 4 May, when the opposition had reached a groundswell, that the PUP informed the public that its Central Council had rejected the proposals.[156] The PUP claimed that unlike the NIP, it had reserved its judgement in order to consult a cross-section of national opinion.[157] A part of the party's problem was that it had accepted the diplomatic nature of the mediation and preferred secrecy to open communication with the population. It was not until the PUP declared its stand that Price disclosed in a radio broadcast on 9 May that his cabinet had, in August 1967, considered and rejected proposals that had been put forward to him.[158] The reason for this late disclosure was clear; it was designed to reassure the population that the PUP government was always in tune with their sentiment and was capable of representing their interests. Accordingly, on 14 May 1968, the PUP government joined the opposition in unanimously rejecting the proposals in the House of Representatives.[159] The decision put the seal on the proposals, since the British government had pledged not to conclude a settlement that was unacceptable to the government. Since then the British government and the Guatemala government have continued their search for a negotiated settlement, although it does not appear that the PUP government is included in all phases of the discussions. Indeed, as we shall see in chapter 11, the PUP government has embarked on its own diplomatic pursuit for support of the Third World countries, especially the Commonwealth Caribbean.

*The impasse.* Although it rejected the Webster proposals, the PUP government nevertheless envisaged an independence conference later in 1968.[160] At the same time, however, the PUP National Executive recommended to the Select Constitutional Committee that the government enter into 'discussion before the date of independence with the United Kingdom regarding adequate defence arrangements'.[161] Significantly the suggestion did not find wide acceptance among the outdistrict representatives in the north who contended that the Guatemalan claim was not sufficient justification for delaying independence.[162]

By imposing upon itself a military condition for taking independence from the British government, the PUP government reduced the constitutional enquiry to an academic exercise. The only outcome of its pursuit of independence since 1968 is the official change of the name of the country to Belize in June 1973. This change was, however, symbolic, and it did not really bring the country closer to independence than when the PUP began to promise it at the time the self-governing constitution was introduced in 1964.

By being so protracted, the internal self-governing constitution is anachronistic. The continued responsibility of the Governor for internal security and the public service forces the PUP government to maintain a close and harmonious relationship with him, especially if he still considers that his role is to govern. Even in the Associated Caribbean States which have full responsibility for their internal affairs, the idea that the British government could pursue their foreign interests and protect their territorial integrity better than they is losing some of its adherents. In these states, beginning with Grenada, independence is gradually but firmly being embraced as the only terminal point of colonial political change. The PUP government has long been committed to this goal but cannot ignore the lingering obstacle to its achievement.

To conclude on this note would however be inadequate. For our analysis of the major events of the phases of the mediation suggests that the PUP government's reluctance is also directly linked to the disunity within the society over its handling of the affair. The picture which emerged was that of an uncertain, if not weak government incapable of commanding national unity on this issue trying to conciliate and responding to the pressures of the opposition elements. The consequences of moving to independence without the dispute being resolved to the satisfaction of the opposition parties and strategic groups like the POU are incalculable. This consideration is, of course, part of a vicious circle. The absence of national unity certainly does not augment the PUP government's bargaining position in the on-going negotiation. Stated differently, it relieves the pressure on the British government to respond positively to the widespread demand in Belize for a military guarantee of the country's independence.

# 9
## Political parties and the political process

In the previous chapter it was suggested that the relationship between the PUP leaders and their followers was changing and that this took the form of a diminution in the role of the party rank-and-file within the political process. Our main contention was that this was not unrelated to the party's ascendancy to office and the legitimization of its power by the British government. To this contention some more related suggestions should be added. One is that it is the cabinet of the PUP government, established in 1964, rather than the party organs – the National Executive Council, the Central Party Council and the Annual Party Convention – that dominates the formulation of party policy. This has come about for a variety of reasons. First, the membership of the cabinet and some of these organs, particularly the National Executive Council, are coterminous. Second, the ministers are assured of control even when they are outnumbered at, for example, the national conferences. Party constituency organizations, party representatives of the National Assembly and local government bodies, and also ancillary organizations, are the main categories represented at the national conferences. But very little in the way of constituency organization has ever actively existed except during a national election, with the result that the influence which emanates from this source is negligible. Local government bodies are also too much the poor relation of the central government for their representatives to be anything but deferential to the views of the superior central government party functionaries. Third, the national conference which is the supreme decision-making body is not held annually as was the case during the party's ascendancy to power. Indeed it has tended to be replaced by district conferences which are held mainly in an election year, and whose role is reduced to confirming the constituency's nominee for the election. Finally, being relatively small, and functionally homogeneous, the cabinet lends itself to the exercise of Price's personal influence much more readily than the Central Party Council which consists of representatives of each constituency, the ancillary party organs, and members of the National Assembly and the National Executive Council.

Another contention is that the party's return to office in 1961 affected the relationship among the parliamentary group of leaders. The idea that it was the government and more specifically the cabinet, and not the party 'at work'[1] dominated the thinking of the PUP leaders to the extent that PUP back-benchers in the House of Representatives were of the opinion that power and influence were being removed from them and felt impelled to chase after it.[2] The fact that this power was being exercised in secrecy probably also added to the fear that Price's personal hold was being institutionalized.

The PUP back-benchers in fact reacted in the mid-1960s to the general concentration of power and influence within the cabinet. They successfully demanded the introduction of the Committee system and a procedural change in the law-making process.[3] The new law-making procedure automatically commits a bill after its first reading to one of eleven Select Standing Committees. This is followed by the second reading of the bill which is next considered by a committee of the whole House of Representatives. It receives its third reading after the report stage.

The object of the Committee system is to democratize the relationship between not only the back-benchers and their leaders, but also the House and the public. Public hearings of Standing Committees are conducted throughout the country depending upon the nature of the subject. The back-benchers do not conceive the committees as merely a conduit for both government and public opinion. They allow cross-examination on important issues with the result that the committees can resemble a political forum. In this way the back-benchers influence the very public opinion that they are canvassing for the House. In a situation where there are more government back-benchers than ministers in the House of Representatives, as was the case until there were cabinet changes after the 1969 election, an unfavourable report of the bill could have ended in deadlock if the back-benchers acted in unison. This diffusion of influence can result, as a minister put it in 1967, in the 'tail wagging the dog'.[4]

Perhaps the PUP back-benchers would have been less radical in their demand if the political system offered them other means of exerting influence. In most post-colonial regimes appointments to quasi-government bodies, such as public corporations, usually solve the problem of the discontented and frustrated back-bencher. Such public offices are, however, few in Belize and most of them are non-remunerative.

Another avenue of upward political and socio-economic mobility which is found in most Commonwealth territories is the appointment of parliamentary secretaries. Resorting to this method can, however, be barely justified in Belize because of the high ratio of ministerial functionaries to back-benchers which it would create in the numerically small House. Within these limitations, the back-benchers' only hope of a measure of influence in the 1960s was Price's adroit handling of ministerial appointments. But in order to retain a balance in racial, cultural and district representation, there was little scope for ministerial changes during the life of an Assembly. Back-benchers, therefore, were not encouraged to regard themselves as potential ministers once the initial appointments were made.

Despite its limited scope, the ministerial method was employed to resolve the problem of the distribution of power and influence. In January 1969, three back-benchers, Fred Hunter, Allan Arthurs and Santiago Peredomo, who had begun a tardy but bitter criticism of the government economic policies in the Committees of the House of Representatives,[5] were appointed parliamentary secretaries.[6] The election in December 1969 enabled Price to extend the use of this method. The three parliamentary secretaries were given ministerial portfolios as was one of their back-bench colleagues, Louis Sylvestre, who was a minister in the 1961 government. Of the four ministers replaced, two of them, Cattouse, Deputy Leader of the party who did not contest the election, and Gwendolyn Lizarraga, had passed their prime; a third, Hector Silva, had retained his seat by literally one vote; the fourth, David McKoy, was appointed a parliamentary secretary. Two young back-benchers, Elito Urbina and Florencio Marin, were also elevated to this post.[7] With these gestures, the number of ministerial personnel in the House of Representatives rose from seven to eleven.

The pressure for power and influence to be shared among the PUP parliamentary representatives was virtually brought to an end when the 1974 general elections reduced their number from seventeen to twelve. Nine had been re-elected and became ministers, and of the three newcomers, two were appointed parliamentary secretaries. This has reinforced the dominance of the Cabinet without rendering the Committee system in the House of Representatives useless since the parliamentary opposition is considerably strengthened.

Another contention is that the PUP leaders bring this highly centralized and personalized type of leadership to bear on their relationship with other institutions within the political process. Institutions such as trade unions are no longer considered as a crucial constituent of the party's influence. On the other hand they are not expected to falter in their support for the government. This is particularly the case with those institutions, such as the denominational schools and the local authorities, whose present economic existence and future well-being depend upon the grace of the political elite. Institutions which are not supportive are looked upon askance.

A contributory factor to the PUP being highly centralized and leader-dominated is the existence of a very limited articulate public opinion. To begin with, the mass media have never been allowed an independent existence. The sole radio network in Belize is government-owned and government-controlled. The opposition parties' demand for the service to be made available to them to voice their viewpoint has met with no success.[8] Sensitive and contentious political issues are seldom discussed and are presented in a light favourable to the government. Second, although the newspapers are locally owned they are either essentially party news-papers or, in the case of *The Reporter*, serve primarily the interests of the business community. Indeed, until this newspaper was established in 1966, the reading public was deluged with the partisan views of *The Belize Times* and the *Belize Billboard* which became defunct in 1969 when a fire destroyed its premises. One was preoccupied with extolling the virtues of the government and the other with denying that there were any.

Organized labour has tended to identify with one of the two major political parties and in any case, lacks the resources to provide a separate outlet to the currents of opinion.[9] Industries are not sufficiently advanced to produce either an income elite capable of providing a firm financial base for sustained trade union activity or an articulate and politically conscious proletariat. Perhaps the only exception is the sugar industry where, as we indicated, the job experience of the cane-farmers has sharpened critical thinking. But this outlook is seldom translated into con-tinuous, open political activity. For one thing the style of Price's leadership discourages organized labour from engaging in public challenges rather than direct representation to the real source of power. For another, workers have not forgotten the disintegrative effect of the deep political involve-ment of the trade unions in the late 1950s. Political activity in the sugar industry is also limited by the migratory and alien character of a large section of the work force. This is the Mexicans who accounted for 20 per cent of the labourers in 1965,[10] and who have no desire to prejudice their tenuous relationship with the political system. The possibility of the critical thinking within the sugar industry being transmitted to other industries is also remote for a variety of reasons. Each region caters for a different type of industry so that the Corozal or Orange Walk cane-farmer has little contact with the Stann Creek citrus worker. Second, the majority of the trade unions have followed suit and tend to organize on an occupa-tional basis. Altogether the parochial outlook which this industrial separa-tion breeds, and the close identification of the trade unions with the political parties, have resulted in a differential orientation of public opinion in the industrial field.

That the rural population is not vocal in its public opinion is hardly surprising. But the same type of civic inactivity exists in Belize City with its educated middle-class population. The more articulate and politically conscious citizens who were once active in literary and debating societies have now retreated to the privacy of their verandahs and clubs where they talk of their disappointment with the political changes that frustrate their political ascendancy. The only issue on which their response was once vocal and strident was the Guatemalan claim when this seemed capable of settlement in the 1960s. A few ultra-conservative Creoles in 1966 formed themselves into a pressure group, Citizens Integrated to Voice the Interests of Country (CIVIC Committee), which adopted an obstinately antagonistic outlook towards the American mediation of the problem and the PUP government's plans for independence.[11] The CIVIC Committee, however, merely duplicated the efforts of the NIP with which its organizers were associated and added very little to public awareness on the issue. Indeed it drew its inspiration less from the responses to its public meetings than from the activities of the British Honduras Freedom Committee of New York[12] and the British Honduras Emergency Committee in London[13] which overseas Belizeans opposed to the PUP government had established to lobby support in the United Nations and the British Parliament respectively. For the CIVIC Committee, mistrustful of the PUP, was of the view that Belizeans were unequal to the task of withstanding the Guatemala claim without the co-operation of the British government and support from the United Nations.

A contributory factor to this general passivity of the middle class is the fact that its largest occupational component is the civil servants who are debarred from criticizing the government in public. In a country where the occupational alternatives to government services are extremely limited, this injunction cannot be lightly violated. There are the widespread fears that it is not possible to differ with the government without being penalized, and that political patronage is becoming the main determining factor of advancement in the civil service. As early as 1962, the POU 'had felt obliged to express fears that the Public Service Commission were relaxing their vigilance and permitting a number of irregularities in appointments and promotions to receive their sanction'.[14] Fear, however, does not only manifest itself in timidity but also in aggressive actions, and the POU has been one of the few organizations to challenge the government openly.

In post-colonial regimes the task of formulating radical public opinion usually devolves on the academic community. Indeed, we observed the role which the American Jesuits played in their secondary schools and related organizations in this regard during the colonial period. These scholastic and religious leaders are, however, less concerned with the state of public opinion than with maintaining their cordial relationship with the PUP government from which they have received encomiums. As Price put it, the American missionaries, especially those from Missouri, which is the headquarters of the Jesuits in Belize, are America's 'best ambassadors to the Caribbean and to Central and South America'.[15]

Until recently, the wider academic community of university-trained Belizeans has shown little willingness to disturb the general political blandness. The Department of Extra-Mural Studies of the University of the West Indies which contributed to the political debate against colonialism in the 1950s, remains a forum for the development of a national consciousness. This is done through the promotion of a national art and culture that is so essential to political self-confidence. It was however with the almost simultaneous but coincidental return of four young University graduates in 1968 that the political process was openly challenged.[16] One of these graduates was Assad Shoman who had won a Belize Scholarship in 1962 and studied law in England. Another was Said Musa who was the runner-up to Shoman, and had entered the same profession. The third was Lionel Del Valle, an economist, and the fourth, Evan Hyde, was an equally outstanding scholar. They seemed to view the Guatemalan claim as having rendered politics in Belize sterile and were willing to reject the *status quo*, characterized by European and American economic and cultural domination,[17] even if it meant sacrificing their careers. For these young graduates had joined the government service, the two lawyers as Crown Counsels, the economist as an Administrative Officer and the journalist as a teacher. It was not long before the government, already perplexed with its failure to produce the necessary social transformation which was now being demanded, decided to terminate the appointment of Musa and Shoman and to refrain from renewing Hyde's.[18] At first this appeared to have little effect upon the political activities of these young radicals, but in a small society, the pressure to conform can be exceedingly overwhelming. Hyde alone had maintained his radicalism, as we shall see in the pages following, but, on the other hand, Del Valle has withdrawn from active politics, and Musa and Shoman have been co-opted by the PUP government as senators, after having been defeated as PUP candidates in the 1974 elections, and in the case of the latter, as Attorney General and also Minister of Economic Development. It must be remembered too, that Belize is cut off from the main traffic of ideas and that political views remain radical long after they become orthodox or outmoded elsewhere.

*Opposition parties*

As we indicated in the previous chapter, the manner in which the PUP continued to dominate the political process cannot be fully understood without reference to the lack of unity within the NIP, between this party and its offshoot, the PDM, and also within UBAD.

*The NIP split and the PDM.* A part of the NIP's problem was that its Leader Goldson alone could claim a certain natural legitimacy or authority owing first to his leading role within the nationalist movement in the 1950s, and second, to his being the only person to provide the party with a continuous presence in the legislature from 1961, and also with its sole representative in the House of Representatives after the 1969 election. This encouraged Goldson to assert a rather personal influence over the definition of party policy, and like the PUP leader, to de-emphasize the party machinery and activity as a bona fide outlet for political participation. Because of the circumstances under which Goldson had broken with the PUP in the mid-1950s, his party policy was essentially narrow, negative and reactive. It was riveted to the Guatemalan claim and apparently confined to opposing the PUP on the issue. The policy had a limited appeal to the young professional middle-class Creoles who joined the party in the later 1950s and early 1960s, especially when it continually failed to advance the party's parliamentary position. This group however recognized that the broadening of the party's focus, especially on domestic issues, was unlikely to be achieved under Goldson's leadership.

In 1967, a member of this group, Dean Lindo, a lawyer and one of three deputy leaders of the party, claimed to have contemplated contesting the leadership of the NIP in that year but deferred to Goldson in the interest of party unity, rather than in the belief that the latter would eventually be able to take the NIP out of the electoral doldrums by concentrating on the Guatemalan issue.[19] It is possible that Lindo refrained from making the move at the time because had he succeeded, the party would have been put in the anomalous situation of having its new Leader outside the House of Representatives and the old inside it. In view of these considerations, the question which arises is, why did Lindo challenge Goldson at the annual party conference two years later in October 1969, and risk the party unity for which he claimed to be concerned, especially as this meeting was expected to be the last before the approaching general election? One possible answer is that the impending election created the opportunity for the potential anomaly in the leadership to be avoided. Indeed, had Lindo wrested the leadership from Goldson, his chances of winning a seat would have been enhanced. As it turned out, he polled 476 or 47.8 per cent of the votes cast and lost the Fort George constituency in Belize City by 30 votes to the PUP candidate, A. A. Hunter, the Minister of Trade and Industry.[20] There is another answer which suggests that Lindo was not conducting a personal campaign for the leadership and that was related to the rise of the UBAD. The significant impact which this organization was making in Belize City not only exposed the sad state into which the machinery of both the PUP and the NIP had fallen, but also threatened to undermine the NIP's middle-class Creole base of support. The sympathy of this group for UBAD was as strong and open as that of the young, the unemployed and the people of the slums of Yarborough. Three members of this Creole group, Rev. Coleridge Barnett, then Principal of Wesley College, Sister Mary Caritas, a Catholic nun, and Edward Laing, a lawyer, were among the witnesses who came forward for the defence in Evan Hyde's trial for sedition in June 1970.[21] The NIP was in a quandary about what steps it should take. The old and more conservative leaders soon resorted, in association with the CIVIC Committee, to a crusade against 'the preachers of hatred and racism'.[22] Following their customary practice with the PUP they seemed bent on provoking a cataclysmic confrontation with UBAD. As one who was not much removed in age and intellectual empathy from the UBAD leader, Lindo must have been aware that the reaction of his colleagues was no answer to the upsurge of Black Power in Belize which was typical of the spread of the movement throughout the Caribbean.[23] Furthermore, although UBAD insisted that it was essentially a cultural organization, it had moved in a more political direction some months before the NIP annual convention in October 1969, when Shoman, Musa and Del Valle, who had formed the People's Action Committee (PAC) in May 1969, approached Hyde about a merger of the two organizations.[24] It was probably the prospect of UBAD becoming a political party, which it had 'reserved the right to do'[25] after it eventually merged with PAC into 'one national liberation movement'[26] called the Revolitical Action Movement (RAM) in October 1969,[27] that finally prompted Lindo to end the delay of his bid for the NIP leadership.

Although he formed the PDM immediately after his defeat and decided to contest the election with the NIP as one party, Lindo continued to speculate about RAM's electoral intentions until his party and the NIP were given the assurance that the new group did not plan to fight the elections.[28] But RAM's decision enhanced the electoral chance of neither the NIP nor the PDM. The NIP lost one of the two seats it had obtained in 1965 and the PDM returned to its independent existence immediately with little indication of its support. Instead of building a strong internal organization, the PDM depended for publicity entirely on its official organ, *The Beacon*, which its Leader founded in 1970, and more than four years elapsed before it held its first public meeting in February 1973.

As a result of the split, the leadership of the NIP was exclusively placed in the hands of the old, ultra-conservative middle-class Creole group of professionals and retired public servants. Any doubts that this was the case were removed when Goldson left the party leadership in the hands of Ulric 'Bunting' Fuller, a retired Creole police inspector, leader of the CIVIC Committee and NIP-appointed Senator, to pursue legal studies in England in 1971. In 1973 Goldson returned with his studies incomplete, and resumed the leadership of the party.

*UBAD*. It should not be inferred from the considerable apprehension which the formation of UBAD in 1970 provoked within the NIP and to a lesser extent, the PUP, that the new movement made an equally significant impact upon the wider multi-racial and multi-cultural society. This was because of the sectional interest which its founder, Hyde, projected. Indeed Hyde's narrow perspective made it difficult for the radicalism of the other young, newly returned professional men to find an institutional expression within UBAD. With its prime objective of promoting 'the interest of the Black man on a national and international level',[29] UBAD offered virtually no accommodation to Del Valle who is a full-blooded Mestizo, and very little to Shoman and Musa who are from Palestinian Arab families in Belize City and San Ignacio, the principal town, in the Cayo District, respectively. Hyde, for example, took the view that Shoman, who had been a guest-speaker on the UBAD rostrum several times had over-stepped his bounds in giving an interview to the *Belize Billboard* in which he authoritatively discussed the aims and programmes of UBAD. As Hyde emphatically put it, in assuring his supporters of 'the direction of the organization', Shoman 'was not and never was an officer of the United Black Association for Development, and therefore had no authority to speak in the name of the organization'.[30] In forming the PAC the three leaders were acknowledging the cultural exclusiveness of UBAD. As they informed Hyde, there was room for an organization 'to deal exclusively with political matters',[31] more so as they could not take their message convincingly to the Indians and Mestizos in the west and north under the auspices of an organization whose name included the word 'Black'.[32] In forming the organization, the three leaders seemed intent on intensifying their fledgling campaign against the North Atlantic economic and cultural domination of their country. From the outset they drew considerable inspiration from the revolutionary activities of Che Guevara and perceived their fight as part of the wider struggle against capitalism and colonialism. But in expressing concern for their image in the north and west, the PAC leaders created doubts about their aims transcending racial and group interest. As Hyde pointed out, some of the UBAD members viewed the emergence of the PAC with suspicion.[33] Nonetheless, the two organizations agreed to exchange public speakers. At the same time they emphasized their respective identities by excluding dual membership on their executive committees.[34]

It was their common opposition to the PUP that was responsible for their merger in October 1969, when the PAC had been four months in existence. Both groups saw in the PUP's search for a defence guarantee of the country's proposed independence the beginning of 'neo-colonialism',[35] which called for a united front. In a document of belief, objectives and programmes of the new movement, the Rockville Declaration, the young leaders claimed that the time 'to end the country's subordination to a foreign culture and to build a society with its own values in which there would be meaningful participation by all our people' was overdue.[36] The leaders did not discount violence as a means of ending the *status quo*.[37] The general tone of the document was curiously reminiscent of the petitions which the PUP submitted to the Colonial Office in the 1950s, and it can be argued that the young leaders were merely continuing the decolonizing process which the PUP had begun.

While it gave impetus to the marriage of UBAD and PAC, the common opposition to the PUP was not sufficiently strong to keep the two organizations together. The unifying influence was overpowered by the difference of opinion within the UBAD group over the compatibility of its cultural aims and the political goals and strategy of the PAC element in the new organization. Ismail Omar Shabazz, leader of the Black Muslims in Belize, a mechanic who was at the time a government employee in the Public Works Department, and to some extent Hyde's mentor, headed a faction which argued that in discarding the name UBAD his colleagues had deferred to the PAC leaders' objections to the word 'Black'.[38] They feared that this marked the beginning of the UBAD group's retreat from its original cultural objectives. There was also the belief among the Black Power element in UBAD that PAC only valued UBAD for its superior organization and support in Belize City and Stann Creek. Other members of UBAD, while not necessarily considering the reference to violence as anything more than rhetoric, thought it at least ill-advised in a situation where it could be seized upon as a possible means of discrediting UBAD as a destructive racialist group. They also resisted the PAC's political ideology, not only for its left-wing orientation, but more important, because its leaders had embraced Che Guevara as their hero. They did not view this choice as accidental; it symbolized not only the revolutionary claims of the leaders, but also aided their efforts to build a mass base among the Indian peasants. These UBAD leaders also saw a connection between PAC's activities, the arrival of Lorenzo Cardenas, allegedly a leading Mexican communist, in June 1969, and Shoman's and Musa's professional visit to him when he was arrested and imprisoned by the PUP government.[39] Identification with this situation was not necessarily advancing UBAD's cultural aim. On the contrary, it may have proved inimical to the extent that it emphasized the country's Latin orientation. Furthermore, other members contended that if UBAD needed to hold a Third World revolutionary leader in reverence, then they had a more appropriate one in Frantz Fanon, and perhaps it was not unimportant that the Rockville Declaration began with a quotation from this leader's celebrated work – *The Wretched of the Earth*.[40] Equally important, UBAD had invoked the name of Marcus Garvey in its cause, patterned its constitution basically on the Universal Negro Improvement Association, and had 'planned a strategy of infiltrating' the organization in Belize with the aim of 'radicalizing it into a black power unit'.[41] At the other end of the UBAD spectrum were those for whom the wider political issues had a stronger appeal and who transferred their support to the PAC element.[42] Hyde, for his part, straddled both positions. He agreed, for example, that considerable discretion had to be exercised in UBAD's identification with revolutionary Third World leaders, and suspended Charles X Egan, a UBAD executive member, for having spoken on a PAC platform in front of a Che Guevara flag in the northern villages. This, he pronounced, 'was adventurism' that would 'be damaging' to UBAD.[43] At the same time Hyde pleaded for a less sectarian outlook among his UBAD associates. It was in the early months of the merger that he wrote a booklet 'Knocking Our Own Ting' in which he essayed that in assisting the British settlers to defeat the Spanish invaders in the Battle of St George's Cay in 1798, the black slaves had done nothing more than determine their masters.[44] As the descendants of these slaves, Afro-Belizeans were 'as oppressed...as their Indian brothers and sisters' by the whole capitalist system.[45] The ordinary Afro-Belizean should therefore avoid the trap into which middle-class Creoles had fallen, of thinking that since they were more acculturated to the dominant Creole norms of the society they were superior to the Latin element. Instead they should recognize that ultimately it is only in a national struggle that both colonized elements would discover their solidarity and necessary interdependence.

This latter viewpoint did not prevail over the debilitating effects of the submergence of UBAD's identity into RAM. The response in Belize City to the public meetings of the new organization was 'relatively poor' because as Hyde observed, many of the 'long time' UBAD members felt alienated and began 'to cut us off'.[46] Nor did the support in the Mestizo towns compensate for the loss. The people in San Ignacio, he noted, were 'polite but unexcited'.[47]

On the whole Hyde recognized that the affiliation with PAC was a liability to UBAD and was undermining his leadership within the latter organization. As he put it, 'UBAD was weak while it was RAM but UBAD as UBAD was a potent political force, more explosive than the opposition National Independence Party. The people of Afro-Honduras were fully aware of our struggle, appreciated our sincerity and understood clearly the message of black dignity, consciousness, togetherism that we had worked so many months to communicate.'[48] Since RAM was also a loosely-knit organization with controversial if not conflicting goals, its fragmentation rather than crystallization was assured. The immediate occasion for the parting of the ways among the RAM leaders was a debate on the attitude that RAM should adopt towards the PUP after the latter won the general election in December 1969.[49] The UBAD leaders argued against temporizing with the PUP. The issue was resolved when Shoman and Musa resigned from RAM in February 1970.[50] The UBAD leaders had regained exclusive control of the organizational machinery which they had brought to RAM. So as not to leave this in doubt, and to retrieve their old image, they reverted to the original name of the organization. But while they embarked on recapturing their original cultural aims, the UBAD leaders recognized that in merging with PAC they had taken a firm step into the political arena from which they could not easily retreat. At a meeting in July 1970 in Belize City this fact was acknowledged. The members and supporters of UBAD voted to constitute the movement as a duly organized political party to be known officially as the UBAD Party for Freedom, Justice and Equality, and began to organize 'in order to take over the government by any means necessary'.[51]

Since the outcome of the relationship between Hyde and the other young radical leaders suggested that the UBAD party would be too sectarian to develop a national appeal, most of the pressures upon the PUP from this element were relieved. Some of the pressures upon the NIP were also removed when UBAD decided to enter into an alliance with it to contest the municipal elections in opposition to the PUP in Belize City in 1971. It was obviously clear to the opposition elements that an alliance was almost a prerequisite to a successful challenge of the PUP hegemony.

The opposition forces again coalesced into the United Democratic Party in late 1973 as Belize moved toward another general election, but not before a fourth opposition party, the Liberal Party, LP, was formed. Even so the alliance was not complete as UBAD stood clear of it, for a variety of reasons. First, it was wary of coalitions since they tended to create dissensions within the party over strategy. The inclusion in the coalition of LP, which was closely identified with the business community and therefore with a philosophy to which UBAD was opposed, added to the latter's reluctance. Finally, because it confined its attention not only to one section of the population but also mainly to Belize City, UBAD entertained correspondingly limited electoral ambitions. It acknowledged this fact by announcing well in advance of the general election its intention to put forward its Leader, Hyde, as the only candidate.

The merger of the LP, the PDM and the NIP into the UDP, immediately raised a problem. Goldson was still in England when the alliance was formed and his return soon after reopened the leadership issue between Lindo and himself. A temporary solution was found in a collective leadership or troika among the rival aspirants who could only have ignored the lessons of approaching the election divided at their own peril. Although the three parties retained their identity within the UDP, their alliance paid handsome dividends. They won six of the eighteen seats and most of their successful candidates belonged to the PDM. This at once settled the question of the opposition leadership within the legislature in favour of Dean Lindo and gave the UDP an undisputed leader.

*Distribution of influence between the PUP and the Opposition Parties*

The significant electoral gains of the UDP in 1974 should not be attributed entirely to the united front which the various opposition elements presented to the electorate. Over the years there had been a gradual shift of influence away from the PUP, which was revealed in the 1961, 1965 and 1969 elections. These three elections are analysed against the background of the two earlier ones in 1954 and 1957. Table 10 illustrates not only the overall strength of the parties, but also the importance of the distinction between Belize City and the outdistricts, and between the main cultural components of the electorate.

Despite the PUP's continuing election success it did not recover in 1961 the urban Creole support which it lost in 1957 to the NIP. Furthermore, this support progressively declined in the 1965 and 1969 elections, with many of the constituencies becoming marginal. Also in the 1965 elections the PUP sustained a loss in every constituency within the Creole complex elsewhere in the country. Toledo North was particularly positive in its

Table 10   General elections in Belize 1954–1974

| Cultural grouping of areas | 1954 PUP | 1954 NP | 1957 PUP | 1957 Opposition parties NP | 1957 Opposition parties HIP | 1961 PUP | 1961 Opposition parties NIP | 1961 Opposition parties CDP | 1965 PUP | 1965 NIP | 1969 PUP | 1969 NIPDM | 1974 PUP | 1974 UDP |
|---|---|---|---|---|---|---|---|---|---|---|---|---|---|---|
| **Creole** | | | | | | | | | | | | | | |
| Belize City | 67.2 | 19.8[b] | 55.9 | 16.5 | 25.6 | 59.4 | 24.5 | 15.2 | 52.9 | 44.9 | 51.7 | 46.5 | 50.2 | 48.8 |
| Belize Rural | 57.6 | 10.3[c] | 68.2 | 10.7 | 19.2 | 70.4 | 12.5 | 14.4 | 68.8 | 27.6 | 70.3 | 26.6 | 59.0 | 29.0[g] |
| **Carib-Creole** | | | | | | | | | | | | | | |
| Stann Creek Town | 58.5 | 37.8 | 56.9 | – | –[e] | 52.2 | 44.2 | – | 50.0 | 48.3 | 54.9 | 43.7 | 43.7 | 56.2 |
| Stann Creek Rural | | | | | | 72.2 | 23.6 | – | 63.2 | 33.1 | 64.9 | 32.4 | 46.0 | 31.8[h] |
| Toledo North | | | | | | 55.5 | 42.3 | – | 43.2 | 54.6 | 53.0 | 45.6 | 44.1 | 55.8 |
| Toledo South[a] | 35.8 | –[d] | 46.1 | 25.9 | 25.9 | 48.0 | 39.6 | 11.8 | 50.1 | 47.2 | 50.3 | 46.8 | 42.5 | 57.5 |
| **Mestizo** | | | | | | | | | | | | | | |
| Corozal North | 60.8 | 35.4 | 82.3 | – | 15.1 | 79.5 | 17.6 | – | 70.4 | 25.1 | 78.0 | 16.7 | 45.4 | –[i] |
| Corozal South | | | | | | 85.5 | 10.4 | – | 83.4 | 11.6 | 79.3 | 20.0 | 56.1 | –[j] |
| Orange Walk North | 61.6 | 34.8 | 64.7 | 23.6 | 7.0 | 57.5 | 40.8 | – | 56.0 | 36.0 | 52.5 | 45.0 | 59.8 | 40.0 |
| Orange Walk South | | | | | | 81.5 | 14.4 | – | 72.8 | 14.7 | 87.5 | 11.2 | 84.6 | 15.4 |
| Cayo North | 87.4 | 14.7 | 50.0 | 6.7 | 21.6 | 70.5 | – | 26.9 | 61.9 | 36.4 | 48.2 | 48.1 | 48.5 | 51.4 |
| Cayo South | | | | | | 61.5 | 5.8 | 30.0 | 59.9 | 36.5 | 50.0 | 39.0 | 62.0 | 38.0 |
| Percentage of total votes | 70.0 | 30.0 | 59.0 | 10.8 | 19.0[f] | 63.2 | 23.4 | 11.4 | 57.8 | 39.3 | 57.6 | 39.8 | 51.3 | 38.1[k] |

[a] Includes the largest Indian village, San Antonio   [b] 10.9% polled by an independent candidate   [c] 33.0% polled by an independent candidate
[d] 51.8% polled by an independent candidate   [e] 42.1% polled by three independent candidates   [f] 9.0% polled by independent candidates
[g] 12.0% polled by independent candidates   [h] 22.1% polled by independent candidates   [i] 54.0% polled by the local Corozal United Front and one
independent candidate   [j] 44.0% polled by the local Corozal United Front and one independent candidate   [k] The remaining percentages are:
UBAD, 0.37; CUF, 4.36: independents, 3.49
Source: British Honduras Gazette and Government Gazette

opposition to the PUP. The party's majority poll of 55.5 per cent in 1961 was turned into a minority of 43.2 per cent in 1965. The PUP regained its support in the 1969 election but the explanation for this cannot discount the split within the NIP at that time.

The rough division of the electorate into urban and rural constituencies in 1961 permits an assessment of the distribution of party influence between 1961 and 1969 from another standpoint. The PUP was much more influential in the predominantly Latin outdistricts than in Belize District, and also much more influential in the villages than in the towns, which in the case of the Mestizo constituencies are in the south and north respectively. Thus the party did not rely simply upon the working class but on the more conservative section of it for support. In other words, the town-dwelling wage labourer in the sugar industry in the north and the citrus industry in the west rather than the village farmer was more likely to desert the PUP.

This analysis suggests that the loss of PUP influence to the NIP was due both to cultural and socio-economic factors. In the case of the second factor the difference between the behaviour of the town and village voter could not be explained in terms of the domestic programmes of the parties, since these were essentially similar. The difference should be explained in terms of the unequal exposure of the town dweller and villager to national leadership. It was only after Goldson became leader in 1961 and reorganized the party that the NIP's penetration of the Mestizo villages began.[52] The premium which the minimal difference in party policies placed upon personal attributes was, however, a drawback to the NIP. Its leaders were full-blooded Creoles and therefore unable to match Price's personal and sectarian appeal to the Latin peasants. The NIP tended therefore to work through influential PUP dissidents to mitigate this cultural liability. The party also adapted itself to local realities by recruiting its candidates from the largest cultural group in the constituencies.

Above all, however, the NIP's influence in both the Mestizo and Creole areas benefited from the collapse of the West Indies Federation in 1962 and the resumption of the Anglo-Guatemalan negotiations in the same year. Consequent upon the demise of the Federation, identification with the West Indies ceased to constitute a drag on the NIP middle-class Creole leadership. On the contrary this relationship became more appropriate after the PUP began to develop closer economic ties with the Caribbean economic association in the mid-1960s.[53] These leaders were, therefore, free to instil fears into the Mestizos, particularly the Mexican descendants in the northern districts of Orange Walk and Corozal, about the eventual outcome of the Guatemalan claim without inviting suspicions of their own motives. Using Price's equivocal past to full advantage, the NIP leaders spared no efforts to unite the various social groups of Creole leaders around their own cultural values. These values, the NIP leaders stated *ad nauseam*, were being threatened by the PUP's attempt 'to re-educate our people into Latin ways, customs, culture and institutions of our neighbour republics' and to proffer 'false notions of our origins and background'.[54] The NIP's concern for the fate of the British-oriented values was by no means solely in response to the Guatemalan threat of absorption. Since little else divided the two parties, the NIP leaders could only have offset Price's nationalist appeal among the ordinary Creoles by voicing their own in cultural terms.

The NIP found little consolation in the progressive decline of the PUP overall support in the 1961 and 1965 elections, although it derived from the results in both cases a certain degree of legitimacy. Noting that proportional representation would have given the opposition six seats in 1961 and seven in 1965 instead of none and two respectively, in 1968 the NIP revived a campaign which it had launched in 1965 for this electoral system to be introduced in national elections. It proposed a mixed system of the West Germany variety. One half of the membership of the House of Representatives should be elected on a constituency basis and the other half from a party list to give each party in the House seats in the exact proportion to the votes it received at the polls. The seats in the Senate were to be allocated in proportion to the votes polled.[55] The PUP however rejected the proposal on the ground that in this culturally heterogenous society its effect was likely to go far beyond the accurate parliamentary reflection of the parties' popularity and frustrate the goal of a unified society. More specifically, the PUP feared that in so far as it encouraged the parties to concentrate on their stronghold, proportional representation would in effect institutionalize both the territorial and cultural divisions.

It is significant that despite the NIP split, the PUP merely succeeded in arresting the loss of support in the 1969 election. The inability of the PUP to capitalize on the divided opposition and regain some of its strength, confirmed the weakness of its own political machinery. Furthermore, this absence of an active party machinery exerted strain upon the unity of the PUP leadership. This eventually resulted in the resignation of Ricalde, the PUP parliamentary representative from Corozal Town since 1957, and the formation in 1973 of the Corozal United Front (CUF) which defeated the PUP in a municipal bye election in the following year. Clearly, the PUP organization admitted of no further neglect. On the other hand, the period between the party split in Corozal and the approaching general election was too short for an effective reorganization of the party and the healing of the breaches. The PUP therefore entered the election divided in the two constituencies in the Corozal District and with the CUF as its principal opponent in both. In Corozal and elsewhere, its weak organization also encouraged the emergence of independent candidates who believed that there was a political vacuum to be filled.

In a way the decline of the party's influence stemmed paradoxically from the relative ease with which it secured its overwhelming success in the past. For, in previous elections, it had only to exploit cleverly the weakness of the opposition in order to win, without being compelled to confront the task of overhauling its own political machinery. Now in 1974 it was unaided by an opposition that had set aside its differences. Furthermore, the PUP was not assisted by the economic conditions in the country. Belize did not escape the widespread economic crisis in 1973 and 1974 that had brought unpopularity, resentment, unemployment and other social problems to the governments of Third World countries. Of course, the sugar industry in the northern districts, Orange Walk and Corozal, fared well as a result of the unprecedented high world market price for sugar, but this made no appreciable difference to the sagging economy in the other parts of the country.

In this connection, it is not surprising that the PUP maintained its electoral support in the north, despite the party split in the area, and sustained its losses mainly in Belize City and the urban constituencies in San Ignacio and Stann Creek districts. It is in Belize City also that the PUP won some of its seats with a very small margin of votes. The results were consistent with our argument that in each District it is the town-dwelling wage labourer rather than his rural counterpart who is likely to become tired of a party that has dominated the scene for more than twenty years without transforming the economy, and accordingly to seek a change. Indeed, in December 1974, less than two months after the general election, the UDP won the Belize City Council elections and brought to an end sixteen years of PUP rule.

The argument that the PUP was itself principally responsible for its loss of influence over the years should not detract from the part that the opposition played in bringing this about in the 1974 election. Apart from presenting a united front to the electorate, the opposition elements, unlike in previous elections, focused attention on the economic problems rather than on the Guatemala issue. This was not only because the latter problem had worn thin and had paid few electoral dividends in the past, but also because the opposition party included the business element that was primarily concerned with the implications of the uncertain economic situation and the government's land ownership policies for their occupational pursuits.

Although the UDP was able to exploit the adverse economic situation to its electoral advantage, it does not offer Belize an alternative in terms of political ideology and economic policies. Considerably influenced by the business element, whose connection with US interests has been noted, the UDP is less likely than the PUP to depart from the orthodox development theories and retrieve the country's heritage from foreign economic domination. Given a more or less common conservative outlook, both political parties are likely to maintain organizations that have little more than a vague feeling of identity with their respective members and supporters except during an election.

*Relationship between Political parties and other institutions*

In addition to political parties, four institutions were clearly involved in the political process in the 1950s. These were the trade unions, the local authorities, the Church and the civil service. They have continued to be important and, as we suggested at the beginning of the chapter, to interact with the political parties. Our analysis of the penultimate stage of decolonization would not be complete without their examination.

THE TRADE UNIONS

*The Christian trade unions.* In Part 2 we traced the inter-relationship between the development of political parties and trade unions in the early 1950s, the fragmentary and debilitating effect which the split in the PUP in 1956 had on the trade union movement, and the manner in which the trade unions disentangled themselves from the political parties as they struggled for survival. By the end of the 1950s, the trade union–party ties were either completely severed or extremely tenuous with the result that the three parties, the PUP, NIP and CDP, contested the 1961 election without trade union support.

Immediately after its electoral victory, the PUP set about rebuilding its trade union base. For a variety of reasons it was not attracted to a single national union. The national leadership which this structure demanded was not available within the party because the few able politicians were immersed in working the new ministerial system of government which in any case, as we argued, was increasingly receiving priority over the mobilization of the population. Nor did the events in the 1950s inspire confidence in the workers in the outdistricts, where the main industries are located, regarding the centralization of trade union authority. Moreover, although poorer in quality than the national leadership, the union leadership in the outdistricts had proved more stable and loyal. The PUP, therefore, fostered regional trade unions in 1961, under the immediate control or patronage of the district-elected representatives. In Orange Walk and Corozal in the north, the Northern Cane Workers' Union (NCWU) was controlled by Jesus Ken, its Secretary-General and at the time (1961) the Corozal South Assemblyman.[56] In the west, the Cayo Labour Union (CLU) was supervised by Hector Silva and Santiago Peredomo, the legislators for Cayo North and Cayo South respectively, who were the auditors and general organizers.[57] In the south, David McKoy, the Stann Creek Rural Assemblyman became the Administrator-General of the Southern Christian Workers' Union (SCU) which, unlike the others was not new. It started with the revival and renaming of the Stann Creek District Union which was an offshoot of the then defunct Christian Democratic Union.[58]

Regional trade unions were by no means a satisfactory alternative to the national general unions that existed in the 1950s which were not confined to individual industries. Each union relied on the main industry in its region – sugar in the northern districts of Orange Walk and Corozal, citrus in the southern District of Stann Creek and timber-cutting and cattle-rearing in the western District of Cayo – for its support. But in matching the industrial structure, the union structure did not enable working-class solidarity, already unsupported by an appropriate ideology, to cut across cultural and local ties. These unions were also too small to attract separately the attention of international trade union organizations and they were inherently too weak to survive on their own. Indeed, the industrial base which the timber-cutting and cattle-rearing activities provided in the western region was so feeble that the CLU soon became inactive, as the static reported membership of 196 throughout the 1960s indicated.[59] The NCWU suffered from the migratory character of a large section of the cane-workers. But for the undying efforts of the hard-core members, the decline of its membership from 345 in 1962 to 175 in 1965 would have been greater.[60] To a considerable extent the union was also self-defeating. Its main purpose was to assist members to cross the barrier from the status of an employee of the sugar company and the large local cane growers to that of an independent farmer. Thus its weakness lay in its success.

Logically enough, and still under PUP inspiration, these embryonic regional unions formed the National Federation of Christian Trade Unions (NFCTU) in September 1962[61] in association with the Christian Workers' Union (CWU) which Pollard formed earlier in the year from a breakaway group of the CDU in Belize City.[62] The Federation did not seek separate registration because each of its constituent unions was to retain its independence under its own district President and General Secretary.[63] Each of its four member unions sent three delegates to a Central Executive Council and received part of the monthly subvention which the Federation obtained from the Caribbean Zone of the Latin American Confederation of Christian Trade Unions (CLASC) to which it was affiliated.[64] From the outset, however, the CWU dominated the Federation. Its leaders, drawn from Belize City, were more able and until the removal of the administrative capital to Belmopan in 1970 were better placed to develop a manageable type of federal organization responsive to government policy. In fact, the CWU representatives made up the sub-committee which drafted the constitution of the Federation.[65] But for the assistance of these officials, the district unions would have been unable to do an effective job of collective bargaining. Indeed, the CWU, recognizing the need for vigorous union activity in Orange Walk, which rapidly developed as a sugar area with the arrival of Tate and Lyle Ltd in 1963, broke out of its self-imposed jurisdiction of Belize City by opening a branch in Orange Walk in 1965.[66] The CWU also extended its activities to the western District of Cayo when the construction of the new capital at Belmopan began in 1966. The influence of the CWU officials was so pervasive and dominant within the Federation that even the Labour Department claimed in 1965 that the outdistrict trade unions were affiliates of the CWU rather than the NFCTU.[67] The upshot was that both the NFCTU and the outdistrict unions were judged by the activities of the CWU officials. The control which the CWU exercised was confirmed when, as we shall see, a split occurred in its leadership in 1968. This had a divisive impact on the NFCTU which resulted in the SCU, the CWU and the NCWU, alternatively referred to as the Northern Christian Union, establishing the National Federation of Workers in September 1969.[68]

The collaboration between the CWU and the outdistrict unions pointed to the reconciliation between Pollard and Price which was mutually desirable. Pollard had been appointed Assistant Executive Secretary for CLASC in the same year, 1962, that he formed the CWU.[69] This placed his claim to the leadership of the local trade union movement beyond dispute. His association with the regional trade union also solved their problem of international affiliation. It was he, as a CLASC organizer, who had revived the union in Stann Creek and as he immodestly put it, the union's application for affiliation with the International Federation of Christian Trade Unions (IFCTU) 'was only a formality' as the three international organizations (IFCTU, CLASC and the Peasants' Federation of Latin America) in accepting him as National Organizer 'had already accepted [the union] as their affiliate'.[70] Moreover, the Catholic and Latin American commitment of CLASC appealed to Price. It lent credence to his claim to be fostering Christian Democracy and strengthened his bond with the Jesuits. As we have seen also, in arranging the international affiliation of the unions Pollard provided them with a reliable source of funds. This probably saved the PUP from many commitments. Despite Pollard's measure of indispensability it was not in his long-term interest to remain alienated from the party which he knew would some day assume full power. For although, as we shall see, his connections were useful to the PUP in the 1960s they were likely to be severed if ever he became a political liability to CLASC in Belize.

At the time that the regional unions were established in 1962, Silva assured the CLU that it would 'be free of political domination' and have 'the privilege of supporting the party of its choice'.[71] No doubt a similar assurance was extended to the other unions. Indeed, over the years the district-elected representatives have developed a tenuous link with their respective trade unions with the exception of Florencio Marin who is an Executive Secretary for the Latin American Federation of Peasants and is closely connected with the unions affiliated to CLASC.[72] On the whole, the PUP is unwilling to proclaim the unions as its own and to develop an overt and visible involvement in their affairs. Reasons for its low profile are not hard to find. In the first place, like the trade unions, the PUP cannot ignore the disintegrative effect of the rigid, naked control on the trade union movement in the previous decade. Second, a very close collaboration with the trade unions is not necessarily compatible with the PUP government's dependence upon expatriate and local investors to fulfil its plans for economic development and its claim to be a 'referee, balancing the conflicting demands of labour and management'.[73] Third, because they are weak, organizationally and financially, the outdistrict trade unions have been displaced by the Town Boards as the principal institution of local political influence. Fourth, the development of party politics since 1960 has discouraged strong structural ties between the PUP and the Christian trade unions. As we indicated, although the party's electoral victories have been overwhelming, they have not had the character of a stampede which one associates with those in the 1950s. If it openly adopts a proprietorial attitude toward the unions the PUP is likely to antagonize union members who support the opposition parties.

There is, however, little doubt that the PUP's aloofness from the unions is more apparent than real. It does not remain indifferent to leadership rivalry within the unions. On the contrary its leaders, without necessarily invoking the name of the party, intervene as partisans in the struggles, with the result that the faction which receives the support usually emerges victorious. The victors may even become unopposed through resignation or expulsions of the vanquished. In either event, the union leaders are even more indebted to the PUP for their positions and can easily become pliable and satellitic. Perhaps this is a more important reason than those proffered earlier for the PUP's apparent loose hold upon the unions. The acquiescence of the union leadership to government policy renders formal party control unnecessary.

A case in point was the leadership conflict within the CWU in 1968.[74] One of the protagonists was Pollard. In 1964 he took up residence in Trinidad from where he worked as a CLASC regional secretary in the Commonwealth Caribbean. Two years later he returned to Belize with a tenuous relationship with CLASC. He soon made his presence felt as Adviser within his old union, the CWU, and General Secretary of the NFCTU, much to the discomfort of the other leaders. In the conflict that developed, Pollard was portrayed as a dissident element bent on splitting the workers over collective agreements and disrupting the cordial relationship between labour and management, particularly in the case of Pauling and Company (Overseas) Ltd, the main British contractors of the new capital project, which the union had carefully established with government assistance.[75] *The Belize Times* threw its political weight on the side of his adversaries by confining its reports to the attacks on him and even reprinting those that the *Belize Billboard* had published at the time of the split in the PUP and the GWU in 1956.[76] As on previous occasions, Pollard left the union and formed another, the Democratic Independent Union (DIU) in 1968, with a fair measure of support in Belize City, Belmopan and Stann Creek.[77] The pattern of events was fully repeated when Pollard quietly withdrew from the union after CLASC discontinued its financial support to him in 1969.[78]

*Other trade unions.* The NIP immediately came to the aid of the DIU.[79] This was primarily as an extension of its opposition to the PUP and part of its preparation for the impending general election in 1969. It was, however, in the arms of the PDM that the DIU eventually fell in 1970.[80] This more or less sealed the NIP's hope of establishing a trade union arm, as the other three unions in Belize were hardly likely to submit to its control or that of any other party. These unions are the General Workers' Development Union (GWDU) which was formed in 1960,[81] the POU, and the National Teachers' Union (NTU) which was registered in 1970[82] as a result of the amalgamation of the British Honduras Union of Teachers (BHUT), which was also registered, and the Catholic Education Association (CEA). The GWDU is a fusion of the GWU and the British Honduras Development Union, and is acutely aware of the fact that both of its progenitors suffered from their embroilment in party politics in the 1950s. Apart from, or because of their specialized membership, the POU and to a lesser extent the NTU are too conscious of their own strength to accept a subordinate still less a subservient relationship with the political parties.

This is not to suggest that these three unions are apolitical and indifferent to the relationship between the PUP and the Christian trade unions. They are affiliated to ORIT and in the case of the POU to other organizations such as the Public Service International (PSI) and the International Confederation of Free Trade Unions (ICFTU). In 1966, the GWDU, the POU and the NTU formed the Trade Union Congress (TUC), largely in response to ORIT's desire to direct its financial assistance to them through a central organization.[83] This move did not simply emphasize the division in the trade union movement in Belize. It also implied that the three unions were resorting to concerted action to counteract the influence of the pro-PUP Christian trade unions. The three unions can therefore appear to be inviting a confrontation with the PUP. Indeed, when their predominantly middle-class Creole membership and the fact that their activities seldom bring them into competition with the Christian trade unions are considered, it can be argued that the POU and the NTU have gone out of their way to do so. The decision of the Trade Union Congress to give affiliation to the DIU in 1972 reinforces this argument.[84] This viewpoint, however, ignores the role which the narrow social field in Belizean society forces the POU members to play. The circumstances under which it can come into conflict with the PUP government and the extent to which this is involuntary can be judged from a detailed examination of the civil service strike which took place in June 1966.

*The role of the POU in the civil service strike.* When their numerical strength, local origin and bureaucratic skills are combined, civil servants are better placed than the other elite groups – lawyers, doctors and school teachers – for fulfilling the social roles in the society.[85] In fact they are brought into contact with each other and with leaders from other components of the political and social elite over and over again. Thus in 1965 Donald Gill was not only the Principal Secretary to the Minister of Local Government and Social Welfare, but also a member of the Cricket Board of which the then Minister, Cattouse, a keen sportsman, was the Chairman. Ednay Caine, then Accountant General, did not only approve the salary of the Principal of Wesley College, but is also a high-ranking lay leader in the Methodist Church. So was Gill who was also a member of the College's Board of Governors. Beside disseminating government news, Rudy Castillo, the Chief Information Officer, was also the Reuter correspondent. None of these civil servants can, however, serve these 'outside' interests too long without running into the government. The Cricket Board is as dependent upon government's patronage as is Wesley College on its financial assistance. In this situation the political awareness of the civil servant is not only heightened but impinges upon his occupational role in the sense that the latter is increasingly looked at in terms of family, religious and social ties and the overall political change within the society.

A logical outcome of this multiple role performance was the POU's interest in the wider community. As its members explained in their famous Stann Creek Declaration on national goals in 1962.

The National Public Service embraces the cream of those sons of the community who, by virtue of the lofty idealism and sacrifices of our parents, have achieved the highest average level of formal education that the nation has to offer or that the national government can provide funds for institutions of higher learning overseas. We fully recognise that a binding obligation follows from this for the public servant consciously to acknowledge and discharge the obligation to be truely [*sic*] servants of the community and this obligation extends beyond the immediate obligations of his paid employment. The public service therefore undertake to assume a front rank position in the battle against ignorance, poverty, disease, crime and any other form of perversity which threatens to blight the face of the nation or to impede the full realisation of national emergence and achievement.[86]

The POU's concern for the wider community certainly led it into strange fields. It also conceived its obligation to the community as being a guardian of 'the basic freedom enshrined in the Universal Declaration of Human Rights and in particular, freedom of worship, of association and assembly,...of free speech, trial by jury and by fair judicial process'.[87] To assume the guardianship of civil liberties is noble, but the POU could hardly have been unaware that it was skirting on the edge of politics. In so far as the threat to these liberties invariably came from the government, any attempt by the POU to honour its self-assigned obligations was likely to bring it into conflict with the ruling PUP. In fact, apart from the NIP, the POU was the only organization to deplore the PUP's claim on the eve of the 1965 general election, that 'the one-party system, with the PUP as the governing party [is] fit and proper' for Belize.[88] The Union felt that it

would not be worthy of calling itself a responsible organization if it failed at this crisis moment to bring to the attention of its members some of the occurrences which reflect insecurity. In the first case except we be insane, could we agree that the best system is a one-party system? Such a system as seen in Ghana, means oppression and eternal slavery for a great number of the inhabitants.'[89]

And in an obvious reply to a PUP criticism of its involvement, the union continued in a subsequent newsletter:

Why should anyone hate us for pointing out to our members that a true pattern of democracy is a two party system and a one party system is dangerous? . . . Yes we know that the two party system was not anointed with any holy oil whereby it has become sacrosanct. But we know too that absolute power can be a dangerous thing and that the world is full of examples even today. On the other hand the world shows today that those countries which pattern their political structures on the British model, have attained a more stable way of life. Workers must be free to express themselves and this type of freedom is taken away from a large number of people under a one party system.[90]

It can be suggested that the POU's protective role was also in their own interest. If the overall political change provided civil servants with opportunities for career advances it also rendered their position insecure. Their attitude had been seriously affected by the lower social status of the political executive. Neither the low educational attainments of the politicians nor the rural origin of most of them reflected the social and urban values of the civil servants. In fact, the civil servants claimed that the PUP exploited these class divisions by holding them up to ridicule on the public rostrum.[91] What was more disconcerting to the civil servants than the ascendancy of the new political elite was the PUP's Central American orientation and the British support for it. They constituted the bulk of the Creole world which all but collapsed in June 1966 when Goldson claimed that the British Foreign Office was favourably disposed to the American mediator's proposals on the Anglo-Guatemalan dispute.[92] As they put it, 'Public Officers as citizens had come to feel that their country was being lost to them and had been unable to secure adequate reassurances.'[93]

Through a process of elimination the POU had reached the conclusion that reassurances were lacking. Neither of its two allied unions, the BHUT and the GWDU, was capable of exerting pressure on the government. Those members of the POU who as citizens were favourably disposed to the NIP appeared to have little confidence in its ability to represent their interests effectively. From its electoral performance the party did not seem capable of effecting a change of government. Nor was the POU prepared to place its faith in the departing Governor, Sir Peter Stallard, who was ultimately responsible for the civil service and offered his good offices to the union. How low was the Governor's personal stock in the eyes of the union became known when a few months before the strike a seemingly innocuous suggestion to invite him to declare open a civil service seminar, jointly sponsored by the Union, the University of the West Indies and the government, was vetoed by the Union.[94] In short, the POU was experiencing a crisis of confidence. For varying reasons, it lacked confidence in the government's role in the Anglo-Guatemalan dispute, the departing Governor, its allied trade unions, and the opposition party. The logical outcome of its own crisis was its interference, sooner or later, in the political process.

On Friday, 30 June 1966, the civil servants began a forty-eight hour sitdown strike. For all practical purposes the strike ended at 12 noon on the following day, Saturday. Though brief, the strike demonstrated the relevance of the small scale of the society by impinging on other relationships within the wider community. The government appealed to the Jesuits of St John's College who quickly gave permission for the use of their students to break the strike. The morality of giving such approval to students entrusted to their care, without the prior knowledge or consent of their parents, was apparently not questioned by the Jesuits. In failing to appeal as well to the other denominational colleges, the government, whatever its views about their likely response, had exposed itself to the charge of looking in one direction for assistance. This failure in effect confirmed the widely held suspicions of an informal alliance between the government and the Jesuits. This in turn brought into sharp relief the conjunction of religious and political attitudes in the society.[95]

It should be stressed that the decision of the civil servants to strike was as much influenced by the smallness of the social field and the many roles they perform in it as by their middle-class background and cultural orientation. When combined, these factors gave rise to particularistic as opposed to universalistic relationships.[96] In other words, relationships of one kind could not be easily distinguished or separated from those of another. As the civil servants told the new Governor, Sir John Paul, 'very often conclusions were made regarding an officer's political affiliation solely on the basis of his family, and on that basis, an officer was sometimes subjected to abuse regardless of how he performed his official duties'.[97] In such a situation the notion of a non-partisan civil service insulated from party politics is irrelevant. Few civil servants are 'pure'. Moreover, possession of this quality is not necessarily a virtue as the holder may often be regarded as ineffective.

Yet it was to this conceptual purity that the new Governor appealed. He informed the Union's Council of Management that 'It was most certainly not for the civil service to arrogate unto itself the right to criticize the government or to try to embarrass it by entering itself in the political arena, and in effect, allying itself with one or other political factions.'[98] Viewed against the post-independence development in other small-scale political and social systems, the old British concept on which the Governor based his argument was not only irrelevant but obsolete. In the new nations the concept is being redefined in terms of a triangular relationship between politicians, civil servants and the military.

Clearly there is a dilemma. The PUP government has tended to look askance upon the more outspoken and radical leaders and question the compatibility of their dual role as civil servants and union representatives. The most important case in point was its ultimatum in October 1972 to the POU President, Curl Thompson, to relinquish his office and membership of the executive and refrain from negotiations in which the union was engaged.[99] The government contended that it was incompatible for Thompson, as a Labour Inspector, to maintain an official standing in the trade union and still give the semblance of impartiality in the performance of his official function.[100] The fact that the POU was the moving spirit of the Trade Union Congress which had at least in one of its other affiliates, the DIU, an implacable and outspoken opponent of the government and the Christian Trade Unions, gave force to the argument. Indeed, Rosado, the Secretary of the National Federation of Workers, claimed that 'his unions have suffered for many years from the partiality of Labour Officers'.[101] Although tenable, the government's argument ignored the fact that history was on the side of the Labour Inspector. Two of Thompson's colleagues, K. C. Dunn, retired Labour Commissioner, and E. A. Pitts, Labour Inspector, functioned in the early 1960s when the Union first became militant in a prominent and executive manner. The government's stand was to be further weakened. For the POU is an affiliate of the Caribbean Public Service Association which elected as its President in 1973 an Assistant Chief Labour Officer who is President of the Guyana Public Service Union.[102]

Thompson ignored the government's demand and was retired in the interest of the Public Service in December 1973.[103] He, however, received a vote of confidence from the POU when he was re-elected President early in 1974, but later resigned from the union after he joined the Liberal Party as one of its founding members.[104]

The problem of the civil servants' role in the political process is not peculiar to Belize. Similar confrontations between governments and individual civil servants over the extent to which the latter can be openly involved in the political process occurred in St Vincent, Dominica and

Antigua during this period and escalated into a strike in the latter two countries. In view of our contention that this conflict arises essentially from the small scale of the society, it is no coincidence that they first came to a head in the smaller territories where relationships are more intense. This sociological problem admits no easy solution and worse still it is ignored in Belize in the redefining of the relationship between the government and the civil servants. In July 1973 a three-man commission drawn from Britain, Canada and India undertook a general review of the public service at the request of the Belize government.[105] The commission deemed the civil strike in 1966 as 'political in character'[106] and noted that a few senior officers took part in the strike. It considered such action reprehensible since 'senior public officers are part of the management of Government', and it was in its opinion 'improper and inconsistent with their obligations to the Government for them to be active members in the Union of this sort'.[107] The commission therefore recommended that all administrative, professional and senior technical officers should be debarred from membership in the union. No objection was, however, raised to these civil servants forming an association (or several associations) of a non-political character, designed to further the interest of the group, and when necessary to make submissions to the government.[108]

Both the twofold recommendation and the assumption upon which it is based are open to criticism. It is misleading to regard civil servants as analogous to industrial managers. At least in theory career expectations in industry recognize few limits. The senior civil servants on the other hand are structurally subordinate to the political executive and cannot enter the latter without a change of occupation. In debarring the senior civil servants from the POU, the commission, by its own acknowledgement that the majority of senior civil servants did not strike in 1966, in effect deprived the union of its restraining influence. In the exclusive hands of the rank-and-file, the union would not only be likely to become more militant, but would be perpetually devoid of experienced leaders since even those that it produces would be lost to it in the normal course of promotion in the civil service. Finally, if our argument about the fundamental nature of the problem is correct, the possibility is remote that the union(s) which senior civil servants are being urged to form would be non-political. In the end, the government may find that it has to contend with two or more highly politicized unions, rather than one as is the present case.

It would be misleading to leave the impression that tension is the dominant characteristic of the relationship between the civil servants and the PUP government and that its nature is wholly political. Ministers are impelled to cultivate a close relationship with their chief advisers precisely because the civil service is the main repository of skill and information. The PUP organization, which is one of the more obvious alternative sources of information, lacks the necessary expertise. The result is that civil servants may be called upon to perform services that are marginal to their normal duties. These requests are not necessarily addressed to the Permanent Secretary but often directly to the officer who can provide the necessary information. In fact, ministers do not allow themselves to be hidebound by formal civil service procedure, and this informality frequently brings them into direct contact with the professional and technical officers. This tendency to overlook formal civil service procedure further blurs the distinction between the roles of ministers and civil servants. Partly because they lack the permanence of civil servants and are under the obligation to account periodically to the electorate, ministers tend to identify themselves with the people by being involved in the execution of programmes. While this may lend weight to the efforts of the officer responsible for implementing the programme it also exposes his judgement to political influences. It also encourages the public to bypass civil servants, particularly field officers, and to want their consultations at the highest level. Thus within the same legally defined relationship weak ministers and strong officials can, and apparently have, produced results totally different from those which would have been produced by a combination of strong ministers and weak or diffident officials.

We can deduce from the preceding analysis of union–party relationships several important consequences for the future development of trade unions in the political process. One is that the division within the trade union movement will persist as long as they are aligned to political parties opposed to each other. A second consequence is that irrespective of whether they are sympathetic or opposed to the government they will not be left to their own devices. A part of their problem is that as in most post-colonial regimes the government is one of the largest employers and have a vested interest in regulating the activities of trade unions. For this reason the union–party relationship is likely to be one-sided with the labour movement's impact upon the political parties being negligible. In this regard the unions share the fate of their counterparts in new nations where the ruling party stifles these organizations and renders them powerless within their embrace.

*Local authorities.*[109] The penetration of party politics into the Belize City Council and the District Town Boards, which began with the decolonization process in the 1950s in general and the introduction of outdistrict elections in 1955 in particular, has continued and has extended to the village councils. This consolidation and spread of party influence has been facilitated by the multiple role performance of local politicians. We have seen that because of local and cultural particularism and the attempt to bring the outdistricts into the national political framework, both the PUP and the NIP recruited their candidates for national elections from among the local leaders. Because they are a more stable and widely recognized institution the Town Boards displaced the trade unions as the point of entry for these aspiring politicians. Indeed, in a few cases the interest in local politics was incidental and the councillors severed their connections with the Town Boards after being elected to the House of Representatives. By and large, however, the district-elected representatives have retained their association with the Town Boards and are also the main link between the party, the town and the administrative capital.

In this situation, where the same functionaries are engaged in national and local politics, national issues are bound to enter the local elections. In the mid-1960s Town Board elections were fought over the Guatemalan claim which was the burning party issue. The NIP transformed the campaigns into a vote of confidence in the PUP government's ability to safeguard the nation's interest in the negotiations with the result that Price invariably felt obliged to conclude personally his party's local campaigns in the elections. On the whole local government election campaigns are really a continuation of campaigns for the national election and the outcome is to be seen not as an end in itself but as the prelude to the next general election.

However national issues and party political considerations do not always transcend all other issues. In municipal elections the town is treated as a single constituency and the voter exercises his franchise in the election of all candidates.[110] If the voters' party loyalty is unswerving all the candidates of a single party can be elected. But in the 1966 elections, only in three of the seven towns were the victories of a single party complete.[111] Corozal and Punta Gorda returned all of the PUP candidates while Monkey River did the same for the NIP candidates. If national party political considerations are also overpowering the PUP should repeat its overwhelming success of the general elections in the local elections. But its fortunes have fluctuated. The towns of Orange Walk, Stann Creek, Monkey River, Benque Viejo and San Ignacio have at one time or another entrusted their administration to the NIP. The mixed party representation on most of the Town Boards and the periodical swing to and from the PUP suggest that in these towns the personality of the individual candidates is of some consequence and that voting is across the party lines. There is certainly not the same life and death political party struggle in these towns as in Belize City where the municipal voter felt the direct impact of national party leadership until the removal of the capital to Belmopan. Unlike its fluctuating fortunes in the District Town Boards the PUP completely dominated the Belize City Council from its return to office in 1961 up to 1974 when it was displaced by the Opposition. It is, however, noteworthy that although personalities appear to play a more important part in the Town Board than in the City elections it is only within the party political framework, as no local leader can realistically aspire to membership of the District Town Board without a party label.

Political parties vie for the control of the District Town Boards not only for the legitimacy which they provide but also because of the central government resources which they command. Control of the local authorities is obviously more vital to the opposition parties than to the PUP. It is the only means by which the former parties can offer the local (and national) electorate facilities in return for their support. Conflicts between the local and central government are, however, more likely to arise when the Town Board is controlled by the opposition. Central government resources can be distributed in a way that would deny such a Town Board, within statutory limits, transactions between the central government and the local population. An example of the central government's astute manipulation of its resources was the control of the new vocational centre in Stann Creek Town. In the 1966 local government election campaign the ruling PUP leaders in their speeches to the electorate held out a vague promise to entrust the administration of the centre to the Town Board.[112] However, the party was defeated and responsibility for the centre was given to the Ministry of Labour whose political head at the time, McKoy, is a resident of Stann Creek Town and the representative of the Stann Creek Rural constituency. In 1972, the PUP expressed its displeasure at being displaced in the local government election in San Ignacio. It reduced the town's annual grant by 55 per cent, demanded the reinstatement of politically appointed officials dismissed as a result of the enforced austerity and requested repayment of sizeable debts incurred by the ousted PUP administration but never pressed during the years it was in office.[113]

Conflict can also arise because the relationship between the District Officer (as the District Commissioner has been restyled), the elected District Assemblyman and the District Town Board is ill-formed. Except in Stann Creek, the District Officer was the chairman of the District Town Board during the colonial period. His leadership role in the community was also unchallenged by the Legislative Councillor who as we saw seldom resided in the constituency. The District Officer has, however, ceased to be intimately involved in the affairs of the wholly elected Town Board which is directly responsible to the Ministry of Local Government and Social Development. His overall status has also been undermined by the constitutional changes and the development of party politics at the district level. Local issues which were brought to the attention of the colonial government through the District Officer are now channelled through the offices of the local politician and the District Assemblyman. This situation is encouraged by the fact that most of the district representatives belong to the ruling PUP, and by the tendency for ministers, when addressing their directives, to overlook the District Officer in favour of the representative. There are, however, issues which must be eventually referred to the District Officer and whose solution depends upon the harmonious relationship between this incumbent and the political representative. But the position of this latter functionary in the local political process has not been formalized. The District Town Board Ordinance,[114] for example, takes no cognizance of him. A narrow legalistic view by the District Officer and the Town Board (if of a different party political persuasion) of their relationship with this representative can therefore result in conflict. There is also the possibility that the over-zealous district representative may impinge upon or seek to influence the work of the District Officer. These conflict situations are basically the result of the development of the institutions of District Officer and political party at different times, and in different contexts, as well as the functionaries' different perception of their role.

There is perhaps a case for reviewing the institution of District Officer in the light of the political changes. In fact, the PUP had suggested to Sir Hilary Blood in 1959 that the institution be politicized.[115] But it should be noted that in those African countries where the District Officer is a politician the change was either preceded or followed by the establishment of a one-party system of government. Since the PUP's proposals, however, a two-party system has more or less been legitimized in Belize and the government is compelled to retain at least the semblance of impartiality at the district level, which the civil servant provides.

In the villages the ruling PUP appears to be adopting a variant of the new arrangement in Africa. It annually sets aside funds for sports and other community projects which can be recommended by the district-elected representative. The funds are administered by the Social Development Department, but the Social Development Officer and the District Officer are not necessarily directly involved in the decision-making process. In the interest of cordial relationship with these officers and to benefit from their administrative experience, the elected representative usually solicits their views before submitting his programme to the Minister of Local Government and Social Development to whom he is directly responsible. By participating in the administrative process the elected representative obtains an insight into the complexities of government and comes to appreciate the need for his demands to be realistic. But perhaps more significant is the fact that participation gives him an opportunity to dispense political patronage. One is encouraged to hold this view when it is observed that the government, in allocating administrative responsibility in Toledo North, the sole constituency which did not elect the PUP candidate in 1965, overlooked the elected representative in favour of the party's Senator who lived in the neighbouring constituency, Toledo South. The bypassing of the elected representative destroyed the sense of impartiality in that the deviant rural community did not expect to receive the full advantages of government-sponsored projects.

Village politics is by no means only about the extraction of resources from the central government and their allocation within the village. It is also party political, as the NIP in the 1960s had been encouraged by its electoral success in the district towns, particularly the Mestizo, also to challenge the PUP hegemony in the villages. Although the NIP's success was infrequent it has brought the village council into conflict with the PUP government, as was the case in 1969 when the NIP won the council election in the Mayan village of Succotz in March. Seven months later the PUP government dissolved the council and ordered new elections on the grounds that it was introducing a new constitution.[116]

The problems in the villages, however, are more social and administrative than political. For one thing the PUP made no attempt to uproot the traditional Alcalde or Patron authority structure in the Indian villages. Apart from the fact that this structure was not an integral part of British colonial rule an assault upon it was not necessary for the party to gain village support. In the first place, as we have just indicated, the PUP's influence was until very recently unchallenged by the NIP. Secondly, its close relations with the Jesuits appealed to the entire Latin peasantry. Thirdly, there has been little local political pressure for change in the traditional village institution. Any diminution of popular allegiance to the traditional authority has been due to the social changes within the villages. Although the Indian villager still spends a great part of the year in the traditional setting he is increasingly involved in the modern market. This has compelled him to produce cash crops for the market rather than for subsistence, especially during periods of unemployment in the sugar, citrus and forestry industries. This is at once reflected in the breakdown of communal activities in the villages.

It was largely in response to the inadequacies of the various self-governing organizations that the government promoted voluntary village councils throughout the country, with the ultimate aim of giving these bodies statutory powers. The long-established and flourishing village councils in four Creole villages – Placentia, Seine Bight, Gales Point and Barranco – boosted the programme. By 1960, these councils increased to fifty-nine in the six administrative districts and over the next four years to ninety-two.[117] These councils function under a standard constitution prepared by the Social Development Department and their programmes are influenced by the welfare orientation of the department. Thus they are essentially community self-help councils through which the department channels and administers its community development programmes.

In so far as the village council symbolizes progress and modernity it is in conflict with the traditional power structure. There is no doubt that it detracts from the prestige of the Alcalde. It seems also that the government's policy is to reduce the Alcalde to a judicial and handy government officer. This redefining of jurisdictional boundaries does not necessarily resolve the conflict between the old and the new institutions. Though the village councils appeal to the young, these leaders are not in a position to provide jobs as is customary among Creole leaders, nor are they necessarily from the elite families of the Indians and Mestizos. And while the young leaders are prepared to embrace the new democratic ideas they are also caught in the vicious net of expectations of reverence, respect and obedience due to elders in the village. This detracts from their drive and initiative. The situation varies from village to village. In some the conflict is so intense that there is a stalemate in which little is attempted except for the efforts of the elders to maintain the *status quo*.

Another problem which hinders the rationalization of the local government arrangement is that of size. The villages are so small in size and population and are so widely dispersed and fragmented that their formation into viable administrative units is a real challenge. When the low social and economic standard and the weight of tradition are added to their small size and population it is difficult to conceive any but the welfare approach to their problem. The village councils are still to prove themselves as community councils and are too new to be given the status of local authorities carrying out statutory functions. The conferring of statutory powers on these councils may not even be desirable, especially if it involves local taxation and paid services since these will undermine the self-help basis of the community development programme of the Social Development Department.

Larger and more integrated local authorities can be created by a tiered structure of local government. In this connection the establishment of non-statutory District village councils comprising the village councils in each administrative district has been officially mooted. The possibility of a link between either the village councils or the proposed District village councils and the District Town Boards is, however, problematical. Under this arrangement the District Town Boards would presumably undertake the major services for the entire administrative region, and the village councils those services of lesser importance. It is, however, doubtful whether these local authorities with their differing approaches to local government will be able to mesh. In any event it is unlikely that the volume of work to be given to local authorities in Belize in the foreseeable future will be sufficient to warrant two tiers of local government. Moreover, the villages at their present stage of economic development are clearly unable to contribute to the additional administrative cost which a two-tiered system entails. It appears, therefore, that the direct administration of these rural areas by agents of the central government will continue indefinitely.

While the local authorities were not a starting-point of the overall process of political change, as the Courtenay Commission had hoped in 1950, they have nevertheless contributed to it. The extension of electoral politics in the 1950s to the six towns on a party political basis led to a change in the backgrounds and experiences of the Town Board members. In turn the Town Boards soon became an important source of admission into the national political process and the focus of local political influence. With the introduction of the village councils political power in the village has been diffused. What is of interest is the extent to which the traditional and modern styles of politics in the Indian villages can co-exist and still more interact. For despite the diminution in allegiance to the traditional authority, the Alcalde system remains an effective means of mediating socio-political relations. On the other hand, the process of modernization throughout the country favours the village councillors, and it is their attitude which would decide whether a multi-structural political system in the villages would develop.

*The Church*. The move towards independence in colonies in which a dual system of educational control by the government and denominational authorities prevailed has not infrequently been accompanied by modification of the relationship. The change is usually from a relationship in which denominational organizations dominated to one in which the increasing power of the government has led to the near eclipse or emasculation of these agencies not only in education but the society as a whole.[118] Belize is one of the countries in which this development has not occurred. On the contrary the PUP reaffirmed its belief that the Church, as an institution, should retain its key position in the country. With its claim to be pursuing social and economic policies that are based on the principles of Christian Democracy, the PUP government appears to accept the assumption that there is a causal connection between the religiosity of a country and the development of democratic institutions. Indeed there is the tendency within the PUP leadership to accept uncritically religion's social function. An editorial in *The Belize Times* in 1967 stated, 'Those who try to confine the Church strictly within the four walls of the church building are attempting the impossible...Church and politics share a joint responsibility...in creating a proper climate for the spiritual, intellectual and material growth of the human person.'[119] The official opposition, at that time the NIP, also assigned to the Church a prominent place in the political process. It claimed that the active role of religion in the education system 'is a precious heritage that all political parties and all far-seeing citizens want to see continued in this country, particularly after the country becomes wholly responsible for its affairs'.[120] Few institutions have been given this assurance of permanent involvement in the political process in general, and the education system in particular, by both major political parties.

In justifying the retention of the system, the government argues that the Church's contribution is of inestimable value because its own financial resources are limited.[121] A UNESCO team, however, which undertook a comprehensive examination of the system of education in 1964 suggested that the present financial arrangement is more expensive to the government than one which was more integrated and government directed would be.[122] Up to 1970, approved secondary schools received salary grants for their principals and one graduate assistant. For those schools with sixth form studies salary grants were also paid for one additional graduate assistant. Since 1971, the government has revised its system of grants to the Churches. A basic annual grant of $12,000 is given to each approved secondary school and an additional grant of $50.00 each year for each student over a minimal number of one hundred.[123] There is no doubt that the voluntary services of priests, nuns and other ministers of religion prevent personnel from consuming a high proportion of the schools' revenue. But under the present grant-in-aid programme for capital expenditure the government probably spends more on secondary education than it would within a more centrally co-ordinated system. It provides 50 per cent of the cost of a project,[124] and given the denominational initiative and rivalry which the government is compelled to support, schools, particularly the Protestant, are not in a position to match the government grant with the result that year after year money set aside by the government is left unspent and 'various schemes have come to nought'.[125] The Tri-partite Survey Commission noted in 1966 that the level of government expenditure was 'disappointingly low',[126] and to overcome this the govern-ment granted loans to the Church organizations to enable them to meet their share of the cost. Since 1966 the whole of the available amount has been allocated.[127]

Even if the government's claim about its financial inability to assume a more positive role is correct, its argument in favour of the denominational system of education still loses its force in the wider social, economic and political context. Expatriate domination of power and authority is still a crucial feature of the influence which the religious bodies exert on the social values of the society. The Roman Catholic Church, which is the pacesetter in education, had only seven Belizeans among its thirty-three priests in 1964.[128] The influence of these Belizean Jesuits within the hier-archy is negligible as only one of them, Father Charles Woods, was a full-fledged Jesuit. Furthermore he resigned in 1969 and marked his return to secular life by contesting the general election in December 1969 as a NIP candidate.[129] The other local priests, of whom there were nine in 1970, are Diocesan priests who work in the outdistrict parishes and usually do not teach in the secondary schools. The Jesuits constitute about 80 per cent of the male clerics in Belize[130] and their position at the apex of the power structure in their denomination and the institution as a whole is assured. A disproportionate number of Belizeans fail to complete the long and exacting studies for the priesthood.[131] As we observed, Price's vocation for the priesthood was tested in the USA. Between 1960 and 1968 five other nationals were sent to the USA to be trained as Jesuit priests but none of them persevered. Whether it is the attraction of American life or the ignominy of failure, these students have not returned to Belize.

The hold which the American Jesuits retain is compounded by the decision-making structure. This assigns a more or less passive role to the lay members. There is no deliberative body comparable to the Anglican and Methodist Synods, and it is only in parish councils that lay influence is entertained. In consequence few of the Catholic laymen can be easily identified with the leadership of the Church. Nor are the Catholic secon-dary schools, with the exception of St John's College, advised by a board of governors as is the case with the Protestant schools.[132]

By itself the relinquishment of expatriate control of the national clerics would not solve the problems that are inherent in the system of dual control. It would not take care of the fragmentation of the educational effort which by 1965, for example, produced in Belize City as many as six secondary schools, with a total enrolment of just over one thousand and managed by four religious denominations, and a farcical situation in Corozal Town where two denominational schools, Catholic and Methodist, had an enrolment of ninety-nine and thirty-four respectively.[133] Of this fragmenting tendency the UNESCO mission in 1964 asked:

If such public funds as are available are absorbed in the maintenance of small uneconomic units established by one denomination, where will the funds be found to see that children of other religious persuasions receive their education, that is, where parents refuse to have their children attend such schools, despite the preparedness of the schools to accept children of other faiths and to make appropriate allowances for their religious instruction?[134]

The question was not merely rhetorical. Democratic principles demand that equal facilities be afforded in education, especially in a country where the political leaders have taken a firm stand on the side of the principles of Christian democracy and social justice.[135] However, in the uneven development of secondary education, the Roman Catholic colleges have a decided advantage. They have been able to acquire far more substantial aid from the United States than have the other denominations from their affiliates in Britain and the West Indies. In acquiring funds from local sources their numerical superiority and the fact that the majority of wealthy people are Roman Catholic have also strengthened the Church's financial position. The overall result is that this Church has at its disposal more funds for development.[136]

The denominational system has also hindered a rational distribution of trained teachers in the primary schools. In 1954, the Catholics established a Teachers' Training College for primary education within two months of the government's establishing St George's Teachers' College.[137] The country was therefore in the unenviable position of having two small training colleges which in 1957, for example, had a total enrolment of twenty-seven students – eighteen at the government college and nine at the Catholic. With an initial enrolment of three students pursuing a two-year course, and an annual intake of five students from 1955 to 1957, the Catholic College did not promise to be a feasible proposition.[138] This is reflected in the distribution of trained primary school teachers. In 1964, for example, the Catholics had 61 per cent of the primary school population and 62 per cent of the teaching personnel but only 8 per cent of the trained teachers. On the other hand the Anglicans and the Methodists with 17 per cent and 14 per cent of the pupils had 20 and 25 per cent of the trained teachers respectively.[139] It was not until the UNESCO mission strongly urged the merger of the two institutions[140] that their separate existence ended in 1965. But the dual system of control precludes a correction of the uneven deployment of the trained teachers with the result that the optimum use of this personnel cannot be nationally realized.

Governmental permissiveness within the system also contributes very little to cultural integration in the Protestant secondary schools. Being almost entirely Roman Catholic Mestizos rarely attend the Protestant schools. It is the Creoles in these schools who are denied the opportunity of cultural and racial interaction since the Catholic secondary schools attract Creoles who are Catholics as well as those who are Protestants but are capable of resisting the pressures of denominational loyalty. Finally, the dual system permits the denominations to plan and implement their programmes with little attention to the government's economic and social goals.[141] Although agriculture is the key to the country's economic development, it is only in the last few years that science has claimed more time in the curriculum than Latin and Bible Study. For years the Catholics struggled to maintain an agricultural college, Lynam Agricultural College, which was established in 1964,[142] but they eventually submitted to the financial burden and ended the venture in 1971.[143]

It was not only the cost of secondary and primary education that suggested greater inter-denominational co-operation and a more nationally integrated and centrally directed system. The relevance of the education system to the needs of the society also called for a reappraisal of the government's passive role. The UNESCO mission noted that the government's Development Plan 'avoids these questions [but] we cannot'. 'Government', the mission declared, 'must accept responsibility for some activities where denominational co-operation fails to mature, and for key expensive institutions; and in any case government should assume wider powers of supervision, and direction if necessary, in matters of vital educational importance while leaving religious matters and purely administrative details in the hands of the denominations.'[144] In consequence the mission proposed an advisory National Education Council, but significantly did not specifically give representation to the Churches. Instead the body was to consist of people from industry, commerce, agriculture and the trade unions, who were more likely to relate the educational plans to the country's social and economic needs.[145]

The government accepted the UNESCO report as 'a fair and reasonable assessment' of the country's education system at that time which also provided 'acceptable guidelines' for development of the system in the future.[146] As we have seen, the two independently run training colleges were amalgamated to form the Belize Teachers' College. In 1969 the government inaugurated one of the two junior secondary schools for pupils between the ages of twelve and fifteen in Belize City which the UNESCO mission had recommended, and had the other one under consideration. At the new capital, Belmopan, it also took the initiative and established the three schools – a comprehensive secondary, a junior and an infant. Other developments have taken place, not necessarily those recommended by the UNESCO team, but in keeping with its recurring theme for a more nationally integrated and supervised system.[147]

At the same time the government has recoiled from several of the UNESCO recommendations that smack of secularism. It yielded to denominational pressures for control of the National Education Council which was established in 1966.[148] Of the fourteen Council members which it proposed in that year, nine were directly connected with the Churches, four were nominees of the denominations, three were principals of secondary schools (one of each of the three main denominations) and two were representatives of the Catholic Educational Association and the British Honduras Union of Teachers. But for the fact that it was legally deemed an abrogation of ministerial power and therefore unconstitutional, the government was prepared to acquiesce to denominational demand to be deeply involved with the Minister in the formulation of policy.[149] In other words the Churches were suggesting that the functions of the National Education Council should be more than advisory. Father F. Ring, the General Manager of the Roman Catholic primary schools, went to the extent of suggesting that 'consultation' was not enough and that 'a super-council on a fifty-fifty scale – six members, three from the government and three from the denominations,' should be 'ultimately responsible for education'.[150]

A similar duel between the protagonists of the denominational system took place over the government schools in the new capital, Belmopan. It ended with a partial settlement which placed the management of the schools under an inter-denominational committee.[151] Even if the denominations remain the dominant partner in this arrangement the fragmentation has been avoided.

But the danger of the secondary education system retaining its divided aims and achieving neither has not necessarily been averted. Like the Protestant schools the government follows the British-oriented education system as its Development Plan speaks of sixth form studies in the United Kingdom context. The Catholic secondary schools also prepare students for the British external examinations. At the same time St John's College has accepted the government's challenge to the schools to make 'their advances themselves' and 'come up with what they like'.[152] Indeed, the government had disregarded the UNESCO mission's advice in its election manifesto in 1965. 'The question of government control', the PUP reiterated in 1966, 'would be contrary to the National Manifesto.' Its policy is not to assume too much of the initiative but 'to support and encourage educational progress in plans devised and set in operation by the private institutions existing in the country – this is a good thing, especially under the present circumstances where government has limited resources'.[153]

The outcome was the government bill in 1967 to confer statutory recognition on the St John's College Associate Degree which is modelled on the North American College pattern and can be awarded to distinguished Belizeans. Protestant fears were presumably allayed when the Premier in concluding the debate expressed the government's willingness to help 'anyone [who] stands ready to come up with another degree... [since] there is nothing wrong to have a diversity of degrees'. The bill, however, ran into fatal opposition in the Senate. The two leading spokesmen on education, Vernon Courtenay and Leslie, both Protestants, were dismayed at the prospect of a proliferation of degrees and the fact that the proposed Associated Degree further complicated the multiple orientation of the education system.[154] They urged their colleagues to refer the bill to a Select Committee of the Senate where it languished until the National Assembly was dissolved in December 1969.

Such opposition to denominational permissiveness is rare and courageous. The political consequences of challenge to the dual system of control are incalculable and few politicians are prepared to cast a critical eye. In fact, *The Belize Times*, in noting the adverse comments of the 1966 Tripartite Economic Commission on the denominational system of education, stated that the commissioners had 'rushed in where angels fear to tread'.[155] Even the UBAD party which has assailed the expatriate clergy as part of its general criticism of North Atlantic influence in the society has stopped short of challenging the deep-seated belief in Belize that Church control is fundamental to a sound system of education. It has called for an ecumenical approach to the problems of fragmentation and proposed that the sixth forms of the secondary schools should be merged into a single entity.[156] Concern for the issue of denominational control has emerged around the fact that there is an upper limit beyond which the expatriate missionaries hesitated to let Belizean teachers advance in the secondary schools. In response to these reservations, the Churches have appointed nationals as principals in some of the schools. The American Jesuits and nuns are, however, apparently less willing than their Protestant counterparts to relinquish their hold, and where this has been done there is probably a tendency to keep the lay teacher at bay in preference to local nuns and priests who have fully internalized the standards, norms and values of their religious superiors.

Perhaps the only immediate threat to the denominational system is the financial inability of the Protestant secondary schools to compete with the Catholic. In view of the loyalty of the Jesuits to the PUP's cause in the past and the tendency for denominational differences to run along racial and cultural lines, there is a strong temptation for the almost exclusively Protestant Creole secondary schools to see themselves as the under-privileged political victims of the government's financial arrangements. The Jesuits are as concerned as the Protestants, as the implication is that the government would be compelled to assume more responsibility for these schools and may well become the main competitor of the Roman Catholic schools. One possible outcome of this step, they contend, is that the government will make inroads into the Catholic domain. While the outlook of the present government postpones such a development, the experiences of the Catholic Church in Mexico and Cuba do not seem to be lost to the Jesuits' sight.

In conclusion, religion has been at once a product and motivator of social and political forces but because of its interaction with these forces it is not always easy to distinguish its response from its influence. Nevertheless, we have been able to identify the most important field, education, in which religious influence remains pronounced in Belize. Through education, the Church has had a formative influence on the country's ideological outlook. It is perhaps the most important factor responsible not only for keeping Belize within the ideologies of the West, but also for the conservative outlook of the politicians. From a geo-political viewpoint this is not without significance for the Central American policy of the United States. Within Belize the hostility to leftist ideologies is so widespread that it is not surprising that the celebrated ex-communist, Douglas Hyde, who was a guest of the St John's College Alumni Association in November 1960 found his audiences in Belize City and the District towns 'receptive' to his anti-communist lectures.[157]

The dominance of the Catholic Church and its marked influence on the educational system is an important factor in explaining this situation. As Douglas Hyde observed at the end of his visit, 'British Honduras has been spared from communist influence so far,...because education has always been on a religious basis, the people were mostly Christian and political leaders reflected that Christian teaching.'[158]

In contributing to a common ideological outlook religion has enabled the major political parties to engage in a rare show of unity. Religion, however, is divisive at the denominational level. Here cultural and racial differences have been emphasized, and the multiple external orientation of the country underlined. Each denomination tends to adopt a sectarian outlook towards the country, thus limiting further the unifying role of the Church. Their general unwillingness to look across denominational boundaries has had unfortunate consequences for the education system.

Once political leaders accept the view that politics should be imbued with religion the prominence and influential position of the Church seems assured. But the consequences of this assurance are not wholly compatible with the country's nationalist objectives. During the past twenty-odd years nationalist sentiment has found expression in politics and the 'Belizeanization' of almost everything except education and the churches. The cultivation of 'Belizean' art and culture is vigorously pursued and officially encouraged, and the civil service personnel is almost all local. This 'Belizeanization' has only recently begun in the secondary schools and its pace is more likely to be dictated by religious considerations than the availability of professionally qualified nationals. Lay teachers in the secondary schools cannot in fact be encouraged by the soft-pedalling of nationalist policy in this field and its subordination to religious considerations, and cannot, therefore, look forward to exercising effective authority. In fact the limited career opportunities in these schools have helped to reduce the attractiveness of the teaching profession.

With control residing in foreign hands the education system must necessarily remain externally oriented. In consequence the local population remains manacled to alien cultural phenomena and policies, and inappropriate ideas. The young Belizean, searching for the freedom and independence, the sense of belonging and of personal worth which other political and social changes are offering freely to him, is caught in the grasp of foreign control of the national schools.

Within this context the Church is to be considered a formidable barrier to further social and political changes. Other powerful and competing interests and claims have however begun to pose a challenge to the Churches' values and position. Urbanization, the provision of university education for an increasing number of youths, and the increasing rejection by the new generation of the foreign domination of any aspect of national affairs, are creating values other than religious ones. It is not inconsistent with a long tradition, that exposure to higher learning would loosen the bonds of religion over the individual. It is therefore likely that the young returning graduates, if only from enlightened self-interest, will be among the first to question the present educational arrangement. An appeal to the primacy of the Church's authority in education may not then be an acceptable answer. It may only ensure that more rapid changes of the system, when they do come, will be extreme.

# 10

# Multiple external orientations: sentiment and reality

In the previous two chapters we saw that the country's relationships with Britain, the United States and Central America were not developing in the manner anticipated by the PUP government. On the contrary these relationships were forcing the government to reorder its orientation. The analysis also revealed that the process of national integration in its manifold aspects – cultural, social and regional – remained problematic and was still conditioned to a considerable degree by the country's marginality to so many external political entities. It now remains for us to explore more fully the country's multiple external orientations with emphasis on its search for regional and international guarantees to ensure its economic viability and enable it to resolve Guatemala's territorial claim and to become independent.

## Economic aspects

*Metropolitan orientations.* The PUP's disenchantment with the nature of American investment, which had set in as early as 1962, proved neither premature nor unjustified. Large, fertile and accessible land was the target of the investors. By 1966 virtually one-half of the 365 persons who owned lands exceeding 100 acres were foreigners.[1] Their numbers were no indication of the size of their holdings. They owned 2,136,000 acres as against 234,000 acres which were in national hands.[2] The data on the ownership of the larger estates of 10,000 acres or more were equally revealing. Only three nationals were among the 50 members of this super-league who together owned 2,000,000 acres.[3] Altogether 90 per cent of the privately owned lands was in the hands of non-nationals.[4] The distribution of the foreign-owned lands by nationality was not disclosed, but even allowing for the corporate holdings of the British-owned BEC Company and the Belize Sugar Industries Ltd, the American ownership must have been substantial.

Indeed American ownership depended to a considerable extent on the BEC not only selling some of its lands but also selling them on conditions

306

and at prices that were beyond the reach of nationals. The company seldom offers small parcels of land for sale, but usually a minimum of 5,000 acres which is more of a business proposition to foreign speculators than the *bona fide* developers.[5] Because of its extremely large share of the private land market, the BEC determines price and the use to which land is put. It is not surprising, therefore, that speculation in land became rife by the mid-1960s. An estate of 11,762 acres in the Orange Walk District, bought for $49,989 in 1959, was sold in 1965 for $329,336. In the same year, 14,085 acres of land on the Northern River was sold for $20,000, double its price eight years earlier.[6] These activities added nothing to the wealth of the country and drew the ire of the government.

What added to the government's disquiet with the American investment was its own timidity to take drastic corrective action. As early as 1963 the United Nations economic mission argued that the speculation would be curbed and the land cultivated only by an increase in land tax, a tax on undeveloped land on a graduated scale, and a capital gains tax which was to be the essential and crowning feature of the entire tax structure.[7] But for four years the government was content to repeat its warning, first issued in 1962, to impose a tax.[8] Far from having a salutary effect on the speculator, the continuous threat merely intensified the speculation to the extent that the resale of very small uneconomic parcels of land had begun by the time the government took action in January 1966.[9] This was limited to a tax on holdings over 100 acres that were under-developed and undeveloped. The government was either too committed to the private enterprise system or, in view of the close relationship between the US investors and the Chamber of Commerce, lacked the political courage to introduce the recommended capital gains tax. In fact, the relevant legislation which is still in force gives the owner the right to fix a reserve for his land where it is to be sold for the recovery of arrears tax. This ensures that he receives the value of the land, less tax, on the open market.[10]

The law also empowered the Minister of National Resources to exempt from the tax holdings whose existing development was maintained and was in his opinion in the interest of that of the country. In 1968 sixteen holdings ranging in size from 1,092 to 627,688 acres were granted the exemption.[11] The arrangement can hardly have been punitive. It was indeed based on the debatable assumption that land in a private enterprise economy 'is held not as of right but in trust from the community'.[12] Even if this was the case, the implication that the interests of the foreign owner and that of the community were identical, or that he should put the host community's above his own, was naive. Instead of being curbed, land speculation continued unabated and the alienation of land to Americans increased. In 1968, Minister A. A. Hunter referred to 'some real estate deals going on in the South...land being bought in the vicinity of $7,000 per acre and this included house and those same lands are now being sold for $4,000 a lot'[13] (about one quarter of an acre). Hunter was even more specific. He cited the cases of Lime Caye which was bought for $4,000 (BH) and sold within a year for $10,000 (US), or nearly $15,000 (BH), and of Southern Long Cay which was bought for $1,340 (BH) and sold the next year for $9,000 (US) or nearly $13,500 (BH).[14] Altogether lands sold to foreigners in 1968 1969 and 1970 have been valued at $637,000, $1,290,000 and $786,000 respectively.[15] However sacred was its private enterprise philosophy, the government had to resort to more drastic measures to halt the alarming rate of alienation and price increases. In December 1973 it enacted the Aliens Landholding legislation.[16] No alien may purchase more than 10 acres outside a town unless he secures a licence from the government Failure to fulfil the licensed conditions for development may result in the cancellation of the licence, in which case the lands and its encumbrances are forfeited to the government. Land owned by aliens at the commence ment of the law is not affected as far as title is concerned, but cannot be sold to another alien unless the prospective buyer has secured a licence Nor can a landholder, national or foreign, bequeath the land to an alien the heir is only entitled to the proceeds of the sale of the property. The reasons for the legislation were not only economic. Since the failure of the Webster mediation in 1968, the government had become more pro prietorial toward the lands that border Guatemala. As the Attorney General put it in introducing the bill, it was necessary to regulate the ownership of land in order to retain 'control of our boundary lines and strategic naval property for our defence'.[17]

Because of the speculative nature of American private investment, Belize is apprehensive about its nascent tourist industry coming too much under American influence. Apart from the country's sub-tropical climate, fishing and boating facilities, its cays provide a convenient location for gambling casinos. And since this type of tourist development is not widespread in the more established Caribbean tourist islands, American investors are convinced that the future of industry in Belize lies in this direction.[18] But the misgivings among Belizeans are many. There is the fear, as George Doxey notes throughout the Caribbean,[19] that the country's economy may fall into the grip of gambling syndicates. Then too, there is concern, particularly within the Church, that these undesirable elements will turn the society into a cultural and social cesspool and force it to develop a political system to service the needs of the tourists.[20]

The government's disappointment with the speculative nature of land investment was matched by a blow from the Hercules Powder Company. After three years the company unexpectedly removed its $5,000,000 (US) resin plant from the Stann Creek District to Nicaragua in 1965, leaving in the lurch about 200 families and a number of ancillary businesses.

The PUP government's hope that the USA would be its principal source of foreign investment was perhaps finally shattered by the Partners of Alliance for Progress. After being kept in uncertainty for several years about its eligibility for this kind of relationship with the USA,[21] Belize was eventually linked to Michigan in 1966. The programme was welfare-oriented, although Price envisaged it as a channel through which his government could 'actively seek foreign investments'.[22] But as far as George Romney, the Governor of Michigan, was concerned, 'the program [was] a people to people program rather than a government to government program'.[23] It was, however, the outspoken President of the Belize Chamber of Commerce, Ismael Gomez, who expressed disappointment in the orientation of the programme. In a press statement prior to his departure for the Fourth Inter-American Conference of the Partners of the Alliance in the USA in 1969, he stated that he felt the 'Partners have concentrated too much on education and health and not enough on business and investment.'[24] He was prepared to tell the conference that if nothing was done in these areas they ought to stop putting it down as part of their programme for the countries in the Alliance. The orientation of the programme remained unchanged and by 1970 the wave of expectancy and enthusiasm had ebbed without leaving many tangible results or promises on the local shore.

This was personally galling to Price because of his own economic and political beliefs. First, as we have seen at the beginning of the nationalist movement in the early 1950s, he had based his case for looking to the USA for investments partly on the fact that most of Belize's imports came from that country. He was also encouraged to hold to this view as the USA share of Belize export constantly rose from 12.4 per cent in 1961 to 33.5 per cent in 1965, as a result of the grant of the sugar quota by the government of that country.[25] While this increase in trade has assumed an even higher order of national importance to Belize, it remains minuscule in USA aggregate trade. In effect Price had pinned his hopes for economic development on a country that had no economic reason to end its passivity toward his country.

Second, Price firmly believed that even if the country was economically unattractive to *bona fide* investors, it was from a geographical and ideological standpoint entitled to American attention and sympathy. As he put it in his address to the Michigan Senate in 1966, Belize lies in a 'critical geo-political area where two ways of life meet in confrontation: the way of communism in Cuba and the way of democracy, Christian Democracy, in Belize'.[26] And as early as 1962, Price had expressed the view that the USA should reward the country for its conservative outlook if only 'to forestall any [communist] move to subvert his people by playing on their misery and poverty which, if unremedied, in time would cause general dissatisfaction'.[27] Five years later, in 1967, he turned his observation and plea into a warning. 'Unless you [USA] build more highways of mutual greatness and hemispheric prosperity and happiness', he told his Michigan Partners of Alliance, 'the growing masses', not only of his country, but those of Latin America and the Caribbean, 'will batter at your gates.'[28] As we saw, such arguments did not win American sympathy in the mediation of the Anglo-Guatemala dispute. It can be argued that it is precisely because the PUP government poses no hemispheric threats that the American response to its economic needs has been so limited.

Instead, therefore, of loosening its ties with Britain, Belize has become more dependent upon it. By the end of 1966, the country was free of British Treasury control, which, as we recall, had been instituted after the disastrous hurricane of September 1931. Nonetheless, it continues to look to the British government for its main source of finance, especially for capital expenditure. Like other developing countries, Belize has found that its efforts to increase the contribution of government saving to development expenditure are frequently frustrated by an inexorable rise in current expenditure.[29] In 1966 the government estimated that the recurrent expenditure would rise at an annual rate of 5 per cent.[30] The Tripartite Economic Survey Commission, however, increased the estimated rate to 6 per cent which called for recurrent expenditure of $14,900,000 in 1971.[31] Even this revised estimate proved conservative, as the 1971 budget provided for recurrent expenditure of $16,100,000 which was 13 per cent higher than the 1970 approved estimates of $15,500,000.[32] To compound the problem the government has been engaged in large-scale construction work since 1968. In addition to the building of the new capital at Belmopan, Belize Airport was reconditioned and various related infrastructural works were carried out. There are several other projects in progress, such as the building of the fifty-mile highway between Belize City and Belmopan. The Tripartite Economic Survey Commission estimated that the government would require from foreign sources $28,750,000 for the three-year period, 1968 to 1970, to undertake these capital works.[33] It could not envisage any substantial source other than Britain which, therefore, it estimated would provide $24,750,000, or 85 per cent of the total.[34] In 1971, the budget provided for a capital expenditure of $13,000,000, excluding the new capital project, which was the largest in the country's fiscal history.[35] Here again, the government was at the mercy of the British sense of its residual imperial responsibility. It noted that the world economy during 1969 and early 1970 was marked by severe inflationary pressures and restrictive fiscal and monetary measures. Since it did not foresee 'any early removal of the restriction on capital'[36] it could not help but acknowledge the 'United Kingdom's contribution largely on a free grant basis'.[37]

The dependence on Britain extends to trade. It is not so much the volume of trade with Britain that is important to Belize, as this dropped from 61 per cent of total exports in 1961[38] to 24 per cent in 1970.[39] What is invaluable is the reciprocal Commonwealth preferential arrangement under which Belizean goods enter Britain. As we indicated in chapter 9, the most valuable arrangement is the negotiated prices paid for the country's main export commodity, sugar, under the Commonwealth Sugar Agreement. Furthermore, the country's overall merchandise trade deficits which increased from $16,500,000 in 1967 to around $26,000,000 in 1971 are traditionally financed mainly with grants from Britain.[40]

One of the problems with this dependence on British aid and trading arrangements is that it is critical to Belize at a time when Britain's ties with the Commonwealth Caribbean are becoming tenuous, largely as a result of Britain's entry into the EEC. This has created uncertainties for the sheltered arrangement under which Belize markets its primary exports to Britain. At best British accession to the EEC exposes Belize to competition from other overseas states associated with the Community. At worst, it might leave the country to face competition in international markets, with the Associated States of the Community being given a competitive advantage in the British market itself.[41]

As we shall see, Belize shares its dependence on British financial aid with the smaller Commonwealth Caribbean countries, and the uncertainties of its British commercial ties with all the Commonwealth countries in the region. Together, the Commonwealth countries are working to safeguard their interests with Britain within the wider context of the EEC. Nevertheless, they are conscious that sooner or later they will become much more closely tied up with the rest of the hemisphere.[42] Unless the USA becomes more responsive to Belize's economic needs, the possibilities of hemispheric aid are restricted. At present the country cannot count on the Inter-American Development Bank (IADB) as a source of financial assistance. This is not so much because of its political status as a colony, but because of its territorial dispute with Guatemala. This effectively blocks Belize's path to the Organization of American States (OAS), membership in which is required to join the IADB. The main source of metropolitan aid within the hemisphere is therefore Canada. The assistance from this source is concentrated in the technical field, especially in manpower development.[43] In the past few years Canada has also evinced an increasing interest in the country's capital expenditure programme, its contribution having risen from 7 per cent in 1968 to 17 per cent in 1973.[44]

Canadian assistance should be seen as much as in a Commonwealth as in a hemispheric context. The Belize programmes were funded from a shared allocation with the Leeward and Windward Islands and Barbados for five fiscal years, 1964–5 to 1969–70, at the end of which Belize received a separate allocation.[45] For a variety of reasons, however, it is still primarily as part of the Commonwealth Caribbean that Belize will be the recipient of Canadian assistance. In the first place, Canada retains a strong disposition, wherever possible, towards considering its aid from the standpoint of the Commonwealth Caribbean area as a whole and to also link it to trade.[46] The most significant case in point in recent years was the Ottawa Conference on Canada–West Indies Relations in 1966 which reviewed the provision for reciprocal preferential tariff treatment in the Canada–West Indies Trade Agreement in 1925.[47] An outcome of the conference was Canada's decision to give a rebate of the preferential duty on sugar to the governments of the Caribbean countries, including Belize, that exported sugar to Canada.[48] In the second place, given Canada's tendency to associate aid with trade, Belize is at a disadvantage because its share of Canada–West Indies trade is relatively small. It is, therefore, likely to gain more from Canada's multilateral assistance than from outright competition with the other territories. Indeed, during 1969 Canada unilaterally announced its intention to discontinue the sugar rebate payments at the end of that calendar year.[49] Instead it made $5,000,000 (US) available to a special Agricultural Development Fund which was created in 1970 to increase agricultural productivity and efficiency in the Commonwealth Caribbean countries. One-half of the Canadian contribution is being administered by the Caribbean Regional Development Bank of which Belize was a founding member in 1970 and to whose capital Canada subscribed $10,000,000 (US) or 20 per cent.[50] Belize is expected to benefit from the Fund since it is the Bank's policy to give prior attention to the needs of the less developed countries in the region. This, of course, does not preclude Belize from receiving bilateral assistance from the other half of the Canadian contribution which the Canadian International Development Agency (CIDA) directly administers. It only means that Belize is spared some of the keen competition with the more developed territories for Canadian aid.

In conclusion, contrary to the PUP's hopes and expectations at the outset of the decolonization process, the principal direction of its metropolitan economic aid remains British. Britain's increasing European orientation and financial difficulties are, however, likely to restrict its willingness and capacity to maintain indefinitely the high level of aid and capital funds. The emergence of Canada as the potential source of financial aid is not altogether a coincidence or unrelated to the USA's seeming indifference to the country's economic needs. Richard Preston suggests that because it has so many problems all over the world, the USA assumes that the Commonwealth Caribbean must remain a British or Commonwealth responsibility.[51] While this viewpoint is highly debatable, Canada is evidently not unwilling to undertake this responsibility since it has more trading and investment interests in the Commonwealth Caribbean than in other parts of the under-developed world.[52] The extension of this responsibility to a small, manageable country such as Belize presents relatively few problems, especially on a multilateral regional basis.

For its part Belize must live with the verdict of continual economic orientation within the framework of the Commonwealth, notwithstanding the PUP's initial eagerness to sever these ties. The verdict, however, is not as severe and disappointing as it may appear. For it is related to the means and not the end. Belize's objective to be an integral part of the Inter-American system can be pursued just as much through closer economic association with Canada as with the USA. Although it has opted for observer status rather than full membership of the Organization of American States, Canada stands at a geo-political crossroad where it cannot deny that part of its destiny lies within the Inter-American system. Finally, in view of Canada's economic domination by the USA, the PUP can still hope that, however indirectly, its preference for the exploration of its natural resources by corporate American rather than British or Commonwealth investors is still a distinct possibility.

*Regional orientation: Central America and the Commonwealth Caribbean.*
It can be argued that the verdict about Belize's economic orientation was not so much one of the USA paramountcy and dictation in the hemisphere, but of the country's economic history. As we recall, the PUP government for years talked with unconcealed hope about its regional economic destiny being in Central America rather than the Commonwealth Caribbean. However, it rarely put its case for its regional orientation in other than sentimental terms. Most of its statements on the subject

placed emphasis on the country's Mayan roots and its Latin heritage of language and culture, and also on the trading links with the USA which could involve Central America in a triangular relationship. Belize's Central American aspirations found enough sympathy for ECLA to agree in 1961 to undertake a study of the possibilities of closer economic ties between the country and Central America. Throughout the 1960s the ECLA secretariat carried out studies on specific sectors of the Belizean economy and finally reported its findings in December 1968.[53]

Essentially the report was an elaboration of Downie's argument in 1959 that Belize should not assume that considerable gains would accrue to its economy from a strengthening of economic ties with Central America. More pointedly, the report advised that the country's accession to the Central American Common Market (CACM) could only result in serious dislocations in the country's economy, unless it was effected gradually and took the form of an associated relationship.[54] The country's developmental possibilities and its trade with Central America and other countries were the focal point of the analysis. The report was concerned with the fact that Belize was the least industrially advanced of the six Central American countries. As a result of the well-known process of economic polarization, it was likely that the accession of Belize to the CACM would have adverse effects on the pace of its industrial development. There was incontrovertible evidence that the integration of countries at different stages of development may, in the absence of special measures, confer a disproportionate share of the gains from integration upon the more industrially advanced countries, sometimes at the expense of dislocating output and employment in the less advanced countries. Competition arising from the freeing of trade might damage the nascent industries in the less developed areas of the Common Market. The economies of conglomeration tend to attract the bulk of new productive activities to more developed countries in the market, and may even drain away from the less developed ones scarce supplies of capital and skills.[55]

On the subject of intra-area trade, the report noted that the country's export trade with Central America was limited, as over the last few decades the CACM countries had never purchased more than 1 per cent of Belize exports.[56] It did not foresee a significant expansion of this export trade resulting from free access to the CACM. The obstacles to such trade were Belize's geographical situation, long distances away from the main consumption centres of the region, the lack of adequate transport facilities and the supply constraints imposed by the country's incipient industrial development. Nor did the report consider Belize's contiguity to Peten in Guatemala an advantage capable of overcoming these obstacles by heavy investments in the construction of adequate transport facilities. The combined population of Belize and of this large adjacent area is less than 150,000 and for many years to come it will constitute a minor outlet for products originating in Central America.[57]

What short-term possibilities of increasing trade exist are not likely to provide sufficient gains to justify Belize's entry into the CACM as a full member. As the report observed, this would imply the renunciation of her present special trading arrangements within the Commonwealth upon which the country's export industries rely.[58] It would also give rise to a considerable increase in internal prices and costs, as a result of adopting the much higher Central American Common tariffs. The report concluded that Belize would be better off with co-operative arrangements whereby it participated in the development of regional industries oriented mainly to overseas markets.[59]

There was nothing new in the report. However, because of its source it had a greater impact than the Downie Report on the PUP government. It brought home to Price the cruel fact that fondness for the country's Latin connections could not alone sustain initiatives toward closer ties between Belize and Central America. No longer could he entertain political attitudes that avoided the alternative. This was to join the Caribbean Area Free Trade Association (CARIFTA) which was established between Antigua, Barbados and Guyana in 1966, and brought together the other Commonwealth Caribbean countries in the same year, 1968, that ECLA reported on Belize.[60]

Almost from the beginning the PUP government evinced an interest in CARIFTA. In October 1967, at the Fourth Conference of the Heads of Commonwealth Caribbean Governments, Price urged the delegates to 'leave the door open in any agreed scheme so that it will not be impossible for Belize to enter at a future date without any penalties'.[61] From then onwards Belize participated as an observer at CARIFTA meetings both at the ministerial and civil service levels. It was, however, not until in early 1971 that Belize applied to join the Free Trade Association. Its application was accepted in March 1971 and membership took effect in May 1971.[62] The country was designated as 'less developed' which meant that it was entitled to special treatment along the lines of that accorded to the Windward and Leeward Islands, including for example, a longer period for maintaining tariff protection of local industries.[63]

By delaying its membership Belize faced the difficulties of negotiation that newcomers to ongoing economic unions normally encounter. The Less Developed Countries (LDC), evidently wishing to restrict their numbers and monopolize their privileges, opposed the extension of this status to Belize.[64] This was done on the grounds that Belize was relatively more developed than some of them, for example, Montserrat, and that the new applicant had had ample and equal opportunity to secure membership at the outset. If anything, despite the PUP government's plea to the contrary in 1967, the LDC argued that more onerous terms should be imposed on Belize for its delay.[65]

Belize could not afford to be daunted by the opposition to its being accorded the LDC status. As the ECLA report pointed out, because of the system of Commonwealth preferences, Belize shares an economically advantageous trading arrangement with the Commonwealth Caribbean.[66] To begin with, the Commonwealth Caribbean has consistently ranked behind Britain and the USA as the country's third largest source of imports. Up to 1960 it was also the third largest market for the country's exports, with the proportion going to those markets falling from 18 per cent in that year to 4.67 per cent in 1970.[67] The bulk of exports which are mainly to Jamaica, consisted almost wholly of lumber. But the market of the Commonwealth Caribbean as a whole was considered by the ECLA report to have a greater potential interest for Belize as an outlet for meat and dairy products.[68] On the one hand an increasing import demand in the territories for these commodities was projected. On the other hand the livestock industry in Belize had tremendous possibilities. There are some 1.5 million acres of land well suited to cattle-raising and the Tripartite Economic Survey Commission observed in 1966 that several potentially large producers are coming on to the scene.[69] The scope for expansion beyond 1970 could be judged from the fact that even allowing for the projected increase in the stock of cattle by that year less than 5 per cent of suitable land resources would be utilized for cattle-rearing.[70] In fact, between 1969 and 1971 the country's cattle population rose by over a quarter.[71]

The ECLA report, however, pointed out that there were tariffs on fresh beef in some of the Commonwealth Caribbean territories and quantitative restrictions in others in order to protect local production.[72] It envisaged that the CARIFTA agreement may be followed by increased trade restrictions *vis-à-vis* third countries, in order to take advantage of possibilities for regional import substitution. The report proceeded to indicate firmly that meat was an obvious possibility, bearing in mind the scope for increasing production in countries such as Guyana, Jamaica and Trinidad and Tobago.[73] The message was clear. Belize stood to lose its potential advantage, and an opportunity to diversify its principal export sector, unless it entered CARIFTA. As A. A. Hunter, the Minister of Trade and Industry subsequently acknowledged, 'the only real economic reason for Belize joining CARIFTA...is the opportunity for exporting agricultural produce to the area. And it is in the agricultural sector that Belize could play a most effective role at this stage.'[74]

The advantages which Belize can derive from the commercial ties with the Commonwealth Caribbean go beyond the expansion of the scope of intra-regional trade. They extend to participation in joint negotiation of external marketing for the region's commodity exports.[75] For example, Belize participated in the renegotiation of the 1925 Canada–West Indies Trade Agreement at the Ottawa conference in 1966, which also dealt with joint arrangement for the receipt of aid and technical assistance from Canada. A more important example was Belize's response to the problems which Britain's entry into the EEC posed for the preferential marketing agreement of its primary products in that country. One way of at least minimizing, if not overcoming these problems, was for Belize to seek membership in the EEC as an overseas associated state for which it would be eligible as a politically dependent territory. From the outset, however, Belize recognized that its trading problems were common to the Commonwealth Caribbean, and joint representation with these countries would augment its external bargaining power.[76] This consideration may have contributed to Belize's decision to enter CARIFTA since the negotiating strategy was worked out within the framework of the Free Trade Association.[77] Indeed Belize confirmed its identity of economic interest with the other CARIFTA countries *vis-à-vis* the EEC when it subscribed to a resolution of the CARIFTA Council of Ministers in July 1972 that CARIFTA, as a group, should seek a single form of relationship with the EEC.[78]

It must be appreciated that Belize carries little weight within CARIFTA, which became the Caribbean Common Market and Community (CARICOM) in August 1973,[79] and its role is largely supportive. Yet it may still be called upon to play a strategic role. Beckford has argued that a Caribbean Common Market would be of little significance and political power among international groupings as long as it is restricted to the English-speaking countries. In his view the viability of this union depends on a further intermediate step toward integration with the Spanish, French and Antillean Caribbean. This in turn should be seen as a precursor to a wider Central American and Caribbean integration, which eventually could provide the basis for a longer-term integration with the rest of Latin America.[80] A trend along this line is already discernible. Three independent Commonwealth countries, Barbados, Trinidad and Jamaica, have joined the Organization of American States, and a fourth, Guyana, has to be content with observer status because of its territorial dispute with a member of that organization, Venezuela. Trinidad already has substantial connection with Latin America because of its oil industry, while Guyana is recognizing that logistically the development of its hinterland can benefit from closer economic ties with its southern neighbour, Brazil.[81] On the other hand, two Latin American countries, Colombia and Venezuela, have been admitted to the Caribbean Development Bank.[82] These two countries, together with the Dominican Republic of Haiti and several Central American countries, have also evinced an interest in membership of CARICOM.[83]

Belize is culturally in a unique position to perform a linking role between the two regional blocks. Drawing strength from its Spanish-oriented element, it could assume the initiative within the Commonwealth Caribbean group to strengthen the growing link and ultimately forge the larger Caribbean and Central American integration.[84] This idea is not new. Belize was at one time conceived as 'a bridgehead of British influence in Spanish America',[85] the difference being that this was based on geographical rather than cultural considerations. In the event of a larger Caribbean regional group, Belize may, after all, realize its hope for a Central American destiny.

*Political aspects*

Because Guatemala still persists in its century-old territorial claim to the whole country, Belize has had to pursue its political relationship with the metropolitan countries, the Commonwealth Caribbean and Central America with a tenacity that was not always evident in the forging of its economic ties. As early as 1962 the PUP government declared its inability to withstand the claim on its own. In that year it rejected the NIP's proposal that the country establish a national defence force, claiming that it would be too expensive and in any case incapable of acting as a deterrent to any military action by Guatemala.[86] The government's policy was to rely on British military protection, to which it was entitled as a colony,[87] and on a diplomatic solution of the problem, as is evident in its concurring with the decision of Britain and Guatemala to submit the dispute to US mediation in June 1965.

As we saw earlier, the PUP government rejected the US mediator's proposals. The implications of its negative and unequivocal response went beyond a diplomatic impasse. As far as Britain and the USA were concerned, Belize had, in effect, decided to take the dispute into its own hands. In the case of Britain, any involvement beyond seeking a diplomatic solution is incompatible with its eagerness to divest itself from a lingering colonial responsibility for defence and foreign affairs. This does not mean that the British government would cease asserting its sovereignty over the territory of Belize. At the same time it would be reluctant to jeopardize its relationship with the Latin American countries which at least sympathized with Guatemala's argument that its territorial claim is in the name of anti-colonialism.

A case in point was the British government's response to a protest by Latin American countries to its military activities in Belize in 1972.[88] In the final week of January 1972 the British government announced that 8,000 servicemen would carry out amphibious exercises in the Caribbean area, including Belize. Five major naval units, including HMS *Ark Royal*, the 43,000 ton aircraft carrier, an assault ship and guided missile destroyer were to take part. At the same time the Second Battalion of the Grenadier Guards was due to arrive at the permanent garrison in Belize. Initial international press reports stated that these moves were designed to underline the British presence at a period when Guatemalan troops were particularly active in anti-guerilla activities in the adjacent areas of Peten.[89] The PUP government, however, later claimed that the Guatemala government began building up its military strength in Peten following the commencement of the British military exercise which had been planned in 1971, and 'given sufficient publicity'.[90] In any case Guatemala thereupon protested at the British show of force, declared a state of alert, broke off negotiation with Britain over their dispute and restated its position that Belize could not be given its independence, which Price had indicated in September 1971 would be in 1972.[91] This was not the most important protest. Within four days of the British announcement, the Inter-American Juridical Committee of the OAS, during its session in Rio de Janeiro, passed a motion proposed by the Guatemalan representative, condemning the exercises as a threat to the peace and security of the continent.[92] The British government's immediate retort was reminiscent of its imperial power. Mr Joseph Godber, Minister of State for Foreign and Commonwealth Affairs, stated in the House of Commons that Guatemala had been informed that the movement of British troops in the British territory was strictly the business of the British government.[93] But the British government retreated from this tough position when the matter was brought before the General Assembly of the OAS in April 1972. It offered to invite an observer from the OAS to verify the number of troops stationed in Belize.[94] This was in response to the Guatemalan charge of a massive increase of British forces and call to the Assembly to demand the removal of the troops and to urge all member states including the USA to impose sanctions against Britain and Belize. The OAS, on a resolution by Uruguay, took up the British government's invitation and appointed an observer, General Alvaro Valencia Tovar of the Colombian Army, whereupon Guatemala withdrew its resolution.[95] In June 1972 the General reported to the Permanent Council of the OAS that the Guatemalan claim about the size of the British forces was exaggerated and that their activities were fundamentally of a defensive nature.[96] The British government's original plan, however, seemed to involve a linking-up of the regular jungle training of the battalion in an air-support exercise from the *Ark Royal*. Clearly such a link-up would have proved politically embarrassing once the Latin American protest had begun. It was, in fact, called off before the issue had reached the General Assembly of the OAS and the naval exercises were completed off the Virgin Islands.[97]

For its part the USA would for a variety of reasons be even less willing than Britain to prejudice its relationship with Latin American countries in general and Guatemala in particular, for the sake of Belize's territorial integrity. First, the support which the US government gave to its ambassador's proposals for the settlement of the dispute suggests that it is more concerned with protecting its own substantial economic investments in Guatemala than with upholding Belize sentiments. Second, the USA may still be indebted to Guatemala for its role in training anti-Castro forces for the Bay of Pigs invasion.[98] In fact Mario Rosenthal claims to have been assured by a person who is in 'possession of the facts', that 'no agreement was reached [on the training of the forces in Guatemala] until Washington had promised unrestricted support in the Belize problem'.[99] Third, the USA may discourage a military solution to the problem as this is likely to restrict Guatemala's defence ability to meet its internal political problems. Indeed, as in so many countries where external threats are minimal, internal security has become the primary reason for the existence of the Guatemalan army. Furthermore, in any serious military confrontation between Guatemala and Britain, the USA would be expected by the OAS charter to support Guatemala in defence of the Inter-American security system even if this exerts a strain on its relationship with Britain.

It is therefore not surprising that neither Britain nor the USA is keen to enter into a bi-lateral arrangement with Belize to defend the latter upon its accession to independence. As the British government stated in October 1969, its interest would be confined to a defence agreement as opposed to a defence treaty which would be a more formal commitment.[100] This evidently falls short of Price's expectations. For as he put it in April 1972, 'When independence comes, it must have a guarantee sufficient to maintain and strengthen our separate existence as an independent state of the Americas.'[101]

In its attempt to extract a firmer commitment from Britain, Belize has also proposed multilateral pacts within both a Commonwealth framework and the Inter-American system. In 1969, at the Commonwealth Parliamentary Association Conference in Trinidad, the Belize Minister of Internal Affairs, Rogers, called for a defence pact involving all the Commonwealth countries in the Caribbean, Canada and the United Kingdom.[102] In talking primarily of a regional defence pact, the Minister's idea was, of course, to reassure the British government that its involvement, however inescapably decisive, would be more or less invisible. Three years later, in February 1972, Price declared that he would like Canada, Mexico and the United States to join with Britain in a multilateral agreement.[103] The linking of Britain to these three countries whose identification with either Latin America or the Inter-American system was greater than that of the Commonwealth Caribbean was obviously intended to reduce still further the visibility of British involvement or at least to protect it against hemispheric criticisms.

Despite its wider context, this second multilateral proposal provides no greater assurance than the first that Britain would not find itself honouring most of the defence commitments. On this matter Mexico had made its position clear as early as 1966. In the past it tended to remind others of its own dormant claims whenever its relationship with Guatemala was at a low point. But following a successful visit to Guatemala in April 1967, the President of Mexico, Gustavo Diaz Ordaz, scornfully remarked that 'between a piece of land and the friendship of the Guatemalan people', the latter 'is worth more to Mexicans'.[104] In his report to Congress in that year he claimed that 'Mexico has not and has never had any territorial ambition in respect of Belize'.[105] Unlike in the previous statement, however, the President took great care not to imply that he was encouraging Guatemala in its claim, for he expressed the hope that the problem would be solved with strict regard to the wishes of the people of Belize.[106] This stand was reiterated two years later when the Webster mediation proposal was published.[107] Unless Mexico reverts to its original position, the most that Belize can hope for is its intervention as a mediator. For economic reasons it may even prefer the problem to persist rather than be resolved too much in Guatemala's favour. For it has in Belize an almost exclusive entrepot mainly for British commodities which enjoy preferential tariff treatment in the colony.[108] This dependence upon re-exports has made Mexico the third largest market for Belize total exports, with its share steadily increasing from some 8 per cent in 1965[109] to 21 per cent in 1970.[110] Mexico would derive fewer tariff benefits from a settlement of the dispute which concedes to Guatemala a measure of control over Belize seaports and brings to an end Belize's participation in the system of Commonwealth preferences.

A Canadian defence presence in Belize is less likely than a Mexican. As Preston points out, despite its membership in NATO for twenty years, Canada still has a deep-seated sentiment against political entanglements and defence commitments in time of peace.[111] A firm defence agreement with Belize, whether bilateral or multilateral, would also besmirch the Canadian image as a peace-keeping force in Third World countries. Third, Canada would be cautious lest it precipitate an avalanche of similar requests from other Commonwealth Caribbean countries as part of its aid programme to them.[112]

On the whole, membership in a collective defence pact that includes the USA, Canada, Mexico or the Commonwealth Caribbean has no greater appeal to Britain than a bilateral pact with Belize. The attempt to draw Britain into a multilateral agreement also reveals the indifference or negative attitude of the other countries that Belize has considered at one time or another towards the proposal. Having made little progress elsewhere, Belize has been showing a remarkable enthusiasm for the strengthening of its relations with the Commonwealth Caribbean and Central American countries, notably Honduras (which is at odds with Guatemala), and the forging of new ones in other Third World countries independent of the British government. The emergence of an expansive and dynamic foreign policy is discernible in the visit of an emissary, Rogers, to Africa and the Middle East to solicit support on the eve of the Conference of Non-Aligned Heads of State in Algeria in September 1973.[113] But this independent outlook had received much of its impetus earlier in the year from a call by Barbados at the Eighth Conference of the Heads of Commonwealth Caribbean Governments in April 1973 for a regional defence arrangement against external aggression.[114] The summit decided that in view of the commitment toward the creation of the Caribbean Community, and mindful of securing the political independence and territorial integrity of Member States of the Community, the four independent CARIFTA countries would seek to establish a Scheme of Mutual Defence against External Aggression and that such a scheme would be devised by a Standing Committee of Caribbean Foreign Ministers. Belize put a seemingly higher degree of importance to the decision than even Guyana and the Bahamas which also worry over the issue of aggression. Indeed, the Prime Minister of the latter country, Lynden Pindling, chose to adopt what seems a rather pragmatic view by stating that he did not see the Mutual Defence System as being any more than an expression of solidarity from his Caribbean neighbours.[115] Price, on the other hand, took a more optimistic view. He recognized that the independent territories lack the human and military resources to back up pledges of solidarity. Nonetheless, he believed that 'their united voice cannot be ignored in today's world, especially in view of the trend toward detente'. On the contrary a show of solidarity 'can prove most valuable' in influencing thinking in the international community toward an understanding of Belize's 'just struggles for an independence that will not be destroyed by the territorial machinations of others'.[116]

The issue of solidarity is not a problem. In October 1968, a few months after the Belize government rejected the Webster mediation, the leader of the Barbadian delegation to the United Nations General Assembly, J. C. Tudor, Minister of State for Caribbean and Latin American Affairs, stated that his government was not satisfied that Belize's aspirations were receiving 'the fullest considerations in all the organizations of the United Nations'.[117] While noting that the British government had promised at the time to hold an early conference to discuss independence for Belize, he wished to be reassured that the Assembly was watching vigilantly over the colony's progress towards 'unfettered and uncompromised nationhood'.[118] More recently, in March 1973, the four independent Commonwealth Caribbean countries criticized Guatemala at the United Nations Security Council meeting in Panama.[119]

These countries have tended to reserve most of their diplomatic offensive for the OAS where they represent Belize's political aspirations as part of their own demands for the rescinding of Article 8 of the OAS Charter. This article excludes countries from membership in the OAS which are the subject of territorial dispute between a member state of the OAS and an imperial power, or which have inherited such a dispute, as in the case of Guyana. A joint resolution by these governments in October 1972 declared the exclusion to be particularly offensive to the English-speaking Caribbean countries since it applies only to countries within this group and, as such, imports into relations between American States connotations of an indefensible discrimination.[120] Among the Commonwealth Caribbean countries, Jamaica has been the severest critic of the Latin American members' stand in general and their attitude towards Belize's call for freedom in particular. At the second session of the General Assembly in 1972, it expressed its inability to reconcile Latin America's anti-colonial tradition with the OAS's evident attempt to deny independence to people in the hemisphere under the cloak of giving solidarity to a member state whose territorial dispute is with a departing imperial power.[121] Much more than Belize itself, Jamaica took a dim view of the General Assembly decision to send an observer to Belize in 1972 in order to satisfy the 'supposed fears' of Guatemala.[122] It was even more concerned that the Permanent Council of the organization to which the observer reported was indifferent to his view that Guatemala's fears were exaggerated.[123]

Unlike the solidarity, the impact of these pressures upon the United Nations and the OAS is open to doubt. For one thing, Belize is removed from those parts of the world, notably Africa, where international attention is focussed on the struggles for self-determination. For another thing, the independent Caribbean countries have little collective weight in the international forums. This is particularly true in the OAS. As newcomers and English-speaking countries they have the problem of establishing their own legitimacy within the Organization. This is not unrelated to the Latin Americans' attitude to the expansion of the Organization. The Latin American countries may recognize the hemispheric destiny of the English-speaking Caribbean countries, and the corollary that their independent development depends upon regional co-operation.[124] Nevertheless, they are likely to view the membership of those countries in the OAS as a contamination of the Latin culture and solidarity. In this regard, Belize, although Spanish-speaking to some extent, is not regarded as a *bona fide* Latin American country. It is seen primarily as a member of the Commonwealth Caribbean States and its accession to CARICOM reinforces this view.

Perhaps also Latin America is reluctant to open its doors to too many Commonwealth Caribbean countries for political and economic reasons. As the Associated States become independent and seek admission into the OAS, they are likely to constitute a Commonwealth Caribbean bloc, and in consequence upset the voting balance. The admission of these countries would merely increase the demand upon the financial and technical resources of the Inter-American Development Bank. The Commonwealth countries have indeed argued that without these resources their efforts to achieve economic independence would be impeded and even jeopardized.[125] Whatever may be the general response to these contentions, the OAS would be under Guatemalan pressure to render little assistance to Belize's economic development unless this is linked to that of Peten. For, in the final analysis and however indirect, it is Belize's economic destiny that Guatemala seeks to control.

In effect, therefore, the diplomatic support of the Commonwealth Caribbean for Belize's political aspirations does not bring the problem substantially closer to solution. The international and regional odds are still against the country's survival as an independent entity. Thus the problem of the country's multiple external association and its future remains as intractable as when the nationalist movement came into existence in 1950.

# Conclusion: decolonization and national integration

This study has related the process of decolonization in Belize in such a way that attention has been focussed on the problem of national integration. Both the process of decolonization and the problem of national integration are multi-dimensional. One of the dimensions of decolonization was the political differences between the young nationalist politicians and the colonial oligarchy. There was nothing novel about this conflict. The political ferment is associated with a specific event, the devaluation of the Belize dollar in December 1949, in the same way as the beginning of nationalist political development in the Commonwealth West Indies is associated with the series of disturbances in the 1930s. Like the situation in those territories the political agitation in Belize climaxed a long period of gestation. It was the memories of the harsh conditions of the 1930s and 1940s that sustained the nationalist movement long after the devaluation of the dollar had been forgotten. Like the movements in many other colonial territories, the PUP had to fight for its legitimacy. It was not until 1960 that the colonial government tacitly recognized the new political elite as its successor. The constitutional structure was then reshaped to accommodate two parallel systems – the colonial and the emergent Belize-controlled governments.

If this new structure was designed to favour nationalist interest there is still considerable difference in opinion as to how this could be achieved. Independence should be the ultimate outcome of this transitional arrangement. But with every unsuccessful attempt to resolve the Anglo-Guatemala dispute the nationalist goal recedes.

The second dimension of decolonization stems from the first. Hardly had the political differences between the young local political elite and the colonial oligarchy begun than the familiar pattern of conflict in a decolonizing situation became evident in Belize. The popular movement was opposed by the old political elite and then torn assunder by internal strife. It is this conflict among Belizeans that has determined the dimension of the problem of national integration. Our analysis shows that this conflict did

325

not arise purely and simply from the cultural and regional differences between the Protestant Creoles in Belize City and the Roman Catholic Mestizos in the outdistricts. The cleavage also arose from the attempt by the upper social stratum to retain its dominance of the political leadership. Indeed, without consideration of social class our picture of Belize society would have been incomplete.

Yet it is exactly this factor of social class that the plural society theory neglects. But before we discuss the inadequacy of this theory with respect to political change in Belize it is appropriate to recall that views expressed on the place of cultural pluralism in the West Indies can be sharply opposed even when they are based on studies of the same society. On the one hand, R. T. Smith maintains that the cultural differences between the Africans and East Indians in Guyana are residual, the East Indians being as much acculturated as the Africans to the Creole norms.[1] On the other hand Leo Despres found that Africans and East Indians in Guyana form separate and comparatively different kinds of social communities.[2] In his view there are no social structures which serve to bring Africans and East Indians together in the expression of a common system of cultural values at the communal level of socio-cultural integration.[3] At the national level it is mainly those government agencies which serve to co-ordinate activities and regulate relations throughout the society that are culturally integrative. Even then, Despres contends, the cultural differences are so formidable that those national, or what he terms 'broker', institutions are unable to generate a national culture equally acceptable to both groups.[4]

The divergent views held on the scope of cultural pluralism in a changing social and political order may well be correct in themselves. Both represent a partial view of the changing order: they are an expression partly of the ambiguities of the concept of cultural pluralism itself and partly of the fluidity in the total social system.[5] Political development in Guyana in the early 1960s was characterized by racial strife. Into the riotous forms of racial expression, however, could have been read several 'hidden' features. R. T. Smith therefore warns that while ethnicity may be invoked and even perceived as the major cleavage in Guyana, it may be an expression of quite different bases of conflict.[6] Despres also recognizes that the conflict was not entirely racial but also resulted from 'ideological factionalism that erupted to the surface within the People's Progressive Party [in the 1950s], the organization of a conservative opposition to the movement, and the internal pressures that were generated by external international developments'.[7] Even M. G. Smith, the principal exponent of the plural society notion in the West Indies, in a foreword to Despres' book concedes that the plural structure of Guyanese society did not retain 'an unchanging character, form, and significance through these [nationalist political] developments', but varied greatly in 'nature, scope, and composition'.[8] But it is precisely these changes in the character of the plural society that R. T. Smith interprets differently.

In our study of Belize, we were confronted with the same problem of identifying and determining the importance of the cultural factor in the political process, even though the cultural differences between the Creole and Mestizo complexes are much more marked than between any two cultural sections in the West Indies. Following Despres' analytical model, most of the institutions and in particular the political parties which we have analysed are 'broker' institutions because they link the outdistricts to the urban headquarters. However, the basic or local institutions were also discussed. The differences between the Indian and Creole family and kinship system and their implications for the traditional local government arrangements in the villages were observed at the outset of the study. The Alcalde system rests on customs that are alien to the Creoles and Caribs; hence its failure in the Carib villages. Social contacts between the Indians and the Creoles, and even between the Maya and Kekehi Indians, are minimized by linguistic differences. Nor is this contact improved by the differing occupational preferences of each group. Within the forestry industries, the domain of the Indian and the Creole is chicle-bleeding and mahogany-working respectively. The location of the two major agricultural export crops, sugar and citrus, in separate regions offers little opportunity for cultural integration. Nor does the organization of most of the trade unions on a regional and industrial basis encourage working-class consciousness to cut across ethnic and cultural affiliations.

Although to a lesser extent, the cultural differences are also maintained in the core remunerative and prestigious occupations. The Creoles virtually monopolize the professions and the civil service. Although there are several industrial and commercial organizations in which both cultural groups are involved, inter-cultural partnerships are limited as personal and family connections, especially among the Mestizos, play a dominant role in the choice of local business associates. The denominational system prevents education from fully exerting its unifying influence. As we have seen, the educational experience of a Creole student in a Protestant secondary school is devoid of social contact with his Mestizo counterpart. And because of their different external connections the Roman Catholic and Protestant educational institutions are incapable of fostering new national values that are equally acceptable to both the Creoles and the Mestizos.

It is when we try to establish the relationship between cultural identity and political behaviour that the structural model of the plural society receives its crucial test. In our discussion of political parties we saw that the conservative opposition to the nationalist movement in the 1950s, though consisting mainly of professional Creoles, was by no means based solely on cultural considerations. It also represented the cream of the Belizean middle class whose members were seeking to deny their defeat by ritualizing the values and positions associated with their previous hegemony. Their apprehension sprang not only from the PUP's Central American orientation but also from the fact that they were being displaced by a new social group which, it should be emphasized, was predominantly Creole.

Preoccupied with their discussion of the new political leaders, the 'plural' theorists tend to overlook the resilience of the old conservative group in the West Indies. That members of this group in various territories are not politically popular does not necessarily mean that they have ceased to influence the political process and act in the interest of their socio-economic class. Many of them in fact return to the political leadership through a variety of channels because the nationalist politicians, determined to retain power, enter into compromises of one kind or another. In Belize where the nationalist leaders never interpreted their role in terms of a radical ideology, the old political elite has had little difficulty in retrieving some of its influence. Despite the political changes, J. W. MacMillan, OBE, a wealthy local white businessman and a Presbyterian Church leader, was a parliamentarian for seventeen years (1948–65) without contesting an election. Nor was it necessary for him to be a PUP member in order to become the first Minister of Education, Health and Housing in the PUP government in 1961. The outstanding case is that of Harrison Courtenay who, after fading from the political scene in the 1950s, became the legal adviser to the PUP government on the Guatemalan and constitutional issues in the 1960s and ended his political career in 1974 as the Speaker of the House of Representatives, but not before he was knighted in 1973. Despite its cultural differentiation the business community became one of the most politically revitalized group in Belize in the late 1960s. Through its weekly medium, *The Reporter*, the Belize Chamber of Commerce continuously exerts pressure upon the political process on behalf of its members and their American associates. If the conflicts within the society are not expressed in terms of social class, it is not because the cultural differences override the economic differences between the business and professional components of the middle class on the one hand and the labouring community on the other. It is rather because of the politicians' belief in the sanctity of private enterprise, and the moderate, divided and inarticulate trade union leadership.

In terms of our own argument at the beginning of the study about elite displacement, we can see that this process has been qualified at several crucial points. The role of the civil servants remains decisive in many spheres. Their relatively vast bureaucratic and professional resources and the sociological setting of their relationship to the wider community ensure this. The business component of the middle class has reasserted its influence and, largely because of the dearth of talent in the PUP, members of the high status families are being readmitted into its political leadership.

If we concentrate on the nationalist politicians it cannot be denied that the major PUP split in 1956 had its source in Price's Central American commitments and their implications for the cultural and social character of an independent Belize. This was expressed in the differing reactions of the two PUP factions to their accommodation within the colonial framework and in the subsequent organizational strategies of the PUP. Although his Creole connections are not tenuous Price had less to lose culturally than the other political leaders from closer political relationship with Guatemala. The cultural groups within the fragmented movement were, however, never completely polarized. While the national leadership of the opposition to the PUP remained highly sectional that of the PUP became more culturally varied. It may be argued that in the absence of ideological differences in Belize and given the PUP's electoral success and consequential ability to distribute favours and rewards, the party had little difficulty in improving its multi-cultural image. At the same time, however, the split and the subsequent developments have not produced a national leader whose culture is primarily Mestizo. All of the outdistrict elected representatives are local notables. Their 'outside' relationship was until the relocation of the capital in 1970 almost entirely with the urban headquarters, Belize City. Also, it was and still is confined mainly to attending meetings of the House of Representatives, the Senate and party caucuses. Again it can be argued that this merely shows that the political integration of Belize society is based upon a system of social relations between cultural units of unequal status and power.

According to the plural society model one also expects that after they had split, Price and Goldson would appeal more and more to cultural sentiments and that the electorate would respond appropriately to it. As we have seen the PUP has not regained its share of the urban Creole support which in fact continuously dropped, except in the 1961 election, from 67.2 per cent in the 1954 election to 50.2 per cent in the 1974 election. This could be attributed entirely to the cultural factor but for the fact that the party's support has also declined in the Mestizo constituencies. The decline is particularly marked among those Mestizos of Mexican origin whose fears of a possible Central American association in which Guatemala is involved had been released by the elimination of the West Indies Federation issue. In other words, they had endorsed Price's Central American policy in the past not because it was inherently advantageous to them but because it was the lesser of two evils. We also noted that the PUP's strength is greater in the villages than in the towns, irrespective of their cultural composition. For example, the percentage of the PUP poll in the predominantly Creole rural constituency, Belize Rural South, was greater in the 1961 and the 1965 elections than in the sizeable Mestizo town constituency, Orange Walk North. In one the PUP received 81.2 per cent of the votes in 1961 and 70.2 per cent in 1965; in the other its share of votes was 57.5 per cent and 56.0 per cent. As we have argued, the explanation for this voting pattern is socio-economic. The difference in behaviour supports Lipset's thesis that communities which are poor and inadequately exposed to the possibilities of change, as are the village communities in Belize, are more conservative than those which are better off and are more aware of a better way of life.[9]

It must be emphasized that until we add the socio-economic dimension to our analysis of multi-racial and multi-cultural societies our picture will never be complete. The West Indies Federation, on which the *middle*-class Creoles had pinned their hopes, is dead, and even if it is resurrected as seems possible with the recent development of regional economic integration the *mass* of Creoles and the Mestizos for differing reasons still would not wish to be saved by it. These Creoles fear the economic competition from a large influx of immigrants – an apprehension which is more a reflection of the slow economic growth than the industry of West Indians. For their part, the Mestizos fear the inevitable reinforcement of the Creole culture.

As an important element in the political process, economic issues came more to the forefront in the late 1960s when a few motivated university graduates returned with new ideas and issues. As V. S. Naipaul, the Trinidadian novelist, observed after a visit to Belize in 1969, 'The sons of people once content with the Premier's benediction go away to study. They come back and curse both parties. They talk of Vietnam and Black Power. They undermine the Negro loyalty to the slave past.'[10] Unlike previous generations of professionals, the group's conception of nationalism appeared to be more than a projection of its status yearning. But as we observed few political figures in this small society can successfully resist the pressures to conform and accept the conventional mould. In consequence the new political figures have either been co-opted into the dominant PUP, withdrawn from active politics or moderated their radical political programme. Nonetheless, Belize has not been completely outdone by the other Third World countries in the assertion of economic nationalism, as is evident in its most recent move to regulate the ownership and use of land by aliens. This was sufficiently drastic to bring the government once more into conflict with the business community which, prompted by the approaching election in December 1974, renewed its quest for allies among the other political parties. Economic considerations are also likely to give rise to political presures upon the government from another occupational group. This group is the Indian and Mestizo sugar growers in the north. If our assessment of their relationship to the national political process is correct, sooner or later they will demand a greater measure of political influence and centrality commensurate with the significant contribution of the sugar industry to the economy. Like most Third World societies, the benefits of incipient economic development are also unevenly distributed, and this produces social and political tensions. These economic issues have been obscured throughout the period of decolonization by the absence of a radical ideological outlook in every political quarter and the preoccupation of the political parties with the Guatemalan claim. The latter issue has encouraged Belizeans to think of their cultural differences as conflicting and incapable of yielding a common social purpose. But although the political implications of the problem for the country's future as a whole should not be underestimated there is a tired air about it and the neglected issues for the first time have a chance of commanding more attention. As this occurs, it is becoming clear that the competition for power and real conflict are going to arise over socio-economic issues although they are still likely to be perceived in cultural terms until the impact of the incipient economic development is deeply felt throughout the country.

# APPENDIX

## Draft treaty between the United Kingdom of Great Britain and Northern Ireland and the Republic of Guatemala relating to the resolution of the dispute over British Honduras (Belize)

Her Majesty The Queen of the United Kingdom of Great Britain and Northern Ireland and of Her other Realms and Territories, Head of the Commonwealth, and The President of the Republic of Guatemala:

Mindful of the request made by Her Britannic Majesty's Government in the United Kingdom and the Government of the Republic of Guatemala to the Government of the United States of America to mediate in the dispute over British Honduras (Belize) and to formulate suggestions on the basis of which the Government of the United Kingdom and the Government of Guatemala might be able to arrive at a final resolution of the dispute;

Taking note, with appreciation, of the suggestions which have been conveyed by the Government of the United States through its representative, Ambassador Bethuel M. Webster;

Reaffirming their desire to strengthen the friendly relations between the peoples and Governments of the United Kingdom and Guatemala;

Recognizing the common interests of the people of British Honduras (Belize), the people of Guatemala, and the other peoples of Central America, and desiring to increase the ties of friendship between the people of British Honduras (Belize) and the people of Guatemala;

Further recognizing that peaceful settlement of the dispute, which for many years has unfortunately harmed the relations of the United Kingdom and Guatemala, is desirable for the successful development of, and the security of, the area concerned;

Desiring to achieve the resolution of the dispute in such a way that the position and rights of both High Contracting Parties are reconciled with the interests and aspirations of the people of British Honduras (Belize), and in such a way that the relationship of British Honduras (Belize) with Guatemala, and consequently, in the near future, with Central America, is constructively resolved;

Have decided to conclude this Treaty and have appointed as their Plenipotentiaries for this purpose;

Her Majesty the Queen of the United Kingdom of Great Britain and Northern Ireland and of Her other Realms and Territories, Head of the Commonwealth:

The President of the Republic of Guatemala:

332

Who, having communicated to each other their respective full powers, which were found in good and durable form, have agreed as follows:

ARTICLE 1

(1) The territory heretofore referred to by Her Britannic Majesty as British Honduras shall be known as Belize after the appointed date mentioned in paragraph (2) of this Article and shall hereafter in this Treaty be referred to as Belize.

(2) On a date hereinafter referred to as 'the appointed date', which shall not be later than December 31, 1970, the Government of the United Kingdom shall grant to Belize its independence from the United Kingdom and shall transfer to Belize supreme authority in respect of Belize. Thereafter sole responsibility for, and the right to exercise, all and any powers, both internal and external, of government, administration, legislation, and jurisdiction shall vest in Belize.

(3) The exercise of the authority described in paragraph (2) shall be consistent with the international obligations of Belize including the treaties under which it has assumed such obligations. The Government of the United Kingdom shall take measure to secure that Belize, on the appointed date, accedes to this Treaty, thereby assuming the obligations, responsibilities, rights and benefits under this Treaty which apply to Belize.

ARTICLE 2

(1) Using one or more transit routes, the products of Guatemala may be exported, and any goods destined to Guatemala may be imported, through Belize without Belize imposing tariffs, duties, taxes, or any other restrictions of that nature. Nothing shall be done to impose restrictions upon the proper use of the transit routes. A transit route is hereby established along the roads indicated in the Annex to this Treaty leading from Belize City and Stann Creek Town to Melchor de Mencos. Other transit routes may be established by decision of the Authority established under Article 9 of this Treaty.

(2) The products of Belize may be exported, and any goods destined to Belize may be imported, through Guatemala without Guatemala imposing tariffs, duties, taxes, or any other restrictions of that nature.

ARTICLE 3

(1) Areas within the ports of Belize City and Commerce Bight, as agreed between Belize and Guatemala, shall be set aside as duty-free ports for the use of Guatemala under the control of the Authority established under Article 9 of this Treaty. Belize and Guatemala may agree to establish other duty-free port areas to be under the control of the Authority.

(2) By duty-free port is meant, for the purpose of this Article, a place to which merchant vessels of all States shall be allowed unrestricted access (within the limits of the facilities available) for loading of goods from, and unloading

of goods destined for, Guatemala. The importation of such goods into, their export from, transit through, or storage within the duty-free port shall be free from any payment of duties or taxes, but no charges reasonably levied for services rendered. Operations necessary for the preservation, sale, shipment or disposal of such goods shall be permitted within the area of the duty-free port, but nothing in this Article shall authorize the manufacture of goods within that area, without permission of the Government of Belize.

(3) The Government of Guatemala shall, at the request of the Government of Belize, make available duty-free areas in Guatemala, as agreed between Belize and Guatemala, for the loading of goods from, and unloading of goods destined for, Belize.

ARTICLE 4

(1) Subject to regulation by the Authority established under Article 9 of this Treaty, Belizeans and Guatemalans may travel freely between and within Belize and Guatemala without presentation of documents other than valid identification documents issued

(a) in the case of Guatemalans, by the authorities of Guatemala; or

(b) in the case of Belizeans, by the authority of Belize; or

(c) in the case of Belizeans or Guatemalans, by the Authority established under Article 9 of this Treaty, pursuant to regulations to be formulated by the appropriate authorities of Belize and Guatemala.

(2) Belizeans shall be accorded in Guatemala the same treatment that is accorded Guatemalans, and Guatemalans shall be accorded in Belize the same treatment that is accorded Belizeans, with respect to the protection and security of the following personal and property rights:

(a) access to courts of justice and to administrative tribunals and agencies, both in pursuit and defense of their rights;

(b) engaging in commercial, industrial, financial and other activities for gain, subject to local labor legislation, and scientific, educational, religious and philanthropic activities;

(c) acquiring and disposing of property, including testate and intestate succession;

(d) obtaining and maintaining patents of invention, rights in trademark, trade names and trade labels;

(e) the assumption of undertakings for, and the making of, payments, remittances and transfers of moneys and financial interests.

(3) The Government of Belize and the Government of Guatemala shall conclude arrangements to secure the return to the one from the other of persons accused or convicted of criminal offenses.

(4) This Article does not affect rights of Belize or Guatemala to deport from their territories undesirable persons.

ARTICLE 5

The transportation and communication facilities of Belize and Guatemala shall, insofar as they involve co-operation between Belize and Guatemala shall, proved and co-ordinated as soon as practicable and, where feasible, integrated, by means to be determined by the Authority established under Article 9 of this Treaty. The Authority shall, as soon as it is established, take steps to achieve this objective. These steps shall include provision by the Authority for the construction or improvement of a road which shall provide an effective link between Belize and Guatemala. The Government of the United Kingdom shall, through its contribution to the funds of the Authority pursuant to Article 9 of this Treaty, assist in that endeavor.

ARTICLE 6

(1) Educational degrees, certificates and diplomas recognized in Belize shall in Guatemala be accorded the same significance as, and shall be recognized as evidence of achievement in the same manner as, those of Guatemala of equivalent level; and educational degrees, certificates and diplomas recognized in Guatemala shall in Belize be accorded the same significance as, and shall be recognized as evidence of achievement in the same manner as, those of Belize of equivalent level. Degrees, certificates or diplomas granted outside Belize or Guatemala shall be excluded from the provisions of this Article.

(2) The Authority established under Article 9 of this Treaty shall organize educational exchange programs under which students from Belize may study at, and receive valid degrees and diplomas from, Guatemalan educational institutions and under which Guatemalan students may study at, and receive valid degrees and diplomas from, Belizean educational institutions.

(3) Exchanges in the cultural field shall also be arranged by the aforementioned Authority.

ARTICLE 7

(1) Belize and Guatemala undertake, through the Authority established under Article 9 of this Treaty, to co-operate in furthering the exchange and use of scientific and technical knowledge, particularly in the interests of increasing productivity and improving standards of living within their respective territories.

(2) Studies and programs relating to cultural and scientific resources of mutual interest and to land use and soil improvement, watershed management and protection, wildlife protection, and nutrition and health of Belize and of Guatemala shall be initiated, and thereafter regulations relating thereto shall be promulgated, under the supervision of the Authority established under Article 9 of this Treaty.

ARTICLE 8

(1) Belizean vehicles of all types, for land, water and air transport, may enter into, and travel in, Guatemala subject to no greater restrictions and conditions than those imposed on vehicles of Guatemala; and Guatemalan vehicles of all types, for land, water and air transport, may enter into, and travel in, Belize subject to no greater restrictions and conditions than vehicles of Belize. Vehicles of Belize traveling in Guatemala shall not be required to be licensed or registered in Guatemala, and vehicles of Guatemala traveling in Belize shall not be required to be licensed or registered in Belize.

(2) Paragraph (1) of this Article:

(*a*) does not pertain to the travel of military vehicles of any type;

(*b*) does not authorize Belizean or Guatemalan vehicles of any type to engage in the schedule carriage by air or otherwise of persons or goods for remuneration or hire, whether such carriage is solely between points in the territories of Belize or Guatemala, or originates at or continues to one or more points outside either of those territories. After the appointed date such carriage shall be regulated by the Authority established under Article 9 of this Treaty, although the negotiation and grant of air traffic or air transit rights and all matters appertaining thereto shall remain a matter to be settled between the Government of Belize and the Government of Guatemala.

ARTICLE 9

(1) The Government of Belize and the Government of Guatemala shall establish an Authority for the purpose of performing the functions conferred upon the Authority in Articles 2 through 8 of this Treaty, and shall take all measures, including the enactment of legislation, as may be necessary to ensure the proper functioning and administration of the Authority.

(2) The Authority shall consist of seven Members. Within 30 days of the entry into force of this Treaty, the Government of Belize and the Government of Guatemala shall each appoint three Members, all of Ministerial rank. Within 45 days of the end of that period, the Members so appointed shall appoint a person of international prominence as the seventh Member, who will serve as Chairman. If the Members are unable to appoint a seventh Member within the period referred to, they shall request the Government of the United States to make such an appointment.

(3) The Authority shall have the powers necessary to enable it to perform its functions, and, in addition to any other powers expressly provided in the present Treaty, the Authority shall have the power to:

(*a*) initiate and perform or supervise studies necessary to the performance of its functions;

(b) promulgate such regulations and issue such directives as may be necessary for the Authority to perform its functions or for the internal administration of the Authority's affairs;

(*c*) take such action to enforce the regulations and directives referred to in paragraph (3)(*b*) of this Article as may be both necessary and consistent with the laws where such enforcement takes place;

(*d*) take steps to obtain technical assistance and external financial support in order to enable it to formulate and to carry out its plans in connection with the exercise of its functions;

(*e*) levy reasonable fees and charges for services performed by it in the exercise of its functions;

(*f*) suggest legislation that may be necessary in Belize or Guatemala for the performance of its functions; and

(*g*) perform other acts which it may be authorized to perform by both the Government of Belize and the Government of Guatemala.

(4) Decisions of the Authority shall be taken by a majority of the three Members appointed by the Government of Belize and the three Members appointed by the Government of Guatemala. In the event of their votes being equally divided the Chairman shall have a casting vote.

(5) The Chairman shall be a full-time servant of the Authority.

(6) The seat of the Authority shall be Belize City, but the Authority may establish other offices at convenient locations.

(7) The Government of Belize and the Government of Guatemala shall by agreement fix the terms of employment and salaries of the Members of the Authority.

(8) The Authority may recruit such staff and acquire such facilities as are necessary for it to fulfill its functions. Its administrative expenses shall be covered by Belize and Guatemala in proportion to their budgetary resources.

(9) Subject to the provisions of paragraph (10) of this Article, the United Kingdom shall pay to the Authority, to assist it to perform its functions under this Treaty, and in such installments and at such times as the Authority may need,

(*i*) the sterling equivalent of United States dollars 4,000,000; and

(*ii*) the balance, if any, of the sum referred to in paragraph (4) of Article 10 of the Treaty, which may be unexpected on the appointed date.

(10) The payments made by the United Kingdom in accordance with the provisions of paragraph (9) of this Article and of paragraph (4) of Article 10 shall not exceed in total in any one year the sterling equivalent of United States dollars 1,200,000. For the purpose of this paragraph, each year shall be deemed to commence on the same day and the same month as those on which this Treaty enters into force. Except as provided in this Article, the United Kingdom shall have no obligation to pay any sum to the Authority.

ARTICLE 10

(1) With a view to developing and strengthening the agricultural, industrial and commercial activities of Belize and of Guatemala, and to permitting the

association of Belize with the economic integration of Central America and ultimately with the broader economic integration of the Hemisphere, the Government of the United Kingdom shall undertake studies relating to the participation of Belize in the institutions and treaties of the Central American economic community.

(2) At such time as Belize should decide to join the Central American Common Market, the Government of the United Kingdom shall arrange to continue for a transitional period (envisaged as being not less than ten years after joining the Central American Common Market) to accord the primary produce of Belize, when imported into the United Kingdom, tariff treatment which is no less favourable than that accorded to such products which are the produce of other Commonwealth countries, insofar as those countries receive that treatment by virtue solely of their membership of the Commonwealth Preference Area. Belize for its part shall give sympathetic consideration to the continuance of preferential tariff arrangements during the same period for goods from the United Kingdom when imported into Belize.

(3) Guatemala shall use its good offices with the other countries of Central America to secure the acceptance of Belize in the various institutions and treaties of the Central American community.

(4) Should the Government of Belize, with the agreement of the Government of the United Kingdom, enter, before the appointed date, into one or more of the institutions of the community referred to in paragraph (1) of this Article, the Government of the United Kingdom shall pay to the Government of Belize such sums, not exceeding in total the sterling equivalent of United States dollars, 1,000,000 and subject to paragraph (10) of Article 9 of this Treaty, as it may need to enable any financial obligations to be discharged which it incurs on such entry and which come due before the appointed date.

ARTICLE 11

(1) Documents of all types duly issued in Guatemala shall not require authentication for acceptance by the courts or administrative authorities or agencies of Belize, and documents of all types duly issued in Belize shall not require authentication for acceptance by the courts or administrative authorities or agencies of Guatemala. The foregoing does not affect the probative efficacy of the documents.

(2) The authorities and courts of Guatemala shall, at the request of the courts of Belize, render judicial assistance in cases pending before the courts of Belize, and the authorities and courts of Belize shall, at the courts of Guatemala, render judicial assistance in cases pending before the courts of Guatemala.

ARTICLE 12

The authorities of Belize and Guatemala shall consult and cooperate in the use of police resources in matters of internal security and mutual interest affecting Belize and Guatemala.

ARTICLE 13

(1) In the formulation and conduct of their foreign policies, the Government of Belize and the Government of Guatemala shall consult and cooperate on such matters of external affairs of mutual concern as may be raised by either the Government of Belize or the Government of Guatemala.

(2) After the appointed date, the Government of Guatemala shall afford assistance to the Government of Belize in the conduct of its international relations. In particular, when requested, the Government of Guatemala shall:

(*a*) act as the channel for communications between the Government of Belize and other governments and international organizations;

(*b*) undertake the representation of the Government of Belize at any international conference at which Belize is entitled to be represented;

(*c*) supply the Government of Belize with information concerning international affairs;

(*d*) undertake the diplomatic protection of nationals of Belize in other countries and perform consular functions on their behalf.

(3) Before the appointed date, the Government of the United Kingdom and the Government of Guatemala shall consult on matters of mutual concern affecting the foreign affairs of the Central American area.

(4) After the accession of Belize to this Treaty, the Government shall support the entry of Belize into the Central American community and into the Inter-American community and in particular into the Organization of Central American States, the Organization of American States, and the Inter-American Development Bank.

ARTICLE 14

(1) After the appointed date, the Government of Belize and the Government of Guatemala shall conclude arrangements concerning matters of external defense of mutual concern to Belize and Guatemala. These matters shall include:

(*a*) Measures considered necessary for the defense of the approaches to Belize.

(*b*) Consultation and coordination in case of any external threat to the security of Belize.

(*c*) The use of port facilities in Belize for repair, refueling, victualing and maintenance of those Guatemalan naval units which have been requested to assist the security forces of Belize in the external defense of Belize.

(2) The Government of Belize and the Government of Guatemala shall establish a Joint Consultative Committee which shall meet regularly to consider those matters of external defense governed by the arrangements referred to in Paragraph (1).

(3) The defence of Belize should be handled within the framework of the

Inter-American Treaty of Reciprocal Assistance signed at Rio de Janeiro on September 2, 1947, to which Belize should become a party, to the end that Belize would not need to conclude bilateral defense arrangements with other countries.

ARTICLE 15

Any dispute as to the application and interpretation of this Treaty shall be settled by negotiation, enquiry, good offices, mediation, conciliation, arbitration, judicial settlement, resort to regional agencies or arrangements, or other peaceful means of the parties' choice.

ARTICLE 16

In view of the foregoing, the United Kingdom and Guatemala affirm that their dispute over Belize has been honorably and finally resolved and accordingly that the mediation by the Government of the United States is concluded.

ARTICLE 17

This Treaty shall be ratified and the instruments of ratification shall be exchanged at Washington, D.C. as soon as possible. It shall enter into force on the date of exchange of the instruments of ratification, provided that if the Government of the United Kingdom does not secure, in accordance with Article 1 (3) of this Treaty, the accession of Belize, this Treaty shall be deemed to have no force and effect and the Parties shall be relieved of all obligations hereunder.

IN WITNESS WHEREOF, the above-mentioned Plenipotentiaries have signed this Treaty and afixed thereto their seals.

DONE in duplicate at Washington, D.C. this...day of..., 196 , in the Spanish and English languages, both equally authentic.

FOR HER BRITANNIC MAJESTY:

• • •

FOR THE PRESIDENT OF THE REPUBLIC OF GUATEMALA:

• • •

# NOTES

NOTES TO PREFACE

1 Lloyd Braithwaite, 'The present status of the social sciences in the British Caribbean' in Vera Rubin (ed.), *Caribbean Studies: a Symposium*, Washington 1960, p. 102.

NOTES TO INTRODUCTION

1 For natural disasters see Ernest E. Cain, *Cyclone*, London 1932; Arthur H. Stockwell, *Cyclone Hattie*, Ilfracombe 1963; and Ray I. Tannehull, *Hurricanes...their nature and history, particularly those of the West Indies and the Southern coasts of the United States*, Princeton 1938.
2 Kevin C. Kearns, 'Belmopan, Prospects of a new Capital', *The Geographical Review*, April 1973, vol. LXIII, no. 2.
3 *Population Census 1970*, Series B, Belmopan, n.d.
4 Kathleen M. Stahl, *The Metropolitan Organization of British Colonial Trade*, London 1951, p. 31.
5 Sir Samuel Hoare, a British Foreign Secretary, who had visited the colony in his capacity as a director of the Company in 1921 wrote an article in which he deplored the neglect of the 'country's considerable natural resources': 'The problem of Crown colony government in the Caribbean', *Nineteenth Century Magazine*, April 1921. Reprinted in the *Belize Independent*, 8 January 1936, p. 8.
6 Stahl, *Metropolitan Organization of British Colonial Trade*, p. 31.
7 *Ibid.*
8 *Ibid.*
9 George L. Beckford, *Persistent Poverty: Underdevelopment in Plantation Economies of the Third World*, London 1972, pp. 246–7.
10 N. S. Carey-Jones, *The Pattern of a Dependent Economy: the National Income of British Honduras*, Cambridge 1953, p. 18.
11 Governor Lynch, Jamaica, to Council of Plantations, C. 01/28 no. 27, 10 March 1671. Cited in J. Burdon, *Archives of British Honduras*, London 1931, vol. I, p. 51.
12 Wayne M. Clegern, *British Honduras: Colonial Dead End 1859–1900*, Louisiana 1967, p. 214.
13 N. S. Carey-Jones, *Pattern of a Dependent Economy*, p. 18.

341

14 *Report of the Tripartite Economic Survey of British Honduras*, May 1966, Belize City, pp. 15–18.
15 Charles Wagley, 'Plantation America: a Culture sphere' in Vera Rubin (ed.), *Caribbean Studies: a Symposium*, Washington 1960, pp. 3–13.
16 Gordon Lewis, *The Growth of the Modern West Indies*, New York 1968, pp. 289–307.
17 West India Royal Commission, 1938–39 Report, London, HMSO 1945 (Cmnd 6607).
18 D. A. G. Waddell, *British Honduras*, London 1961, pp. 109–42.
19 R. T. Smith, *British Guiana*, London 1962, pp. 163–83.
20 Selwyn D. Ryan, *Race and Nationalism in Trinidad and Tobago*, Toronto 1972, pp. 120–27.
21 Morley Ayearst, 'A note on some characteristics of West Indian political parties', *Social and Economic Studies*, September 1954, vol. 3, no. 2.
22 C. H. Grant, 'The civil service strike in British Honduras: a case study of politics and the civil service', *Caribbean Quarterly*, September 1966, vol. 12, no. 3, University of the West Indies, pp. 37–49.
23 D. A. G. Waddell, *British Honduras*, p. 129.
24 *The Daily Clarion*, 22 August 1945.
25 *Ibid.*
26 J. C. S. and M. C. S. Sologaistoa, *Guide to British Honduras*, London 1919, p. 83.
27 The *Belize Billboard*, 1 October 1950.
28 *Ibid.*
29 Selwyn D. Ryan, *Race and Nationalism in Trinidad*, p. 433.
30 Burton Benedict (ed.), *Problems of Smaller Territories*, London 1967.
31 D. P. J. Wood, 'The smaller territories: some political considerations' in Burton Benedict (ed.), *Problems of Smaller Territories*, p. 33.
32 Gordon Lewis, *The Growth of the Modern West Indies*, pp. 289–307.
33 *The Belize Times*, 9 May 1968.
34 G.B. House of Commons Debates, 21 May 1968, vol. 765, col. 275.
35 Derek Courtenay, 'Constitutional development: Antigua', *Parliamentarian*, vol. XLVII, no. 3, July 1966, pp. 253–5.
36 *Belize: New Nation in Central America*, Belizean Independence Secretariat, February 1972, p. 2.
37 In the West Indies the terms 'East Indians' and 'Amerindians' are used to refer to descendants from India and to the Aboriginal Indians respectively. In most of the territories the prefix 'East' is not normally used whereas in Belize this prefix is retained and that in Amerindian is discarded. The use of these terms in the study follows the practice in Belize.
38 *Population Census of Belize 1970*. Working population – Part 1, Belmopan, p. 12.
39 *Census of British Honduras 1960*, Kingston, 2 vols.
40 Algar Robert Gregg, *British Honduras*, London 1968, p. 59.
41 *West Indian Census 1946*, Part E Kingston, p. 14.
42 D. A. G. Waddell, *British Honduras*, p. 17.
43 Douglas MacRae Taylor, *The Black Carib of British Honduras*, New York 1951.

44 Jocelyne Kharusi, 'Patterns of migration and indices of urbanization in Belize, British Honduras', unpublished M.A. thesis, McGill University 1970.

45 *Report of the Sugar Industry Commission of Enquiry (1963) British Honduras* (Chairman Gilbert Rodwell Hulse), March 1971, p. 8.

46 J. Eric Thompson, 'Ethnology of the Mayas of Southern and Central British Honduras', p. 3 in *Field Museum of Natural History, Anthropological Series*, vol. XVII, no. 2, Chicago 1930.

47 J. Burdon, *Archives of British Honduras*, vol. 3, p. 306.

48 *British Honduras Gazette*, no. 44, 23 August 1958.

49 Stephen L. Caiger, *British Honduras: Past and Present*, London 1951, p. 179.

50 R. T. Smith, *The Negro Family in British Guiana*, London 1956, pp. 191–4, and M. G. Smith, *The Plural Society in the West Indies*, Berkeley 1965, pp. 307–8.

51 M. G. Smith, *Stratification in Grenada*, Seattle 1962.

52 Douglas Taylor, *The Black Carib of British Honduras*.

53 A second such area centred in Peru and included parts of what are now Ecuador, Bolivia, and north-western Argentina. The resilience of this early civilization in these areas has been such that about one-half of the population of Peru, Ecuador and Bolivia still live as Indians. See George I. Blankstein, 'The Politics of Latin America' in Almond and Coleman (eds), *The Politics of the Developing Areas*, Princeton 1960, pp. 455–531.

54 J. E. S. Thompson, *The Rise and Fall of the Mayan Civilization*, London 1954, pp. 100–23.

55 J. Burdon, *Archives of British Honduras*, vol. 1, p. 4.

56 *Ibid.*, vol. 3, pp. 6–22.

57 *Ibid.*

58 *The Handbook of British Honduras for 1888–1889*, compiled by Lindsay, Bristowe and Wright, London 1889.

59 *Local Ordinance 31, 19 March 1858*, chap. 13. Cited in *The Handbook of British Honduras for 1891 and 1892*, p. 132.

60 'The Battleground', *Tropical Battleground 1851–1951, a Centenary Handbook of the Roman Catholic Mission in British Honduras*, p. 4.

61 *The Handbook of British Honduras for 1888–1889*, pp. 201–2.

62 *Ibid.*

63 Grant D. Jones, 'Political Brokers and Social Change in Northern British Honduras'. Unpublished paper, presented at the Tenth Annual Meeting of Northeastern Anthropological Association held in conjunction with the American Ethnological Society in Ottawa, 9 May 1970.

64 Peta M. Henderson, 'The context of economic choice in the rural sugar-growing area of British Honduras', unpublished M.A. Thesis, McGill University 1969.

65 C. H. Grant, 'Rural local government in Guyana and British Honduras', *Social and Economic Studies*, vol. 16, no. 1, March 1967, pp. 57–76.

66 D. A. G. Waddell, *British Honduras*, pp. 62–5.

67 For a discussion of the sociological aspects of the Creole language, see

S. R. R. Allsopp, 'The linguistic dilemma in British Honduras, *Caribbean Quarterly*, vol. 11, nos. 3 and 4, September–December 1965, and N. Ashcraft and Grant D. Jones, 'Linguistic problem in British Honduras', *Caribbean Quarterly*, vol. 12, pp. 65–7.

68 *Belize: New Nation in Central America*, p. 14.

69 J. Burdon, *Archives of British Honduras*, vol. 3, p. 224. Also J. E. S. Thompson, *Ethnology of the Mayas of British Honduras*, p. 32.

70 Colin Rickard, *Caribbean Power*, London 1963.

71 G.B. Colonial Office, *Conference on the Closer Association of the British West Indian Colonies, held at Montego Bay 1947*, pp. 82–4.

72 W. H. Knowles, *Trade Union Development and Industrial Relations in the British West Indies*, California 1959, p. 103.

73 Gordon Lewis, *Growth of the Modern West Indies*.

74 Ivan Oxaal, *Black Intellectuals Come to Power: The Rise of Creole Nationalism in Trinidad and Tobago*, Cambridge (Mass.) 1968.

75 *Report of the Constitutional Commissioner* (Sir Hilary Blood) 10 October 1959, Belize, p. 4.

76 James D. Cochrane, *The Politics of Regional Integration: the Central American Case*, New Orleans 1969.

77 *Carifta and the New Caribbean* (Commonwealth Caribbean Regional Secretariat), Georgetown 31 May 1971, and *From Carifta to Caribbean Community* (Commonwealth Caribbean Regional Secretariat), Georgetown 1 May 1972.

78 Economic Commission for Latin America (ECLA), *Annual Report*, 30 March 1961–15 May 1961 (E/3486, E/CN. 12/573/Rev. 1), p. 4.

79 Economic Commission for Latin America (ECLA), *Possibilities of Economic Co-operation between British Honduras (Belize) and Central America*, December 1968 (E/CN. 12/809/Rev. 1). Hereinafter ECLA Report, 1968.

80 Information obtained from Department of Extra-mural Studies, University of the West Indies, Belize City.

81 Information obtained from Ministry of Information, Belize City.

82 Lloyd Braithwaite, 'The social sciences in the Caribbean' in Vera Rubin (ed.), *Caribbean Studies: a Symposium*, p. 106.

83 For example, the 'plural' viewpoint is cogently argued in M. G. Smith, 'Social and cultural pluralism', *Annals of the New York Academy of Sciences*, vol. 83, art. 5, January 1960. For the opposing argument see Raymond T. Smith, 'Social stratification, cultural pluralism and integration in West Indian societies' in *Caribbean Integration: Papers on Social, Political and Economic Integration*, Third Caribbean Scholars Conference, Georgetown 4–9 April 1966. Institute of Caribbean Studies, University of Puerto Rico, Rio Piedras, 1967.

84 R. T. Smith, 'People and change', *New World Quarterly*, Guyana Independence Issue, vol. 2, no. 3, p. 49.

85 M. G. Smith, *Stratification in Grenada*.

86 Leo A. Despres, *Cultural Pluralism and Nationalist Politics in British Guiana*, Chicago 1967.

87 M. G. Smith, *The Plural Society in the West Indies*, p. 310.

88 Leo A. Despres, 'Ethnicity, resource competition and plural theory', unpublished paper, 1971, p. 12. See also Leo Despres, 'Differential Adaptation and Micro-cultural Evolution in Guyana', pp. 263–86 in Norman Whitten Jr and John F. Szwed (eds.) *Afro-American Anthropology: Contemporary Perspectives*, New York 1970.

89 R. T. Smith, 'People and change', p. 53.

90 Lewis A. Coser, *The Functions of Social Conflict*, Illinois 1956, pp. 78–9.

NOTES TO CHAPTER 1

1 J. Burdon, *Archives of British Honduras*, vol. 2, pp. ix–xii, hereinafter referred to as *Archives*. Narda Dobson has suggested that the three volumes of this archival material be used with caution since it was compiled by 'a team of amateurs' and the importance of dates and careful quotation was not always appreciated. Narda Dobson, *A History of Belize*, London 1973, p. 338.

2 L. M. Bloomfield, *The British Honduras–Guatemala Dispute*, Toronto 1953.

3 For the compromise over Canada and Guadeloupe see Eric Williams, *From Columbus to Castro, the History of the Caribbean 1492–1969*, London 1970, pp. 90–1.

4 D. A. G. Waddell, *British Honduras*, pp. 27–56.

5 T. D. Vickers, *The Legislature of British Honduras*, Belize 1955.

6 L. M. Bloomfield, *The British Honduras–Guatemala Dispute*.

7 J. Burdon, *Archives*, vol. 1, p. 5.

8 Wayne Clegern, *British Honduras*, pp. 68–96.

9 *Honduras Almanack 1826;* Bridges, *Annals of Jamaica, 1828*, vol. 1, p. 408 and vol. 2, p. 139.

10 Stephen L. Caiger, *British Honduras*, chaps. 1–4.

11 J. Burdon, *Archives*, vol. 1, p. 5.

12 *Ibid.*

13 *Ibid.*, p. 2.

14 Add. MSS Long Papers, Book 1, chap. 12.

15 Mary Williams, *Anglo-American Isthmian Diplomacy 1815–1915*, Washington 1916.

16 Sir Thomas Modyford, Governor of Jamaica to Lord Arlington, Secretary of State, 18 March (or 31 October) 1670, *Archives*, vol. 1, pp. 49–50.

17 Answer on Behalf of King of Spain to Memo of Her Britannic Majesty, 13 July 1913. *Archives*, vol. 1, p. 61.

18 Board of Trade to George I, 25 September 1717, *Archives*, vol. 1, p. 65.

19 Definitive Treaty of Peace, Versailles, 3 September 1783, *Archives*, vol. 1, p. 137; Guatemala Ministry of Foreign Affairs, *The White Book; controversy between Guatemala and Great Britain relative to the Convention of 1850 on territorial matters*, Guatemala 1938.

20 Stephen L. Caiger, *British Honduras*, chap. 6, pp. 79–88.

21 Wayne Clegern, *British Honduras*, p. 6.

22 *Ibid.*

23 L. M. Bloomfield, *The British Honduras–Guatemala Dispute*, pp. 8–9.

24 J. Burdon, *Archives*, vol. 1, pp. 20–1.
25 *Ibid.*, vol. 2, p. 292.
26 Guatemala Ministry of Foreign Affairs, *The White Book*, 1938 (Mexico from time to time put forward claims to Belize).
27 Stephen L. Caiger, *British Honduras*, p. 130.
28 Mr Miller to Under-Secretary of State, 20 February 1835, *Archives*, vol. 2, p. 366.
29 *Ibid.*
30 Gordon Ireland, *Boundaries, Possessions, and Conflicts in Central and North America and the Caribbean*, New York 1971, p. 124; R. A. Humphreys, *The Diplomatic History of British Honduras, 1638–1901*, London 1961, pp. 47–59.
31 R. A. Humphreys, *The Diplomatic History of British Honduras*, p. 59.
32 *Ibid.*
33 *Ibid.*, p. 79.
34 For the British viewpoint see: R. A. Humphreys, *The Diplomatic History of British Honduras*; L. M. Bloomfield, *The British Honduras–Guatemala Dispute*; D. A. G. Waddell, 'More on the Belize Question', *Hispanic American Historical Review*, vol. 40, May 1960, pp. 230–33. For the Guatemalan viewpoint in English see, in addition to the Guatemala Ministry of Foreign Affairs, *The White Book*; Wayne Clegern, 'New light on the Belize dispute', *American Journal of International Law*, 1958; 'A Guatemalan defence of the British boundary of 1859', *Hispanic American Historical Review*, vol. XL, no. 4, November 1960; and Robert Peragibe, *The Question of British Honduras*. Second Series: A defence of the viewpoint of the Guatemalan Government, Rio de Janeiro, 1939.
35 D. A. G. Waddell, 'Developments in the Belize Question 1946–1960', *American Journal of International Law*, vol. 55, no. 2, April 1961, p. 460.
36 *Ibid.*
37 *Ibid.*
38 Guatemala Ministry of Foreign Affairs, *The White Book*.
39 G. B. Central Office of Information, *British Honduras: The Guatemalan Claim*, London, October 1962.
40 *Ibid.*
41 R. A. Humphreys, *The Diplomatic History of British Honduras*, pp. 145–50.
42 *British Honduras: The Guatemalan Claim*, p. 9.
43 Definitive Treaty of Peace, Paris Article XVII, 10 February 1763, *Archives*, vol. 1, 87–8.
44 *Ibid.*
45 Definitive Treaty of Peace, Versailles, Article VI, 3 September 1783. *Archives*, vol. 1, pp. 137–8.
46 Stephen L. Caiger, *British Honduras*, p. 90.
47 Definitive Treaty of Peace, Versailles, *Archives*, vol. 1, pp. 137–8.
48 Convention of London, 14 July 1786, *Archives*, vol. 1, pp. 154–6.
49 George Dyer to 'Your Lordship', 12 February 1790, Duke of Portland to Governor Balcarres, 26 June 1799, *Archives*, vol. 1, p. 183 and p. 272.
50 Convention of London, 14 July 1786, *Archives*, vol. 1, p. 156.

51 Evans Report, 1948, p. 253.
52 Lieutenant-Governor to Governor, Jamaica, 28 October 1867, *Archives*, vol. 3, p. 296.
53 *Ibid.*
54 Census 1861, 1 April 1861, *Archives*, vol. 3, p. 238.
55 Assembly 1866, Lieutenant-Governor's Speech, 31 January 1866, *Archives*, vol. 3, p. 267.
56 Lieutenant-Governor to Governor, Jamaica, 17 May 1867, *Archives*, vol. 3, p. 267.
57 J. Eric Thompson, 'Ethnology of the Mayas of British Honduras', *Anthropological Series*, p. 33.
58 Wayne Clegern, *British Honduras*, p. 61.
59 Assembly 1866, Lieutenant-Governor's Speech, 31 January 1866, *Archives*, vol. 3, p. 267.
60 *Ibid.*, pp. 279, 349.
61 Wayne Clegern, *British Honduras*, p. 61.
62 G.B. Colonial Office, *British Honduras: Financial and Economic Position*, Report by Sir Alan Pim, March 1934, Cmd. 4856, p. 127 (hereafter *Pim Report, 1934*), p. 27.
63 *Ibid.*
64 Wayne Clegern, *British Honduras*, p. 92.
65 T. D. Vickers, *The Legislature of British Honduras*, pp. 1–4.
66 Narda Dobson, *A History of Belize*, p. 338.
67 Report of Commission to investigate claims to occupied land, 9 March 1818, *Archives*, vol. 2, p. 207.
68 Pim Report, 1934, p. 15.
69 Laws 1765–1810. Meeting of Committee, 25 July 1787, *Archives*, vol. 1, pp. 164–5.
70 *Ibid.*
71 Evans Report, 1948, p. 236.   Fraudulent ownership existed before 1812 as there is a reference to 'fictitious Collusive Copartnership' in *Archives*, vol. 1, p. 161.
72 Pim Report, 1934, p. 127.
73 *Ibid.*
74 Kathleen M. Stahl, *The Metropolitan Organization of British Colonial Trade*, p. 31.
75 Pim Report, 1934, p. 127.
76 Annual Report of the Forest Department, Belize, March 1929, p. 1.
77 *Ibid.*
78 *Ibid.*
79 Pim Report, 1934, p. 23. Almost every economic activity was subordinated to the interest of the forestry owners. Belize has some excellent pasture lands but cattle were selected neither for beef production nor dairy, but primarily for the purpose of producing oxen for timber haulage in the rivers.
80 British Honduras Government, 'Report of the Agricultural Commission, October 1917, Belize City (unpublished); *Report of the Economical and Natural Features of British Honduras in Relation to Agriculture, with*

*Proposals for Development,* by W. R. Dunlop, 1920, Belize City (unpublished). G.B. Colonial Office, *Report on the Forests of British Honduras with Suggestions for a Far Reaching Forest Policy* by C. Hummel, 1925, London: Waterlow and Sons; *Report on Development of Agriculture in British Honduras* by H. C. Sampson, 1929, London: HMSO.

81 Pim Report, 1934, p. 24.

82 Annual Colonial Report, 1914, Belize, p. 20.

83 *Ibid.*, 1918, p. 8.

84 *The Daily Clarion,* 22 January 1931.

85 Richard Hofstadter, William Miller and Daniel Aaron, *United States: the History of a Republic,* New Jersey 1961, p. 635.

86 G.B. Colonial Office, Minutes from Colonial Office to Treasurer, 25 August 1931, CO 123/334 1931, File 8535/31.

87 G.B. Colonial Office, Governor to Secretary of State, 19 March 1931, CO 123/334, File 85301/31.

88 G.B. Colonial Office, *Interim Report of Finance Committee,* October 1931, CO 123/334, File 85353.

89 This section relies heavily on Sir John Burdon's three volumes on the *Archives of British Honduras.*

90 Two classical works are L. J. Ragatz, *The Fall of the Planter Class in the British Caribbean,* London 1928, and Eric Williams, *Capitalism and Slavery,* North Carolina 1944. Two other important and recent sources are Elsa Goveia, *Slave Society in the British Leeward Islands at the End of The Eighteenth Century,* Yale 1965, and Edward Braithwaite, *The Development of Creole Society in Jamaica, 1770–1820,* London 1971.

91 Colonel Arthur to Lord Bathurst, 7 November 1816, *Archives,* vol. 2, p. 187.

92 *Ibid.*

93 Mr Hyde an Inhabitant of the Settlement of long standing, temporarily in London, to the Under Secretary of State for the Colonies, Mr Lefevre, 28 January 1834, *Archives,* vol. 2, p. 352.

94 Colonel Arthur to Lord Bathurst, 7 November 1816, *Archives,* vol. 2, p. 187.

95 Magistrates Meeting, 19 February 1819, *Archives,* vol. 2, p. 187.

96 Narda Dobson, *A History of Belize,* p. 150.

97 Superintendent to Earl Bathurst, 6 February 1825, *Archives,* vol. 2, p. 284.

98 Capt. George Henderson, *An Account of the British Settlement of Honduras,* London 1809, p. 60.

99 Narda Leon, 'Social and Administrative Developments in British Honduras 1798–1843', unpublished B.Litt. Thesis, University of Oxford, 1958, p. 203.

100 Superintendent to Secretary of State, 29 October 1833, *Archives,* vol. 2, p. 350.

101 Narda Dobson, *A History of Belize,* p. 156.

102 *Ibid.*

103 *Ibid.*

104 A singular exception is Narda Dobson's *A History of Belize,* pp. 165–79.

105 Colonel Arthur to Earl Bathurst, 16 May 1820, *Archives*, vol. 2, p. 228.

106 Magistrates' Meeting, 19 February 1819, *Archives*, vol. 2, p. 215.

107 *Ibid.*, p. 216.

108 *Ibid.*, p. 241.

109 Laws 1765–1810, 21 October 1791. Regulation respecting Obeah, *Archives*, vol. 1, p. 195.

110 *Ibid.*

111 Superintendent to Earl Bathurst, 18 February 1825, *Archives*, vol. 2, pp. 284–5.

112 *Ibid.*

113 Colonel Arthur to Earl Bathurst, 10 January 1822, *Archives*, vol. 2, p. 247.

114 *Ibid.*, 28 September 1821, *Archives*, vol. 2, p. 241.

115 *Ibid.*, 7 October 1820, *Archives*, vol. 2, p. 235.

116 *Ibid.*, 10 January 1822. *Archives*, vol. 2, p. 247.

117 *Ibid.*

118 *Ibid.*, 7 October 1820, *Archives*, vol. 2, p. 235.

119 Secretary of State to Superintendent, extract from a letter from Dr Lushington, 28 October 1827, *Archives*, vol. 2, p. 298.

120 Census 3, 31 December 1826, *Archives*, vol. 2, p. 293.

121 Public Meeting, 30 June 1828, *Archives*, vol. 2, p. 302.

122 Legislative Meeting, 4 and 5 July 1831, *Archives*, vol. 2, p. 330.

123 Extract of a letter from Dr Lushington to Secretary of State, dated 28 October 1827, March 1828, *Archives*, vol. 2, p. 299.

124 *Ibid.*, p. 300.

125 Public Meeting, 4 March 1816, *Archives*, vol. 2, p. 184.

126 Letter from Dr Lushington to Secretary of State.

127 Private letter from Superintendent to W. H. Hay, 12 July 1828, *Archives*, vol. 2, p. 302.

128 Magistrates' Meeting, 8 August 1810, *Archives*, vol. 2, p. 140.

129 Public Meeting, 24 August 1810, *Archives*, vol. 2, p. 166.

130 Magistrates' Meeting, 26 January 1814, *Archives*, vol. 2, p. 166.

131 Secretary of State to Superintendent, 1 December 1834, *Archives*, vol. 2, p. 362.

132 Public Meeting, 28 June 1817, *Archives*, vol. 2, p. 201.

133 Public Meeting, 10 July 1820, *Archives*, vol. 2, p. 230.

134 Colonel Arthur to Secretary of Lieutenant-Governor, Jamaica, 26 November 1821, *Archives*, vol. 2, pp. 243–4.

135 R. T. Smith, *British Guiana*, London, pp. 29–33.

136 *Ibid.*, pp. 33–37.

137 Rev. Robert Cleghorn, *A Short History of the Baptist Missionary Work in British Honduras 1822–1939*, London 1939.

138 *The Centenary Number of the Methodist Records*, 1927, Belize City 1927.

139 *The Handbook of British Honduras for 1888–1889*, p. 143.

140 Newport to Horton, 12 January 1825, CO 123/36. Cited in Narda Dobson's *A History of British Honduras*, p. 159.

141 *The Handbook of British Honduras for 1888–1889*, p. 146.

142 *Ibid.*, p. 144.

143 *The Methodist Record*, 1927, p. 7.
144 Secretary of State to Superintendent, 25 October 1827, *Archives*, vol. 2, p. 296.
145 *The Methodist Record*, 1927, p. 9.
146 Legislative Meeting, 4 July 1832, *Archives*, vol. 2, p. 336.
147 Meetings of Inhabitants and Slave Proprietors, 21 and 26 October 1833, *Archives*, vol. 2, p. 349.
148 Mr Hyde, an Inhabitant of the Settlement of long standing, temporarily in London, to the Under Secretary of State for the Colonies, Mr Lefevre, 28 January 1834, *Archives*, vol. 2, p. 352. Narda Dobson states that the Order-in-Council was drafted for Trinidad, *A History of Belize*, p. 170.
149 *Ibid.*
150 Rawle Farley, 'The Rise of the Peasantry in British Guiana', *Social and Economic Studies*, vol. 2, no. 4, 1954.
151 Census 4, 31 December 1832 and Census 5, 31 December 1835, *Archives*, vol. 2, p. 343 and p. 382.
152 Superintendent to Secretary of State, *Archives*, vol. 2, p. 384.
153 *Ibid.*
154 Superintendent to Superintendent Liberated Africans, Havana, 17 April 1844, *Archives*, vol. 3, p. 73.
155 Letter from Superintendent to Mr Miller, 22 January 1885, *Archives*, vol. 2, p. 365.
156 Secretary of State to Governor, Jamaica, 4 July 1861, *Archives*, vol. 3, pp. 241–2.
157 Stephen L. Caiger, *British Honduras*, p. 127.
158 D. Morris, *The Colony of British Honduras; Its Resources and Prospects*, London 1896, p. 122.
159 Secretary of State to Governor, Jamaica, 5 September 1864, *Archives*, vol. 3, p. 257.
160 Lieutenant-Governor to Governor, Jamaica, 23 October 1868, *Archives*, vol. 3, p. 310.
161 Stephen L. Caiger, *British Honduras*, p. 127.
162 Superintendent to Secretary of State, 10 August 1838, *Archives*, vol. 2, p. 401.
163 D. Morris, *The Colony of British Honduras*, pp. 122–3.
164 *Report on Social and Economic Conditions in Belize for 1931*, Belize, p. 13.
165 D. Morris, *The Colony of British Honduras*, p. 122.
166 *Ibid.*, p. 123.
167 *Ibid.*, p. 120.
168 *Report on Social and Economic Conditions in Belize for 1931*, p. 13.
169 *Ibid.*
170 Superintendent to Governor, Jamaica, 10 March 1856, *Archives*, vol. 3, p. 188.
171 *The Methodist Record*, pp. 18–21.
172 *Ibid.*, p. 20.
173 Superintendent to Governor, Jamaica, 1854, *Archives*, vol. 3, p. 201.
174 Superintendent to Governor, Jamaica, *Archives*, vol. 3, p. 127.

175 Census of British Honduras, 7 April 1960, *Archives*, vol. 2, pp. 6–7.
176 Lieutenant-Governor's General Remarks on the Settlement, June 1859, n.d., *Archives*, vol. 3, 219.
177 *The Handbook of British Honduras for 1888–1889*, p. 302.
178 Lieutenant Governor's General Remarks on the Settlement, June 1859, *Archives*, vol. 3, p. 221.
179 57 Geo. III C 53. Cited in Narda Dobson, *A History of Belize*, p. 79.
180 *Ibid.*
181 T. D. Vickers, *The Legislature of British Honduras*, p. 2.
182 *Ibid.*
183 Morley Ayearst, *The British West Indies*, London 1960, p. 100.
184 Convention of London, *Archives*, vol. 1, pp. 154–6.
185 Lord Sydney, Secretary of State to Captain Despard, 1 December 1784, *Archives*, vol. 1, p. 149.
186 Laws 1765–1810; Burnaby's Laws, 9 April 1765, *Archives*, vol. 1, pp. 100–6.
187 *Gazette 1884*, 1 November 1884, *Archives*, vol. 3, p. 353.
188 The Earl of Balcarres to Colonel Barrow, 29 January 1798, *Archives*, vol. 1, p. 243.
189 Extract of Accounts of the Battle of St George's Cay, September 1798 to February 1799, *Archives*, vol. 1, pp. 252–68.
190 Superintendent to Governor, Jamaica, 19 April 1851, *Archives*, vol. 3, pp. 144–5.
191 Governor, Jamaica to Superintendent, 19 August 1842, *Archives*, vol. 3, p. 111.
192 Laws 1881, 13 December 1870, *Archives*, vol. 3, pp. 323–4.
193 G.B. Colonial Office, Governor to Secretary of State, CO 123/342, 1933, File 15539.
194 *Ibid.*
195 *Ibid.*
196 For the various categories in which Crown colony Government can be classified see Colin Hughes, 'Semi Responsible Government in the West Indies', *Political Science Quarterly*, September 1953, pp. 338–53.
197 Barbados, the Bahamas, Bermuda and Guyana also retained their representative constitutions. See Martin Wight, *The Development of the Legislative Council, 1606–1945*, London 1946.
198 Governor to Secretary of State, CO 123/342, 1933.
199 T. D. Vickers, *The Legislature of Belize*, p. 8.
200 *Ibid.*
201 *Ibid.*
202 Governor to Secretary of State, CO 123/342, 1933.
203 G.B. Colonial Office, *West Indies and British Guiana*, Report by Hon. E. F. L. Wood, Cmd. 1679, London 1922, p. 102. Like so many other Colonial Office commissions to the West Indies, Mr Wood's visit to Belize did not materialize.
204 Governor to Secretary of State, CO 123/308, 1933.
205 *Ibid.*, CO 123/314.
206 *Ibid.*, CO 123/315.

207 G.B. Colonial Office, Governor to Secretary of State, CO 123/315, File 41353, 1923.
208 *Ibid.*

NOTES TO CHAPTER 2

1 Lucian W. Pye, *Politics, Personality and Nation Building*, Yale 1962, p. 103.
2 West India Royal Commission Report (Chairman Lord Moyne), HMSO London, July 1945, Cmd. 6697.
3 Legislative Council Debate, 31 December 1949.
4 Stephen L. Caiger, *British Honduras*, p. 160.
5 Governor to Secretary of State, 16 September 1933, CO 123/335.
6 Belize, *The Hurricane Reconstruction Loan Ordinance*, no. 22 of 1932, 5 May 1932.
7 *The British Honduras Constitution (Amendment) Ordinance*, no. 17 of 1932, 2 March 1932.
8 Evans Report, 1948, pp. 272–3.
9 Legislative Council Debate, 17 June, 1946, p. 39.
10 Sir Alan Burns, *Colonial Civil Servant*, London 1949, p. 129.
11 Governor to Secretary of State, MP 1673/33, 20 January 1934.
12 *Ibid.*, MP 98/34, 1 February 1934.
13 Evans Report, 1948, p. 237.
14 Pim Report, 1934, p. 43.
15 *Land and Property Tax Ordinance*, chap. 24. Consolidated Laws 1924.
16 Pim Report, 1934, p. 43.
17 Governor to Secretary of State, MP 1141/32, 10 May 1934.
18 *Ibid.*
19 Governor to Secretary of State, MP SS 231/33, 20 January 1934.
20 Governor to Secretary of State, MP 516/34, 3 May 1934.
21 Pim Report, 1934, p. 24.
22 *Ibid.*
23 Governor to Secretary of State, 0600/76, 3 November 1939.
24 *Ibid.*
25 Governor to Secretary of State, MP 2515/33, 23 January 1934.
26 Evans Report, 1948, p. 237.
27 Pim Report, 1934, p. 43.
28 Governor to Secretary of State, MP 427/34, 5 April 1934.
29 *Ibid.*, 0600/76, 3 November 1939.
30 *Ibid.*, 02287/37, 2 October 1939.
31 K. J. Post, 'The Politics of protest in Jamaica, 1938', *Social and Economic Studies*, vol. 18, no. 4, December 1969.
32 A. Soberanis G. and L. D. Kemp, *The Third Side of the Anglo-Guatemala Dispute over Belize or British Honduras*, Belize 1949, p. 10.
33 *Ibid.*
34 Governor to Secretary of State, 362/31, 15 August 1932.
35 Department of Labour Annual Report, 1942.
36 *Ibid.*

37 Governor to Secretary of State, no. 183, 11 August 1931.
38 Governor to Secretary of State, MP 1413/34, 28 November 1934.
39 Legislative Council Debate, 6 November 1941.
40 *Ibid.*, 6 April 1943.
41 West India Royal Commission Report, pp. 437–8.
42 Legislative Council Debate, 11 March, 1941.
43 *Ibid.*, 6 April 1943.
44 *Ibid.*, 11 March 1943.
45 Pim Report, 1934, pp. 123–6.
46 Evans Report, 1948, p. 275.
47 Sir Alan Burns, *Colonial Civil Servant*, p. 130.
48 G.B. Colonial Office, *Report of Labour Conditions in the West Indies* by Major St J. Orde Brown, Cmd 697, 1939, p. 19.
49 Report of the Committee on the Banana Industry, Sessional Paper 46 of 1937, 12 January 1938.
50 Governor to Secretary of State, SS 362–32, 15 August 1932.
51 Colonial Secretary's letter (20 May 1935) to B. H. *Agricultural Journal*, vol. 1, no. 2, April to June 1935, p. 51, Belize City.
52 *Ibid.*
53 *Ibid.*
54 Governor to Secretary of State, 1719–34/7, 27 December 1934.
55 Report of the Committee on Local Food Production, Sessional Paper 24/1942, 18 November 1942.
56 Secretary of State to Governor, SS 362–32, 15 August 1932, B.H. no. 162.
57 *Ibid.*
58 *Ibid.*
59 *Ibid.*, also MP 238/34, 14 May 1934.
60 *Ibid.*
61 *Ibid.*, MP 1656/34, 28 November 1934.
62 Report of the Committee on Local Food Production, 18 November 1942.
63 Governor to Secretary of State, 1330/49(1), 7 February 1950.
64 Governor to Secretary of State, 0600/76, 3 November 1939.
65 Governor to Secretary of State, File 02005/37, 12 January 1938.
66 *Ibid.*
67 Legislative Council Debate, 16 February 1943.
68 *Ibid.*
69 Annual Report of the Labour Department, 1942.
70 *Ibid.*
71 *Ibid.*
72 Legislative Council Debate, 27 February 1945.
73 *Ibid.*, 19 June 1942.
74 *Ibid.*
75 Evans Report, 1948.
76 Governor to Secretary of State, 6 June 1949.
77 Governor to Secretary of State, 1330/49(1), 7 February 1950.
78 *Ibid.*, 482/47/27, 12 February 1948.
79 *Ibid.*
80 It was not possible, from the slow rate of repayment, to foresee the liquidation

of these debts in the immediate future. At the beginning of 1948, for example, 293 borrowers owed $150,883 and by December of the same year the number of debtors had been reduced to only 267 owing a total of $132,321 of which $8,132 were arrears of interest. In fact a few payments were still being made in 1967.

81 Governor to Secretary of State, 743/49, 12 August 1949.
82 *Ibid.*
83 Governor to Secretary of State,, telegram no. 478, 31 October 1949.
84 *Ibid.*, CO 1556/85/91.
85 N. S. Carey-Jones, *Pattern of a Dependent Economy*, p. 141.
86 Ministry of Finance, Belize, n.d.
87 Governor to Secretary of State, 28 October 1949.
88 G.B. House of Commons Debates, 23 October 1949, vol. 470, col. 351.
89 N. S. Carey-Jones, *The Pattern of a Dependent Economy*, p. 141.
90 *Ibid.*
91 W. M. MacMillan, *Warning from the West Indies*, London 1936, p. 37.

NOTES TO CHAPTER 3

1 Governor to Secretary of State CO 123/337, 11 January 1932.
2 For example see Legislative Council Debate, 17 June 1946, p. 26.
3 Secretary of State to Governor CO 123/336, 20 January 1932.
4 *Ibid.*, CO 123/335, 1 February 1932.
5 *Ibid.*
6 *Ibid.*
7 *Ibid.*
8 *Ibid.*
9 Governor to Secretary of State, CO 123/336, 28 January 1932.
10 *British Honduras Constitution (Amendment) Ordinance 1932* (no. 17 of 1932), section 9.
11 Morley Ayearst, *The British West Indies*.
12 G.B. Colonial Office, Minutes, CO 123/337, File 94670, 29 April 1932.
13 *Ibid.*
14 *British Honduras Constitution Ordinance 1935* (no. 13 of 1935).
15 Secretary of State to Governor, CO 123/337, 24 June 1932.
16 Governor to Secretary of State, no. 183, 11 August 1931.
17 G.B. Colonial Office, Minutes, CO 123/335, File 85364, 22 September 1931.
18 *Ibid.*
19 *Ibid.*
20 Letter to Brigadier-General Sir Samuel H. Wilson (Private Secretary) Colonial Office from Oliver V. G. Hoare, CO 123/335, 24 September 1931.
21 Governor to Secretary of State, MP 1413/34, 28 November 1934.
22 *Ibid.*, CO 123/335, 28 January 1932.
23 For example see G.B. Colonial Office, Minutes, CO 123/337, File 94670, 29 April 1932.
24 Governor to Secretary of State, CO 123/350, File 85366, 2 January 1935.
25 Governor to Secretary of State, CO 123/335, 17 December 1931.
26 G.B. House of Commons Debates, 20 December 1935, vol. 307, col. 2134.

27 The *Belize Independent*, 5 February 1936.
28 W. M. MacMillan, *Warning from the West Indies.*
29 Legislative Council Debate, 20 November 1945, p. 88.
30 *Ibid.*
31 *Ibid.*
32 *Ibid.*
33 The issue was indeed vexatious since the colony contributed 79.3 per cent of the total revenue between 1935 and 1944.
34 Legislative Council Debate, 20 November 1945, p. 88.
35 *Ibid.*, p. 89.
36 *Ibid.*, 17 June 1946, p. 26.
37 *Ibid.*
38 Narda Dobson, *A History of Belize*, p. 306.
39 Legislative Council Debate, 5 June 1947.
40 The British government agreed to cancel the unpaid balance of the loan, although the Belize government was to continue to claim repayments of the sums re-lent from the original loan to individuals and organizations. These payments were to be credited to an elemental disaster fund.
41 Governor to Secretary of State, 482/47/38, 13 February 1948.
42 *Ibid.*
43 *Ibid.*
44 *Ibid.*, March 1923.
45 *The Handbook of British Honduras for 1925*, compiled by H. E. C. Cain and M. S. Metzgen, Belize.
46 *Ibid.*
47 *The Electoral Qualification Ordinance 1935* (no. 13 of 1935). This high qualification was abolished in 1945 and became the same as that for the voter.
48 Governor to Secretary of State, CO 123/315, 11 January 1932.
49 Personal interviews.
50 For example see Registrar General's Department Reports, 1931, 1932, 1933, 1934.
51 *Tropical Battleground 1851–1951*, Jesuit Mission Bureau, St Louis, 1951.
52 Norman Ashcraft and Cedric Grant, 'The development and organization of the education system in British Honduras', *Comparative Education Review*, Columbia University, vol. xii, no. 2, June 1963.
53 B. H. Easter, *Report on an Enquiry into the Educational System of British Honduras, 1933–1934*, Belize City 1935.
54 'Fifty Years in British Honduras', *The Jesuit Bulletin*, vol. 23, no. 5, 1944.
55 Annual Reports of the Education Department, 1936–1938, 1940–1943.
56 *Tropical Battleground, 1851–1951.*
57 J. C. Dixon, *Report on the Initiation of Jeanes Supervision in British Honduras, 1936*, Atlanta, Georgia, p. 5.
58 Several books on the Colonial Office make this point. See particularly those by Sir Charles Joseph Jeffreys for reference.
59 Personal interview with E. O. B. Barrow.
60 Draft Despatch from the Colonial Secretary to the Governor of British Honduras, dated 18 March 1933, CO 123/336. Of the five district

commissioners in 1933, three were expatriates. In the case of one whose 'career had been in the army and in business in the East and in British Honduras. . .it was discovered after his appointment at the age of forty-eight that he had been an undischarged bankrupt'. Little was known of the qualifications and background of another except that he first served as a Police Sergeant in 1895 (according to the Colonial Office List) before being appointed a District Commissioner in 1919, and that in 1931 he was sixty-three years old. The third had been a detective with the London Metropolitan Police before being appointed Assistant Superintendent of Police in the colony. It is instructive to compare these qualifications and careers with those of the two Belizean District Commissioners. One was Ezekial Grant, the lawyer, who had an impressive civil service career before being called to the bar. The other, Antonio Alcoser, a Mestizo Mexican immigrant, had an equally impressive civil service career having previously served in three of the key departments, Customs, Treasury, and Survey. (Note on District Commissioners CO 123/336.)

61 *Report of the Commission on the Unification of the Public Service in the British Caribbean Area, 1948–1949* by Sir M. Holmes, Col. no. 254, 1949, p. 12.

62 Governor to Secretary of State, CO 123/34, File 85353. Service in Belize, in fact, was at best seen as a prerequisite for a more important assignment in the Colonial Service, and the minimum tour of duty seldom expired without the officer feeling that his transfer was overdue.

63 Pim Report, 1934, p. 51. Over and above the salary reduction, Belize also offered salaries and other conditions of service which were much less than those in other parts of the Empire because it had rejected the principle of expatriate allowance along with the West Indian Colonies. See G.B. Colonial Office, *Report of the Commission on the Unification of the Public Service in the British Caribbean Area, 1948–1949* by Sir M. Holmes, Col. no. 254, 1949.

64 The financial situation necessitated the amalgamation of several posts and departments. Pim Report, 1934.

65 See British Honduras Annual Reports for the 1920s and 1930s.

66 *The Daily Clarion*, 9 April 1931.

67 *Ibid.*

68 *The Handbook of British Honduras for 1925*, p. 396.

69 Personal interview with the prominent members of the Debating Society and the Progressive Party such as Sir Harrison Courtenay and E. O. B. Barrow.

70 In 1925 there were ten registered Friendly Societies. *The Handbook of British Honduras for 1925*, pp. 400–1.

71 *The Daily Clarion*, 10 January 1936.

72 Sir Alan Burns, *Colonial Civil Servant*, London 1949, pp. 142–3.

73 *British Honduras Census Report, 1931*.

74 A. Caldecott, *The Church in the West Indies*, London 1898, p. 43.

75 *The Handbook of British Honduras for 1888–1889*, p. 114.

76 Naturally, the Anglican Church took official precedence. Governors, colonial secretaries and other expatriate officials were invariably members

of the Anglican Church or at least extended their patronage to it. The accommodation of the Anglican Rectory in the same compound as the Governor's and Colonial Secretary's residence was also indicative of the high status of their denomination.

77 Stephen L. Caiger, *Honduras Ahoy! The Church at Work in Central America*, London 1949, p. 24.

78 *Ibid.*, p. 14. Archbishop Arthur Dunn was Bishop of the Diocese for twenty-seven years, 1917–43, and Archbishop of the West Indies for seven years, 1936–43. His local *protégé*, Archbishop Hulse, served for about fifteen years, 1933–48 and spoke Spanish.

79 *Ibid.*, p. 23.

80 *Ibid.*

81 *Ibid.*

82 *The Jesuit Bulletin in British Honduras*, October 1944, vol. XXIII, no. 5, p. 85.

83 *Ibid.*

84 Sir Alan Burns, *Colonial Civil Servant*, p. 143.

85 *Ibid.*

86 C. H. Grant, 'Rural Local Government in Guyana and British Honduras', *Social and Economic Studies*, vol. 16, no. 1, March 1967.

87 *The Sower*, vol. 1, *Co-operatives in the Mission Fields*, no. 4, Belize, 16 March 1947, p. 1.

88 *Tropical Battleground 1851–1951*: A Centenary Handbook of the Roman Catholic Mission in British Honduras, 1951, p. 15.

89 *The Sower*, vol. 1, no. 4, p. 3.

90 *Tropical Battleground*, p. 5.

91 J. C. S. and M. C. S. Sologaistoa, *Guide to British Honduras*, 1919, pp. 80–6. St Catherine's Academy was started for girls in 1883. The Sisters of the Holy Family (black), the Pius Mission and Pallotine also established missions throughout the country but their convents tended to attract the less wealthy.

92 *The Jesuit Bulletin*, 1946, vol. 23, no. 3, p. 4.

93 *Mangrove*, vol. 14, no. 1, February 1947, p. 25.

94 Norman Ashcraft and Cedric Grant, 'The development and organization of the education system in British Honduras'.

95 J. C. Dixon, *Jeanes Supervision in British Honduras*, p. 103.

96 Legislative Council Debate, 13 February 1945, p. 19.

97 *Ibid.*

98 As late as 1947 Catholic parents were reminded that it was a 'violation of their sacred duty' to send their children to non-Catholic schools, *The Sower*, vol. 2, *My Church and Education*, no. 2, 2 March 1947, p. 1.

99 Legislative Council Debate, 13 February 1945, p. 19.

100 *The Daily Clarion*, 12 August 1935.

101 Personal interview with a Jesuit priest.

102 *Ibid.*

103 Admittedly the senior civil servant could speak knowingly of annual rates of pay, and hopefully of assisted overseas passages when on vacation leave, and of retiring benefits, however penurious these last may have been.

On the other hand employment in the civil service could not compete with a successful business enterprise as a source of wealth.

104 The Club came into existence around 1940 as an amalgamation of the Belize Golf Club and the Belize Polo Club. For information of these progenitors see Sir Algernon Aspinall, *The Pocket Guide to the West Indies*, London 1907, p. 408.

105 Its Founding President was L. P. Ayuso, a businessman and at the time an elected representative of the Legislative Council.

106 *The Handbook of British Honduras for 1925*, p. 390.

107 *Ibid.*

108 Governor to Secretary of State, CO 123/337, File 94670, 28 October 1933.

109 *Ibid.*

110 Governor to Secretary of State, CO 123/337, 21 April 1933.

111 *Ibid.*, CO 123/337, 28 October 1932.

112 *Ibid.*

113 Secretary of State to Governor, CO 123/337, 24 June 1932.

114 Governor to Secretary of State, CO 123/337, 28 October 1932.

115 *Ibid.*, CO 123/342, File 15539, 21 April 1933.

116 *Ibid.*

117 *Ibid.*

118 *Report of the Commission of Inquiry on Constitutional Reform 1951* (Chairman Harrison Courtenay) 25 April 1951, p. 9. Hereinafter Courtenay Constitutional Report.

119 Governor to Secretary of State, CO 123/337, 28 October 1932.

120 Governor to Secretary of State, CO 123/342, 21 April 1933.

121 *Ibid.*

122 *Ibid.*

123 Lucian Pye, *Personality and Nation Building*, p. 109.

124 *British Honduras Constitution Ordinance, 1935*.

125 Legislative Council Debate.

126 *British Honduras Constitution Ordinance, 1935*, Belize.

127 *British Honduras Census Report, 1946*.

128 Courtenay Constitutional Report, 1951.

129 Legislative Council Debate, 27 March 1935.

130 *Government Gazette*, 14 December 1935, p. 459.

131 *Ibid.*

132 *Ibid.*

133 Courtenay Constitutional Report, 1951, p. 13.

134 *The Daily Clarion*, 29 January 1936.

135 A. Soberanis G. and L. D. Kemp, *The Third Side of the Anglo-Guatemala Dispute over Belize or British Honduras*, Commercial Press, Belize 1949, p. 4.

136 Governor to Secretary of State, 1 August 1799, *Archives*, vol. 2, p. 123.

137 A. Soberanis G. and L. D. Kemp, *The Third Side of the Anglo-Guatemala Dispute*, p. 8.

138 *Ibid.*

139 *Ibid.*

140 Gordon Lewis, *Growth of the Modern West Indies*, p. 343.

141 *Conference on the Closer Associations of the British West Indies Colonies,* Col. no. 218, London 1948.
142 Guatemala, Ministry of Foreign Affairs, *The White Book.*
143 D. A. G. Waddell, 'Development in the Belize Question, 1946–60, *The American Journal of International Law,* vol. 55, no. 2, 2 April 1961, pp. 463–4.
144 *Ibid.*
145 *British Caribbean Standing Closer Association Committee,* 1948–49. Report Chairman Sir Hubert Rance.
146 The *Belize Billboard,* from 1948 to 1956.
147 Courtenay Constitutional Report, 1951.
148 Evans Report, 1947.
149 For the group's pro-federation and anti-Guatemala arguments the best source is *The Daily Clarion.*
150 Legislative Council Debate, 1 March 1948.
151 D. A. G. Waddell, 'Development in the Belize Question'.
152 A. Soberanis G. and L. D. Kemp, *The Third Side of the Anglo-Guatemala Dispute,* p. 11.
153 *Ibid.,* p. 3.
154 *Ibid.,* p. 4.
155 *Ibid.,* p. 11.
156 *Ibid.*
157 *Ibid.*
158 *Ibid.*
159 Governor to Secretary of State, File 66985/48, 24 January 1949.
160 Labour Department Annual Report, 1943.
161 Governor to Secretary of State, File 1138/48/20, 6 April 1950.
162 For example see the issues for March and April 1949.
163 Two of the nationalist leaders, Philip Goldson and Leigh Richardson, were regular contributors.
164 *The Methodist Record,* p. 41.
165 A. Soberanis G. and L. D. Kemp, *The Third Side of the Anglo-Guatemala Dispute,* p. 10.
166 *Ibid.*
167 *Mangrove,* August 1942.
168 *Ibid.,* February 1947.
169 The *Belize Billboard,* 3 February 1954.
170 *Ibid.*
171 *Ibid.*
172 Personal interview with E. O. B. Barrow and others.
173 The *Belize Billboard,* 29 September 1949, p. 1.
174 Legislative Council Debate, 26 September 1949, p. 20.
175 *Ibid.,* p. 12.
176 *Ibid.*
177 *Ibid.*
178 *Ibid.,* 31 December 1949.
179 Legislative Council Debate, 31 December 1949.
180 The *Belize Billboard,* 16 September 1949.

181 G.B. House of Commons Debates, 23 October 1949, vol. 470, col. 350.
182 Legislative Council Debate, 31 December 1949.
183 *Ibid.*
184 *Ibid.*
185 Martin Kilson, *Political Change in West Africa,* Cambridge, Mass. 1966, p. 48.

NOTES TO CHAPTER 4

1 *The Daily Clarion,* 29 June 1950.
2 The *Belize Billboard,* 5 February 1950.
3 *The Daily Clarion,* 27 April 1950.
4 *Ibid.*
5 *Ibid.,* p. 2.
6 The *Belize Billboard,* 30 April 1950.
7 *Ibid.*
8 The *Belize Billboard,* 9 February 1950.
9 *Ibid.,* 2 February 1950.
10 *Ibid.,* 5 February 1950.
11 *The Daily Clarion,* 2 March 1950.
12 Sir Samuel Hoare, *The Problems of Crown Colony Government in the Caribbean,* April 1921.
13 *Ibid.*
14 *Ibid.*
15 *Ibid.*
16 Governor's Despatch to Secretary of State, File 1748/3, 3 December 1935.
17 *Ibid.,* CO 12042/49, 3 July 1949.
18 *Ibid.,* 5 February 1950.
19 *Ibid.*
20 *Ibid.*
21 The *Belize Billboard,* 9 February 1950.
22 *The Daily Clarion,* 14 March 1950.
23 The *Belize Billboard,* 9 February 1950.
24 *Ibid.*
25 *The Daily Clarion,* 7 March 1950.
26 The *Belize Billboard,* 6 February 1950.
27 *Ibid.,* 9 February 1950.
28 *Ibid.,* 5 February 1950.
29 *The Daily Clarion,* 2 March 1950.
30 The *Belize Billboard,* 14 September 1950.
31 *Ibid.,* 22 January 1950.
32 *Ibid.,* 2 February 1950.
33 *Ibid.,* 6 August, 1950.
34 *Ibid.,* 25 June 1950.
35 *Ibid.,* 9 February 1950.
36 *Ibid.,* 20 August 1950.
37 *Ibid.*
38 *Ibid.*

39 Legislative Assembly Debate, 27 June 1961.
40 *Ibid.*, 19 January 1950.
41 For example, Governor's radio broadcast on 15 January 1950. Reproduced in the *Belize Billboard*, 15 January 1950.
42 Governor to Secretary of State, no. 43/50.
43 The *Belize Billboard*, 14 September 1950.
44 *Ibid.*
45 *Ibid.*
46 *The Daily Clarion*, 6 February 1950.
47 *Ibid.*
48 *Ibid.*
49 *The Daily Clarion*, 11 January 1950.
50 *Ibid.*
51 *Ibid.*, 12 January 1950.
52 *Ibid.*, 14 January 1950.
53 The *Belize Billboard*, 23 March 1950.
54 *The Daily Clarion*, 11 February 1950.
55 See pp. 115–16.
56 *The Daily Clarion*, 10 August 1950.
57 *Census of Population of British Honduras*, 1946, p. xxvii.
58 *Ibid.*, table 37, p. 24.
59 *Mangrove*, vol. iv, no. 1, February 1947, pp. 27–8.
60 *The Daily Clarion*, 30 January 1950.
61 Thomas Hodgkin, *Nationalism in Colonial Africa*, London, p. 150.
62 The *Belize Billboard*, 17 August 1950.
63 *The Daily Clarion*, 29 June 1950.
64 The *Belize Billboard*, 17 August 1950.
65 *Ibid.*
66 D. A. G. Waddell, *British Honduras*, p. 109.

NOTES TO CHAPTER 5

1 The *Belize Billboard*, 1 October 1950.
2 *Ibid.*, 20 July 1950.
3 *Ibid.*, 1 October 1950.
4 *Ibid.*, 6 August 1951.
5 Minutes of the Town Council, Belize, 10 July 1951.
6 The PUP amendment which was moved by Price read: 'That the Resolution be not considered until the currency of this country is restored to its former and traditional value, until import controls are abolished, until the conventions of the international labour organizations are extended to this country, until the green curtain cutting off workers from natural association with their fellow citizens has been lifted and until a democratic constitution liberates the people from colonial rule.'
7 The *Belize Billboard*, 16 July 1951.
8 Legislative Council Debate, 6 August 1951. Fuller moved the resolution as follows: 'Whereas members of my constituency have petitioned me to bring forward to the Honourable members of this Council the disgraceful

attitude of the majority of the Belize City Council as was indicated in a petition presented to His Excellency the Governor on July 24, 1951; and whereas the petitioners feel that Honourable members of this Council are in duty bound to uphold the prestige and loyalty of the British Crown, be it resolved that this Council requests His Excellency the Governor to dissolve the Belize City Council on the grounds referred to in the petition dated July 24, 1951.'

9 *Gazette Extra-Ordinary*, 8 August 1951.

10 *The Daily Clarion*, 22 August 1951.

11 Courtenay Constitutional Report, 1951, p. 7.

12 *The Daily Clarion*, 22 August 1951.

13 Courtenay Constitutional Report, 1951, p. 5.

14 *Ibid.*, p. 20.

15 *Ibid.*

16 *Ibid.*, p. 9.

17 *Ibid.*, pp. 9–10.

18 *Ibid.*, p. 12.

19 *Ibid.*, p. 15.

20 *Ibid.*, p. 12.

21 *Ibid.*, pp. 12–13.

22 *Ibid.*, p. 10.

23 W. J. M. Mackenzie, *Theories of Local Government* (Greater London Papers) no. 2, 1961.

24 Courtenay Constitutional Report, 1951, p. 1.

25 *Ibid.*, p. 13.

26 *Ibid.*

27 *Ibid.*

28 *Ibid.*, pp. 16–18.

29 *Ibid.*, p. 18.

30 *Ibid.*

31 Personal interviews with former NP officials.

32 This argument should not be pressed too far, for as F. G. Bailey points out, 'a literate man in a village may share his pleasure by reading aloud to his audience'. F. G. Bailey, *Politics and Social Change. Orissa in 1959*, London 1963, p. 109.

33 The phenomenal growth in union membership in the early years of nationalist activities was more political than industrial in character. For since the GWU and the PUP had the same leadership, workers were expected to reward the union for bargaining on their behalf more by their political support than by the paying of dues. This understanding was formalized when the GWU established a fund to promote its political objectives as we observed, gained representation on the PUP executive, and finally contested the 1954 election in association with the party.

34 Report of a Select Committee of All the Unofficial Members of the Legislative Council, Sessional Paper no. 40 of 1952.

35 *Ibid.*

36 Legislative Council Debate, 28 July 1952, pp. 6–12.

37 The 1951 Sierra Leone Constitution, for example, provided for a mixed franchise.

38 C. H. Grant, 'Local Government in Guyana and British Honduras', *Social and Economic Studies*, vol. 16, no. 1, March 1967.

39 G.B. Colonial Office, *Constitutional Reform in British Honduras*. Despatch of the Secretary of State for the Colonies to the Governor, no. 3, 17 January 1953.

40 *Ibid.*

41 Legislative Council Debate, 30 January 1953.

42 *Ibid.*, 28 July 1952, pp. 6–12.

43 *Memorial for a Democratic Constitution for British Honduras*, July 1951. See also the *Belize Billboard*, 13 June 1951.

44 The *Belize Billboard*, 16 October 1953.

45 *Ibid.*, 5 October 1950.

46 *Ibid.*, 29 October 1950.

47 *Ibid.*

48 *Ibid.*, 22 December 1952.

49 *Ibid.*, 19 November 1950.

50 B. C. Roberts, *Labour in the Tropical Territories of the Commonwealth*, London 1964, p. 91.

51 The *Belize Billboard*, 14 August 1951.

52 *Ibid.*, 21 November 1951, p. 4.

53 Edwin Lieuwen, *US Policy in Latin America*, New York, pp. 88–92.

54 This was the period of McCarthyism in the United States.

55 Governor to Secretary of State, Telegram no. 31, CO 849/48/10 66985/48, 24 January 1949.

56 The *Belize Billboard*, 3 September 1951.

57 *Ibid.*, 17 March 1952.

58 *Ibid.*

59 *Ibid.*

60 *Ibid.*, 24 September 1951.

61 *Ibid.*, 17 March 1952.

62 *Ibid.*

63 *Ibid.*, 20 September 1952.

64 *Ibid.*, 11 September 1952.

65 *Ibid.*, 17 March 1952.

66 G.B. Colonial Office, 'British Honduras. Report of an Inquiry held by Sir Reginald Sharpe, Q.C. in Allegations of Contacts between the People's united Party and Guatemala', 1954. Cmd 9139. Hereinafter Sharpe Report, 1954.

67 'British Guiana: Suspension of the Constitution', Cmd 8980, Ocober 1953.

68 Cf. London (United Press Service Report). The *Belize Billboard*, 11 March 1954.

69 The *Belize Billboard*, 12 March 1954.

70 Sharpe Report, 1954, Paragraph 11.

71 *Ibid.*

72 The *Belize Billboard*, 24 March 1954.

73 Legislative Council Debate, 30 January 1953.

74 The *Belize Billboard*, 11 March 1952.

75 *Ibid.*, 16 March 1952.

76 *Ibid.*, 20 March 1952.

77 Legislative Council Debate, 2 June 1952.

78 See chapter 3, table 8.

79 *British Honduras Gazette*, March 1954.

80 *Ibid.*, April 1954.

81 *Ibid.*, 13 February 1954.

82 *Ibid.*, March 1954.

83 The *Belize Billboard*, 30 April 1953.

84 *British Honduras Gazette*, April 1954.

85 *Ibid.*, May 1954.

86 The *Belize Billboard*, 6 October 1956.

87 *Ibid.*, 6 October 1950.

88 *Ibid.*, 14 July 1952.

89 *Ibid.*, 2 February 1951.

90 *Ibid.*

91 *Ibid.*

92 The amended section of the letter reads 'Our criticism, because it is often couched in strong terms is open to misunderstanding. But we intended at no time to create disrespect or malice against Your Excellency, or to bring the Government of British Honduras into disrepute; and if at any time anything which we may have said or written is susceptible to that interpretation we wish here and now to withdraw any such statements unreservedly, and admit that there never was any foundation for any of the charges which we made, as subsequent events have shown that our charges lacked foundation. We regret making the charges which form the basis of these prosecutions.'

93 The *Belize Billboard*, 2 February 1951.

94 *Ibid.*

95 The list of party councillors for 1950 is not available but most of them were re-elected in April 1951. See the *Belize Billboard*, 1 May 1951.

96 The *Belize Billboard*, 24 April 1951.

97 *Ibid.*, 26 January 1956.

98 *Ibid.*, 5 October 1950.

99 *Ibid.*, 21 November 1950.

100 *Ibid.*

101 *Ibid.*

102 *Ibid.*, 25 November 1951.

103 *Ibid.*, 21 November 1951.

104 *Ibid.*, 24 March 1954.

105 Bauer in his book *La Controversia Sobre El Territorio de Belice* states that Gabriel Angel Castaneda shows that the word 'Belize' is derived from the Mayan language and is made up of the words *be* (a preposition which means 'towards') and *likin* (which means 'east'). Together 'Belikin' means towards the east. The *Belize Times*, 4 November 1958.

106 Wallace traded in logwood and had as his source of supply the area around the 'Old River' off the Belize River. The Spaniards, whose ships

and settlements the English buccaneers raided from time to time could not pronounce the letter 'W'. For them it represented the sound of 'B'. Hence Ballace and later on Belize. Spanish historians give another version claiming that Belize comes from the word 'baliza' which means a buoy. There is a fourth but less endearing version by J. O. S. Thompson, the renowned Mayan archaeologist, who claims that the word is indigenous but simply means 'muddy'.

107 The *Belize Billboard*, 11 September 1952.
108 *Ibid.*, 14 July 1952.
109 *Ibid.*
110 British Honduras Annual Report 1954.
111 *Report of Delegation to London*, Belize, n.d.
112 *Ibid.*, p. 5.
113 The *Belize Billboard*, 14 January 1952.
114 *Report of Delegation to London*, p. 12.
115 *Ibid.*
116 Legislative Assembly Debate, 31 December 1954.
117 The *Belize Billboard*, 9 August 1956.
118 *Ibid.*
119 *Ibid.*
120 Price did not have an office as such in the Government Department and was not expected to write in files.
121 The *Belize Billboard*, 9 August 1956.
122 During the first session of the Legislative Assembly, which lasted from June 1954 to April 1955.
123 For example see 'Volume of speeches by Goldson, Member for Social Services', *Social Views*, Belize, July 1956.
124 The *Belize Billboard*, 4 January 1955.
125 *Ibid.*, 31 January 1956.
126 *Ibid.*
127 *Ibid.*, 7 March 1956.
128 *Ibid.*
129 *The Daily Clarion*, 31 August 1951.
130 The *Belize Billboard*, 2 July 1951.
131 *Ibid.*, 7 March 1951.
132 *Ibid.*
133 *Ibid.*
134 *Ibid.*, 29 July 1956.
135 Courtenay Constitutional Report, 1951, p. 5.
136 The *Belize Billboard*, 8 July 1956.
137 *Ibid.*, 8 August 1956.
138 *The Belize Times*, 29 September 1956.
139 The *Belize Billboard*, 14 September 1956.
140 *Ibid.*, 28 September 1956.
141 *Ibid.*
142 *Ibid.*, 30 April 1953.
143 *Ibid.*
144 *Ibid.*, 12 August 1956.

145 Labour Department Annual Report, 1955.
146 *The Belize Times*, 6 October 1956.
147 Auditor's Report of the GWU for 1950, 4 July 1951.
148 Labour Department Annual Reports, 1954–1956.
149 *Ibid.*, 1955.
150 The *Belize Billboard*, 6 October 1956.
151 Personal interview with Trade Union leaders.
152 The *Belize Billboard*, 15 March 1955.
153 *The Belize Times*, 15 October 1956.
154 *Ibid.*
155 *Ibid.*
156 Labour Department Annual Report, 1956. The reported membership fell from 10,500 in 1954 to 700 in 1956.
157 *PUP Manifesto*, 1957, Belize.
158 See *The Belize Times* for February and March 1957.
159 The *Belize Billboard*, 2 March 1957. Also *Social Views*, July 1957.
160 *British Honduras Gazette*, April 1957.
161 *Ibid.*
162 *The Belize Times*, 22 October 1956.
163 *Ibid.*, 29 September 1956.

NOTES TO CHAPTER 6

1 G.B. Colonial Office, *British Honduras*, London, December 1958, pp. 23–4.
2 Guatemala Foreign Ministry Official (Snr Jose Mendonza), press interview in Belize City, the *Belize Billboard*, 27 November 1957.
3 The organization had a chequered career because of the ideological differences between the pro-communist government in Guatemala and the anti-communist government in El Salvador. The differences had reached their climax with the withdrawal of Guatemala from the organization in 1953. Following the overthrow of the Arbenz regime in 1954, however, Guatemala rejoined ODECA which began to function in 1955.
4 *Hispanic American Report*, vol. 6, no. 4, April 1953, p. 12; vol. 7, no. 6, June 1954, p. 15; no. 12, December 1954, p. 11; vol. 8, August and October 1955, p. 356, p. 460. Cited by D. A. G. Waddell, *British Honduras*, p. 128.
5 Legislative Assembly Debate, 7 June 1957.
6 G.B. House of Commons Debates, 27 November 1957, vol. 578, col. 1159–62.
7 The *Belize Billboard*, 29 November 1957.
8 G.B. House of Commons Debates, 27 November 1957, vol. 578, col. 1159–62.
9 The Governor took action on the grounds that Price by secretly negotiating with the Guatemalan Minister had violated Rule 14(2) of the B. H. Letters Patent, 1954, in that he had not discharged his obligation in a manner consistent with his oath of allegiance.
10 Legislative Assembly Debate, 6 December 1957. See also *Broadcast by Governor Thornley* on 2 December 1957 and *Government Gazette Extraordinary*, 23 December 1957, pp. 645–8.
11 D. A. G. Waddell, *British Honduras*, p. 129.

12 Legislative Assembly Debate, 6 December 1957.
13 *The Belize Times*, 1 December 1957.
14 Personal interviews with former PUP officials.
15 The *Belize Billboard*, 9 March 1958.
16 *Ibid.*
17 *Ibid.*, 1 March 1958.
18 Personal interview with Pollard.
19 British Honduras Annual Report, 1958.
20 *The Belize Times*, 18 November 1958.
21 *The Daily Clarion*, 24 March 1958.
22 For example, see Legislative Assembly Debates in 1959.
23 *The Belize Times*, 8 January 1957.
24 *Ibid.*
25 Labour Department Annual Report, 1959.
26 The *Belize Billboard*, 16 May 1959.
27 Personal interview with Jesuit priest.
28 The *Belize Billboard*, 18 January 1958.
29 *Ibid.*, 14 February 1958.
30 Blood Report, 1959, p. 16.
31 *Ibid.*
32 *Ibid.*
33 *The Belize Times*, 7 May 1960.
34 The *Belize Billboard*, 6 July 1958.
35 *Ibid.*, 12 January 1961.
36 *Ibid.*, 7 November 1958.
37 *Ibid.*, 8 November 1960.
38 Legislative Assembly Debate, 18 December 1957.
39 Blood Report, 1959.
40 Jack Downie, *An Economic Policy for British Honduras*, Belize, 24 October 1959 (Hereinafter Downie Report).
41 Blood Report, 1959, Appendix E, Joint constitutional proposals by the National Independence Party and Christian Democratic Party, pp. 20–22; Joint supplementary proposals for constitutional reform by the National Independence Party and Christian Democratic Party, pp. 23–4.
42 *Ibid.*, p. 11.
43 Legislative Assembly Debate, 13 November 1959.
44 Blood Report, 1959, p. 20.
45 *Ibid.*, p. 17.
46 *Ibid.*, p. 18.
47 *Ibid.*, p. 20.
48 For example, Ydigoras Fuentes celebrated the centenary of the Anglo-Guatemala Treaty with a ceremony in which a symbolic re-occupation of 'Belice' was carried out on a concrete map of Guatemala.
49 *Extracts of Guatemalan Speeches and Documents on the Disputed Claim of Guatemala to Sovereignty over British Honduras*, Belize, Appendix A. Guatemalan Government Decree of 8 August 1958, pp. 2–3.
50 *Ibid.*, Appendix F, President Fuentes' Christmas Message to the Army, 24 December 1958, p. 4.

51 Legislative Assembly Debates, 23 November 1958 and 17 January 1959.
52 *Ibid.*, 16 January 1959.
53 *Ibid.*, 20 March 1959.
54 *Ibid.*
55 Blood Report, 1959, p. 17.
56 Legislative Assembly Debate, 20 March 1959.
57 Blood Report, 1959, p. 18.
58 *Ibid.*, p. 5.
59 *Ibid.*, p. 23.
60 *Ibid.*, p. 7.
61 *Ibid.*, p. 24.
62 *Ibid.*
63 *Ibid.*
64 *Ibid.*, p. 1.
65 *Ibid.*, p. 10.
66 *Ibid.*, pp. 4–5.
67 William Tordoff, *Government and Politics in Tanzania*, Nairobi 1967.
68 Blood Report, 1959, p. 4.
69 *Ibid.*
70 Downie Report, 1959, pp. 28–9.
71 Blood Report, 1959, p. 4.
72 A. Gilmour, *Report of the Financial and Economic Prospects of British Honduras*, 13 January 1956, pp. 34–5. R. J. C. Howes, *Report on an Enquiry into Salaries and other conditions of service including Recommendations for Increased Efficiency in Organisation and Administration in the Civil Service of British Honduras*, Government Printer, Belize City, 1956, pp. 10–11.
73 G.B. Colonial Office, *Her Majesty's overseas civil service: statement on policy regarding organization*. Cmd 9768, London 1956.
74 So as not to be outdone Sir Hilary argued that had the expatriates asked for been available, quasi-ministers would have been better served, and members of the local civil service would have had the advantage of working under, and being trained by, those who had just the knowledge necessary to teach them.
75 Blood Report, 1959, p. 4.
76 Legislative Assembly Debate, 20 March 1959.
77 Blood Report, 1959, p. 5.
78 *Ibid.*
79 *Ibid.*
80 *Ibid.*, p. 11.
81 *Ibid.*, p. 6.
82 *Ibid.*, p. 12.
83 *Ibid.*, p. 1.
84 *Ibid.*, p. 6.
85 *Ibid.*, p. 11.
86 *Ibid.*, p. 6.
87 Legislative Assembly Debate, 13 November 1959.
88 *Ibid.*

89 *Ibid.*
90 *Ibid.*
91 *Ibid.*
92 *Ibid.*
93 *Ibid.*
94 *Ibid.*
95 See above.
96 Legislative Assembly Debate, 13 November 1959.
97 *Ibid.*
98 *Ibid.*
99 Blood Report, 1959, p. 5.
100 The *Belize Billboard*, 7 November 1959.
101 Legislative Assembly Debate, 13 November 1959.
102 *Ibid.*
103 *Ibid.*
104 *Ibid.*, 18 December 1959.
105 *Ibid.*
106 *Ibid.*
107 *Ibid.*
108 *Ibid.*
109 *Ibid.*
110 The *Belize Billboard*, 25 October 1959.
111 *Ibid.*, 5 November 1959.
112 For an overview of the economy in the mid-1950s; see David L. Gordon
    *The Economic Development of British Honduras*, December 1954. Gordon
    was an official of the International Bank for Reconstruction and
    Development and prepared the report at the request of the government
    of British Honduras.
113 Downie Report, 1959, p. 7.
114 *Ibid.*, pp. 3–4.
115 *Ibid.*, p. 7.
116 *Ibid.*
117 The demographic figures were somewhat arbitrary and, as Downie
    conceded, difficult to justify.
118 Downie Report, 1959, pp. 12–13.
119 *Ibid.*, p. 7.
120 *Ibid.*, p. 9.
121 *Ibid.*, p. 12.
122 *Ibid.*, pp. 18–25.
123 The fact that, unlike Sir Geoffrey Evans, he was the sole investigator
    should also be considered. He was not given equal opportunity to benefit
    from specialist advice in various aspects of an inauguration plan. Finally,
    he did not set out to write an economic survey of Belize but assumed
    'a knowledge of the country and its economic position in those who read
    my report' (p. 1) and described that position only so far as was necessary
    to substantiate his findings and recommendations. In fact, as regards the
    detailed organization of a settlement scheme, he admitted that he could
    'do no better than recommend renewed study of the report of the Evans

Commission as a starting point for those concerned in planning it'
(p. 14).

124 Downie Report, p. 13.

125 The cost worked out at $16,000 to $20,000 for each family.

126 *Ibid.*, p. 6.

127 The *Belize Billboard*, 8 November 1959.

128 *Ibid.*

129 *Ibid.*

130 Sir Hilary Blood, 'British Honduras: land of opportunity', *Journal of the Royal Commonwealth Society*, vol. 3, 1960, pp. 83–6.

131 *The Belize Times*, 8 November 1959.

132 Downie Report, 1959, p. 12.

133 *Ibid.*, p. 5.

134 *Ibid.*, pp. 11–12.

135 *Ibid.*, pp. 23–4.

136 *Ibid.*, p. 11.

137 *Ibid.*

138 Legislative Assembly Debate, 20 November 1959.

139 *Ibid.*

140 *PUP Manifesto*, n.d., p. 2.

141 Downie Report, pp. 11–13.

142 *Ibid.*, p. 14.

143 The *Belize Billboard*, 9 December 1959.

144 *Ibid.*

145 *Ibid.*, 24 December 1959.

146 *Ibid.*

147 *Ibid.*, 14 January 1960.

148 *Ibid.*

149 Legislative Assembly Debate, 20 March 1959.

150 The *Belize Billboard*, November 1959.

151 Personal interview with Harrison Courtenay.

152 Labour Department Annual Report for 1959 and 1960.

153 *First Plenary Meeting of the Working Committee*, 14 January 1960.

154 Personal interview with Pollard.

155 *Third Plenary Meeting of the Working Committee*, 19 January 1960.

156 *Ibid.*

157 *The British Honduran*, October 1959.

158 *Third Plenary Meeting*, 18 January 1960.

159 *First Plenary Meeting*, 14 January 1960.

160 *Third Plenary Meeting*, 18 January 1960.

161 *Fourth and Final Plenary Meeting*, 25 January 1960.

162 Personal interview with delegates.

163 G.B. House of Commons, *Report of the British Honduras Conference*, Cmd 984, 17 February 1960.

164 Draft Minutes of the Final Session of the British Honduras Conference, 17 February 1960.

165 *Ibid.*

166 *Ibid.*

167 *Ibid.*
168 D. A. G. Waddell, *British Honduras*, p. 13.
169 Draft Minutes of the Final Session of the British Honduras Conference.

NOTES TO CHAPTER 7

1 *British Honduras Gazette*, 25 March 1961, pp. 194–6; *Government Gazette*, April 1965, pp. 293–5 and 10 February 1970, pp. 11–14.
2 The *Belize Billboard*, 25 March 1961.
3 *Government Gazette*, 1 April 1965, pp. 203–95.
4 *The Reporter*, 31 October 1969.
5 Sir John Mordecai, *The West Indies: The Federal Negotiations*, London 1968.
6 *The Belize Times*, 24 March 1961.
7 G.B. House of Commons Debates, 29 April 1968, vol. 763, col. 798–801.
8 *The Belize Times*, 15 May 1968.
9 The *Belize Billboard*, 3 July 1966.
10 *Ibid.*
11 Sir Colin MacGregor Knight, *Findings of Commission of Inquiry*, 2 June 1967, Belize City.
12 C. H. Grant, 'The Civil Service Strike in British Honduras', *Caribbean Quarterly*, vol. 12, no. 3, September 1966.
13 The *Belize Billboard*, 19 June 1966.
14 *Ibid.*, 26 June 1966.
15 *The British Honduras Weekly Newsletter*, 27 August 1962.
16 Report of the Sugar Industry Commission of Enquiry (1969), March 1971, Belize.
17 *Ibid.*
18 George L. Beckford, *Persistent Poverty*.
19 Peta M. Henderson, 'The Context of Economic Choice in the Rural Sugar-Growing Area of British Honduras'. Unpublished M.A. thesis, McGill University, April 1969.
20 Report of the Sugar Industry Commission of Enquiry.
21 Report of the Tripartite Economic Survey of British Honduras, May 1966, p. 55. Hereinafter Tripartite Economic Commission Report.
22 *Ibid.*
23 *The Reporter*, 23 January 1973.
24 Evan Hyde, *The Crowd Called UBAD: the Story of a People's Movement*, Belize City 1970.
25 House of Representatives Debate, 7 January 1966.
26 *Gazette Extraordinary*, 29 April 1968, pp. 213–19.
27 *Economic Commission for Latin America, Possibilities of Economic Co-operation Between British Honduras (Belize) and Central America*. E/CN 12/809 Rev. 1, December 1968. Hereinafter ECLA Report, 1968.
28 *The Belize Times*, 23 March 1971.

NOTES TO CHAPTER 8

1 Legislative Assembly Debate, 26 January 1962.
2 *Gazette Extraordinary*, 30 November 1960, p. 599.
3 *How We Are Governed*, Government Information Services, Belize City.
4 *The PUP Government and the Guatemalan Claim*, Government Information Services, Belize City, p. 3, n.d.
5 *Ibid.*
6 Legislative Assembly Debate, 27 June 1961.
7 *The PUP Government and the Guatemalan Claim*, p. 5.
8 Press Release from the Party Leader of the People's United Party, Belize, 15 July 1958.
9 *The PUP Government and the Guatemalan Claim*, p. 5.
10 *Ibid.*, p. 6.
11 *Ibid.*
12 Legislative Assembly Debate, 27 June 1961.
13 *The British Honduras Weekly Newsletter*, Department of Information, Belize City, 23 July 1962, p. 6.
14 *British Honduras Report for the Years 1962–63*, Belize City 1965, p. 3. See also Tripartite Economic Commission Report, May 1966, pp. 53–5.
15 *Ibid.*
16 *Ibid.*
17 *The British Honduras Weekly Newsletter*, 3 December 1962, p. 4.
18 Legislative Assembly Debate, 15 June 1962.
19 *British Honduras Report for the years 195F–61*, HMSO, London 1963. pp. 1–2.
20 Legislative Assembly Debate, 15 June 1962.
21 *Ibid.*, 17 October 1958, p. 19.
22 *The British Honduras Weekly Newsletter*, 18 June 1962.
23 *Ibid.*, 23 July 1962.
24 Legislative Assembly Debate, 28 January 1963.
25 *Ibid.*
26 United Nations Department of Economic and Social Affairs. *British Honduras; Agriculture, Economy, Housing, Urban Public Utilities and Transport Development* (TAO/BRHO/1), 17 June 1963, p. 353.
27 *Ibid.* Cited in the Tripartite Economic Commission Report, 1966, pp. 4–5.
28 Tripartite Economic Commission Report, 1966, p. 106.
29 Legislative Assembly Debate, 28 January 1963.
30 *Ibid.*
31 *Ibid.*
32 *Ibid.*
33 *British Honduras Weekly Newsletter*, 7 January 1963, p. 3.
34 Report of the Sugar Industry Commission of Enquiry (1969), Belize City, March 1971.
35 Legislative Assembly Debate, 28 January 1963.
36 *The British Honduras Weekly Newsletter*, 17 September 1962, p. 2.
37 Legislative Assembly Debate, 28 January 1963.
38 *The British Honduras Weekly Newsletter*, 14 April 1962, p. 10.

39 Arthur Lewis, *The Agony of the Eight,* Bridgetown 1965, p. 6.
40 ECLA Report, 1968.
41 *Daily Telegraph and Morning Post,* 2 January 1962, p. 14. See also Mario Rosenthal, *Guatemala,* New York 1962, p. 303.
42 *The Belize Times,* 6 March 1962.
43 *The Economist,* 28 April 1962, p. 33.
44 For a full text of the comminique see *The British Honduras Weekly Newsletter,* 21 April 1962, pp. 1–2.
45 *The British Honduras Weekly Newsletter,* 17 March 1962, p. 1.
46 *Ibid.,* 31 March 1962, pp. 1–2. Sagastume was released from prison in December 1962 and deported to Guatemala. The Governor also exercised the prerogative of clemency towards Rosado.
47 *The British Honduras,* Information Department, Belize City, July 1960, p. 3.
48 *The PUP Government and the Guatemalan Claim,* pp. 7–9.
49 *Ibid.,* p. 15.
50 *Ibid.,* p. 22.
51 *Ibid.,* pp. 7–13.
52 *The British Honduras Weekly Newsletter,* 28 April 1962, pp. 1–2.
53 *Ibid.,* 21 May 1962, p. 1.
54 Legislative Assembly Debate, 7 June 1963.
55 *Ibid.*
56 Blood Report, 1959, p. 21.
57 British Honduras Report for 1961–62, HMSO, p. 3.
58 *British Honduras Gazette,* 30 November 1960.
59 Cf. p. 195.
60 Legislative Assembly Debate, 7 June 1963.
61 *Ibid.,* 6 January 1962.
62 *Ibid.,* 19 June 1962.
63 *Ibid.,* 28 January 1963.
64 *Ibid.,* 6 January 1962.
65 *Ibid.*
66 *The Belize Times,* 6 March 1962.
67 Cf. pp. 227–8.
68 Legislative Assembly Debate, 6 July 1962.
69 *Ibid.,* 7 June 1963.
70 *Ibid.*
71 *The British Honduras Weekly Newsletter,* 29 April 1963, p. 5.
72 Legislative Assembly Debate, 7 June 1963.
73 *Ibid.*
74 *Ibid.,* 17 June 1963.
75 *Ibid.*
76 *Ibid.,* 7 June 1963.
77 Cf. p. 207.
78 Legislative Assembly Debate, 7 June 1963.
79 Blood Report, 1959, p. 16.
80 Cf. p. 208.
81 Legislative Assembly Debate, 7 June 1963.

82 *Ibid.*

83 *The British Honduras Weekly Newsletter,* 24 June 1963, p. 2.

84 *Ibid.,* 1 July 1963, p. 1.

85 Legislative Assembly Debate, 17 July 1963.

86 *The British Honduras Weekly Newsletter,* 24 June 1963, p. 1.

87 Legislative Assembly Debate, 17 July 1963.

88 *The British Honduras Weekly Newsletter,* 24 June 1963, p. 1.

89 Legislative Assembly Debate, 7 June 1963.

90 *Ibid.*

91 *Ibid.*

92 *Ibid.*

93 *British Honduras Gazette,* 6 January 1964, p. 18.

94 *Ibid.,* pp. 19–20.

95 *British Honduras Constitution Ordinance, 1963,* no. 33 of 1963, 30 December 1963.

96 *British Honduras Gazette,* 6 January 1964, p. 21.

97 House of Representatives Debate, 31 March 1965.

98 *Address to the United Nations Trusteeship Committee by Hon. Linberg Rogers, Minister of Internal Affairs, accompanied by Senator V. H. Courtenay, Vice-President of the Senate,* n.d., Belize City, Government Printer, p. 4.

99 Legislative Assembly Debate, 7 June 1963.

100 *British Honduras Weekly Newsletter* 4 August 1963, p. 1.

101 *The Economist,* 9 September 1967, p. 878.

102 House of Representatives Debate, 5 April 1968.

103 *Ibid.,* 17 June 1966.

104 *The PUP Government's Manifesto for Belizean Progress,* 1965, Belize City, p. 1.

105 House of Representatives Debate, 5 April 1968.

106 Minutes of the Meeting of the Joint Special Select Committee, 19 April 1968, p. 2.

107 The *Belize Billboard,* 8 May 1968.

108 Minutes of the Meeting of the Joint Special Select Committee.

109 POU's Memorandum to the Clerk, National Assembly, 4 June 1968.

110 *The Reporter,* 14 March 1968.

111 *The B.H. Chamber of Commerce Proposals for an Independence Constitution,* 2 October 1968, p. 3.

112 Minutes of the Meeting of the Joint Special Select Committee, 15 May 1968, p. 1.

113 Courtenay Constitutional Report, 1951, p. 9.

114 Minutes of the Meeting of the Joint Special Select Committee, 8 May 1968, p. 4.

115 Legislative Assembly Debate, 18 June 1962.

116 Minutes of the Meetings of the Joint Select Committee, 8, 15 and 29 May 1968.

117 *Ibid.,* 12 June 1968, Appendix B.

118 *Ibid.,* 31 July 1968, Appendices A, B, C, D, E.

119 *Ibid.*

120 *Ibid.*, 19 June 1968, p. 2.
121 *Ibid.*
122 *Ibid.*, 12 June 1968, p. 3.
123 *Ibid.*, p. 2.
124 *Ibid.*
125 *Ibid.*
126 Legislative Assembly Debate, 6 July 1962.
127 Minutes of the Meeting of the Joint Special Select Committee, 12 June 1968.
128 *Ibid.*, 12, 19 June 1968.
129 *Ibid.*
130 Draft Treaty, *Gazette Extraordinary*, 29 April 1968, pp. 213–19.
131 The *Belize Billboard*, 3 July 1966.
132 *Ibid.*
133 *Ibid.*
134 *Ibid.*
135 *Ibid.*
136 *The Belize Times*, 21 May 1968.
137 Cited in the *Belize Billboard*, 10 June 1966.
138 The *Belize Billboard*, 19 June 1968.
139 C. H. Grant, 'The Civil Service Strike in British Honduras'.
140 United Nations General Assembly A/AC 109/SR 548, 5 October 1967.
141 *Address to the United Nations Trusteeship Committee by Hon. Linberg Rogers, Minister of Internal Affairs, accompanied by V. H. Courtenay, Vice-President of the Senate*, n.d., Belize City, Government Printer.
142 The *Belize Billboard*, 27 April 1968.
143 Draft Treaty, Article 1.
144 *Ibid.*, Articles 9 and 14.
145 *Ibid.*, Article 3.
146 *Ibid.*, Articles 13 and 14.
147 *The Belize Times*, 9 May 1968.
148 Draft Treaty, Article 6.
149 Cited in Mario Rosenthal, *Guatemala*, New York 1962, p. 291.
150 *Ibid.*, pp. 288–93.
151 House of Representatives Debate, 29 April 1968.
152 The *Belize Billboard*, 30 April 1968.
153 *Ibid.*, 4 May 1968.
154 *Ibid.*, 3 May 1968.
155 *Ibid.*
156 *The Belize Times*, 4 May 1968.
157 *Ibid.*
158 *Ibid.*, 9 May 1968.
159 House of Representatives Debate, 14 May 1968.
160 *The Belize Times*, 27 April 1968.
161 Minutes of the Meeting of the Joint Special Select Committee, 29 May 1968, Appendix A.
162 *Ibid.*, 12 June 1968.

NOTES TO CHAPTER 9

1  For example, it was the government's and not the party's achievements that were emphasized in the 1965 election campaign, see *Your Government of 1961–1965 at Work*. GIS Belize City, n.d. Also *The Belize Times*, 22 December 1964.

2  This initially took the form of the Revision of the Standing Orders of the House of Representatives in 1966. (*Standing Orders of the House of Representatives*, 1966.)

3  *Standing Orders of the House of Representatives*, 1966.

4  I am grateful to the Minister for permission to quote from his notes for his meeting on 2 February 1967 with the PUP members of one of the Standing Committees.

5  House of Representatives Debate, 19 July 1968.

6  *Official Gazette*, 11 January 1969, pp. 12–13.

7  *Ibid.*, 15 December 1969, pp. 721–6.

8  House of Representatives Debate, 9 June 1967.

9  *The Belize Times*, 4 May 1971.

10  *Manpower Report*, March 1966, p. 16. Issued by Labour Department.

11  *The Testimony of the People of British Honduras*, presented by CIVIC Committee to Lord Shepherd, British Minister of State for the Commonwealth, 6 October 1969 (hereinafter CIVIC Committee Testimony).

12  See, for example, the Committee's petitions to the United Nations on the Anglo-Guatemala dispute. UN General Assembly A/AC 109/PET 1970.

13  The Committee, for example, produced a series of Research Papers on the implication of the Webster proposals in 1968.

14  *British Honduras Civil Service Association*, 40th Annual General Meeting, 11–12 May 1962, p. 17.

15  *The Belize Times*, 15 March 1967.

16  *The Crowd Called UBAD*, p. 16.

17  *Ibid.*, chapters 8 and 9.

18  *Ibid.*

19  Interview with Dean Lindo, August 1974.

20  *Official Gazette*, 10 January 1970, pp. 11–14.

21  *The Beacon*, 11 July 1970.

22  *The Crowd Called UBAD*, p. 33.

23  V. S. Naipaul, 'Power to the Caribbean People', *New York Review of Books*, 3 September 1970, pp. 32–4 and 'British Honduras: twilight of a colony', *The Daily Telegraph Magazine*, no. 247, 4 July 1969, pp. 6–10.

24  *The Crowd Called UBAD*, p. 48.

25  *Program of the Nation of UBAD–RAM*, n.d., p. 1.

26  *The Crowd Called UBAD*, p. 48.

27  *Ibid.*

28  *Ibid.*, p. 49.

29  *UBAD Constitution*, n.d.

30  *The Crowd Called UBAD*, p. 23.

31 *Ibid.*
32 *Ibid.*, p. 24.
33 *Ibid.*
34 *Ibid.*
35 *The Crowd Called UBAD*, p. 47.
36 *The Rockville Declaration*, n.d., p. 1.
37 *Ibid.*, p. 2.
38 *The Crowd Called UBAD*, p. 48.
39 *Ibid.*, p. 24.
40 *The Rockville Declaration*, n.d., p. 1.
41 *The Crowd Called UBAD*, p. 9.
42 *Ibid.*, p. 24.
43 *Ibid.*
44 Evan Hyde, *Knocking Our Own Ting*, Belize City.
45 *Amandala*, 15 October 1969, pp. 2, 4.
46 *The Crowd Called UBAD*, p. 48.
47 *Ibid.*
48 *Ibid.*, p. 60.
49 *Ibid.*, p. 53.
50 *Ibid.*
51 *Ibid.*, p. 87.
52 *National Independence Party, 1958–1968*, n.d.
53 House of Representatives Debate, 7 and 8 April 1967.
54 CIVIC Committee Testimony, p. 2.
55 NIP letter to Minister of Internal Affairs and Health, 27 June 1968, cyclostyled.
56 *The Belize Times*, 5 May 1961.
57 *Ibid.*, 23 May 1961, p. 1.
58 *The Belize Times*, 16 February 1962.
59 Labour Department Annual Report, 1969, table xi.
60 *Ibid.*, 1965.
61 *The Belize Times*, 16 February 1962.
62 *Ibid.*
63 *Ibid.*
64 Letter from Nicholas Pollard to *The Belize Times*, 21 September 1969.
65 *The Belize Times*, 16 February 1962.
66 Labour Department Annual Report, 1965, p. 2.
67 *Ibid.*
68 *The Belize Times*, 21 September 1969.
69 *The Belize Times*, 16 February 1962.
70 *Ibid.*, 19 January 1962.
71 *Ibid.*, 23 May 1961.
72 *Ibid.*, 27 September 1968.
73 *Ibid.*, 18 January 1968.
74 *Ibid.*
75 *Ibid.*, 17 February 1968.
76 *Ibid.*, 21 August 1968.
77 The *Belize Billboard*, 11 August 1968.

78  *The Belize Times,* 30 March 1968.

79  Annual Labour Department Report, 1968.

80  *The Beacon,* 10 July 1971, p. 1.

81  Labour Department Annual Report, 1970.

82  *Ibid.,* 1969.

83  Interview with Labour Official, December 1966.

84  *Vanguard,* October 1972, p. 14.

85  C. H. Grant, 'The civil service strike in British Honduras: a case study of politics and the civil service', *Caribbean Quarterly,* vol. 12, no. 3, University of the West Indies, September 1966.

86  POU 45th Annual General Meeting, 1–2 March 1963, p. 27.

87  *Ibid.*

88  *The Belize Times,* 7 February 1965.

89  *POU Newsletter,* 9 February 1965, p. 1.

90  *Ibid.,* 22 February 1965, pp. 2–3.

91  Resumé of the meeting held between the Governor and the POU, 28 July 1966.

92  The *Belize Billboard,* 12 June 1966.

93  Meeting between Governor and POU.

94  The author was one of the organizers and lecturers of the seminar.

95  C. H. Grant, 'The civil service strike in British Honduras'.

96  For a discussion of these kinds of relationships see Burton Benedict, 'Sociological aspects of smallness' in Burton Benedict (ed.), *Problems of Smaller Territories,* London 1967, pp. 45–55.

97  Meeting between Governor and POU.

98  *Ibid.*

99  *Vanguard,* October 1972.

100  *Ibid.,* January 1973.

101  *The Belize Times,* 7 January 1973.

102  *Vanguard,* June 1973.

103  *Ibid.,* January 1973.

104  *Ibid.,* June 1973.

105  Report of the Commission of Inquiry on a Review of the Public Service in Belize 1973 (Chairman, Sir Charles H. Hartwell). Belize City, 5 July 1973.

106  *Ibid.,* p. 38.

107  *Ibid.*

108  *Ibid.,* p. 39.

109  This section is based on my article, C. H. Grant, 'Rural local government in Guyana and British Honduras', *Social and Economic Studies,* University of the West Indies, vol. 16, no. 1, March 1967, pp. 57–76.

110  The *Belize Billboard,* 13 June 1962.

111  The *Belize Billboard,* 1 January 1967.

112  I attended these meetings.

113  *The Beacon,* 13 March 1973.

114  *Laws of British Honduras, 1958,* District Town Board Ordinance, chapter 136.

115  Blood Report, 1959, p. 18.

116 *The Reporter*, 5 December 1969.
117 *Report on Policy for Social Development Services 1965–70*, by A. V. S. Lochhead, 22 January 1965, p. 10.
118 Swarna Jayawerra, 'Religious organizations and the state in Ceylonese Education', *Comparative Education Review*, vol. XII, no. 2, June 1968, pp. 159–79.
119 *The Belize Times*, 7 February 1967.
120 The *Belize Billboard*, 5 May 1959.
121 Senate Debate, 13 December 1966.
122 Report of the UNESCO Educational Planning Mission to British Honduras, 1964, Paris, September 1964.
123 *Belize: New Nation in Central America*, Belize City, n.d., p. 47.
124 Norman Ashcroft and Cedric Grant. 'The Development and Organization of Education in British Honduras', *Comparative Education Review*, vol. XII, 2 June 1968, p. 178. Hereinafter 'Education in British Honduras'.
125 *Tripartite Economic Survey 1966*, p. 79.
126 *Ibid.*
127 Norman Ashcroft and Cedric Grant, 'Education in British Honduras', p. 178.
128 *Annual Report of the Registrar General Department, 1964*, Belize.
129 The *Belize Billboard*, 4 December 1969.
130 Compiled from the Registrar of Marriage officers, Registrar General's Department, Belize City.
131 Interview with a Jesuit priest, August 1969.
132 *Ibid.*
133 Annual Education Report, 1964/65, p. 68.
134 UNESCO Report, 1964.
135 *The Government's PUP Manifesto for Belizean Progress*, n.d., Belize.
136 Norman Ashcraft and Cedric Grant, 'Education in British Honduras', p. 178.
137 *Triennial Report of the Education Committee*, Belize, p. 66.
138 *Ibid.*
139 UNESCO Report, p. 20.
140 *Ibid.*
141 *Ibid.*, p. 25.
142 *Ibid.*
143 *Ibid.*
144 *Ibid.*
145 *Ibid.*
146 J. A. Bennett, 'The development of education in Belize, 1914–1965', unpublished M.A. thesis, University of London.
147 *Ibid.*
148 Minutes of the First Meeting of the Health, Education and Welfare Committee of the House of Representatives, 1 March 1967.
149 *Ibid.*
150 *Ibid.*
151 *The Beacon*, 13 June 1970.
152 House of Representatives Debate, 2 December 1966.

153 Senate Debate, 13 December 1966.
154 *Ibid.*
155 *The Belize Times,* 25 February 1967.
156 *Amandala,* 30 March 1972.
157 The *Belize Billboard,* 20 November 1960.
158 *Ibid.,* 18 November 1960.

NOTES TO CHAPTER 10

1 *Belize Government, Rural Land Utilization Tax. A Beneficial, Just and Equitable Piece of Legislation.* Government Printer, Belize City, n.d. p. 7. See also House of Representatives Debate, 7 January 1967. Hereinafter *Rural Land Utilization Tax.*
2 *Ibid.*
3 *Ibid.*
4 *Ibid.*
5 Information obtained from the Lands Department, Ministry of Agriculture, Belize.
6 *Rural Land Utilization Tax,* p. 2.
7 *Ibid.,* p. 5.
8 *Ibid.*
9 *Ibid.,* p. 7.
10 *Ibid.*
11 House of Representatives Debate, 22 November 1968.
12 *Rural Land Utilization Tax,* p. 7.
13 House of Representatives Debate, 8 November 1968.
14 *Ibid.*
15 Dennis McFarlene, *The National Accounts of Belize 1968–1970,* Kingston, 1971/030.
16 Aliens Landholding Ordinance 1973, no. 31 of 1973, 31 December 1973.
17 House of Representatives Debate, 17 December 1973.
18 *The Belize Times,* 27 January 1967.
19 *The Senate of Canada, Proceedings of the Standing Senate Committee on Foreign Affairs on Canada–Caribbean Relations,* no. 5, 18 March 1969, p. 83.
20 The *Belize Billboard,* 28 September 1967.
21 'Report on British Honduras', *Latin American Report,* vol. v, no. 1. August 1962, p. 23.
22 'Address by Premier George Price to the Michigan Senate', *Journal of the House,* no. 29, 8 March 1967, p. 509.
23 *Ibid.*
24 *The Reporter,* 16 May 1969.
25 ECLA Report, 1968, p. 87.
26 'Michigan Senate', *Journal of the House,* March 1967, p. 510.
27 'Report on British Honduras', *Latin American Report,* p. 22.
28 'Michigan Senate', *Journal of the House,* March 1967, p. 511.
29 Tripartite Economic Commission Report, p. 107.
30 *Ibid.*

31 *Ibid.*
32 *The Budget Speech for 1971*, Ministry of Finance, Belize, n.d., p. 5.
33 Tripartite Economic Commission Report, p. 117.
34 *Ibid.*
35 *The Budget Speech for 1971*, p. 5.
36 *Ibid.*
37 *Ibid.*, p. 7.
38 ECLA Report, 1968, p. 87.
39 *Annual Report of the Economic Commission for Latin America, 1971*, p. 169.
40 *Ibid.*, p. 168.
41 ECLA Report, 1968, pp. 1–2.
42 *United Nations General Assembly 1702nd Meeting*, 22 October 1968, p. 7.
43 Canadian International Development Agency (CIDA), Report on Canadian Development Assistance to the Commonwealth Caribbean. Cyclostyled, n.d., p. 1. Hereinafter CIDA Report.
44 Information obtained from officials of the Ministry of Finance, Belmopan.
45 CIDA Report, p. 2.
46 *Proceedings of the Standing Senate Committee on Foreign Affairs on Canada–Caribbean Relations*, p. 101.
47 *Ibid.*
48 *Ibid.*
49 *Ibid.*
50 CIDA Report, pp. 12–13.
51 Richard A. Preston, 'Caribbean defence and security. A study of the implications of Canada's special relationship with the commonwealth West Indies', *South Atlantic Quarterly*, vol. LXX, no. 3, Summer 1971.
52 Kari Levitt and Alister McIntyre, *Canada–West Indies Economic Relations*, Private Planning Association of Canada and McGill University, Canada 1967.
53 ECLA Report, 1968, p. 104.
54 *Ibid.*, p. 66.
55 *Ibid.*, p. 67.
56 ECLA Report, 1968, p. 17.
57 *Ibid.*, p. 72.
58 *Ibid.*
59 *Ibid.*, p. 73.
60 Commonwealth Caribbean Regional Secretariat, *CARIFTA and the New Caribbean*, Georgetown 1971.
61 Belize joins CARIFTA, *The New Belize*, March 1971, Belize, p. 8. Hereinafter Belize joins CARIFTA.
62 *Ibid.*, p. 9.
63 *Ibid.*, p. 8.
64 Belize joins CARIFTA, p. 8.
65 *Ibid.*
66 ECLA Report, 1968, pp. 26–7.
67 Trade Report for 1970, p. 8.
68 *Ibid.*, p. 26.

69 Tripartite Economic Commission Report, pp. 22–8.
70 *Ibid.*
71 *The Economist Intelligence Report, Quarterly Economic Review of the West Indies, Guyana, British Honduras, Bahamas and Bermuda,* no. 3, 1971.
72 ECLA Report, 1968, p. 26–7.
73 *Ibid.,* p. 27.
74 Belize joins CARIFTA, p. 9.
75 ECLA Report, 1968, p. 27.
76 *The Belize Times,* 15 May 1967.
77 *The Economist Intelligence Report,* no. 4, 1972, October 1972, p. 2.
78 *Ibid.*
79 Commonwealth Caribbean Regional Secretariat, *From CARIFTA to Caribbean Community,* Georgetown, May 1972.
80 Cedric Grant and George Beckford, 'British Honduras: two views', *New World Quarterly,* vol. III, no. 4, 1967, pp. 51–5.
81 *Proceedings of the Standing Committee on Foreign Affairs on Canada–Caribbean Relations,* no. 5, March 1969, p. 83.
82 *The Economist Intelligence Report,* no. 3, 1972, 12, July 1972, p. 2.
83 *Ibid.*
84 Cedric Grant and George Beckford, 'British Honduras', p. 52.
85 Wayne M. Clegern, *British Honduras,* p. 157.
86 Legislative Assembly Debate, 18 and 19 June 1962.
87 *Ibid.*
88 *The Belize Times,* 28 January 1972.
89 Cited in *The Reporter,* 4 February 1972.
90 *The Belize Times,* 5 May 1973.
91 *Ibid.,* 10 September 1971.
92 United Nations *Report of Committee on Colonialism,* A/AC 109/L824, 21 August 1972, p. 5.
93 *Ibid.,* p. 6.
94 *Ibid.,* Also *The Belize Times,* 23 April 1972.
95 *Ibid.*
96 United Nations *Report of Committee on Colonialism,* A/AC 109/L824, 21 August 1972, p. 5.
97 *The Economist Intelligence Report,* no. 2, 1972, 21 April 1972, p. 15.
98 Edwards Galeano, *Guatemala: Occupied Country.* Monthly Review Press, New York.
99 Mario Rosenthal, *Guatemala,* p. 303.
100 United Nations *Report of Committee on Colonialism,* Supplementary no. 23 (A/8023 Rev. 1), vol. IV, p. 247.
101 *Ibid.,* A/AC 109/L824, 21 August 1972, p. 5.
102 *The Reporter,* 18 October 1969, pp. 1, 4.
103 United Nations *Report of Committee on Colonialism,* A/AC 109/L824, 21 August 1972, pp. 4–5.
104 The *Belize Billboard,* 6 April 1967.
105 United Nations *Report of Committee on Colonialism,* A/7623/Add. 7, 11 November 1969, p. 214.

106 *Ibid.*

107 *Ibid.*

108 Trade Report for 1970, Ministry of Finance, pp. 61–4.

109 ECLA Report, 1968, p. 17.

110 Trade Report for 1970, p. 8.

111 Richard Preston, *Caribbean Defence and Security*, p. 327.

112 *Ibid.*

113 *The Belize Times*, 9 September 1973.

114 *Ibid.*

115 *Sunday Advocate News*, 1 July 1973, p. 10.

116 *Ibid.*

117 United Nations Plenary Session, 1702nd Meeting, 22 October 1968, p. 8.

118 *Ibid.*

119 For example see address by S. S. Ramphal, Minister of Foreign Affairs, Guyana. *New Dimensions of Preventive Diplomacy*, Georgetown, March 1973, p. 16.

120 Address by Dudley Thompson, Minister without Portfolio, Jamaica, OAS General Assembly, E 47/73, 6 April 1973, pp. 7–8.

121 *Ibid.*, E 63/72, 15 April 1972, p. 13.

122 *Ibid.*, E 47/73, 6 April 1973, p. 6.

123 *Ibid.*

124 United Nations Plenary Session, 1702nd Meeting, 22 October 1968, p. 5.

125 OAS General Assembly, E 47/73, 6 April 1973, pp. 7–8.


NOTES TO CONCLUSION

1 R. T. Smith, *British Guiana*, pp. 141–78.

2 Leo Despres, *Cultural Pluralism and Nationalist Politics in British Guiana*, Chicago, p. 271.

3 *Ibid.*

4 *Ibid.*

5 For a similar argument on the place of tribalism in the modern African situation, see A. L. Epstein, *Politics in an Urban African Community*, Manchester 1968, p. 229.

6 R. T. Smith, 'People and change', *New World Quarterly*, Guyana Independence Issue, vol. 2, no. 3.

7 Leo Despres, *Cultural Pluralism and Nationalist Politics*, p. 281.

8 *Ibid.*, pp. xii–xiii.

9 S. M. Lipset, *Political Man*, London 1963, p. 63.

10 V. S. Naipaul, 'Twilight of a Colony', *The Daily Telegraph Magazine*, no. 247, 4 July 1969, p. 10.

# SELECT BIBLIOGRAPHY

## OFFICIAL REPORTS

### UNPUBLISHED OFFICIAL CORRESPONDENCE

This consists of original despatches exchanged between the Governors of Belize
and the Secretaries of State for the Colonies on record in the Public Record Office,
London, and in some cases in the Archives, Belize City. Those in Belize City have
not been filed or indexed. Of those in London, the following volumes are in the
series CO 123/: 315, 316, 334, 335, 336, 337, 342, 350.

### DEBATES

These are debates of the Belize Legislative Council, 1942–1954 (Belize City),
the Belize Legislative Assembly, 1954–1965 (cyclostyled from 1957 onwards: Belize
City and Foreign Office Library, London), the Belize House of Representatives,
1965–1970 (cyclostyled: Belize City) and Senate, 1965–1970.

### ANNUAL DEPARTMENTAL REPORTS OF BELIZE

The most important were those of the Labour Department, the Education
Department, the Social Development Department, and the Forestry Department.

### OTHER REPORTS, 1934–1973

Pim, Alan. *British Honduras, Financial and Economic Position*, Cmd 4586, HMSO,
London 1934.
Easter, B. H. *Report of an Enquiry into the Educational System of British Honduras
1933–1934*, Government Printer, Belize City 1935.
Dixon, J. C. *Report on the Initiation of Jeanes Supervision in British Honduras*,
Atlanta, Georgia 1936.
Brown, Major St J. Orde. *Report of Labour Conditions in the West Indies*,
Cmd 607, HMSO, London 1939.
Evans Geoffrey (Chairman). *Report of the British Guiana and British Honduras
Settlement Commission*, Cmd 7533, HMSO, London 1948.
Lord Moyne (Chairman). *West India Royal Commission Report*, Cmd 6697,
HMSO, London 1948.
Sir M. Holmes. *Report of the Commission on the Unification of the Public Service
in the British Caribbean Area 1948–1949*, Col. no. 254, London 1949.
Courtenay, W. H. (Chairman). *Report of the Commission of Inquiry on
Constitutional Reform 1951*, Government Printer, Belize City 1951.

Ramage, R. O. *Report on an Enquiry into Salaries and Matters of Organisation in the Civil Service of British Honduras,* Government Printer, Belize City 1951.

Sharpe, Reginald. *Report of an Inquiry into Allegations of Contacts between the People's United Party and Guatemala,* Cmd 9139, HMSO, London 1954.

Howes, R. J. C. *Report of an Enquiry into Salaries and other Conditions of Service including Recommendations for Increased Efficiency in Organisation and Administration in the Civil Service of British Honduras 1956,* Government Printer, Belize City 1956.

Downie, Jack. *Report on an Economic Policy for British Honduras,* Government Printer, Belize City 1959.

Blood, Hilary. *Report of the Constitutional Commissioner 1959.* Government Printer, Belize City 1959.

*Census of British Honduras 1960.* Kingston. 2 vols 1960.

*Report of the British Honduras Constitutional Conference held in London, July, 1963.* HMSO, London 1963.

*Report of the UNESCO Educational Planning Mission to British Honduras,* Paris 1964.

Government Information Service. *The Premier Speaks,* Belize City 1964.

Ramage, R. O. *Report on a Review of the Public Service in British Honduras,* Government Printer, Belize City, 1965.

Clayton, G. (Chairman). *Report of the Tripartite Economy Survey of British Honduras, May 1966,* Belize City 1966.

Webster Bethuel. *Draft Treaty Between the United Kingdom of Great Britain and Northern Ireland and the Republic of Guatemala Relating to the Resolution of the Dispute over British Honduras (Belize),* New York 1968.

*Economic Commission for Latin America, Possibilities of Economic Cooperation Between British Honduras and Central America,* E/CN 12/809 Rev. 1, December 1968.

Hulse, Gilbert Rodwell (Chairman). *Report of the Sugar Industry Commission of Enquiry (1969), British Honduras,* March 1971.

Hartwell, Sir Charles H. (Chairman), *Report on the Commission of Inquiry on a Review of the Public Service in Belize,* Belize City 1973.

*NEWSPAPERS*

The *Belize Billboard* and *The Belize Times.*

*BOOKS*

GENERAL

Ayearst, Morley. *The British West Indies,* Allen and Unwin, London 1960.

Beckford, George L. *Persistent Poverty: Underdevelopment in Plantation Economies of the Third World,* Oxford University Press, London 1972.

Benedict, Burton (ed.). *Problems of Smaller Territories,* Athlone Press, London 1962.

Burns, Sir Alan. *Colonial Civil Servant,* Allen and Unwin, London 1949.

Caldecott, A. *The Church in the West Indies,* Cass Library of the West Indies, London 1898.

Commonwealth Caribbean Regional Secretariat. *CARIFTA and the New Caribbean,* Georgetown 1971.

Coser, Lewis A. *The Functions of Social Conflict,* Routledge and Kegan Paul, Illinois 1956.

Despres, Leo A. *Cultural Pluralism and Nationalist Politics in British Guiana,* Rand McNally and Company, Chicago 1967.

Galeano, Edwards. *Guatemala: Occupied Country,* Monthly Review Press, New York 1969.

Ireland, Gordon. *Boundaries, Possessions, and Conflicts in Central and North America and the Caribbean,* Harvard University Press, New York, 1971.

Kilson, Martin. *Political Change in West Africa,* Harvard University Press, Cambridge, Mass. 1966.

Knowles, W. H. *Trade Union Development and Industrial Relations in the British West Indies,* University of California Press, California 1959.

Levitt, Kari and McIntyre, Alister. *Canada–West Indies Economic Relations,* Private Planning Association of Canada and McGill University, Canada 1967.

Lewis, Gordon. *Growth of the Modern West Indies,* Monthly Review Press, New York 1968.

Lipset, S. M. *Political Man,* Doubleday Press, London 1963.

MacMillan, W. M. *Warning from the West Indies,* Faber and Faber, London 1936.

Mordecai, Sir John. *The West Indies: The Federal Negotiations,* Allen and Unwin, London 1968.

Oxaal, Ivan. *Black Intellectuals Come to Power: the Rise of Creole Nationalism in Trinidad and Tobago,* Schenkman Publishing Company Inc., Cambridge, Mass. 1968.

Pye, Lucian W. *Politics, Personality and Nation Building,* Yale University Press, New Haven and London 1962.

Ratnam, K. J. *Communalism and the Political Process in Malaya,* University of Malaya Press, Kuala Lumpur 1965.

Rickards, Colin. *Caribbean Power,* D. Dobson, London 1963.

Rosenthal, Mario, *Guatemala,* Twayne Publishers, New York 1962.

Ryan, Selwyn D. *Race and Nationalism in Trinidad and Tobago,* University of Toronto Press, Toronto 1972.

Smith, M. G. *The Plural Society in the West Indies,* University of California Press, Berkeley 1965.

Smith, M. G. *Stratification in Grenada,* University of California Press, Berkeley 1962.

Smith, R. T. *British Guiana,* Oxford University Press, London 1962.

Stahl, Kathleen M. *The Metropolitan Organization of British Colonial Trade,* Faber and Faber, London 1951.

Thompson, J. E. S. *The Rise and Fall of the Mayan Civilization*, University of Oklahoma Press, London 1954.

Tordoff, William. *Government and Politics in Tanzania*, East African Publishing House, Nairobi 1967.

Williams, Mary. *Anglo-American Isthmian Diplomacy 1815–1915*, American Historical Association, Washington 1916.

BELIZE

Bianchi, William J. *Belize: The Controversy between Guatemala and Great Britain over the territory of British Honduras in Central America*, Las Americas Publishing Company, New York 1959.

Bloomfield, L. M. *The British Honduras–Guatemala Dispute*, Carswell Company, Toronto 1953.

Burdon, John Alder. *The Archives of British Honduras*, Sifton Pread and Company, London 1931–35. 3 vols 1935.

Caiger, Stephen L. *Honduras Ahoy! the Church at Work in Central America*, SPG, London 1949.

Caiger, Stephen L. *British Honduras: Past and Present*, Allen and Unwin, London 1951.

Carey-Jones, N. S. *The Pattern of a Dependent Economy: The National Income of British Honduras*, Cambridge University Press, London 1953.

Clegern, Wayne M. *British Honduras: Colonial Dead End 1859–1900*, Louisiana State University Press, Baton Rouge 1967.

Dobson, Narda. *A History of Belize*, Longman Caribbean, London 1973.

Humphreys, R. A. *The Diplomatic History of British Honduras 1638–1901*, Oxford University Press, London 1961.

Taylor, Douglas MacRae. *The Black Carib of British Honduras*, Viking Fund Publications in Anthropology, no. 17, Werner–Gren Foundation, New York 1951.

Vickers, T. D. *The Legislature of British Honduras*, Printing Department, Belize, British Honduras 1955.

Waddell, D. A. G. *British Honduras: A Historical and Contemporary Survey*, Oxford University Press, London 1961.

*ARTICLES*

Ashcroft, Norman and Grant, Cedric. 'The development and organisation of the education system in British Honduras', *Comparative Education Review*, Columbia University, vol. XII, no. 2, June 1963.

Ayearst, Morley. 'A note on some characteristics of West Indian political parties', *Social and Economic Studies*, vol. 3, no. 2, September 1954.

Belize joins CARIFTA. *The New Belize*, Belize, March 1971.

Blood, Sir Hilary, 'British Honduras: land of opportunity', *Journal of the Royal Commonwealth Society*, vol. 3, 1960.

Braithewaite, Lloyd, 'The social sciences in the Caribbean' in Vera Rubin (ed.), *Caribbean Studies: a Symposium*, Washington 1960.

Grant, Cedric. 'The civil service strike in British Honduras: a case study of politics and the civil service', *Caribbean Quarterly*, University of the West Indies, vol. 12, no. 3, September 1966.

Grant, Cedric. 'Rural local government in Guyana and British Honduras', *Social and Economic Studies*, vol. 16, no. 1, March 1967.

Grant, Cedric and Beckford, George. 'British Honduras: two views'. *New World Quarterly*, vol. III, no. 4, 1967.

Courtenay, Derek. 'Constitutional development: Antigua', *Parliamentarian*, vol. XLVII, no. 3, July 1966.

Jayawerra, Swarna. 'Religious organizations and the state in Ceylonese Education', *Comparative Education Review*, vol. XII, no. 2, June 1968.

Kearns, Kevin C. 'Belmopan, Prospects of a new Capital', *The Geographical Review*, vol. LXIII, no. 2, April 1973.

Naipaul, V. S. 'Power to the Caribbean People', *New York Review of Books*, 3 September 1970.

Naipaul, V. S. 'British Honduras: twilight of a colony', *The Daily Telegraph Magazine*, no. 247, 4 July 1969.

Preston, Richard A. 'Caribbean defence and security. A study of the implications of Canada's "Special Relationship with the Commonwealth West Indies"', *South Atlantic Quarterly*, vol. LXX, no. 3, 1971.

Smith, R. T. 'People and change', *New World Quarterly*, Guyana Independence Issue, vol. 2, no. 3, 1966.

Thompson, J. Eric. 'Ethnology of the Mayas of Southern and Central British Honduras in Field Museum of Natural History', *Anthropological Series*, vol. XVII, no. 2, Chicago 1930.

Waddell, D. A. G. 'Developments in the Belize Question 1946–1960', *The American Journal of International Law*, vol. 55, no. 2, April 1961.

Wagley, Charles. 'Plantation America: a cultural sphere' in Vera Rubin (ed.), *Caribbean Studies – A Symposium*, Washington 1960.

Wood, D. P. J. 'The smaller territories: some political considerations' in Burton Benedict (ed.), *Problems of Smaller Territories*, Athlone Press 1967.

## THESES

Bennett, J. A. 'The development of education in Belize 1914–1965', unpublished M.A. Thesis, University of London, 1969.

Henderson, Peta M. 'The context of economic choice in the rural sugar-growing area of British Honduras', unpublished M.A. Thesis, McGill University 1969.

Kharrusi, Jocelyne. 'Patterns of migration and indices of urbanization in Belize, British Honduras', unpublished M.A. Thesis, McGill University 1970.

Leon, Narda. 'Social and administrative developments in British Honduras 1798–1843', unpublished B.Litt. Thesis, University of Oxford 1958.

# INDEX